STENDHAL

STENDHAL

JONATHAN KEATES

CARROLL & GRAF PUBLISHERS, INC.
NEW YORK

First Carroll & Graf edition 1997
First paperback edition 1998

Carroll & Graf Publishers, Inc.
19 West 21st Street
New York, NY 10010

Library of Congress Cataloging-in-Publication data is available.
ISBN: 0-7867-0545-0

Manufactured in the United States of America

To

Sam and Hazel Hackett

CONTENTS

INTRODUCTION

'Stendhal was a most singular character,' pronounced Henry James at the beginning of an article published in *The Nation* on 17 September 1874, and promptly went on to demolish outright the first attempt in English at outlining the writer's life and achievements. 'We have seldom seen a book more in need of complete revision,' he declared witheringly of Andrew Archibald Paton's *Henry Beyle* (otherwise *De Stendhal [sic] A Critical and Biographical Study*) 'both as to matter and to manner. It contains hardly an opinion which is not ludicrously erratic and hardly a quotation a foreign phrase or a proper name which is not misspelled or misprinted. But the author writes with a garrulous *bonhomie* – that of an easy-going cosmopolite, well advanced, apparently, in years – which will soften the edge of the reader's displeasure; and he is to be thanked at any rate for bringing Beyle once more before the world . . .'

James's essay on Paton's book, veined characteristically with his own brilliant *aperçus* of the novelist's strengths and weaknesses (though he judged *Le Rouge et le Noir* unreadable) may stand alongside its hapless victim as a warning to those embarking on a biography of Stendhal, more especially to his English-speaking biographers, of whom there have not been many. Since F. C. Green and Matthew Josephson published their studies in 1939 and 1946 respectively, only Joanna Richardson (1974) and Robert Alter (1979) have ventured to consolidate on these achievements with the aid of a vast amount of fresh material made available during the past forty years.

Neither faced an overwhelming number of French counterparts. The enormous interest in the whole phenomenon of Henry Beyle, whether as a writer, a personality, a lively mind or simply an inexhaustible source of apposite quotation on every conceivable subject, developed in France since the end of the nineteenth century, has rather surprisingly failed to find expression in the relatively straightforward business of recreating his life. With the exception of Victor del Litto's moderately proportioned biography published in 1965, no serious effort was made towards extending the domain so amply and authoritatively claimed by Henri Martineau's monumental *Le coeur de Stendhal* (1951) until Michael Crouzet's massive *Stendhal ou Monsieur Moi-même* (1990) which, despite its reprehensible lack of either an index or an adequate corpus of notes, must surely be seen as the greatest of all existing Stendhalian chronicles.

Something of this neglect, enhanced by the presence of a voluminous critical literature and – perhaps rather provokingly – by any number of books investigating single aspects of his life, must derive from the way in which we are nowadays content to view Stendhal. He has become a victim of what might be termed 'the iceberg syndrome', whereby only a small part of an immense literary output is visible above the waterline of published availability. The *New Yorker* cartoon which shows a wife berating her husband with the words 'Stendhal said this, Stendhal said that, didn't anyone else say anything original?' underlines however obliquely the superficial level on which we tend to invoke his presence among us. For many readers he is represented by two novels which they have a certain difficulty in finishing. Nobody quite dares to deny him his allotted status, yet by the same token, especially outside France, this cold respect has not been matched by the kind of enquiring curiosity which might have drawn more of his considerable *oeuvre* into the purview of a general readership.

To a degree Stendhal himself is to blame. We call him a novelist, yet fiction forms merely a part of his overall achievement, and we might just as well pin on him the labels of critic, art historian, musicologist, journalist, biographer, diarist and letter writer, in all of which areas he excelled. Our modern concern with specialization, with the need to be seen to cultivate a particular 'field', is embarrassed by his versatility, coupled as this is with an extraordinary fluency in the manipulation of a style so shorn of outward flourishes and self-conscious touches of art that it effectively resists adequate translation. Formally too he satisfies none of our customary desires that a writer's work should fit over his life and personality like a piece of expert tailoring. Several of his most interesting projects, such as *Lamiel* and *La Vie de Henry Brulard*, are unfinished; others, like *La Chartreuse de Parme*, end (for some) unsatisfactorily. His journals, scarcely kept with a Pepysian precision, eventually existed simply as marginal jottings and fly-leaf notes in the various books he read. Two substantial volumes of the *Oeuvres complètes* are dedicated to the abortive efforts at playwriting he kept up almost until the last decade of his life.

Yet amid this scatter of *disjecta membra*, of books whose titles seem to have little or nothing to do with their subjects, of shameless and abundant plagiarisms, of texts which seem at first glance to be made out of nothing more consistent than opinions and digressions, lies the evidence of an intensely absorbing personality, of that 'restlessness of a superior mind' which Henry James singled out as the writer's most endearing quality. To say, as is often said, that Stendhal's one and only subject was himself is an absurdly reductive cliché, but there can be no doubt of his primacy in the reader's attentions even in works as apparently straightforward in their intentions as *La Vie de Rossini* and the *Histoire de la peinture en Italie*.

Thus, though the task of assembling a new biography of Stendhal was always likely to be a daunting one, I have been assisted throughout by the astonishing candour of his own writings. Whatever his faults – and he is nothing if not frank about those – few literary artists have been more generous with their self-disclosures. As if to emulate him, Stendhal scholars have been comparably liberal with their talents and energies, exemplified in the work of figures such as Henri Martineau, François Michel and the stupendous Victor del Litto, whose labour of more than half a century as editor, critic and exegete, as well as in promoting Stendhal studies in France and abroad, represents an unparalleled dedication to the writer's cause. As in all scholarly domains, however, there is traditionally little charity shown to initiates in the field, and the pages of *Stendhal Club*, the quarterly review dedicated to every aspect of Henri Beyle, his life and work, are well seasoned with vitriol, evidence perhaps that, as one distinguished *beyliste* has observed, every enthusiast for the man and his books likes to feel that he or she alone holds the key to their significance.

With this in mind I may as well point out that the focus of this biography has been first of all on the interests of the general reader, in whom I have been bold enough to assume a basic command of French. Secondly, for obvious reasons, I have tended, at certain points in the book, to concentrate on features of Stendhal's career which are more likely to interest English and American readers than their counterparts in continental Europe. This is what the French would call an 'Anglo-Saxon' biographical study – that is to say a straightforward birth-to-death narrative, without much hypothesis or personal intervention, based on no initial psychological premises, and supported by reference notes, an index and suggestions for further reading.

In this context I offer little but the blandest generalities on individual works: I'm conscious, what is more, that certain of them, such as the *Chroniques italiennes*, have been treated much too sketchily. At least once, in Chapter 9, I have relaxed the strict chronological sequence altogether, so as to allow the significant number of interesting projects undertaken during Stendhal's early years in Paris after 1821 to be discussed in a balanced connection with the development of his social milieu. Space has compelled the omission of certain details which more expansive studies such as those of Martineau and Crouzet can embrace without difficulty. I should like to have been able to tackle, for example, the question of Stendhal's involvement with the Didier insurrection at Grenoble in 1816, to have investigated more fully the rich documentary sources of *Le Rouge et le Noir*, to have fleshed out the origins of *La Chartreuse de Parme*, both Renaissance and contemporary, and to have spent far longer on the endlessly fascinating *Lamiel* and its multifaceted inspirations.

My hope must inevitably be that others, armed with more time, money and academic resources than I am able to command, will produce biographies of greater depth and detail. The aim of the present sketch is to provide an impetus towards broader general interest in the career and personality of a man who, like his contemporary Coleridge and his near-contemporary Dr Johnson, achieved immortality through being as much as through writing. Finally let me say that I reject entirely the ridiculous caveat which urges biographers not to love their subjects too greatly. I cannot begin to say how much pleasure a deepening acquaintance with Henri Beyle and his work has given me, and I hope readers of this book will catch the contagion of my love and admiration for him.

Acknowledgements

Most of the research for this biography was conducted in the library of the Taylorian Institute, Oxford University, to whose staff, unfailingly courteous and painstaking with their assistance, my sincere thanks.

I am grateful also to the following institutions: The British Library, The London Library, The Institute of Romance Studies at London University, The Bodleian Library, Oxford, the Bibliothèque Nationale and the Bibliothèque de l'Arsenal, Paris, the Musée Stendhal de Grenoble, the Biblioteca Nazionale, Florence, the Biblioteca Marciana, Venice, the Biblioteca Estense, Modena, the New York Public Library, the City of London School Library.

The idea for this book was originally proposed by Julian Evans. My thanks to him for so fortunate an inspiration, to my publisher Christopher Sinclair-Stevenson for alternately encouraging and belabouring me, to my editors Neil Taylor and Emily Kerr, and to my agent Felicity Bryan.

Special acknowledgement is due to my former colleague Dr P. J. S. Whitmore for his invaluable supply of Stendhaliana culled from a reading of scholarly periodicals, and also to Claire Tomalin and Rupert Christiansen, both of whom might have presented a better account than mine of Stendhal's life, but who both graciously stepped aside in my favour. I am always abjectly grateful to my colleagues in the English Department of the City of London School, whose forbearance has sometimes been pushed to impossible limits.

My thanks finally to the following for help and encouragement of various kinds: Candida Brazil, Helen Ellis, Dr Renato Ferrari,

Mrs G. Fallows, the late Gianni Guidetti, Alan Hollinghurst, Ian Irvine, Sonia Keates, Timothy Keates, Alastair Laidlaw, Robin Lane Fox, Dr Gilles Lorquet, Gerard McBurney, Alison Millar, Patrick O'Connor, Mary Sandys, Charles-Edouard Saint-Guilhem, Terence De Vere White.

I am thankful most of all to the dedicatees of this book, my godfather Professor C. A. Hackett and his wife Hazel. Though I have not yet investigated the possibility of Stendhalian echoes in the poetry of Arthur Rimbaud, the present study may perhaps go some way towards acknowledging their infinite kindness and support throughout my life.

Suggestions for Further Reading

As noted earlier, the literature of Stendhal studies constitutes an immense area, impossible to encompass adequately in this brief supplement. In addition to the works already mentioned in the notes, the following may be recommended.

On every aspect of Stendhal, man and works, the quarterly review *Stendhal Club* remains true to its traditions of meticulous detail, exhaustive research and enlivening moments of dry humour and contentiousness. Further reference material will be found in the remarkable three-volume *Fichier Stendhalien* compiled by François Michel, 15,000 references to items in works by or on the writer, published in 1964. A detailed analysis of Stendhal's finances is provided by Lily R. Felberg's *Stendhal et la question d'argent au cours de sa vie* (1975). Beyle's politics are examined in considerable depth in H. F. Imbert's *Les Métamorphoses de la Liberté* and his intellectual background is covered by V. del Litto's important study *La Vie intellectuelle de Stendhal*.

Among early essays on Stendhal, the best are those by Auguste Bussière (1843) Paul Bourget (1885) and Hippolyte Taine (1894). In the present century Louis Aragon (*La lumière de Stendhal*, 1954) and Paul Valéry (*Variétés* II) have offered some of the liveliest responses by modern French writers to his genius. Also warmly recommended in this context are the *Lezioni su Stendhal* by Giuseppe Tomasi di Lampedusa (currently available in the edition published by Sellerio, Palermo, 1977).

On the works in general, classic studies are those by Jean Prévost (*La Création chez Stendhal*) and Henri Martineau (*L'Oeuvre de Stendhal*) both published in 1951, Maurice Bardèche's *Stendhal*

Romancier and Georges Blin's *Stendhal et les Problèmes du Roman* (1958). *Im Hotel de la Mole*, in Erich Auerbach's *Mimesis* (1946) remains one of the most stimulating essays on *Le Rouge et le Noir.*

English and American readers will enjoy Robert M. Adams's spirited *Stendhal: Notes On A Novelist* (1959) Michael Wood's urbane and unorthodox *Stendhal* (1971) and F. W. J. Hemmings's *Stendhal: A Study Of His Novels* (1964). Two outstanding recent studies are those by Roger Pearson (*Stendhal's Violin* 1988) and Anne Jefferson (*Reading Realism In Stendhal* 1989).

CHAPTER 1

THE CHILDHOOD OF H.B.

'I have written the life of several great men,' Stendhal once scribbled on the flyleaf of a copy of Richardson's *Clarissa Harlowe*. 'This was the kind of work which I enjoyed best. I no longer have the patience to search for materials and to weigh up contradictory opinions. It has occurred to me that I might embark on a life all of whose incidents I know extremely well. Unfortunately the subject, myself, is entirely unknown. I was born at Grenoble on the 23rd January, 1783 . . .'

Stendhal bitterly loathed his home town, 'the capital of pettiness', but clung affectionately to memories of its surrounding countryside. The Dauphiné is the name given to the mountainous region of south-eastern France which lies between the Rhône and the Savoyard passes leading into Italy. Its landscape of Alpine crags, fir forests, swift-flowing rivers and wooded vales dotted with farms and little manor houses appeals alike to the romantic *paysagiste* and to more restless travellers, ready to scramble up the beetling rock faces of the Deux-Soeurs in the Massif du Vercors, to tramp across the Grésivaudan valley towards the banks of the Isère, which cuts a slick line through the plain, or to walk the shuttered Gothic cloister of the Grande Chartreuse, where Thomas Gray in 1742 left a Latin poem in the monks' album, and where Matthew Arnold a century later seized on the monastery as a potent image of intellectual dislocation from the modern world.

If it is true that environment determines the temper of a people, then this terrain is the perfect mirror of regional history and character. A long habit of rebellious independence among the *dauphinois* lies rooted in the singular political dispensation confirmed at the end of the thirteenth century, whereby the entire territory, including the city of Vienne and the counties of Die and Valence, became a principality, administered by the successive Dauphins, or Crown Princes, of France. By this arrangement, freedoms of a kind not enjoyed elsewhere in the kingdom were guaranteed. A local parliament upheld rights and privileges, protested regularly against unjust taxation and enjoyed the continued support of landowners and magistrates by its gestures of autonomy in the face of royal coercion. The loyalty of the humblest peasant, sharpened by the sense of aggressive wariness derived from living in a frontier zone, was first of all to the Estates of the Dauphiné and some way afterwards to the King of France. Not for nothing was banishment to a neighbouring province such as Bresse or Provence considered the worst doom that the parliament could possibly pronounce.

By temperament, the *dauphinois* were seen as coarse-mannered, boastful spendthrifts, noted for both their dogged patience and extreme secretiveness. In addition to the two last qualities, Stendhal himself was proud to inherit the stubborn integrity and absolute scorn for hypocrisy which he saw as crucial to the local character. 'The nature of the *dauphinois*,' he wrote, 'is distinguished by a tenacity, a depth of intellect, a liveliness and a refinement which one might seek in vain in either of the neighbouring provinces of Provence or Burgundy.' Elsewhere he noted that, 'in this region, covered with snow for six months of the year, since enforced idleness encourages people to occupy themselves with the making of ideas, the inhabitants have the misfortune of being original'. His fellow countrymen were wholly incapable of falsehood. 'It is utterly beyond the nature of any *dauphinois* to become anyone's dupe. Even while bending the knee before the most triumphant hypocrisy, he can scarcely avoid incurring odium by showing, through some imprudent detail or other, that he has not been deceived.'

Doubtless these thumbnail sketches, like everything else Stendhal wrote, were intended ultimately to relate to his own notion of himself as a creature of invincible perspicacity and sophistication, yet it is hard to imagine him belonging anywhere else than in this corner of France which peers over into Italy. His father's family were peasants of the Vercors region, south-west of Grenoble, settled around the town of Saint-Jean-en-Royans, whose names appeared in official documents as Beile, Baile, Belle or Beyle. Stendhal was ready enough to boast of noble descent, but the social position of the Beyles was firmly established only in the seventeenth century, when Jean Beyle, son of Ambroise, set up as a draper in Lans and married Alix Clapasson of Sassenage in 1656.

It was as the captain-castellan of the Sassenage mountains that their elder son, Pierre, automatically gained a noble title, while the younger, Joseph, became a distinguished local lawyer, *procureur* of the Parlement de Grenoble and deputy bailiff of the Graisivaudan. When illness forced Joseph to give up his work in Grenoble, he handed on his duties to his son, Pierre, who subsequently made a most advantageous match, in 1734, with the daughter of the *grenoblois* merchant and banker Pierre Dupéron.

All the Dupéron girls married lawyers, but of the three Jeanne appears to have been the liveliest and was certainly the most fecund, bearing thirteen children in all. Ten daughters survived, but only one son, Chérubin, brought up to follow in his father's profession and made a *procureur* by special decree in 1764, when he was only seventeen years old. The Parlement, in granting the boy his certificate, presumably bore in mind the fact that his father's early death had left him with the unenviable task of providing for his sisters, only four of whom managed to find husbands. Earnest, dedicated and hardworking, Chérubin gathered practical experience and professional credit, so that by the year of his marriage in 1781, he was within reach of one of the highest legal honours Grenoble could offer, a seat among the forty advocates of the city's consistory court.

Whether Chérubin Beyle married for love or merely to consolidate his status as a successful lawyer is hard to say, though substantial sums of money in the form of a dowry and settlements certainly entered the calculation. His bride was Henriette-Adélaïde-Charlotte Gagnon, the twenty-three-year-old daughter of a distinguished local doctor, who brought with her a portion of 20,000 francs and the expectation of a sizeable inheritance from her aunt Elisabeth. She was, as Stendhal himself tells us, plump, fresh-faced and very pretty, endowed with a noble serenity of demeanour and ceaselessly busy, preferring to do everything for herself rather than put her servants to work. Her favourite reading was Dante's *Divine Comedy*, of which she had five or six different editions in the original Italian.

Grenoble, where the newly married Beyles settled and brought up their three children, has never been noted either for architectural beauty or for charm of situation. Then as now, the grandeur of the mountainous backdrop set off a city whose rapid growth as a provincial capital had been directed by practical rather than aesthetic considerations. Cularo, the stronghold of a Gaulish tribe, the Allobroges, had been raised to civic status in AD 379 by the Emperor Gratian, with the sonorous title of Gratianopolis, and its subsequent development had always been governed by the line of Roman fortifications, strengthened during the Middle Ages and completed with the thrusting star-points of Vaubanesque ramparts which became such a familiar feature of frontier cities during the late seventeenth century.

Travellers sardonically noted the depressing colours of the two rivers embracing the town. The Isère, even when purged by winter rains and floods, was a perpetual dirty grey, while the Drac stayed a muddy yellow. Even the most benign visitor could hardly ignore the pervasive stench of urine wafted from the dark, foetid alleyways, a *grenoblois* particular lasting into the present century, when a guidebook writer could still observe, nostrils wrinkling with distaste: 'It is necessary to have been accustomed from childhood to such disgusting spectacles, such revolting odours, in order to suffer them without strenuous protest . . . . the houses are often as filthy as the streets; the majority of passageways and staircases resemble public rubbish heaps.'

Unable to spread outwards, Grenoble had to make do with growing upwards, in a series of tall, dismal, barrack-like apartment buildings arranged around dank, sunless courtyards, and it was on the second floor of one of these, number 14 Rue des Vieux-Jésuites, that Chérubin and Henriette Beyle settled after their marriage. The street, poky and charmless, remains more or less as it always was, though it has been renamed Rue Jean-Jacques Rousseau to commemorate a brief visit by the celebrated

Swiss in 1768. A plaque commemorates the birth here, on 23 January 1783, of the Beyles' only surviving son, Marie-Henri.

He was not their first child. A year previously, an earlier Henri had died after only four days. Psychology makes much of the spectral sibling within the life of the family, and the burdens of remorse and self-reproach no doubt lay as heavily upon the Beyle household as on any other. Some at least of the tension which was to develop between Stendhal and his father may have been due to frustrated expectations connected with his dead brother which he himself was intended to fulfil.

On the day after his birth the boy was baptized Marie-Henri in the church of Saint Hugues. His two godparents were his grandfather, Dr Henri Gagnon, and Marie Rabit, widow of his father's noble cousin, Jean-Baptiste Beyle. If in naming her as godmother, Chérubin hoped to strengthen links with the grander branch of the family, he was to be disappointed, for she died the following year at the age of eighty.

It is typical of Stendhal that his earliest childhood memory should foreshadow the perpetual ambiguities of his adult relationships with women. Marie-Louise-Marguerite Pison du Galland was the wife of his mother's cousin, Alexis, a promising young advocate and banker who had been a witness at the Beyles' wedding. Fifty years later he wrote:

> I see her now, a woman of twenty-five, rather plump and wearing a great deal of rouge. Apparently it was this rouge which annoyed me. As she sat in the middle of a field known as the Glacis de la porte de Bonne, her cheek came exactly level with mine. 'Kiss me, Henri,' said she. I didn't want to. She grew angry. I bit her hard. I remember the incident, probably because I was made instantly to feel guilty for it and the matter was endlessly referred to.

The episode shows, of course, the writer as he would have wished us to see him, *contra mundum*, recusant, out of step, the unconventional anti-hero of an entirely conventional childhood episode. Madame Pison du Galland might nevertheless have known better, for Henri's kisses were exclusively reserved for his mother, with whom, as he frankly tells us, he was in love. He wanted, he says, to cover her with kisses, adding, 'and that there should be no clothes. She loved me passionately, kissed me often, and I returned her embraces with such ardour that she was often obliged to leave the room.' The intensity of his passion was unforgettable. 'She could not be offended by the liberty I took in revealing my love for her: if ever I find her again I shall tell her of it once more. For herself she took no part in it . . . as for me, I was as criminal as possible, frenzied in my adoration of her.'

Her death in childbirth on 23 November 1790 was due to the clumsiness of the *accoucheur*, apparently chosen out of pique towards another male midwife who was a great deal better at his job. Around two o'clock in the morning, little Henri, staying at his grandfather's house, awoke to find the entire household in tears. When the old maidservant, Marion, told him his mother was dead, he was incredulous: 'Why couldn't the doctors make her better? Shall I never see her again?' Hearing the priest, Abbé Rey, assuring the tearful Chérubin that Henriette's death was 'God's work', the boy found the reality still more impossible to accept. Only on the following day, when he went into the drawing room and saw the coffin under its black pall, was he overcome with violent despair. The very sound of Grenoble's cathedral bells, heard many years afterwards, was enough to remind him of this moment, 'inducing a sombre, arid sadness empty of tenderness, the sort of sadness which is akin to anger'.

After the funeral, Henriette's husband ordered her room to be closed, and it stayed sealed for ten years, Henri alone being entrusted with a key and permitted to study mathematics there at a table covered with a waxed cloth. The date of his mother's death remained momentous for him. In *Vie de Henry Brulard*, the amazingly confessional account of his early life, first conceived in Italy when he was nearly fifty, but made public almost half a century after his death, he noted with laconic significance: 'At this point my moral life began.'

It is by no means unusual for a sensitive child to blame the premature death of one parent on the unfortunate surviving partner, and this certainly happened to Chérubin Beyle. Stendhal was entirely candid in expressing a profound detestation of his father. The wretched man was accorded no mitigating virtues except a reverence for his dead wife's memory:

> He was an excessively dislikable man, always concerned with the purchase and sale of property, very sharp, accustomed to dealing with peasants, an arch-*dauphinois*. . . . What is more, he was extremely wrinkled and ugly, becoming silent and disconcerted even in front of women, whose presence was necessary to him.

Religiosity brought on by Madame Beyle's death made Chérubin increasingly ridiculous and there was even talk of him taking holy orders, though this idea was mercifully scotched by his desire to hand on his advocate's practice to his son at his death.

None of these aspects of Chérubin's character hurt Henri as much as an absolute failure to love the boy for himself rather than for what he represented in terms of an heir to name, status and wealth. A complete coldness developed between the two of them, which the years never succeeded in dissipating. The city of Grenoble, which Stendhal – not, we may suppose, without an awareness of the punning potential in its first syllable – referred to by the ancient Gaulish name of Cularo, was frequently identified both in spirit and appearance with the money-grubbing, culture-disdaining ethos of his father, to whom he attributed the prevailing joylessness of his childhood and adolescence.

This at any rate is the father whose reality Stendhal invites us to accept. Readers of his novels, accustomed to the blurred edges between fiction and truth in these works, and indeed to the way in which the true so often threatens to engulf the fictive, may well be somewhat wary of the portrait of Beyle *père* which emerges from *Vie de Henry Brulard*. Here as elsewhere, Stendhal is so downright as regards his own version of his life that our automatic impulse is to want to contradict him – a reaction he would surely have enjoyed. In the case of Chérubin Beyle, alas, there seem to have been very few factors to mitigate his son's harsh verdict. At best his obsession with the getting rather than the spending of money can be viewed as provident thrift, while his dry meticulousness and emotional detachment must in part have been the results of a legal training which stood him in good stead as he gradually climbed the professional ladder towards becoming one of Grenoble's forty consistorial advocates.

To join this self-elected band of senior lawyers brought privileges along with kudos. Once accepted, Chérubin would have found himself exempted from a number of local taxes and accorded the permission to hunt which marked him as a gentleman. The consistorial advocates were in essence a minor aristocracy, even if their hereditary rights had been abolished in the sixteenth century by Henri II. Chérubin's snobbery, as a member of a family only recently risen from among small tradesmen and peasant farmers, would undoubtedly have been flattered by such distinctions, of a kind calculated to push him further towards royalism and reaction in the coming revolutionary decade of the 1790s. 'Beyle' was now a respected *grenoblois* name, to be proclaimed by a coat of arms with which the lawyer sealed his letters.

'My father,' wrote Stendhal at the full tide of filial resentment, 'loved me only as the bearer of his name, but never as a son.' Yet the more we examine the writer's character, tastes and reactions, the closer, however ironically, he appears to the hated Chérubin. The two shared not just the doggedness and prudence typical of their *dauphinois* heritage, but also an essential secretiveness and reserve. Not for nothing did Henri's friend François Bigillion say of the family: 'You are Beyles, thus always hiding something. Perhaps this is just because of the way you appear or the way in which I look at you, but you haven't the kind of openness which strikes one at first meeting; it's necessary to get to know you.'

More significant than this, in view of the novelist's adult relationships, are the indications of his father's suppressed emotional life. The piety and moral earnestness which Chérubin evidently hoped to teach the young Henri by example covered springs of deep sensitivity, though one of the more astounding features of *Vie de Henry Brulard* is Stendhal's pitiless refusal, even as he enumerates such essential traits, to concede their humanity. He tells us how his father wept for the dead Henriette, how he rocked his daughter Zénaïde to sleep on his knee, of his passionate enthusiasms and his need for women. None of these details, however, is allowed to soften the portrait the writer resolutely thrusts upon us of a cold, formal hypocrite, meriting all his son's loftiest contempt.

The trouble seems to have been that Chérubin was a bore. Endless letters to Henri on such topics as viticulture, merino sheep and dairy farming were no substitute for the warmth and charm that had vanished from the house with the death of the enchanting Madame Beyle, who, as Stendhal had good reason to believe, never really loved her husband. To whom, amid the gloomy, joyless atmosphere prevailing in the Rue des Vieux-Jésuites, was the boy Henri to turn for attention and love?

Not, it appeared, to his mother's youngest sister, Séraphie Gagnon, now taking her place in the family as the kind of sour-faced maiden aunt who lives by bullying and manipulating her relatives and by pretending to martyr herself on the altar of domestic duty. Whatever compassion we may feel towards Séraphie, charged with managing the Beyle household and provided with little in the way of emotional or material recompense, evidence scarcely softens Stendhal's portrait of an ignorant, vindictive, mean-spirited harridan.

She hated her nephew as much as he loathed her. The boy's maturing cynicism, that rational intelligence inherited as a birthright from the enlightened France of Voltaire, Diderot and Condorcet in which he was born, stood entirely at odds with his aunt's strenuously exhibited Catholic piety, which, according to him, brought priests flocking to her deathbed. A ferocious royalist, whom the news of Louis XVI's execution sent into a paroxysm of hysterical rage, she mistrusted the written word as an agent of progress and a malign influence on young minds, the more so because Henri was so avid a reader. Without a sense of humour and hopelessly insensitive to the subtler gradations of feeling in others, whether children or adults, she quickly assumed the role of uncontested tyrant in a family whose members found it opportune to suppress their instinctive reactions rather than challenge her authority head on.

It is easy to see where the problem lay. Among the three Beyle children, Henri, for whatever reason, was the one most calculated to remind his aunt of her own childlessness. Anything that made her notice him was thus worthy of punishment, but the effect of her spiteful domestic edicts and neurotic rages penetrated more deeply than she can possibly have imagined. The adult Stendhal, for all his appearance of hardbitten detachment, nurtured a raw sensitivity which, when wounded, took comfort in bitterness and scorn. What gives *Vie de Henry Brulard* its singular vividness, muddled and rambling document though the work appears, is a sense that the creative act of writing it was in itself a judgement on those involved in the author's early life. His ultimate victory over Séraphie is to preserve her for us as the archetypal family ogress, the wicked stepmother of Stendhalian romance, yet something of her spirit seems ironically to inform his withering denunciation of her. Probably it is going too far to declare, in the words of an earlier biographer, that she 'deformed his character and depraved him', but the edges of his cynicism and asperity and of his instinctive revolt against banal orthodoxy were unquestionably sharpened through their incessant skirmishes.

Mingled with Henri's detestation of her was a curious erotic ambivalence, on which he is as candid as ever:

> Each morning she used to walk out bare-legged, without stockings, in the courtyard. I was seized with such a devil that the legs of my very worst enemy would have made an impression on me. I should willingly have fallen in love with Séraphie, conceiving a delicious pleasure in squeezing this relentless foe in my embrace.

Whatever its true nature, such a feeling did nothing to dampen his joy when, on 9 January 1797, Séraphie, aged only thirty-six, died after a long illness. The termagant who had dragged him out on long, boring walks, who had tried in vain to censor his reading, who had labelled him an impious liar and criminal, was dead at last, and the boy, hearing a servant say 'she has passed away', sank to his knees on the kitchen floor to thank God for so great a deliverance. He was not alone. The entire family, after a week of decent sorrow, heaved a sigh of relief. Even his father, whom he characteristically suspected of a liaison with her, seemed thankful for the passing of this household devil.

By then, in any case, Henri's fear of Séraphie had been replaced by smouldering rage. One evening, incensed by the continual sneaking of his younger sister, Zénaïde, he pencilled a caricature of her on the wall of the corridor outside his grandfather's dining room, captioned with the words: 'Caroline Zénaïde B-- telltale'. The customary after-supper card party was in progress, with the family and their guests playing boston, a French game whose technical terms were derived from the American War of Independence.

When Séraphie discovered the offending sketch, drawn in the guise of a framed portrait, her fury broke up the party. Two of her cousins, Antoinette Romagnier and Justine Colomb, happening to be present, were enlisted in support, but the pair, both of whom were as irritated by her fussing as they were devoted to Henri, rose from the table as though ready to go home, a move which merely made her more angry. As she advanced on the unrepentant culprit, he seized a wicker-bottomed chair to defend himself, holding it in front of him while he backed down the corridor towards the kitchen with his aunt in pursuit. There he remained, weeping indignantly at her stream of obloquy, bitterly ashamed of his tears, until it was time for supper. He had after all been right about Zénaïde, towards whom he remained coldly suspicious for the rest of his life. With his other sister, Pauline, a closeness developed only when he left Grenoble and found in her an intelligent and lively correspondent. In the Beyle household itself, the sole source of emotional warmth and friendliness came from the servants, united in their dislike of Séraphie and a certain protective fondness for Henri.

He discovered an ally in his grandfather's valet, Vincent Lamberton, known as Lambert. The young man's initial rejection of his attachment with the occasional cuff round the ear only made Henri more fond of him. Intelligent, ambitious and eager to free himself from a menial position, Lambert had bought a mulberry tree and begun to cultivate silkworms. One day, climbing to pick the leaves, he fell off a ladder, and the resultant concussion led, after three days of blindness and delirium, to his death at the age of twenty-three.

The effect on Henri was devastating. Lambert was the first person beyond his immediate family circle for whom he had felt any genuine love:

> The pain of Lambert's death was of a kind I have experienced throughout the rest of my life, a meditative, tearless, inconsolable sorrow. I was shattered and always on the point of collapsing as I entered, ten times a day, the room where my friend lay, and looked at his handsome face as he died. I shall never forget his beautiful black eyelashes and the air of health and strength which the fever only accentuated. . . . Once, in Italy, I saw a picture of Saint John watching the crucifixion of his friend and his God, and I was suddenly reminded of everything I experienced twenty five years before with the death of 'poor Lambert' as we always called him thereafter. I could fill five or six pages with my precise and enduring recollections of such terrible grief. They nailed him in the coffin and carried him away . . . . *Sunt lacrimae rerum.*

A week or so later, Séraphie received one of her nephew's rare marks of approval when she vented her anger on the servant who brought her soup in the faience dish that had been used to catch Lambert's blood. As Henri burst into uncontrollable tears, she scolded him and he ran into the kitchen crying, 'Infame, infame!' In nearly forty years he would never forget Lambert and 'the paroxysms of love, enough to burst a blood vessel' he had felt towards the young man.

There was always the refuge of his grandfather's house in the Place Grenette. Stendhal treasured the memory of Dr Henri Gagnon not merely as a loving and companionable presence in the background of a lonely childhood, but also as symbolizing that part of his inheritance he most valued and wanted others to notice, that lively, pleasure-loving, *désinvolte* side to his character which he believed was the legacy of an Italian ancestry. Had not his great-aunt Elisabeth, after all, told him that Dr Gagnon was born in Avignon, 'a city of Provence, the land where oranges came from, as she said with a sigh'? And had she not spoken also of an Italian forebear named Guadagni or Guadanianno, guilty of 'some little murder', who had found sanctuary in the Pope's domain of Comtat-Venaissin during the seventeenth century?

Despite this obvious impulse towards wish-fulfilment by one of the most famous of all literary Italophiles, Stendhal's early biographers were disposed to give him the benefit of the doubt. Paul Arbelet, in his monumental *La Jeunesse de Stendhal* (1919), even went so far as to produce an Italian connection in the person of a Johannes Gagnoni, mentioned in a fifteenth-century diocesan charter as settled at Bédarrides, between Avignon and Orange. Subsequent research has revealed, however, that either Elisabeth Gagnon or her nephew or both of them were romancing. Gagnon is a common enough name in the Midi, deriving from a generic word for the young of any farm animal (for example, the *limousin* word for a piglet, *gagnoun*) and the origins of the doctor's family were among humble Provençal peasants, without even the glamour of an unpunished crime, living at Monteux near Carpentras.

It was Jean Gagnon who, towards the end of the seventeenth century, became a military surgeon and moved to Avignon itself. Nobody has yet discovered why his son Antoine, an army doctor like his father, set off northwards to Grenoble, where he married Elisabeth Senterre, a draper's daughter, in 1718. Their son Henri, born ten years later, began his studies at Montpellier, the best-regarded medical school in France, and may have intended to follow family traditions by becoming a regimental surgeon. The desultory and ultimately inconclusive War of the Austrian Succession brought fierce fighting to France's south-eastern frontiers, and Henri Gagnon had his first and only taste of soldiering at the bloody battle of L'Assiette on 17 July 1747, when a French force was defeated by the troops of the King of Savoy, holding the Mont Cenis pass.

Prudently returning to Montpellier to complete his degree, Henri Gagnon at length set up in practice in his native city. As one of the consultant physicians at the Grenoble general hospital, he was admired as much for the soundness of his diagnoses as for the charm of his bedside manner. Among the first local doctors to practise smallpox vaccination, he also experimented with herbal treatments for venereal disease and extended his scientific interests to embrace meteorology and astronomy. His significance in Grenoble society increased with the Revolution, when, during an outbreak of putrid fever in 1799 among wounded soldiers returning from the Italian campaign, he was asked to provide a concise report on the dubious issue of the town's sanitation. In its recommendations of fresh air, sound diet and a scrupulous moderation in the use of purgatives and stimulants as a basis for medical treatment, Gagnon's memorandum shows an admirably enlightened practicality. The document's stylistic clarity suggests, what is more, that he left something more useful to his grandson than mere affectionate recollections.

The doctor cut a distinguished if somewhat eccentric figure among his fellow citizens. Though sporting a fine head of hair, he felt it more appropriate to his position to continue wearing, long after the fashion had died out, an enormous powdered peruke with three rows of curls. He made a point of never riding in a carriage and always carrying his three-cornered hat under his arm as he moved with rheumatic stiffness through the streets of Grenoble, leaning on an elegant little boxwood cane inlaid with tortoiseshell.

His popularity, whether among the poor, whom he often treated free of charge, or with the nobility, whose medical confidences a strong dash of snobbery made him relish, derived from an indulgent gentleness of manner. Stendhal, however grateful for his grandfather's presence among the dramatis personae of a tragicomic childhood, never fails to emphasize what he calls the 'à la Fontenelle' aspects of Dr Gagnon's character, the irritating readiness to put up with Séraphie's rages, the reluctance to speak out when really necessary, those negative qualities of prudence and discretion which prevented him from assuming roles of genuine political and social prominence during the early days of the Revolution.

Gagnon had nevertheless contributed his share to the cultural life of Grenoble, as a founder member of the Académie Delphinale in 1772 and as the initiator, in the same year, of a proposal for establishing a public library in the town. The doctor's literary tastes were those of a true son of the Enlightenment: tolerant, liberal, easygoing in matters of religion and morality. Stendhal tells us that he kept a little bust of Voltaire, whom he had visited in his Swiss retreat at Ferney and whose name he never mentioned without a smile of affectionate respect. Predictably perhaps, his favourite writer was Horace, whose mood of well-tempered sensual enjoyment harmonized with Gagnon's own domestic philosophy.

It was natural that Henri, responsive, intelligent and apparently without any friends of his own age, should come under the influence of a man in whose company he spent so many of his waking hours. The house in the Place Grenette, with its terrace overlooking the square, was far more of a home to him than the death-marked Rue des Vieux-Jésuites. Even though we know, from an inventory taken at Chérubin Beyle's death, that the boy's father was a reader of surprisingly catholic tastes (his library included the *Encyclopédie, Paradise Lost*, Voltaire, Beccaria, Locke, Montesquieu and Richardson) it was Dr Gagnon who fostered that retentive curiosity which was eventually to make Stendhal one of the best-read writers of the early nineteenth century.

In his grandfather's library the boy was given more or less complete freedom, though certain works needed more surreptitious inspection than others. Scarcely turned ten years old, Henri was reading, under the doctor's direction, Voltaire's tragedies and the same author's masterly *Siècle de Louis XIV* and *Histoire de Charles XII*. To discovering James Bruce's *Voyage to the Sources of the Nile*, in French translation, he attributed his 'lively enthusiasm for all the sciences of which the writer speaks. Hence my love of mathematics.' Even the turgid *Séthos, Histoire ou Vie, tirée des monuments, anecdotes de l'ancienne Egypte*, a three-volume didactic romance by the Abbé Terrasson, was a mine of interest, if only because its educational aims were disguised, however thinly, within fictional trappings.

Other books required to be read in secret. Stendhal remembered that when the news of Louis XVI's execution was brought to Dr Gagnon's house, he was pretending to study while secretly reading the Abbé Prévost's *Mémoires d'un homme de qualité*, the novel which contains within it, as a detachable narrative, the author's best-known work, *Manon Lescaut*. Rousseau too was officially forbidden him, but he managed to get hold of the enormously popular *La Nouvelle Héloïse*, and though he was later to abhor its influence on the writers of his generation, he still felt that the novel's emphasis on emotional sincerity and warmth of heart had been fundamental in developing his own regard for honesty at all costs as a measure of human greatness.

Not all Dr Gagnon's recommendations were enthusiastically accepted. However markedly Voltairean in its merciless economy and clarity the mature Stendhalian manner, Henri, as child and adult, showed no special love for the author of *Candide*, 'legislator and apostle of France, her Martin Luther'. A marginal jotting in a volume of Schlegel, dated 15 March 1821, lists, beside Buffon and Madame de Staël as Stendhal's antipathies, 'Voltaire, extremely and for ever'. Molière, for whom he was later to develop an enduring admiration, held no charms for a boy in search of poetry and romance, whose favourite reading included *Don Quixote* (much disapproved of by Chérubin because it made his son laugh) and Ariosto's *Orlando Furioso*. Bored to death by Racine, a favourite of his father's, he despised him as a contemptible hypocrite who, according to legend, had died of disappointment at not attracting suitable notice from Louis XIV.

Corneille was a different matter. The verve and passion of his lines and the courage of a writer unafraid to take risks and make costly artistic mistakes were more likely to appeal to Stendhal than the formal perfections of a dramatist like Racine who covered his tracks so successfully. What was more, the older playwright was a decided favourite with his beloved great-aunt Elisabeth, a figure of positively heroic proportions among the cast of *Vie de Henry Brulard*. She possessed all those qualities in which her niece Séraphie was so notably deficient, and several which, morally at least, might have lent her brother, Dr Gagnon, a more impressive personality. She was brave, dignified, reticent and entirely independent, and from what Stendhal tells us, there is every reason to believe that she despised the rest of her family for their failure to rise to her level.

Elisabeth's role as an elderly maiden aunt, the 'Tatan' of her nephew and nieces, was scarcely an enviable one. Even if she was supposed to have been crossed in love as a young girl, any chance of marriage had been sacrificed to the needs of her widowed brother and his family. Her life was essentially a prolonged self-suppression: when Henri's mother died, a favourite niece, she refused to weep, and Stendhal recorded that he never once saw her cry. In recompense, however, she became the embodiment of an unimpeachable integrity, the source of 'all the honour, all the lofty and crazy impulses of the family'.

The standard by which she judged others was that of her father,

Jean Gagnon, whom she remembered weeping with rage when the Austrians were preparing to capture Toulon in 1746. It was impossible to imagine his son, the witty Voltairean doctor, manifesting this sort of patriotism. As for Chérubin Beyle, he would at once have begun calculating what profit he could make out of the operation. The fact that Stendhal felt, on this point as on others, an immediate sympathy with his great-aunt was important in distancing him from the bourgeois atmosphere surrounding him, one of cowardly opportunism and infinite variations on the themes of deceit and hypocrisy. He may not always have been true to the spirit of Elisabeth's sternly expressed morality, but at any rate he tried as far as possible to show himself worthy of it.

In artistic matters her yardstick was Corneille's classic tragedy of love and honour *Le Cid*, in which the hero's struggle to sustain his moral identity was bound to appeal to her imagination. Elisabeth's ultimate accolade for anything she admired, a word, an action, a book, was 'beau comme le *Cid*', and since the great paladin himself was a Spaniard, it was natural that Stendhal should think of his aunt, obsessed by honour like some Castilian hidalgo, as having 'a Spanish soul'.

Henri was taken to a performance of *Le Cid* by his uncle, Romain Gagnon, but anyone less Cornelian in spirit it is hard to conceive of. As depicted by Stendhal, this handsome libertine cynic walks into the world of Henry Brulard from the genteelly scabrous pages of *Les Liaisons Dangereuses* or the novels of Restif de la Bretonne. If, as Dr Gagnon was in the habit of saying, 'my son has read nothing', he was still a natural charmer, whose personal and social gifts were enhanced by a none too strenuous practice of the law and by an allowance from his father, with which, as Stendhal succinctly notes, 'he bought embroidered coats and kept actresses'.

It was Henri's delight, at the house in Place Grenette, to go upstairs in the evening to his uncle's rooms, to watch him take off these elegant coats and change into a dressing gown before supper, which was served at nine o'clock each night. Then the boy would take up the silver candlestick and solemnly light Romain downstairs. They were always, he remembered, tallow rather than wax candles, but the Gagnons made much of the fact that they were specially made of goat's fat from the mountains around Briançon in the eastern Dauphiné.

Romain's glamour made him into another of those figures whom his nephew's imagination eagerly set up against the hated Chérubin, so utterly devoid of elegance or panache. 'Young, brilliant and lively, my uncle passed easily for the most attractive man in the city,' he wrote, 'to the point at which, years afterwards, Madame Delaunay, seeking to justify her virtue against too many imputed blemishes, said, "All the same, I never yielded to Monsieur Gagnon *fils*."'

Doubtless it was from among Romain's books that Henri, probably by then an adolescent, got hold of Choderlos de Laclos' *Les Liaisons Dangereuses*, that fictional archetype of male sexual freebooting aided by female duplicity and competitiveness, which Stendhal later came to believe had been conceived or actually composed in Grenoble, where the author's regiment had been stationed for some years.* Still more exciting was a pile of paperbound novels which his uncle had thrown aside as pulp reading, but which Henri, forbidden to touch them by Dr Gagnon, seized upon avidly. The most alluringly trashy was evidently the much-reprinted *Félicia ou mes fredaines*, attributed to the Chevalier de Nerciat, a mildly pornographic tale in which the eponymous heroine, urged by her uncle not to waste time over scruples but to gather her rosebuds while she may, takes him at his word, recounting her erotic adventures to the curious reader.

Ironically this novel, of no literary merit whatever, confirmed Henri in his resolve to become a writer, even if at that stage it was as a dramatist rather than as a novelist that he aimed to succeed. Equally significant was the influence of works such as *Félicia*, not to speak of *Les Liaisons Dangereuses*, on Stendhal's view of sex as essentially a matter of successfully achieved conquests à la Don Juan. After his death, in one of the most penetrating tributes paid to the singularity of his genius, his friend Prosper Mérimée would recall that 'he always seemed convinced

* In Chapter 6 of *Vie de Henry Brulard* he claims to be able to identify Mme de Merteuil as a certain Mme de Montmaur, who owned an estate near his grandfather's at Voreppe.

by the idea, much canvassed under the Empire, that any woman may be taken by storm and that it is up to every man to attempt it'. We must make what we please of the military metaphor, though it is hard not to equate such a point of view with the image of thrusting, restless imperial acquisitiveness provided by that ultimate totem Napoleon Bonaparte.

As an earlier role model, Romain Gagnon remained immensely attractive to his nephew, who described him as 'bringing joy into the family'. In 1790 he had married the charming Cécile-Camille Poncet, and the pair had later gone to live close to her parents at Les Echelles on the borders of Italian Savoy, in a small, two-storey house with a conical roof, where a mountain stream called the Guiers plashed on the rocks below amid a surrounding landscape of forests, meadows and the heights of the Grande Chartreuse in the distance.

Stendhal, unlike most of his contemporaries, was wholly unsentimental in the matter of natural description. At certain points where he introduces it into his fiction, it even appears forced and uncomfortable, and he was at pains to distance himself, whatever his admiration for Sir Walter Scott, from the kind of northern-romantic descriptive vein which so influenced later writers such as Manzoni in *I Promessi Sposi*. He was strongly sensitive, nevertheless, to the enchantment of a rural scene, whether experienced directly or recalled from youthful expeditions to his father's country house, Furonières, in the Drac valley south of Grenoble.

Les Echelles, however, was the place his memory cherished best of all, for its identification with that absolute happiness which became his talisman in adulthood. As he embarks on his account of a stay there in 1791 when he was eight years old (presumably intended as a distraction from the shock of his mother's recent death) we can feel Stendhal's narrative control, even in the context of a work as subjectively disorganized as *Henry Brulard*, dissolving beneath the pressure of an almost unbearable joy.

'It was for me,' he recalls:

> like a stay in heaven, everything was quite ravishing. The noise of the Guiers, a torrent flowing some two hundred paces before my

> uncle's windows, became a sacred sound for me, transporting me instantly to heaven.
>
> Words start to fail me already. I must start working these passages over and transcribing them. . . . Where can I find language to paint such perfect happiness, enjoyed with pleasure and without satiety by a sensitive soul, almost to extinction and madness?
>
> I don't know whether I might not give up the enterprise. I can't describe, it seems, this happiness, ravishing, pure, fresh, divine, except by enumerating the evils and boredom which were so notably absent. A sad enough means of depicting happiness.

No more Séraphie, no more priests, no more Chérubin and studying Latin in the Rue des Vieux-Jésuites. Here instead was beautiful Aunt Camille, of whose white thigh he caught a fleeting glimpse as she stepped from the carriage and who became 'an object of the most ardent desire'. Here was Uncle Romain, surrounded by a perpetual atmosphere of amorous badinage, whether involving Camille's sister or Fanchon, the chambermaid. They all doted on Henri, to whom his grandfather had encouragingly said, 'You're ugly, but no one will ever criticize you for that.' There were parties at the house of Monsieur Bonne of Berlandet, where Henri went for donkey rides and threw stones at a girl of whom he grew jealous and for a punishment was lifted into the high branches of an apple tree by an army officer, 'le grand Corbeau', who had been rejected by Camille in favour of Romain. There were excursions to a nearby grotto, walks in the woods and hunting trips along the banks of the Guiers. How they laughed when Corbeau's fishing line got tangled in a tall tree, with a fat trout still hanging on the end of it!

A return to Grenoble meant going back to the drudgery of learning, along the lines set out by Chérubin Beyle. He was the sort of careful father, not unlike the fatally misguided Prince Consort moulding the unfortunate Albert Edward as a model Prince of Wales, who views children as essentially idle, perverse and naturally disposed to crime, so that the idea of recreation and free time as both necessary and educative is seen merely as a passport to unregenerate wickedness. He meant well, with his little lectures on parental solicitude and filial duty, but the premise from which he began, a belief that his son was fundamentally wicked, was calculated to erode still further the already dubious basis of their relationship.

The preceptor chosen for his son has passed into French literary history as the ogre-pedagogue *par excellence*, a monster against whose practices and principles his most famous pupil spent the rest of his life in conscious revolt. Though Stendhal, on at least one occasion, acknowledged that his judgement of the Abbé Jean-François Raillane was more than a trifle harsh, he never forgave him for poisoning the atmosphere of his childhood and stifling any impulse he may have had towards making friends with boys of his own age. So traumatic indeed was 'la tyrannie Raillane' that Stendhal viewed his ultimate deliverance from the Abbé's tutelage as crucial in the shaping of his destiny. Without this escape (whose precise circumstances are never properly established *Vie de Henry Brulard*) he would, he believed, almost certainly have been turned into a scheming hypocritical Jesuit or else into a dissolute army officer.

Raillane, though born in Avignon, was without any of those saving meridional graces Stendhal was prepared to claim on behalf of the Gagnons. Small, thin, pinched, with a greenish complexion, he had a shifty look, 'abominable eyebrows', and could be memorably summed up in the almost untranslatable phrase 'un noir coquin' (literally, 'a black rogue', though there is clearly more to it than this). In addition to all his other faults, Raillane's was that besetting sin of tutors and schoolmasters, the compulsion to be forever dispensing precepts and injunctions, so that every circumstance is transformed into a lesson.

His discourse, Stendhal notes witheringly, was like that of some modern government newspaper, forever warning against the dangers of liberty. All around them his wretched charges from among the various good families of Grenoble beheld images of the freedom which they themselves were denied by his insidious watchfulness. On a walk along the banks of the Isère, for example, they looked on enviously as other youngsters played and swam in the river: the Abbé, prophesying the swimmers' imminent death by drowning, turned Henri and his companions, the pleasant but intellectually unpromising Chazel and the pretty, blond, shy

Reytiers, into perpetual cowards, succeeding very well in Stendhal's case, who never learned to swim.

The Abbé's practice was to lodge with his pupils' families, and he duly installed himself in the Rue des Vieux-Jésuites. With him he brought his orange trees in pots, beside which Henri was forbidden to eat his breakfast because the breadcrumbs would attract flies which would eat the plants. Next to the boy's bedroom he installed an enormous cage containing some thirty canaries, fed on egg yolks and filling the damp, lightless rooms with the smell of their droppings.

The symbolic implications of this cage, though Stendhal is not at pains to emphasize them, are obvious, and the picture of 'la tyrannie Raillane' which his narrative, snarling and merciless, essentially outlines, is a Romantic incarceration reminiscent of Beethoven's *Fidelio* or Byron's *The Prisoner of Chillon.* The language in which it is couched is that of an enforced alienation from society, in what, at least obliquely, appears to the writer to have been a deliberate attempt to warp his character into the moral deformity appropriate to a future burgher of Cularo–Grenoble. In this sense, however ironically, the Abbé shaped the course of Stendhal's life as essentially that of a refugee in restless self-banishment from the banal solutions of greed, gain and petty emotional suppression held out to him by almost everyone during his first seventeen years of existence.

Like Day & Martin's blacking factory with the mature Dickens, this early trauma was to stay with Stendhal for ever. On 4 December 1835, returning from Rome to the grind of his official duties in Civitavecchia, Consul Beyle, as he then was, fell in with a beautiful young woman from Lyons whose glance cruelly tormented him during the last eight leagues of the journey. When she asked his help in finding a cheap place to stay, he imagined he could scarcely fail with her, but something in that engaging countenance awakened the spectre of Abbé Raillane. 'The aquiline nose, a shade too small, of this attractive Lyonnaise recalled that of the Abbé, so much that I could not even look at her and pretended to fall asleep in the carriage.'

The 'noir coquin' himself was not without defenders. Writing to her sister on 26 April 1803, the wife of one of his early pupils,

Augustin Périer, described Raillane as 'an enlightened man, full of intelligence and readiness to teach, severe but honest, with much that is useful and interesting in his conversation. . . . There can be few Catholic priests so devoid of prejudice and so exalted in feeling.' A colleague drew a sympathetic pen portrait of a punctilious little man in a capacious brown overcoat, his face, with its finely chiselled features, framed by high-piled hair tied in a cue with an embroidered muslin ribbon. During the Revolution he was forced into hiding, moving rapidly from house to house until finally caught, when an order was given to deport him to the Ile de Ré. Before this could be carried out, however, the government of the Directory countermanded the decree, apparently concerned that there might not be enough good teachers left in Grenoble and willing to utilize his proven experience.

Struck from the list of proscribed *émigrés* and allowed full rights and liberties (subject to an oath upholding the Constitution) Raillane opened his own academy, a boarding school which survived the various changes in French politics and was still flourishing in 1830. An inspector's report implies that the establishment was well run, orderly and conducive to its pupils' happiness. The Abbé was helped by his sister-in-law, who was 'full of activity, endowed with intelligence and a mother to the children, to all of whose reasonable wishes she is attentive'. A year later the July Revolution was starting to make the students fractious and demanding, with bad results in all subjects.

The political events which caught up with the Abbé Raillane in 1799 had been significantly anticipated by developments in Grenoble and the Dauphiné as a whole. Throughout the 1780s the region witnessed rising tension between the wealthy bourgeoisie and the more overweening members of the local nobility, dominating the Parlement de Grenoble. This ancient assembly nevertheless fought tenaciously to retain the Dauphiné's peculiar condition of semi-independence, and by 1787 its members were clamouring for the recall of the States General, the French national assembly, which had not met for a hundred and fifty-nine years.

Royal commissioners were finally sent to wind up the Parlement's activities and to reform, by the same token, the entire administration, legal and financial, of the Dauphiné. Such a direct assault on local autonomy was bound to stir up popular feeling among the *grenoblois*. On 7 June 1788 a hostile crowd, reinforced by contingents from the surrounding countryside, surged through the city, seizing control of its various gates to prevent the commissioners from leaving the town. While the troops, led by the military governor, the Duc de Clermont-Tonnerre, tried to hold back an enraged mob armed with paving stones, a hail of tiles clattered down from the high rooftops, giving the day its name in the annals of Grenoble, 'La Journée des Tuiles'. Though the riot was finally quelled, and in the short term achieved nothing whatever, there was no question of any further serious resistance to the gathering momentum of revolt against central authority. Pioneered by the lawyers Jean-Joseph Mounier and Joseph Barnave, the constitution proposed by the recalled Parlement, favourable both to aristocrats and to untitled property owners such as Chérubin Beyle and Henri Gagnon, rapidly became a popular model for a future national government.

By the end of 1789, however, the Dauphiné and its chief cities had been overwhelmed by the speed and violence of successive events detonated by the fall of the Bastille. Attempts to re-establish order in the countryside after a wave of château-burnings merely fuelled local resentment, and the moderate Mounier fell out with Barnave, whose extremism made him more obviously a man of the hour, even if four years later a secret correspondence with the imprisoned Louis XVI and Marie-Antoinette would bring him at last to the guillotine.

The news of the King's execution on 21 January 1793 was greeted by a loyal declaration from the council of the newly formed Department of the Isère, assuring the government that in 'letting fall, beneath the stroke of the law, the guilty head of the last tyrant of the French, the Assembly had deserved well of the nation, had honoured France and could only be repudiated by cowards'. The ten-year-old Henri Beyle thought the same. While the rest of the household in the Rue des Vieux-Jésuites wrung its hands in horror and alarm at the sovereign's fate, Henri continued quietly working in his father's study. It was seven o'clock in the evening when the sound of the Lyons mail coach was heard in the street outside. 'I must go and see what the monsters have done,' said Chérubin. 'I hope they'll have executed the traitor,' thought Henri. Coming back into the house, his father said with a sigh, 'It's over, they have murdered him.' At that point, writes Stendhal, 'I was seized with one of the most fervent impulses of joy I ever knew in all my life.'

Stendhal was at no stage especially sympathetic towards either violent revolution or towards the kind of idealized view of the proletariat which distinguished certain of his Romantic contemporaries in England and Germany. The child's delight at the news of an event which elsewhere throughout France was hailed with little genuine rejoicing may have had more to do with his ingrained opposition to the bourgeois conservatism embodied by his father than with any particular political sophistication.

His sense of the occasion's momentousness, which made him shut his eyes 'so as to enjoy this great event in peace', was matched by a similar reaction the following year to one of the few manifestations of the Reign of Terror to take place in Grenoble. On a June morning in 1794, Henri sat by the window reading Virgil with his fat, ignorant Latin master, Durand, while a crowd gathered in the Place Grenette to witness the execution of two priests named Ravenas and Guillabert. Where Dr Gagnon was frozen with horror, Séraphie enraged and Elisabeth more impenetrably plunged than ever into one of her haughty Spanish silences, Stendhal says that he felt only pleasure, writing the word in English to emphasize the horrifying incongruity of his emotion. Challenged on his implacability by the family confessor, Monsieur Dumollard, Henri reminded him that only twenty years previously the Parlement had sentenced two Protestant ministers to death. There was, maintained Dumollard, a certain difference. The boy's reply was glacially lofty: 'They were condemned for religion: these died for betraying their country.'

Henri's acute, multifaceted sensitivity quickly alerted him to the inherent vulgarity of Jacobinism. Once, on the pretext of going to meet Aunt Elisabeth at a friend's house, he went to a reunion of the Jacobin club which had taken over the church of Saint André. What he had innocently expected to be a meeting of heroic patriots, after the fashion of those republican Romans so popular with the painters of the period, turned out to be a disorderly, decidedly common assembly, characterized by the attendance of women of the lowest class and entirely lacking in revolutionary glamour. From henceforth his enduring image of the Jacobins was one of ugliness and grime.

One by one, the sterner and more excessive aspects of the French Revolution began to manifest themselves in *grenoblois* daily life. In 1792 the 'Ça ira' was heard for the first time in the Place Grenette, where the citizens danced the Carmagnole, lists of *émigrés* were posted throughout the town and the royal arms and all noble escutcheons were removed from palaces and churches. In the spring of the following year the arrival, at the invitation of the *Société populaire des amis de la Liberté et de l'Egalité*, of André Amar and Jean-François-Marie Merlino, government officials armed with lists of suspected enemies of the Republic, was the signal for a general round-up of the less enthusiastic beneficiaries of the new political order.

A deputy to the Convention from the Isère department and a vociferous supporter of the King's death sentence, Amar was no stranger to Grenoble. He had been, indeed, a colleague of Chérubin Beyle, both as an advocate of the Parlement and as a member of the same masonic lodge, suitably if ironically named 'L'Egalité'. His intimate acquaintance with the upper orders of *grenoblois* society made the preparation of a proscription list an easy matter. His letter to the Committee of Public Safety, couched in appropriate language, spoke of 'the insolent aristocracy' parading 'its audacious front beneath the tacit but unmistakable protection of the constituent authority. . . . Here we have found nothing but the rump of the Parlement and spirits opposed to the tyrant's death.'

The roster of 162 names included, among the clergy, that of Abbé Raillane, and among those of the nobility several of Dr Gagnon's patients. Though the doctor himself was not named, Chérubin Beyle was one of those arrested and imprisoned. For sixty-five days, from 5 May to 9 July, he was kept in the former convent of Sainte-Marie-d'en-Haut, where he was permitted to receive food from his family and allowed out for walks on parole. In August, when the authorities were growing particularly nervous over Grenoble's exposed position close to the frontier with

Piedmont, now at war with France, he was jailed once more for a similar term. This time the age of most of the prisoners rescued them from a cheerless incarceration throughout the sharp *dauphinois* winter.

In 1794 Chérubin was finally cleared of all suspicion. The watch committee of Claix, where he held his country property, confirmed that 'citizen Belle [sic]' was 'not at all counter-revolutionary'. Nevertheless it is hard not to suppose that some ancient jealousy of Amar's had triumphed over their masonic bond, and that the arrest was in the nature of a revenge, as Beyle himself believed. Henri's response was as pitiless as might be expected. 'But,' said he to his father at supper, 'Amar put you down as notoriously *suspect* of not loving the Republic, whereas it seems to me that you *truly* do not love it.' While his outraged family condemned him to silence throughout the meal, he merely reflected with saturnine detachment on the accuracy of his semantic distinction.

Dr Gagnon, however consistently disdainful of Jacobin commonness and revolutionary extremism, remained unscathed. He was clearly far too significant a figure in the city to be harassed by inquisitors and threats of denunciation. It was not long before he was called upon to assist in organizing Grenoble's own Ecole Centrale, following the official decree of 25 February 1795, establishing such schools throughout France. Deliberately running counter to the educational principles of the Ancien Régime, which regarded literature as the pivotal feature of the curriculum, the Ecoles Centrales reflected the practicalities of an enlightened pedagogy incorporating a study of sciences, modern languages, drawing and legislation, and reserving grammar for the attention of the higher forms of sixteen years and over.

The school, now the Lycée Stendhal, was inaugurated on 21 August 1796*, with an elaborate ceremony in which the 'jeunesse intéressante, douce espérance de la patrie' was addressed by a variety of officials employing the ageless rhetoric of French public oratory, before Dr Gagnon rose to his feet. Adducing the use of

* '*4 fructidor, an IV*', according to the Revolutionary calendar. I have used modern dating to avoid confusion.

telegraphy, developments in gunnery and the benefits of chemical knowledge in warfare as proof that scientific study was of real value to an embattled nation, he took a well-aimed swipe at the Terror and its principal perpetrators in causing the deaths of artists and *savants*. By now the Directory had assumed power, and a benign idealism, the legacy of Rousseau and the *philosophes*, pervaded educational thinking. The doctor, who had lived to witness, for a brief but halcyon moment, the triumph of most if not all of his cherished principles in the school's creation, spoke fervently of 'forsaking systems in favour of seeking truth by way of experience', a phrase revealing a remarkable similarity in outlook between Gagnon and the Stendhal his grandson Henri Beyle would later become.

Stendhal always recognized his good fortune in having attended the Ecole Centrale de Grenoble. This and its sister schools would last barely a decade before Napoleon's repressive government saw fit to close them for good. Both in curriculum and discipline they were the most advanced institutions of their kind in Europe, and it was to be more than a century before anything comparable emerged elsewhere in the field of secondary education.

The pupils could choose their course and relinquish them as they saw fit. Perceiving what many teachers and parents still fail to grasp, that punishment merely for the sake of reprisal or as an assertion of authority is negative and useless, the educationalists forbade beating, encouraging instead an appeal to the pupil's sense of shame. There were to be nature walks, outings of different kinds and plenty of holidays, especially those designed to celebrate the various Republican virtues and triumphs.

It was all a far cry from 'la tyrannie Raillane', even if Henri did find his fellow students somewhat common and uninspiring. The teaching staff included several exceptionally gifted and eminent figures, including the literature master Jean-Gaspard Dubois-Fontanelle. A prolific writer, he had published novels, travel books, a life of Pietro Aretino and a translation of Ovid, as well as a celebrated tragedy, *Ericie ou la Vestale*, attacking fanaticism and monastic vows. Henri's original exercise books for Dubois' lessons survive, and from them we can reconstruct the wide-ranging course, which involved a survey of artistic genres (including pastoral poetry and opera) the copying out of extracts and the study of eloquence. Dubois' taste, especially in foreign literature, was immensely catholic, but his favourite books outside the French tradition were mostly written in English. He introduced his pupils to Milton, Ben Jonson, Dryden, Addison and 'Ossian', though he was less enthusiastic about the rule-breaking Shakespeare, on whom he held that Voltaire had improved in his translation of Hamlet's 'To be or not to be'.

Henri, who had already begun to fall under the Shakespearian spell, was not as appreciative as he should have been towards the gouty little man with the absurd peruke and the dumpy German wife, maintaining that 'he had practically no influence on my character'. The restless adolescent much preferred lessons with the Abbé Gattel, who taught logic and 'general grammar', basically philosophy studied in relation to the use of language as a vehicle for original thought. Under Gattel's tutelage, Stendhal first encountered the ideas of Hobbes and Locke and the writings of Helvétius and Condillac. The philosophical and theoretical grounding he received in these classes remained with him for the rest of his life, and the combative grittiness and ruthless clarity of his prose style owes much to this early training in rigorous abstraction.

Not for nothing, therefore, was his favourite subject mathematics. 'I loved them and I love them still,' he tells us, 'for themselves, as not admitting hypocrisy or vagueness, my two pet aversions.' The mathematical discipline monopolized Henri so completely that when one of his friends told him that his hair was too long, he complained that getting it cut would be a waste of a valuable half hour's study. 'I worked like Michelangelo in the Sistine Chapel.' Soon abandoning the dull classes of Monsieur Dupuy de Bordes, one of whose former pupils was none other than Napoleon Bonaparte, and the plodding standard textbook, Etienne Bezout's *Cours complet de mathématiques*,* he turned instead to the far more stimulating Louis Gabriel Gros, an inspired geometry teacher and a convinced Jacobin.

* To which Napoleon had in fact addressed a poem which began, 'Grand Bezout, achève ton cours'.

Their lessons together, Stendhal implies, had to be carried on in secret, as Gros' politics made him unacceptable either to the Gagnons or to Chérubin Beyle. His academic brilliance was matched by a thoroughgoing negligence in matters of dress. Another of his pupils, Romain Colomb, Stendhal's cousin and executor, remembered Gros appearing at school in baggy nankeen breeches without stockings, but identified this with his 'perfect image of pure, modest, disinterested republicanism'. Stendhal himself paid tribute to his maths master both in *Le Rouge et le Noir*, where he appears by name as 'the one honest man' in the town of Verrières, and more significantly in *Lucien Leuwen* as the republican newspaper editor Gauthier:

> This M. Gauthier was a huge, Herculean young man with beautiful blond hair which he wore too long. It was his only affectation – simple gestures, obvious sincerity, and an extreme energy which could be turned towards anything, rescued him from vulgarity . . . he was a true fanatic, yet beneath his passion for a France ruled 'by herself alone' lay a fine spirit. . . . Upon a giant body, Gauthier had the head of a genius, and splendid blond hair curling most attractively.

The mingled appreciation of physical beauty and moral integrity is significant. Gros was the first adult whom Henri, already so maturely alert to the insufficiencies of those around him, could genuinely and unreservedly admire.

Held in almost as much regard was the Jacobin bookseller Falcon, president of the club of which the boy had gained such a dismal impression from his one clandestine visit. Henri liked Falcon the more because Chérubin and Aunt Séraphie were so vehement in their detestation of him. After the Terror had died down, the authorities forbade 'those who had participated in the horrors committed under the tyranny' to gather at his shop, and the *grenoblois* made up a doggerel song about:

> Falcon dans sa boutique
> Avec toute sa clique,
> Chacun fait la nique,
> Ils poussent des holà! ha ha, ha ha!

O, les tristes figures
Qu'ils ont, je vous assure;
ils ont tous l'encolure
De craindre le trépas: ha ha, ha ha!

In his fine powdered wig and scarlet coat, with the tricolor hung outside his shop at the news of each fresh victory of the French armies, Falcon became for Henri both the perfect image of republican virtue and of the *dauphinois* regional character at its indomitable best.

It was natural enough that Henri, his susceptible affections starved during a lonely childhood, should feel able to hope at last for friends on joining the Ecole Centrale. The Romantic ideal of friendship, with its powerful homoerotic undertones, found no real fulfilment, however, among his classmates, who were neither lively or crazy enough, lacked nobility and refinement, and could be summed up as merely a bunch of selfish scamps. Yet, difficult as they in their turn found him, a surly, vindictive loner who deliberately hung back from their various sports, Henri gathered together a small handful of companions who, with one tragic exception, would remain close to him until the end of his life.

Louis Crozet, small, ugly and nervous, earned respect for his fiercely articulate intelligence and a readiness to speak as he found, qualities which Henri was to appreciate later when, as young men in Paris, they undertook a study of Molière and philosophy together. Louis de Barral, reliable if somewhat dour, was one of the few schoolfriends for whom his admiration remained untempered by the bitterness of age and experience: writing in 1835, when both were in their early fifties, Stendhal affirmed 'He is the person in the world who loves me best, and there's no sacrifice I wouldn't perform for him'. As for the brilliant Piedmontese mathematical prodigy Giovanni Plana, whose family had long been settled in Grenoble, the writer, with his competitive passion for assessing the greatness of his contemporaries, soon placed him among the likeliest talents of his generation. 'If nothing turns Plana aside, he'll be a great man in ten years' time', and indeed he was, becoming director of the royal observatory in Turin and a highly distinguished astronomer.

There was one friend whom destiny was to cast in the most unenviable role regarding our acceptance of *Vie de Henry Brulard* as a faithful record of its author's early years. By the time he came to write the book, Stendhal's friendship with Joseph-Désiré-Félix Faure was to all intents and purposes over. If we take its many derogatory references to him at their face value however, the real significance of Faure in Stendhal's life beomes all too easily blurred. For at least ten years the two were the closest of companions and correspondents, even if Henri seems to have grown increasingly disappointed by his friend's tendency to depressive gloom, using the English word 'Happy' with obvious irony to translate his Latin forename. Félix was to be useful to him, not merely as a comrade in arms during the Napoleonic campaigns, but also as a legal advisor in unscrambling the complexities, disadvantageous as they ultimately proved, of Chérubin Beyle's estate, Only later, when a successful career was crowned with a peerage and an important role in public life during the 1830s, was he metamorphosed into a correlative for all those unresolved feelings of frustrated wordly ambition which helped in some measure to bring *Brulard* into being.

One of his friends, Maurice Diday, played the role of second in a duel fought with a fellow student from the art classes conducted by Louis-Joseph Jay, less impressive as a painter than as a teacher inspiring his pupils by playing on their competitive instincts. One afternoon, as they worked vigorously away at life drawing, a big boy named Odru got in Henri's way and was rewarded with a powerful slap. A moment later Odru, pulling away his chair, pitched him on the floor. The already smouldering animosity between the pair, originally created by Henri's caricature of Odru as 'Odruas Kambin' (alluding to his pronunciation of the phrase 'quand bien') crackled into life as the pair challenged one another to a duel with pistols.

Stendhal, recalling the incident years later, was not at all sure where they managed to obtain their weapons, but remembered that somehow they ended up at the Porte de Graille, overlooking the river. Unable to shake off the crowd of fellow students who came after them, they moved away again as twilight fell, into the ditch running below the city ramparts. Here the customary ritual began, with the loading of the pistols and the marking out of paces. Henri fixed his eyes on a distant hilltop, shaped like a flattened cone, and awaited the moment.

It never arrived. Neither gun went off, and the affair concluded with a grudging peace, on which the infuriated Odru and his stern opponent refused absolutely to shake hands. Henri's reputation, whatever his own doubtful feelings as to the propriety of a duel ending in this damp-squib fashion for someone brought up on Aunt Elisabeth's *espagnolisme* and the ideals of *Le Cid*, was made among his schoolfellows. The gloomy rebel, alienated through his own dourness and malice, was now a figure of dignified confidence, preparing to take his place among the Ecole Centrale's earliest prizewinners.

'L'affaire Odru', essentially an absurd squabble between two peevish adolescents, emphasizes that unostentatious courage which is one of Stendhal's most appealing characteristics. His sense of personal honour was uncompromised either by boasting or by the kind of pompous military rodomontade so typical of the Napoleonic age. He was brave and he knew it, yet he lacked the necessary brag to carry it off handsomely. 'In moments of great danger,' he wrote, 'I'm natural and simple'. It was not long before he was to face a great many such moments.

A more bizarre test of Beyle's courage took place some time later when he rallied several friends in the cause of defacing a notice which hung on the Fraternity Tree planted, according to revolutionary principles, in Place Grenette. The tree itself, 'an unfortunate young oak . . . thirty feet high', had been decorated by Stendhal's drawing teacher Louis-Joseph Jay with a placard showing a crown, sceptre and chains above a moralizing inscription. On a cold, dark evening, the conspirators, including his cousin Romain Colomb and the schoolfellow Fortuné Mante with whom he later entered on a business venture at Marseilles, surrounded the tree and levelled a pistol at the offending decoration. When the loud bang aroused the soldiers in the adjacent guardhouse, the boys fled across the square, Henri and his cousin running towards what had once been his grandfather's apartment, now rented out to the Mesdemoiselles Codé, former proprietors of a draper's shop. They found the two old women huddled over their Bible, terrified by the noise and hastily explaining their plight, the cousins joined them at their devotions. When the soldiers burst in and asked whether 'these citizens' had spent the evening in the ladies' company, they were answered by the Mesdemoiselles Codé with an unblinking affirmative. Nobody ever named the culprits afterwards, though next morning it was obvious that the whole school knew of the affair. What puzzled Stendhal afterwards was why the devout spinsters should have lied. He could only guess it was because of their veneration for Dr Gagnon, whose exclusion for political motives from the Grenoble education committee had inspired the schoolboys' daring prank. Looking back on the incident, he would always recall it with pride.

'Freed from tyranny, my soul gained a certain resilience. By degrees I lost my obsession with that exhausting sentiment, impotent hatred.' Henri was ready, in short, to fall in love, and the ideal object presented itself during the winter and spring of 1797–8. In the stuffy, smelly old theatre of Grenoble, where the management, for economy's sake, lit the chandeliers only a moment or so before the overture, and where there were so few dressing rooms that the performers had to take turns getting changed, a visiting theatrical troupe was giving a season of comedies and operas. Among the stars was Mademoiselle Virginie Kubly*, who took the *jeune première* role in Pigault Lebrun's sentimental *Claudine de Florian*, the story of a Savoyard peasant girl who, after her seduction by a young man of fashion, follows him to Turin and becomes his servant.

The play, mingling *larmoyante* romanticism with the approved revolutionary view of virtuous proletarians abused by heartless gentlefolk, was wildly popular with *grenoblois* theatregoers, but for Henri Beyle the focus of attraction was increasingly Mlle Kubly. When anyone named her in his presence, he felt faint and 'there was a kind of storm in my blood'. He grew secretly enraged at anyone calling her, according to perfectly acceptable practice, 'la Kubly' instead of 'Mademoiselle'. It was the beginning of

* Arbelet (op.cit.) gives the name as 'Cubly'; others follow Stendhal's spelling.

'some four or five months of the most intense happiness and sensual delight, bordering on pain, that I have ever known'.

For the first time, through the medium of Virginie Kubly's wretched little voice trilling the airs of Gaveaux and Grétry, Stendhal encountered the lyric song which monopolized his musical passion for the rest of his life. He was entranced not merely by the idea of Kubly herself, the calf-love of a spoony adolescent, but by what her singing represented, the access to a world of powerful sensation, significant on its own account. Much is made of the fact that Stendhal was not a Romantic in the traditional sense of the term, and his distinctive singularity within the artistic context of his period partly arises, indeed, from the distance he kept from its climate of turbid enthusiasm. Yet his unashamed surrender to feeling and his inflexible belief in the primacy of emotion, expressed again and again in his personal writings, make him archetypally the child of his age.

He found out Mlle Kubly's lodging in the Rue des Clercs, and on days when he felt especially brave, walked from one end of the street to the other, greatly relieved at not meeting her. One morning, sauntering in the chestnut avenue of the Jardin de Ville, a popular spot for gallant assignations with the famously flirtatious *grenobloises* and thus forbidden to Henri in the bad old days of Aunt Séraphie, he caught sight of his idol coming towards him. Among the innumerable diagrams included in the manuscript of *Vie de Henry Brulard*, *aides-mémoire* to a reconstructed emotional life, the most amusing plots Henri's flight across the gardens, tortured by the anguish occasioned through a mere sighting of La Kubly.

Stendhal would fall in love with other actresses more talented and successful, but he never forgot Virginie Kubly. In 1811, for example, we find him writing: 'Twelve years ago, the Italian style, that of Alfieri's tomb by Canova, would have bored me; no doubt I wanted art to produce figures like Mlle Kubly. Nowadays a small figure with affected French graces would make me sick at heart.'

As for Virginie herself, she made little impact on the theatrical scene. Her modest career ended in the unrewarding occupation of playing elderly female companions in repertory seasons at provincial theatres. A single glimmer of immortality was cast upon her by the man whom as a boy she may or may not have glanced at one morning, before he ran away in confusion among the trees of the Jardin de Ville.

Many years afterwards, sitting beside Lake Albano, north of Rome, Stendhal amused himself by tracing in the dust the initials of the women he had loved. The first of these was 'V' for Virginie, but it might almost as easily have stood for Victorine, sister of his friend François Bigillion, a classmate at the Ecole Centrale. Bigillion was candid, unpretentious and sincere, the son of what Stendhal calls a 'bourgeois de campagne', living in the village of Saint-Ismier, who had rented a little apartment in Grenoble where his two boys might stay during the school terms. François, together with Victorine and their brother Rémy, 'a humorist and a true *dauphinois*', lived in the Rue Chenoise, where Henri used to sup with them off the walnut table spread with an unbleached holland tablecloth and eat brown bread, something he had never encountered before.

Though Stendhal says he was not at all in love with the thirteen-year-old Victorine, his recollections suggest otherwise. 'We lived, in those days, like young rabbits playing about in a wood and nibbling the wild thyme.' Victorine, as the housewife, used to give Henri bunches of raisins in vineleaves, which he enjoyed quite as much as the sight of her charming young face. Lively and pensive by turns, her countenance seemed to him to match the apartment's lattice windows, dark despite their southerly aspect. She possessed what Stendhal liked to think of as a truly 'Allobrogian' beauty (alluding to Grenoble's Gaulish founders) and a bosom he found especially alluring.

Yet for all this he was reluctant, after his experience of frustrated desire for Mademoiselle Kubly, to fall in love again. Victorine Bigillion may have seemed more attractive because her brothers guarded her so jealously, but she was important to him as a confidante rather than as an object of passion. When Stendhal was rash enough to mention the Bigillions to his own family at dinner, the concerted bourgeois snobbery of Beyles and Gagnons was devoted at once to cutting them down to size. Wasn't there a daughter, some chit of a country girl? The uncle was keeper of the gaol in Place Saint André. A twelfth-century Bigillion ancestor may have welcomed Saint Bruno to the Grande Chartreuse, but Victorine's jolly, pleasure-loving father was scarcely on intimate terms with the first families of the town, and was the sort of person expected to raise his hat to Dr Gagnon.

Making a feeble excuse, Henri left the table and spent the next few days nursing the wounds of scorn. On the cover of his new edition of Bezout's mathematics course he drew a wreath and inscribed a capital 'V' in the midst of it. When in 1806 he happened to return to Grenoble, he heard from an acquaintance that Victorine was in love. 'Talking of the person she had loved for so long,' added his friend, 'she said, "he is not handsome, but nobody will ever reproach him for his ugliness . . . he was the cleverest and most charming of all the young men of my time." In a word, she meant you.'

The incident at the supper table was one of several which conspired to round off the process of Stendhal's alienation from his family and its narrow world. They had sought to deny him the kind of elementary freedom in the choice of friends, books and pastimes which was granted without serious reservation to most of his younger contemporaries. While Chérubin Beyle tried to impose his acquisitive ideals on the son he saw in terms of an heir to the family name, the Gagnons were equally at fault in inculcating their provincial notions of family pride. None of them could have guessed that by attempting to create a middle-class stereotype, they had simply provided the reactive chemistry for the production of its opposite. In assessing personality, tastes and opinions, Stendhal's ultimate criterion would henceforth be the capacity to transcend that banality and limited vision which typified the households of Rue des Vieux-Jésuites and Place Grenette.

There was one obvious means by which he could escape. His growing obsession with mathematics would surely lead him towards the kind of academic success his family were convinced he could achieve, and armed with this, he might at last flee Grenoble for a wider world. 'In those days,' he says, using one of those acutely potent images which add still greater vitality to the tone of rueful anger clothing the narrative of *Vie de Henry Brulard*:

> I was like some great river about to plunge down a cascade, like the Rhine above Schaffhausen, smooth-flowing but ready to hurl itself down an immense waterfall. My waterfall was a passion for mathematics, which, firstly as a way of leaving Grenoble, the very incarnation of bourgeois life and literally of nausea, and later for its own sake, monopolized me completely.

The lessons with Gros, paid for by Aunt Elisabeth with a characteristic mixture of noble disinterestedness and disapproval of their secrecy, inevitably bore fruit. In his teacher Henri 'saw a great man and did not become a scoundrel'. After a morning entirely devoted to discussing politics, Gros astonished his pupil, accustomed to the ways of money-grubbing *dauphinois*, by refusing to accept payment. 'He took possession of my soul, I adored and respected him to such an extent that I may have displeased him.' Quadratic and cubic equations became 'a glimpse of Heaven', a pleasure 'like that of reading some engrossing novel'. It may all have been set down in Bezout, but handled by Gros, such material was like a voyage 'to the farthest frontiers of science'.

In the autumn of 1799 examinations were held for third-year pupils of the Ecole Centrale, with a view to certain of the brighter candidates going on to study at the Ecole Polytechnique in Paris. The mathematics tests were conducted orally at the blackboard by an astute and erudite engineer named Dausse, one of the school's original founders, whose questions were deliberately tough and unsympathetic. Henri's eloquent answers, the result of fifteen months' passionate engagement with the subject, won him first prize, announced by an official proclamation in which Dausse spoke of 'Citizen Beyle's exactitude and brilliant facility'. Triumphant, the seventeen-year-old Henri swaggered through the Jardin de Ville, a retinue of loyal friends in tow, including François Bigillion, to whom he loftily remarked: 'At such a moment, a man might forgive all his enemies.' 'Quite the contrary,' rejoined Bigillion, 'at such a moment one should confront one's enemies and crush them.' The riposte, as Stendhal subsequently conceded, was as typical of Bigillion's common sense as his own remark characterized 'that exaltation *à l'espagnole* of which all my life I have been the victim'.

The official requirement of a second examination was deferred and finally put off *sine die* through the laziness of the school's mathematics master, Monsieur Dupuy, keener to harvest his grapes than to be testing Citizen Beyle in statics and conic sections. Obliging both of them, he wrote out a bogus certificate of proficiency, and Henri was now fully qualified to submit himself as a candidate for the Ecole Polytechnique. On 30 October 1799 he was escorted towards the Lyons mail by his family, including his father, his uncle and the faithful cousin Romain Colomb. Uncle Gagnon offered him some money, which Henri was tactful enough to refuse, well aware of the giver's extravagance. In the fragment of autobiography written over a period of fifteen days during the summer of 1832 and entitled *Souvenirs d'Egotisme*, Stendhal recalled the look of paternal tenderness in his uncle's beautiful eyes as he addressed a word in season to him:

> At this moment you are full of an insufferable pride because of your success in mathematics, but this counts for nothing. No one gets anywhere in the world without women. . . . Your mistresses will forsake you, remember that: at moments like these, one seldom appears more ridiculous, and in the eyes of other women one is simply meat to throw at dogs. So in the first twenty-four hours after that, make a declaration to some other woman, a chambermaid for want of a better.

If only I had followed his advice, thought Stendhal. The speech has an air of fictional serendipity about it, of being what his uncle ought to have said, if he did not actually say it, as a man of the world. Are we, on the other hand, to believe Romain Colomb, who tells us that he and Henri shed tears at parting? Towards one lacrymose figure, however, the departing hero was wholly pitiless. Of the weeping Chérubin Beyle, Stendhal notes, with unsparing sincerity, 'the sole impression made on me by his tears was that he looked very ugly'.

CHAPTER 2

OFFICIER DE CAVALERIE

The idea of the young man journeying from the provinces to the capital in search of fame, glamour and success is one of the favourite clichés of fictional invention and literary history. Balzac's Eugène Rastignac and the figures of Samuel Johnson and David Garrick on the road from Lichfield to London are the incarnations of a buoyant optimism which no kind of cynical wisdom after the event can destroy. There at the feet of our hero lies the city, which his talent and good looks will take by storm. Whether or not matters actually turn out thus is scarcely important. The romance of untested possibilities is eternal and made all the brighter by the callowness of the youth confronting its challenges.

So it should have been for Henri Beyle, setting out from Grenoble for Paris in the autumn of 1799. The journey, made in the company of one of his father's friends, Monsieur Rosset, was by way of Lyons, Moulins and Nemours and took almost ten days. At Nemours the travellers received news of the momentous *coup d'état* of 18th brumaire (9 November) which brought General Bonaparte to absolute power, and the idea of Napoleon as King of France intensified Henri's excitement, already heightened by the imagined scenario he had devised for his arrival in Paris. 'My idea was that a pretty woman, a Parisian far lovelier than Mme Kubly or my poor Victorine, would have a carriage accident while I happened to be nearby, or else run into some sort of danger from which I should rescue her and afterwards become her lover.'

Nothing of the sort occurred. Monsieur Rosset set down his

charge at a hotel on the corner of Rue de Bourgogne and Rue Saint-Dominique, in what is nowadays one of the smarter residential quarters of central Paris, west of the Boulevard Saint-Germain, and Henri was free to seek out his former schoolfellows who had entered the Ecole Polytechnique the previous year. When the hotel turned out to be too expensive, he moved to a room nearby, in the modern Rue de Constantine, built on what in Stendhal's time was part of the Quinconce des Invalides. Then the moment arrived for him to go and call on his relations.

Noël Daru was a cousin of Chérubin Beyle, a native *grenoblois* who had accumulated a significant fortune during the Revolution and trimmed his sails skilfully according to the prevailing political ideology. Now he lived in an apartment over the *porte-cochère* of the house he had bought in Rue de Lille, together with the good-hearted and modest little wife he had married for her estate, of whom Stendhal notes: 'I never met anyone more devoid of celestial fire. Nothing in the world could stir her soul towards nobility or generosity. For people like this, a selfish prudence, upon which they pride themselves, replaces all angry or generous emotion.'

Something of his parents' worthy but essentially unlovable nature had transmitted itself to their immensely successful eldest son, Pierre, shortly to become one of the most influential if one of the least warmly regarded among Napoleon's ministers. A man of considerable literary pretentions, he had undertaken translations of Cicero, Terence and Catullus, written a series of poems entitled *Washington ou la liberté de l'Amérique septentrionale*, and tried his hand at tragedy and comedy. His version of Horace, published in 1798, was already widely admired, and he was to go on to write one of the earliest authoritative modern histories of the Venetian Republic.

Appointed Secretary for War (his official title was 'Inspecteur aux revues et Secrétaire général à la guerre') Pierre Daru subjected the French army to a thorough reorganization from top to bottom. To his efficiency the Grande Armée owed much of its devastating impact as a fighting machine. Though Talleyrand remarked ambiguously of him 'he is an ox, and all his intelligence is devoted to hard work', Napoleon himself was more frankly admiring. Daru, whom he created a count, was 'a regular work-horse, a man of rare capacities, my best administrator'. Stendhal's later employer, Comte Molé, sardonically described him as prouder of writing third-rate books than of all his sterling efforts to overhaul the military establishment.

It was this bookish bureaucrat and his family who were to influence the course of Stendhal's life for the next decade. Seldom entirely unreserved in his praise of others, Stendhal was notably ungenerous in assessing the man whose kindness and influence may be said to have plucked him from shabby obscurity, and who, with a stroke of the pen as it were, set him literally on the road towards the source of some of the most untrammelled happiness he was ever to experience. While not absolutely ungrateful, he seems to have felt no genuine sympathy with Daru, either as relative or as a *littérateur*. His cousin was his superior only because he worked so hard. Otherwise the tone Stendhal adopts in writing of his benefactor is that of an all too characteristic impatience and contempt. Daru's *La Cléopédie ou la Théorie des Réputations en littérature* was 'like the sort of poem written by Jesuits in 1700, facile and dull'. He kept the family waiting for dinner while he plodded away at the office, then came home cross and bleary-eyed, looking like an overworked ox. Perhaps, though Stendhal does not say this in so many words, what he most resented about Pierre Daru was all that he owed to him.

Evidently, however, there was a powerful reminiscence of the Beyle–Gagnon household in the Darus, with their bourgeois hypocrisy, their gospel of toil and profit, and a pride in Pierre's literary achievements which did not extend to any real concern with books in general. Visiting the house in Rue de Lille, the seventeen-year-old Henri was consumed with embarrassment, and matters were hardly improved by his apparent lack of interest in taking the exam for which he had been sent to Paris in the first place. Mathematics, the monopolizing obsession of the previous year, had after all been simply a key to unlock the provincial prison door.

The boy had a new ambition, one it would not have been possible to share with his prosaic cousins. While still at Grenoble he had begun a comedy entitled *Selmours*, in the English manner of Goldsmith, Colman and Cumberland which had gained popularity all over Europe during the final decades of the eighteenth century. Now he began seriously to meditate a career as a comic dramatist, working rigorously to an ideal formula which he was clearly convinced might be evolved from a close study of dramatic form and technique. Nothing, it seems, ever quite persuaded Stendhal that a successful comedy might involve a little more than cutting out well-tried patterns and stitching them together, and with this methodical aim in mind he sat down to study François Cailhava's *Art de la Comédie*, a treatise on comic style which he naïvely supposed would offer him the necessary alchemical secret.

Paris was singularly unforthcoming in its recognition of Henri's fancied talent as a dramatist. In fact the city was a serious disappointment to him. It was attractive solely because it was not Grenoble. Otherwise the streets were muddy, there were no mountains, and, presumably through neglecting to feed himself adequately, he contracted a stomach disorder for which his fellow lodgers sought the dubious ministrations of the army surgeon who treated them for venereal disease. Gulping down the prescribed black draught, Henri, huddled beside the little stove in his room like a prison cell, found himself thinking 'Good God, what a disappointment! Is there anything left to hope for?'

To his rescue came the kind, loyal Darus, who offered him a large attic in Rue de Lille, engaged an eminent physician, Dr Portal (whose face, with its resigned air, as if he were already inspecting a corpse, terrified Henri) and provided him with a nurse during his three weeks of sickness and delirium. His hair fell out, and there is no reason to suppose that it ever properly grew back again: the mature Stendhal of his various portraits is always shown wearing some descendant or other of the toupee he purchased following this youthful illness.

There was no palliative or concealment offered, on the other hand, for the awful *gaucherie* he displayed at the long, ceremonious family dinners. This first experience of Parisian cooking inspired him with a detestation which was to last a lifetime. Things might have gone better if the ice of formality had cracked sufficiently for him to shine according to his initial fantasy, as the kind of debonair young rake he had read about in novels. As it was, by remaining solemn and tongue-tied among the very last sort of people calculated to flatter this idea, he appeared second-rate even to himself.

Tongue-tied he remained in Noël Daru's presence, when the old man tackled him on his embarrassing reluctance either to enter the Ecole Polytechnique or at least to begin studying for the following year's examinations. When at last Henri impudently ventured to point out that his family had left him more or less free to decide his own future, Monsieur Daru answered, with devastating understatement: 'That is all too obvious.' A week or so later, all thoughts of further education were put aside for ever when Pierre Daru announced that cousinly patronage had procured the boy a clerical job at the Ministry of War.

It was better than nothing, even if Henri, set to copying a letter, disgraced himself by spelling *celà* with a double 'l'.* He could argue about Racine with his fellow clerk Mazoïer and cry up the merits of Shakespeare, whose beauties he had begun to discover in Grenoble, reading the plays in Letourneur's translation, borrowed from François Bigillion's uncle, a monk named Morlon. The paragon of French classical drama seemed merely an unctuous courtier, wholly without simplicity or naturalness, in comparison with the man who could make Imogen in *Cymbeline* exclaim:

Now peace be here,
Poor house that keepst thyself!

Such partisanship was to become one of Stendhal's enduring critical concerns. From the literary quarrels of the young clerks in Napoleon's Ministry of War sprang *Racine et Shakespeare* (1823), a major contribution to the polemic skirmishing of French Romanticism.

As portrayed in *Vie de Henry Brulard*, the Ministry seems to have been almost self-parodyingly bureaucratic in its practices, and Stendhal, subsequently to become an efficient and dependable

* Stendhal seems to have taken pride in his spelling mistakes as offering proof of his own spontaneity: 'J'en fais beaucoup et je les aime.'

civil servant under two very different regimes, found himself instinctively copying Pierre Daru's dry secretarial style in the drafting of official correspondence. His cousin, he was quick to perceive, worked through inspiring fear in his subordinates, a fear designed to screen his essential timidity. Even if Stendhal never learned to love his patron, he grudgingly acknowledged his tireless, self-punishing industry as an essential component in the machinery of imperial government.

Life beyond the office was entirely lacking in romance or opportunity. Outside the windows, at the far end of the Ministry garden, stood two pollarded lime trees, against which the office staff were in the habit of urinating. 'They were the first friends I made in Paris,' says Stendhal, expressing his lifelong devotion to trees, 'and I felt sorry for them, clipped as they were, contrasting them with the splendid limes of Claix [his father's estate] lucky enough to flourish in the mountains. But should I have wished to return to those mountains?' The fact that the answer was a decided affirmative need not surprise us. There was nothing to detain Henri in Paris, but the chance to leave it arrived in a form which was totally irresistible.

Though Napoleon Bonaparte had first come to prominence as the victor of a series of brilliantly managed battles with the Austrians in northern Italy, it was these same Habsburg battalions which now threatened to reverse everything France had achieved in its Italian campaign. A counter-attack needed preparing, swiftly and in secret, and by early May 1800 the troops were ready to march, with a reserve force following in support. To join this reserve army, setting off towards Dijon on 7 May, Pierre Daru sent his young cousin, the humblest unit of a rearguard which seemed unlikely to witness any serious fighting.

Till the end of his life Stendhal retained a certain untarnished innocence which coloured his pride and vulnerability as a lover and fuelled his optimism even at the more lonely and disillusioned moments of middle age. Fiction and autobiography, in their unique Stendhalian blend, consecrated this heroic *naïveté* in a sequence of young men, Octave de Malivert, Julien Sorel, Lucien Leuwen, whose intelligence and callowness in a world largely peopled by charlatans, time-servers and bores mirror their creator's attempt to recover all the better versions of himself. Watching Henri Beyle starting out on his brief career as a soldier, we look forward to the ultimate archetype fashioned from the experience as a kind of desirable improvement on its realities, the figure of that most winning among nineteenth-century *jeunes premiers*, Fabrice del Dongo.

As the army left Geneva, where Stendhal hastened to seek out the birthplace of Jean-Jacques Rousseau, an episode occurred which by its very nature was a gift to this imaginative self-projection as the innocent adventurer. He had been ordered to take charge of a sick horse belonging to Pierre Daru, who had set out some time earlier. Fresh and skittish after its convalescence, the animal no sooner felt the weight of Henri and his heavy portmanteau on its back than it galloped away across a field towards the shore of a neighbouring lake. The terrified rider, who had only once or twice before been in the saddle, expected to be hurled head first into the water when he was overtaken by a servant belonging to a cavalry captain named Burelviller who, unknown to Henri, had been asked to look after him on the road to Italy.

Burelviller, one of various surrogate-paternal 'good sorts' in Stendhal's early years, was evidently delighted to take the young man under his wing and acted towards him 'as an excellent tutor does towards a prince'. The captain, whom Stendhal decribes as 'this desiccated roué of twenty-eight or thirty who appeared the very antithesis of feeling', admired the evidence of impulsive courage offered by his protégé at Lausanne when a surly Swiss in charge of billeting sarcastically cast doubt on the notion of honour among French officers. Henri had instinctively made to draw his sword, but Burelviller held him back. Only later did he admit to knowing nothing at all of swordsmanship. 'So what would you have done if the rascal had challenged us?' asked Burelviller. 'I'd have run at him,' rejoined Henri without a moment's thought.

As they crossed the mountains, little auguries began to appear of that talismanic happiness – *le bonheur* – to which Stendhal accorded a perpetual numinous significance. At Rolle, near Geneva, he heard church bells ringing as he looked out across the expanse of the lake under a spring sky and felt, as never so keenly afterwards, the absolute perfection of rapturous delight. From that moment, somewhere around 24 May 1800, he could date the beginnings of contentment.

The cold mist came down while the troops wound their way up the Saint Bernard Pass. Now the very opposite of restive, Henri's mount kept threatening to stumble, while he himself was soaked to the skin. The groups of infantrymen they passed swore at them and looked quite prepared to steal their horses, but if the ascent was bad enough, coming down was predictably worse as they teetered along the edge of a precipice, with the bodies of a score or so of dead mules and horses littering the ice of a frozen lake below. By night in their bivouacs they were so plagued by mosquitoes that Henri had one eye completely closed up.

So far they had met with no serious opposition, but below Aosta, under whose Roman triumphal arch, Stendhal later recalled, he made a wish that this present existence might last for ever, the fortress of Bard was holding out against the French vanguard, apparently under the notion that Napoleon himself was leading the assault. The inevitable sketch map in *Vie de Henry Brulard* graphically illustrates the fort's position on top of a plateau above the village, and the author's annotations comically revive his fear that Daru's horse, which he still rode, would bolt, owing to the army rule that the reins were to be held between two fingers only. Yet despite the appalling thunder of the guns, this, considered Henri, was true sublimity, even if a little too close to danger for his comfort.

Staying the night in the village at the house of a friendly parish priest who taught him the Italian words *donna* ('woman') and *cattivo* ('bad'), and how to say 'How many miles from here to Ivrea?', next morning he followed the road through the hills of Piedmont and down at last onto the plains of northern Lombardy, until on 1 June he arrived, with Burelviller still sedulously looking after him, in the town of Novara, the last place of any size and substance before the frontier – or former frontier – between the Kingdom of Savoy and the Habsburg domains was reached.

Nowadays Novara is a prosperous industrial city on the main railway line from Milan to Turin, and though its historic centre is attractive enough, we may not find it especially easy to associate anywhere so ordinary with one of the most significant experiences in Stendhal's life, the moment indeed at which Italy seized and held him to her in perpetuity.

War in those days was seldom so annihilatingly total as to kill off the pleasures of peace in their entirety, and the obsession with opera, which during the latter half of the eighteenth century had stifled the composition of most other kinds of music throughout Italy, was the last enjoyment Italians were ever likely to surrender. Thus it was almost inevitable that the French reserve army's arrival at Novara should have coincided with a series of performances at the Teatro Nuovo*, which included Domenico Cimarosa's opera *Il matrimonio segreto*.

Born in Naples in 1749, Cimarosa was universally regarded as one of the greatest operatic composers of his age, and an absolute master of the *opera buffa* comedy genre which he had helped to pioneer during an international career which took him everywhere from London to St Petersburg. The gradual modern revival of such comic masterpieces as *Le astuzie femminili* and *Il pittore parigino* has enabled us to appreciate the extraordinary impact of his music, with all its wit and fecundity of invention, on his contemporaries (including Mozart, whose *Don Giovanni* and *Le nozze di Figaro* plainly reflect a Cimarosan influence) but for over a century after his death in 1801 his only work to hold the stage was *Il matrimonio segreto*, first produced at the Burgtheater in Vienna in 1792 and based on an English play, David Garrick and George Colman's comedy *The Clandestine Marriage* (1766).

It was a performance of this opera that June evening in Novara which changed Stendhal's life. Though the sound of the church bells at Rolle may have been the summit of happiness, here in the theatre his enthusiasm was more keenly focused. The brio and irony of Cimarosa's comedy appealed to his own sense of humour, but it was the Italian music, with its tuneful directness of engagement, which captivated and transfigured him, so that he

* Rebuilt in 1873 as the Teatro Coccia and named after the Novarese master Carlo Coccia, first professor of harmony and composition at the London Royal Academy of Music, about whose talents Stendhal was always somewhat lukewarm.

reeled homewards inspired with a new determination 'to live in Italy and listen to such music as this'.

How musical was Stendhal? Early attempts at learning the violin and clarinet and taking singing lessons merely shamed him with their revelation of his technical limits. With his customary candour he acknowledged that he possessed no genuine feeling for instrumental or choral music and that 'only vocal melody seems to me the result of genius'. Yet he always retained some primitive impulse towards composing on his own account. During his early Italian years, whenever he went to the theatre before a new operatic première to buy the word-book, he used to make up music for all the arias and concerted numbers, and 'sometimes that evening I thought my own melodies loftier and more tender than those of the composer himself'.

French lyric drama, with its curious abhorrence of easily singable tunes, said nothing to him, and the best French songs in his judgement never transcended the crudity of popular ballads. Even the *Marseillaise*, 'infinitely better than anything else ever made up by a Frenchman', was scarcely equal to anything in his favourite composers, Cimarosa and Mozart. The success of works like Meyerbeer's *Robert le Diable* in 1833 merely underlined his impression of his countrymen as musical barbarians. What, had he lived to hear him, would Stendhal have thought of that archetypal mirror of Gallic influences, the German master of *tragédie lyrique*, Richard Wagner?

In one of those fascinating moments in *Vie de Henry Brulard* where we hear Stendhal reasoning aloud with himself, tearing off successive layers of question and speculation to arrive at the truth of his personality, he asks: 'Do I enjoy music as a symbol, as a recollection of youthful happiness, or purely for its own sake?' Acknowledging that 'laziness and a lack of opportunity for learning the dull physical aspects of music, namely how to play the piano and write down my ideas', were what prevented him from expressing in notes what he set down elsewhere in printed words, he nevertheless believed that in the end an instinctive passion for music transcended all those more narrowly symbolic associations it possessed for him.

The attachment to Cimarosa, and more especially to *Il matri-*

monio segreto, remained undying. Stendhal rightly perceived in the Neapolitan composer an artistic forerunner of Mozart and Rossini in extending the range and versatility of *opera buffa*, and returned again and again to his theatrical masterpiece for inspiration and delight. In 1806 he wrote of feeling the work 'vibrating on my soul as fully as when I saw it for the first time', and his devotion was unaltered thirty years later when he declared: 'I don't know how many leagues on foot or days in prison I should endure just to hear *Il matrimonio segreto*.' In the novels Cimarosa's music is used again and again as an emotional correlative and reference point. Julien Sorel, in *Le Rouge et le Noir*, bursts into tears on hearing one of the heroine Carolina's arias, and his clandestine romance with Mathilde de la Mole imitates the plot of the Italian libretto. Fabrice del Dongo, hero of *La Chartreuse de Parme*, falls in love with Clelia to the strains of their creator's favourite air, *Quelle pupille tenere*, from *Gli Orazi ed i Curiazi*, a literary ancestor, as one critic has suggested, of Proust's more famous 'petite phrase de Vinteuil' in *A la recherche du temps perdu*.

Stendhal could never make up his mind as to whether or not he had taken part in a battle soon after leaving Novara. Not surprisingly, his memory tended to carry him at one bound from the provincial opera house to that *sanctum sanctorum* of Italian lyric art, the Teatro della Scala at Milan, a theatre from which he would never thereafter be absent if he could help it and which symbolized for him the pure distillation of unclouded happiness. When he entered Milan some time around 10 June 1800, his first visit to La Scala was almost literally an entrance onto a wholly new stage of his existence.

Whatever the intensity of Stendhal's involvement with Milan and the men and women he met there during the next thirty years, it is hard for any modern visitor to the sprawling brown metropolis of northern Italy – European business capital, leader in industrial design, arbiter of world fashion – to imagine how the novelist could ever have found it so limitlessly entrancing. Why did he push his symbiotic absorption with the city to the extent of demanding as his epitaph the words 'Arrigo Beyle, Milanese'? Why, other than from sheer Stendhalian contrariness, should he have spent nearly half a book entitled *Rome, Naples et Florence* talking about Milan? What, even after significant encounters with the other great cities of Italy, held him in perpetual thrall to this, his earliest love?

As with other Italian towns, a glance at the map of present-day Milan shows its obvious development through a sequence of concentric rings created by thoroughfares marking the former line of ancient defensive walls. The city Stendhal knew was in reality very small, extending only as far as the modern ring of streets running outwards from the Castello Sforzesco and following the line of the Naviglio, a canal which originally formed a species of moat overlooked by a girdle of ramparts. Dominated by the massive Duomo, the largest Gothic building south of the Alps, central Milan was further enriched by a handsome assembly of Renaissance and Baroque palaces and churches, and the convincing impression of a capital city was rounded off by the construction, in 1772, of the austerely grandiose Palazzo Reale as a residence for the Austrian viceroy.

When Milan became a part of the Habsburg domains in 1714, a remarkable transformation of its whole atmosphere and character began, whose effects remained potent until the very year, 1859, when the city was assumed into a united Italy. The fundamental irony, not perhaps sufficiently appreciated nowadays but certainly apparent in the eighteenth century, was that the enlightened rule of Empress Maria Theresa and her son Joseph II, should have enabled Milan to achieve a far more intellectually and culturally stimulating atmosphere than that of Vienna, which, for all its active musical life and the presence of numerous aristocratic *illuminati*, remained in comparison a provincial backwater.

It is no exaggeration, indeed, to claim that Milan, during the latter half of the eighteenth century, was the most exciting city in Europe for anyone interested in the cirulation of new concepts, whether in political theory, sociology, jurisprudence or economics. Its salons rivalled those of Paris, and its intellectuals breathed a free air under the comparatively benign and well-ordered Habsburg government. Here the Verri brothers, Pietro and Alessandro, founded their Accademia dei Pugni (Academy of the Fists) and published the brilliantly combative reformist journal *Il Caffè*, which, though it only lasted for two years, became one of the most influential contemporary channels for enlightened debate and polemic. Here their friend Cesare Beccaria wrote his classic study of the relationship between justice and society, *Dei delitti e delle pene* (1764), instantly outlawed by such autocrats as Empress Catherine of Russia and the Prussian monarch Frederick II as potentially subversive in its lethally well organized attack on the chaos and barbarity underlying Ancien Régime legal institutions. Here too the cunning satirist Giuseppe Parini put Milanese sophistication to a severe test with his *Il Giorno* (1763–5), a sequence of indiscreet glimpses into the daily round of trifling idleness among the Lombard aristocracy.

It was this aristocracy, nevertheless, which proved among Italy's most receptive to the fashionable ideals of the French Revolution. The groundwork laid by this enlightened atmosphere was to make Milan into one of the principal centres of opposition to Habsburg hegemony in Italy after the fall of Napoleon. Much better educated than their counterparts in other Italian states, these noble families were noted for their friendliness to strangers. 'There is no place in Italy, perhaps I might have said in Europe, where strangers are received in such an easy, hospitable manner as at Milan,' wrote the English traveller Dr John Moore, and Stendhal, arriving twenty years after him, found that in this respect nothing had altered.

In a memoir of Napoleon begun in 1837, which carries the hero's career as far as the battle of Rivoli (1797) and then maddeningly breaks off after two chapters of circumstantial digression, Stendhal launches, with typically vigorous irrelevance, into a description of the atmosphere in Milan at the time the tatterdemalion French army first arrived at its gates, following the crucial fight at Lodi in 1796. 'The entry of the French into Milan was a day of rejoicing for the Milanese as much as for the army,' he tells us, though he might just as well be describing – and as it turns out, actually is – the prevailing air of the city at the time of his own arrival with the second wave of French military power to re-establish control four years afterwards. 'Plaudits rent the air, the prettiest women were at the windows; from the very evening of this wonderful day, the French army and the people of Milan were fast friends.'

He goes on to praise the atmosphere of true equality among the various social classes, created by a lack of invidious privileges separating nobility and bourgeoisie. He speaks of 'les bons Milanais', 'cette ville aimable', 'le bon sens et la bonté de la société milanaise' and recalls the happiness and wisdom of Maria Theresa's government under her viceroy Count Firmian. He remembers above all the beauty and grace of the Milanese women as they drew up each evening for the *corso* at the Porta Orientale in little carriages known as *bastardelle* from which they could easily converse with the young French officers who bought them ices at the café of the Corsia dei Servi. None of these subalterns, says Stendhal, ever really wanted to leave Milan, and it would have been hard to find more than twenty of them who thought seriously of promotion. 'They all loved music, and would have covered a league in the rain just to secure a seat in the pit at La Scala. None of them, however prosaic, ambitious and greedy he might later have become, ever forgot his stay in Milan. It was the most glorious moment of a glorious youth.'

Scarcely had he arrived than Stendhal encountered his cousin, Martial Daru, who took him to the palace where he was living in Corso di Porta Nuova (now Via Alessandro Manzoni). This was the newly built Casa d'Adda, the work of the neoclassical architect Girolamo Arganini, who gave it the kind of grandeur, in its courtyard, staircase and gallery, calculated to appeal to the wide-eyed French boy making his first encounters with the visual impact of Italian design. 'I was spellbound, it was the first time architecture produced such an effect on me.' Almost at once Stendhal was treated to a dish of *cotolette alla milanese*, veal cutlets fried in breadcrumbs, still the most famous culinary speciality of Milan, and one which would always recall the city to Henri.

Martial Daru, younger brother of the sober, industrious Secretary for War, in no way resembled Pierre. He was a lively, sociable fellow, an inveterate womanizer whose familiarity with the great world and its pleasures was bound to impress the callow young cousin from Grenoble. Something of his early influence coloured for ever Stendhal's attitude to women as fair game for the sexual freebooter. It was difficult for him to write of his friends and relatives without drawing attention to their emotional and intellectual shortcomings, but when Martial died in 1827 (as a result, according to Henri, of an overdose of aphrodisiac beverages) he was affectionately recalled as 'mon ami protecteur', the master who taught him the little he knew of the art of amorous success.

Presumably Martial was officially billeted on the household of the Marchese Febo d'Adda, since the palace appears in a contemporary list of military lodgings, and Pierre Daru had set up his office there. Stendhal spent only a fortnight in the palazzo, however, before moving to the Casa Bovara, in Corso di Porta Orientale (modern Corso Venezia), an altogether more modest palace built by the Abbate Giovanni Bovara in 1787, and at this period occupied by Claude Petiet, so-called 'minister extraordinary to the Cisalpine Republic' but effectively civil governor of Lombardy under re-established French rule. Petiet lived there with his attractive wife, Anne, their daughter and their two sons. Also in the house was Petiet's secretary Henri-Constantin Mazeau de le Tannière, who appears to have taken the fullest possible advantage of Mademoiselle Petiet's proximity.*

Ten years afterwards, returning to the city for the first time and trying to pick up the threads of old acquaintance, Stendhal noted in his journal something of the peculiar character of this first Italian experience. Its singularity derived, as he felt, from an extreme reaction to the moral conditioning attempted by his family. The word 'virtue' was so repugnant to him that he yearned to be a roué and found the notion of obtaining happiness from a virtuous woman wholly inconceivable. He envied his friends' talents for making conquests and keeping mistresses, while he himself awaited the ideal romantic moment, along the lines of that fortunate carriage accident of which he had dreamed when first arriving in Paris. A woman's love would have enhanced his charm and taught him the social graces he still badly needed:

* See Stendhal's journal entry for 21 May 1801: 'Mazeau, whom they went to annoy while he was in bed, stripped off his nightshirt and went to see them in this condition. The girls were obliging.'

> The two years of sighs, tears, bursts of love and of melancholy which I spent in Italy without women, in this climate, at this period of my life, probably gave me this inexhaustible fount of sensibility which nowadays, at twenty-eight years of age, makes me feel everything to the utmost detail.

As a compensating pleasure or as a spur to yet stronger sexual frustration there was always La Scala. Giuseppe Piermarini's superb auditorium had been opened barely twenty years when Stendhal began to frequent it. Like all Italian theatres at that period, its role as the principal meeting place for the fashionable world was quite as significant as its function in showing off the newest operas and most brilliant vocal talents of the day. The atmosphere can scarcely have altered when that liveliest of Romantic travellers Sidney Owenson, Lady Morgan, visited it on her tour of Italy in 1820. Praising its 'sober magnificence' and 'solemn splendour', she emphasized that cunningly achieved effect of fantasy which the interior of the house contrives to produce even in our own time. She was fascinated by the deep boxes where:

> the ladies take off their large bonnets and hang them . . . exactly as at Paris. . . . The most scrupulous ladies of the highest ranks come alone in their carriage to the opera. As soon as they have entered their box and have glanced their eye along the circles, giving or returning the Italian salutation, which has something at once infantine and coquettish in its beckoning gesture, they turn their back to the scene, and for the rest of the night hear and see nothing out of their society. . . .

Stendhal was overwhelmed by the theatre's handsome dimensions and by the sheer beauty of the spectacle. Braving one of the typical pea-soup Lombard fogs, which he was convinced had given him a cold, he went to the first night of the carnival season on 27 December. 'You can scarcely have any idea,' he told his sister Pauline:

> of the beauty of the decorations and the sumptuousness of the costumes: illusion is complete in a theatre like this one at Milan.

> Just imagine the Place Grenette covered over, with every balcony hung with taffeta curtains of many colours; the smallest boxes are the size of my bedroom at Grenoble. Inside each one, everybody has lighted candles, a table with cards, and usually some refreshments are brought in for the ladies.

We know little of what Stendhal actually heard and saw at La Scala during this first visit to Milan. In a journal entry during the crucial year of 1811, he mentions Johann Simon Mayr's two-act comedy *Che Originali!* (under its later title of *Il melomane italiano*) as 'one of those operas which contributed, ten years ago, towards forming my taste for Italian music'. He also records on 20 September 1801 'a superb spectacle', Nicola Zingarelli's *Il mercato di Monfregoso*, 'without contradiction the finest opera I have heard in Italy, whether for its enchanting music, or for the quality of its little arias, perfectly placed'. The star soprano was Elisabetta Gafforini, who was evidently part of the Casa Bovara circle, since her name figures eight days earlier among a party of friends, including Mazeau and Auguste Petiet, who were on their way to Venice. Stendhal later recalled her as 'comic song in all its perfection . . . A livelier creature, more sparkling, more gay, more on fire, will surely never appear again to bring trifling pleasure to sensible people'.

One of those going to Venice with La Gafforini was a certain 'Mme Grua', the earliest mention, indeed, of somebody who was to play a major role in Stendhal's Milanese life in future years, but towards whom on this occasion he kept a bashful distance. Angela Pietragrua was the daughter of a draper, Antonio Borroni, contracted as a supplier of clothing to the French army. Married at sixteen to a clerk in the weights-and-measures office, she was later described by Stendhal as a 'grande et superbe femme', endowed at that stage with a kind of Junoesque voluptuousness, subsequently to turn into something more emphatically majestic. Clearly he made no specially devastating impression on her at their first meeting, since when they saw each other again, she failed to recognize him. Once Beyle had reminded her of who he was, she merely exclaimed, 'It's the Chinaman!', implying, as he saw it, that she remembered him for his gaiety and wit, though she was more likely to have been referring to his narrow eyes. Otherwise there is absolutely nothing in his 1801 journal entries to indicate the extent of Angela's initial impact on him.

Meanwhile he took clarinet lessons and fought a duel with Auguste Petiet, possibly over a certain Mme Martin, receiving a sabre wound in the left foot. Officially he was still not attached to any particular regiment, but in October, thanks once again to his provident cousin Pierre Daru, General Oudinot awarded Henri a provisional commission as a second lieutenant in the cavalry. Daru's letter of recommendation reminds Oudinot that 'this young man has been well educated and knows mathematics'. Given his criticism of Henri's spelling while still a clerk in his Paris office, the boy would have been wryly amused to note that the Minister's own rendering of several French words – 'rapeller', 'faitte', 'occuppé' – was not quite what might have been expected from the noted *littérateur*, translator of Horace and author of the *Cléopédie*.

A week after Daru's letter to Oudinot, Stendhal's commission as a subaltern in the 6th Dragoons regiment was confirmed. Founded under Louis XIV at the end of the seventeenth century, the regiment had distinguished itself as part of the revolutionary army at the battles of Valmy and Jemmapes, and was currently basking in the glory earned on the field of Marengo. The splendid uniform included a white cloak, a dark-green coat with scarlet facings and a helmet adorned with a kind of bandeau or puggaree of tiger-skin.

Doubtless Henri, whom the secretary Mazeau had jokingly described as 'looking like a sick lion', felt he appeared to better advantage as dashing Second Lieutenant Beyle of the 6th Dragoons, but military *élan* and *panache* were to be as elusive for him at this stage as for his hero Fabrice del Dongo. For one thing, Pierre Daru was touchingly anxious to keep him out of danger, and seems to have contrived, with Oudinot's blessing, that he should not spend more time than was absolutely necessary with his regiment. When the chance of a battle actually offered itself during the autumn of 1800, once both French and Austrian armies had regrouped in the eastern Lombard plains south of Lake Garda, the commander-in-chief, General Brune, simply kept up desultory delaying tactics, while a disgruntled Stendhal wrote to his sister from the camp at Bagnolo near Brescia, where it poured with rain and he had his first encounter with *polenta*, the maize meal which until recently was the staple diet of rural north Italy and whose appearance on the table as a species of rubbery custard forms the severest of gastronomic tests for the traveller.

Matters looked a great deal more promising by the new year. One of Stendhal's many appealing characteristics for the biographer is his mixture of candour, self-reproach and genuine modesty in talking about himself, but we would give anything to know more about the exact nature of the courage he apparently displayed at the battle of Castelfranco on 12 January 1801. Five years later the general who led the vanguard across the River Brenta, Claude-Ignace Michaud, offered to renew his original citation of Beyle's exemplary conduct, adding praise for the young officer's intrepidity, zeal, exactitude, intelligence and administrative skills. Forsaking his usual reluctance to commend without reserve, Stendhal wrote of 'this good and great man' who heaped him with kindnesses and received him in his house like a son.

One of those rare creatures who ask for nothing when others around them are jostling for advantage amid petty jealousies and intrigues, Michaud endeared himself to his staff, as well as to his fellow generals, by a realistic assessment of his own limitations and a fatherly tenderness to those under his command. Towards Henri, whom he named as his aide-de-camp almost as soon as the new campaign began, he was especially indulgent. 'I like this little Beyle a lot,' he said, 'he's full of spirit . . . but he's too frank and too sharp.'

In his new role Henri followed Michaud through the various towns and cities of Lombardy, the Veneto and Emilia. At Reggio, where he sketched out a five-act comedy, *Les Quiproquos*, he had what must have been his earliest contact with the landscape which ultimately provided a context for the most famous of all his Italian works. The city, birthplace of his beloved Ariosto, lies halfway between Parma and Modena, and all three towns of this fertile plain were to offer him materials he needed from which to shape *La Chartreuse de Parme*. He tells us in a later journal that he got as far as Florence, though there is no mention of any Tuscan experience in the records he kept at the time.

The spring of 1801 found him back in Milan and preparing to set out for Bergamo, where he flung himself into the theatre as soon as he arrived. A performance in Italian of Jean-François Regnard's classic seventeenth-century comedy *Le légataire universel* was less than satisfying, but the aspiring dramatist was undeterred and actually sat down to translate another play in the current repertoire, Carlo Goldoni's *Zelinda e Lindoro*. Borrowing the text from a bookseller in the upper town and relying on his old teacher Gattel's adaptation of a standard Italian grammar, he hacked out a French version of the play in two weeks. By no means among the Venetian dramatist's best works, its appeal to Stendhal lay in that slight tinge of melancholy which often deepens the resonances of Goldonian laughter, as well as in the fondness they both shared for portraying love as a generous and ennobling passion. He went on to read widely in 'le charmant Goldoni', and that wholly unforced naturalness in the playwright's dialogue, enabling the characters to reach emotional truth as if by pure instinct, had an enduring influence on the nature of his own artistry as a novelist.

The translation of *Zelinda e Lindoro* must have helped to distract Stendhal from the sudden wretchedness of his own situation when he was seized by a prolonged fever and vomiting, against which continued doses of ipecacuanha, cassia and senna were unavailing. He had no real friends on Michaud's staff, and now matters were made worse by the arrival of a curt letter from the colonel of his regiment, Jacques Le Baron, demanding his instant return to headquarters, on the perfectly justifiable pretext that since Pierre Daru himself had issued an order stating that only lieutenants who had served in two campaigns could be appointed aides-de-camp, Stendhal's current position, obtained thanks to the Minister's influence, was an anomaly.

Henri dawdled somewhat longer at Bergamo nevertheless, entranced, between purging and vomiting, by the loveliness of its surrounding hills, reading Metastasio, discussing the rumours of a pro-Austrian conspiracy among the higher-ranking officers and making tart comments on several of them – Brunet, 'a thief, vain, stupid and tattling'; Franceschi, 'a coward'; Foy, 'has an inflammation of the testicle' – in his journal. Soon after leaving the town for Brescia, he summed up, in that thinking-aloud fashion which became an obsessive characteristic, his resolutions, projects and personal limitations as he saw them at that moment. For a boy of eighteen and a half, this short assessment has a remarkable, almost chilling clarity in its expression and organization. The voice has a touch or two of sober maturity, even if we know just how callow Stendhal still was.

'Let us enjoy the present to the full,' he writes:

> for our moments are numbered. An hour spent in worrying has nevertheless brought me that much closer to death. Let us work, for work begets pleasure, but let us never worry. Let us reflect calmly before taking up our position: the decision once made, we must never change our minds. With stubbornness anything is possible. Give us talent; one day I shall regret the time I wasted.
>
> A great source of consolation is that you cannot enjoy everything at once. You create an elevated notion of yourself by observing your own superiority in a particular field, the spirit is exalted by this reflection, you compare yourself to your inferiors and assume a feeling of superiority towards them. Then you are mortified to find them more successful than you in some other line which commands their attention. It would be too cruel for the same men to possess every type of superiority; I don't even know whether the apparent happiness arising from this would not swiftly turn into boredom. You must try, however, to achieve this superiority, because, even though never absolute, it exists and is generally the source of success. It gives, what is more, a feeling of assurance which is decisive.

Stendhal would spend the rest of his life never quite attaining this ideal equilibrium. Doubtless it would have been a bleak consolation to him to say that his personality becomes more interesting to us because of the ways in which he registered his failure to achieve his aims. There is something positively prophetic in the nature of his self-questioning when he continues:

> I must gain worldly experience so as to be able to choose my pleasures. Why should I be astonished at my awkwardness with women, at not succeeding with them and at shining in society only

> when argument is strong or the conversation turns on the mass of characters and passions which form the object of my study?

Brescia, like Bergamo so lately ruled by the Republic of Venice and marked by a Venetian stateliness in the white Istrian marble façades of its palaces and churches, was somewhat more hospitable towards the occupying French, and Stendhal was a welcome guest in the palazzo of the liberal Count Lechi, a noted patron of the arts. He observed nevertheless that there was something in the Brescian air which made the officers forget their traditional gallantry and behave with outright rudeness to the aristocrats with whom they lodged.

His journal entry for 1 August 1801, with melancholy precision, notes stage by stage a method for making love to a respectable woman, learned from a fellow officer:

> While she is lying down, you start kissing and titillating her and she begins to like it. Custom however decrees that she should still keep you at a distance. Then, without her guessing your intentions, you put your left forearm on her neck, under the chin, as if to strangle her. . . .then you take your organ between the index and middle finger of the right hand, holding them tightly, and put it quietly into her machine . . . You have to cover the decisive movement of your forearm with little pretended moaning noises.

There is nothing to suggest that Henri ever put any of this into practice while on his first Italian visit.

On 18 September he left Brescia for Milan, on his way to rejoin the regiment. After a week in the city, spent buying new accoutrements, going once more to La Scala, watching a grand firework display in honour of General Murat and eating excellent lunches at a café by the Porta Orientale, he set off into Piedmont, passing the battlefield at Marengo on the way, still littered with the bones of men and horses. The regiment itself was at the town of Bra, south of Turin, a place Stendhal found utterly charmless and in which he fell ill once more, this time from catching a chill after wading across a river while out hunting. By the time the 6th Dragoons, returning to France in compliance with the terms of the Treaty of Amiens, reached Saluzzo, Second Lieutenant Beyle had grown decidedly pensive under the influence of a fever which had lasted on and off for two months. His doctor, Luigi Maria Depetazzi, a much admired Piedmontese physician, told him roundly that his recurring malady, along with certain symptoms of nostalgia and melancholy, was that of ennui, which plenty of exercise, work and company would cure. Gloomily the patient noted down the chief circumstances of his life so far – 'born 23 January at Grenoble', 'left for Paris 8 Brumaire year VIII', et cetera – as if in preparation for imminent death. Sick leave put a period to his first brief spell in uniform. It was five years before he put on another and ten before he saw Italy again.

In the end, what his earliest Italian visit had offered was a kind of pledge, an earnest of the much stronger relationship which lay ahead, in the form of little intimations as to possible sources of future happiness. Milan, the opera, Angela Pietragrua, the pleasures of bowling down the roads of Italy in search of art, fine women and good music – these would all be savoured more richly when he was older and more subtly attuned to each of them. For the time being, as a refuge from dullness and disillusion, Italy could be transformed into the perfect imagined paradise of desire.

•

CHAPTER 3

TILL THE MIDNIGHT FOR EVER

Stendhal's return to France in January 1802 was scarcely the glorious homecoming of the seasoned campaigner. Still a second lieutenant, he did not relinquish his commission until 5 October of that year, but there was no further demand for his services in a nation committed, for the time being at least, to peace with its principal enemies, Austria and Great Britain. Perhaps not very willingly, he went home to Grenoble and promptly fell in love with the sister of his friend Edouard Mounier.

Victorine-Marthe-Marie Mounier was the daughter of a linen draper whose growing disenchantment with the course of the French Revolution drove him to quit Grenoble in 1790 and settle in Weimar, at that time the capital of one of Germany's most enlightened princely states and already celebrated for its association with such writers as Goethe and Schiller. Involved, as we have seen, in the revolutionary disturbances in his native city, Jean-Joseph Mounier opened, while at Weimar, his own school of political science, taking as his pupils the sons of the local aristocracy, several young Englishmen and various German princes. Only after eleven years did Mounier deem it safe to return with his family to Grenoble, where Henri Beyle, newly arrived from Italy, made their acquaintance.

The nature of Henri's passion for Victorine reflected his earlier feelings of unease in the presence of a virtuous woman. Should we believe Paul Arbelet, who declares, in his romanticized account of their relationship, that her father's strict teachings, 'the sadness of mourning and exile, the precocious gravity required of her in her role as elder sister in a motherless family, besides her noble dwelling in Weimar, together with the titled persons who lived there, must all have offered Mademoiselle Victorine lessons in melancholy, nobility and dignity'? Shadowy though she always appears amid the almost unbroken parade of idealized mistresses, projected wives, surrogate mothers and substitute sisters which stretches across Stendhal's life, Victorine aroused serious emotions which her lover, even if he never actually declared them, continued to nurse for several years.

One means of keeping in touch, however indirectly, was through a correspondence with her brother Edouard. Some sixteen of these letters survive, written in a style which, depending on the reader's mood, looks either like a remarkable anticipation of its author's most mature literary manner or else like an affected man-of-the-world loftiness deliberately calculated to impress by its throwaway elegance of phrase and its rhetorical feints in the direction of something truly lapidary. Behind certain passages we can detect Stendhal's wish to show himself to the Mounier family as a young man of honourable intentions, with the obvious aim of attaching Victorine herself:

> I believed that all women were sensitive, but I saw only vapours and vanity. I repent of having created a chimera which I sought after for five years. I want to use all my powers of reason to drive it away, yet it always returns. I have given it a name, eyes, a physiognomy; I see it incessantly, speak to it occasionally, though it never replies, and like a child, after having kissed my doll, I weep because it cannot return my kisses.

Apart from Edouard Mounier, Stendhal's principal correspondent during this period was his sister, Pauline Beyle, three years his junior but evidently a highly intelligent and responsive reader whom her brother viewed as a favourite pupil, with a literary taste awaiting the right kind of formation. The letters to Pauline, sustained, with two or three intervals, for some sixteen years, are a conscious offloading of Henri's critical opinions on books and authors past and present, and a reflection of a distinctly pedagogical impulse which seems to have reached its most intense pitch during his second stay in Paris, after the return from soldiering in Italy. When we hear him beginning, 'I am sad, my dear Pauline, so I shall console myself with you. I want to talk to you about the moral principles of literature', the note of self-indulgence is characteristic. He copies out a snatch of André Chénier – a rare demonstration of interest in poetry on the part of a prose writer notoriously deaf to its attractions; he tells her to read Voltaire's *Zadig* and *La Vie de Charles XII*, Quintus Curtius, Corneille, Racine, Montesquieu's *Grandeur des Romains*, Condillac's history, La Bruyère and Molière; he urges her to learn Italian and English and to correct her studies of astronomy, along the Ptolemaic lines approved by the church, through reading Lalande's *Abrégé d'astronomie*, which will put her right as regards the motion of the earth around the sun. He becomes dogmatic, even pompous: 'You are in your seventeenth year: consider that it is passing never to return, and that in three years' time you will reproach yourself for all those moments lost in speaking to people who only have false ideas.' As in his letters to Mounier, we can feel him straining towards the epigrammatic, the old-young man posing as a *philosophe*, ready with those generalizations on human conduct for which French always seems so fatally well adapted as a literary language.

Comparatively few of Pauline's letters to her brother have survived to show us how she took his unabashed epistolary lecturing. Those which do exist nearly all belong to the earliest phase of their exchange, when Pauline, whom Stendhal had certainly not overestimated as a kindred spirit, was perishing of boredom in the very same Beyle-Gagnon orbit he had so recently abandoned. Chérubin, now much exercised by a project for breeding merino sheep, which he assured his son would make them both very rich, was as conversationally dreary as ever, and when he was not in the house the talk of sermons, masses, cooks and servants was dull enough to drive Pauline out of the room: 'I am 18¼ years old; for some years now I have lived amidst unchanging tedium. Recently I began to think this might be coming to an end. This gave me courage to bear it, but at present I have no hope left. Life will be a burden to me if it continues thus.' Henri must have hugged himself with relief at having put such a world behind him.

Not that his life in Paris, sharing lodgings with his schoolfriend Félix Faure in the Rue Neuve Saint Augustin, was necessarily more glamorous or fraught with exciting possibilities. In May 1802 he began taking English lessons with a Mr Dawtram, and later from an Irish Franciscan friar, John Baptist Hickey. The journal entries for the year diminish to a trickle of dry little jottings, through which we can chart the progress of his newly awakened interest in Adèle Rebuffel, with whose family he had formerly lodged on first arriving in the city. Here his style of courtship was somewhat different from that adopted towards Victorine Mounier. To lay siege to the virtuous Adèle he began a liaison with her mother Magdeleine, which gave him a pretext for those regular visits so doggedly chronicled throughout September and culminating in the blunt announcement:

'Je fous Mme R depuis le commencement de fructidor.'

Whether Stendhal actually loved, or was in love with either Adèle Rebuffel or Victorine Mounier is questionable. Doubtless it mattered to receive some sort of assurance from Edouard that his sister had read the latest stylistic flourish from the Beylian pen or for fourteen-year-old Mademoiselle Rebuffel to present him with a lock of her hair, but in the end, as with his various other fancied passions, the source of emotion was not so much genuine love as the sense that his heart ought to be in a state of perpetual amorous engagement. Being in love, regardless of the outcome, became a necessary condition for the rest of his life.

For consolation and philosophic reassurance there were always books. The omnivorous reading habit developed during a lonely boyhood in Grenoble was as powerful as ever, and his letters and journals are a logbook of critical judgements forming and reforming, of shifting tastes and dawning enthusiasms. To Edouard Mounier he writes guardedly of the interest aroused by Mme de Staël's first novel *Delphine*, which has 'infatuated all our pretty women with its Ossianic style'. In a letter to Pauline he reels off a republican tirade from Alfieri's *Timoleone* and counsels her to read

La Fontaine, Boileau and the *Andromaque* of Racine. At the Bibliothèque Nationale he spends nearly six hours studying a translation of Terence's *Andria* and Goldoni's *La finta ammalata*. A few days later he records his determination to 'de-Gagnon-ize my taste' and to 'de-Rousseau-ize my judgement', but his reaction against Rousseau, for whom he was so passionate during his boyhood, had already begun when, soon after returning to Paris, Stendhal began an intensive study of the works of the influential eighteenth-century *philosophe* Claude-Adrien Helvétius.

What he seems most of all to have admired in Helvétius' two major treatises, *De l'esprit* and *De l'homme*, was not their positive views on human perfectibility, which age and experience caused him swiftly to question, but their concept of virtue and the general good of mankind as things dependent on circumstance and individual interpretation. When Julien Sorel, awaiting the guillotine in Chapter 74 of *Le Rouge et le Noir*, proclaims, 'There is no such thing as natural law: the expression is merely a worn-out morsel of stupidity . . . the men we honour are simply rogues who have been lucky enough not to get caught red-handed', his voice is charged with a truly Helvetian cynicism. In his enthusiasm for a thinker who fundamentally influenced Jeremy Bentham and the Utilitarians, Stendhal was consciously rejecting the Rousseauesque idealism which animated so many of his proto-Romantic French contemporaries. The sense often communicated by his books, of a writer consciously swimming against the tide in a need to establish authority for the sardonic worldliness of his viewpoint, derives from this indelible Helvetian impress.

Yet it would be wrong to portray Stendhal as ideologically in thrall to a single philosophical viewpoint. Writing to Mounier on 15 December 1803, he spoke of the devastating initial effect on him of *De l'esprit*, 'to the extent that for several days I actually doubted friendship and love', but acknowledged ultimately that Helvétius, having probably never experienced either sentiment at first hand, was incapable of writing about them or explaining them adequately. In the same letter he compares Rousseau's *Contrat Social* favourably with Montesquieu's *L'Esprit des Lois*, though we know that the latter, acquainted with Helvétius and holding him in warm regard, was destined to set an enduring mark both on Stendhal's political and social attitudes and on his literary style.

Doubtless it sounds like a statement of the obvious to say that books and ideas played a significant part in Stendhal's formation as an imaginative writer, but it is hard to think of another nineteenth-century novelist, even a self-conscious intellectual like George Eliot, who makes us quite so intimate with their successive phases of critical and emotional engagement as a reader. For this reason we should be reluctant to tie Stendhal down to anything like consistency in tastes or interests. Again and again we catch him in the act of enjoyment, irritation, scepticism or contempt. His loyalties in reading were not fixed and his enthusiasms came and went according to the moment's needs. He had encountered Helvétius, however, at a crucial instant, and the initial fascination never wholly left him.

Once his resignation from the army was confirmed, from 5 October 1803, Henri Beyle could turn freely towards the world which had fascinated him since his schoolboy passion for Virginie Kubly, the realm of the drama, the Parisian theatres and the art of acting. An entire volume might be addressed, indeed, to the nearly always hopeless flirtation of nineteenth-century novelists and poets with the stage. The reasons for an almost total absence of inspired dramatic invention in Europe between Schiller and Ibsen must be explored elsewhere: Stendhal nevertheless takes his place beside all those others, Keats with *Otho the Great*, Henry James with *Guy Domville*, who tried and failed to lasso their genius around the runaway horses of tragedy and comedy.

The Parisian theatre, in these early years of the new century, was entering one of its most glittering phases, having quickly recovered from those undignified agit-prop absurdities it had witnessed during the more *enragé* moments of the Revolution. At the Comédie-Française, for example, audiences could enjoy the varying styles of such actresses as Sophie Volnais, a heartrending Iphigénie, the mistress of Marshal Junot to whom she accredited several children by less distinguished fathers, Louise-Françoise Contat, the original Suzanne of Beaumarchais' *Le Mariage de Figaro*, who boasted the Comte d'Artois (the future Charles X) among her lovers, nicknamed by her fellow actors 'L'Impératrice' for her haughty demeanour, and the legendary Mademoiselle Mars, Anne-Françoise-Hippolyte Boutet, destined to play Dona Sol in Victor Hugo's notoriously controversial *Hernani*, but at this first stage of her career mostly cast in *ingénue* roles or as a delightful Chérubin.

Stendhal's favourite was Josephine Duchesnois, who in 1802, only a few months after an unpromising introduction at the Comédie-Française, where she was judged too ugly and stupid to succeed, made a triumphant debut as Phèdre, wearing a cloak presented by her namesake the future Empress Joséphine. In his theatrical column for the *Journal des Débats*, the famously captious critic Julien-Louis Geoffroy ecstatically evoked the sound of her voice, 'sweet, sonorous and touching', her features, 'a moving picture upon which all the soul's affections are portrayed' and her gift for stirring others through her own involvement: 'it is her heart that speaks, and all other hearts listen'.

A month or so later, the young actress's rival, Marguerite-Joséphine Weymer, known as Mademoiselle George, was brought on at the same theatre as Clytemnestre in Racine's *Iphigénie*. At only fifteen she was already able to establish an easy dominion over the spectators by her majestic beauty, though her acting merely consisted in copying what she had learned from her teacher, the actress Raucourt. Geoffroy's loyalty all too readily wavered, and the wretched Duchesnois suddenly found herself cold-shouldered, soon becoming the victim of continual sniping from her former partisan.

Theatrical life in Paris has always relished battles, from the days of the Querelle des Bouffons between the supporters of Gluck and those of Piccinni to the legendary 'Bataille d'*Hernani*', but it was many years since a combat as exciting as this one promised to be had divided the audience at the Comédie-Française. Partisans, known as Georgiens and Carcassiens, the latter in unflattering allusion to Duchesnois' thinness, took to wearing favours in their hats to signal a preference. To his wife's enthusiasm for Duchesnois, Napoleon responded by taking George as a mistress.

Matters came to a head on 19 February 1803, when Duchesnois appeared at the Comédie as Aménaïde in Voltaire's tragedy *Tancrède*. The rigid stipulations which governed casting at the theatre meant that George had already acquired the right to play queens and empresses, while Duchesnois was expected to content herself with what were loosely known as 'amoureuses', the roles of the lovestruck princess and the innocent heroine. News of this had spread among the Carcassiens, who of course thronged the parterre, eager for their star, who, as a somewhat acid notice in the *Journal de Paris* pointed out, 'seemed in truth somewhat frightened by the convulsive enthusiasm which greeted her entry and made her lose her nerve: thus we refrain from criticizing her extreme weakness and the total extinction of her voice in the opening scene'.

'We shall not report', continues the writer:

> upon the revolting incident which followed the tragedy. Suffice it to say that after having vociferously demanded the representation of *Phèdre* by Mlle Duchesnois in place of Mlle George, some twenty hotheads climbed across the orchestra onto the stage, thus mutinously to impart the supposed wishes of the public to the actors, and that, without the prompt arrival of a sizeable armed force, this band of intriguers might have perpetrated the most indecent excesses.

The demonstrators, judging from police records, were a motley assortment from every walk of Parisian life. There was an army officer, a maker of barometers and a wine merchant's son, there were three students from the Ecole Polytechnique, a Danish count and a fourteen-year-old boy, apparently a connoisseur of tragedy. Among the crowd was Henri Beyle, whose enthusiasm for Duchesnois rapidly turned into a decided penchant. On 18 March 1803, in telling Mounier about the salons he visited (one of them featured music, dancing and the presence of Madame Récamier) he mentioned 'an *ancien régime* circle where I am known as M de Beyle' and the liveliest of all, Monsieur Dupuy's Saturdays:

> where there are *savants* of every shade, speaking every language, from every country. Mlle Duchesnois comes here often with her master Legouvé! Here they speak Greek, *Greek*, just think of the significance of that word! If you were here you would shine. I can't imagine how you can live at Rennes. You have the means, so come

to Paris. Find work here and you certainly won't miss your Bretons.

Stendhal was evidently enjoying Paris far more than he had ever thought possible under the starchy aegis of the Daru family before his soldiering in Italy. A jotting in his notebook underlines his new mood:

> I reflected that there never was a man as happy as I am at this present moment. . . . My dear grandpapa has parted with four louis for my sake. Such attentions are charming, and in the provinces four louis are worth ten. He is proud of my career as an artist. Oh yes, I'm sure of it! This life is delightful, it gives the soul more of a capacity for loving, and with such a grandfather, can I have too much of that?

Still more pleasure seemed within reach when his friend Louis Crozet promised to introduce him to Duchesnois in her dressing room. Stendhal had started noting down stray details about her mode of life, the fact that she went to bed at three and got up at midday, that her *maître de langue* (what would nowadays be called a dialogue coach) arrived at one o'clock, that she was not to be visited in the mornings, and that she frequented the salon of the Marquise de Montesson, morganatic widow of Philippe Egalité, Duc d'Orléans. He even sat down to write a campaigning article against Geoffroy and the Georgiens, signing himself 'Junius' and attacking his enemy's 'journalistic absurdities' and 'pompous gibberish'. Many years afterwards he would come to appreciate Geoffroy, for all his appalling lapses of judgement, as 'the liveliest and most intelligent of journalists', and admit that when he used to dine at the Café Hardy in the Boulevard des Italiens off a delicious plate of spatchcocked kidneys, the dinner never tasted quite so good on days without one of the critic's spirited reviews for company.

The attack on Geoffroy was not published, and Crozet, whom he asked to show it to Mlle Duchesnois, evidently failed to do so. Nevertheless, on the evening of 24 April 1804, Henri finally achieved his ambition. After a day at the Bibliothèque Nationale, following the course of intensive reading on which he had now embarked (today it was a translation of Cesare Beccaria's *Ricerche intorno alla natura dello stile* (1770) and the *Lettre sur les occupations de l'Académie française* (1716) of Fénelon) he had gone to the theatre to see Népomucène Lemercier's tragedy *Agamemnon*, in which Duchesnois was playing opposite François-Joseph Talma, the greatest French actor of the day. The journal notes an earlier performance at which Stendhal was unhappy with both of them, but this time he considered that 'the scene in which the murder is proposed was divinely played'.

Following the play, Crozet took Henri backstage to see Duchesnois. He thought her charming, much less plain in real life than he had imagined,* with a strong definition to her face, 'highly appropriate to depicting the passions.' As usual, however, he was gravelled for lack of felicitous compliments and felt that in future he had better write down in advance what he had to say. All he could produce in the way of remark was to tell Duchesnois that *Agamemnon* and Beaumarchais' *La Mère Coupable* were the two most moral contemporary plays.

Feeling encouraged nevertheless, he began to make a habit of calling at her dressing room whenever he was at the Comédie. The practice was as well established in Paris as anywhere else, and the actress at first seemed friendly enough towards him, even though Stendhal himself was not so entirely smitten as to be unable to judge her performances dispassionately. A brilliant *Bajazet*, in which she excelled as Roxane, was followed by a distinctly mediocre *Iphigénie*. He was determined, all the same, to become her lover, with a definite eye to promoting the comedy on which he was at work, *Les Deux Hommes*.

The features of Stendhal's obsession with Mlle Duchesnois were those of any other stage-struck young man's infatuation, and the journal chronicles them remorselessly. Following his custom when writing about friends and mistresses, even, as here, about an imagined mistress, he gave her a codename, 'Ariane', after the heroine of a tragedy by Thomas Corneille. When she called for a defender against Geoffroy's constant attacks, he ran

* He notes later (10 May 1804) that on this occasion she was not wearing her chemise.

home, dashed off a three-page article and hurried across Paris to hand it to her concierge. Even when, a week later, she showed that she had not even read it, by asking whether his name was not Lebel, he was scarcely discouraged, simply noting that: 'I behaved well: I was right to see her.'

It was one thing to be able to spend an hour in Duchesnois' company at her house in Rue Saint-George while her *maître de langue* made a third, but quite another actually to enter her list of lovers, which included the doctor Anthelme Richerand (later Stendhal's personal physician) and the Comte de Valence, one of Bonaparte's generals. Slowly Henri's own good sense diluted the initial ardour, and he began to perceive that his Ariane's offstage allure was as variable as her dramatic gifts. As 1804 drew to a close (or rather, as the Revolutionary Year XII became Year XIII) his interest in the theatre took a different turn altogether, and the idea of a love affair with an actress suddenly became a reality.

Writing for the stage was meanwhile monopolising Stendhal's energies. Desperate to succeed as a comic dramatist, he read eagerly among the playwrights of the past, Terence, Machiavelli, Goldoni, analysing styles, moods, effects, and night after night he visited the theatres, cramming his notebook with observations on technique, jottings which show just how determined he was to penetrate the alchemical formulas and *magna arcana* of genius. Characteristically he embarked on an analysis of the sources of laughter, an anticipation, as it were, of Henri Bergson's famous *Du rire*, written a century later, and sedulously copied out the definitions, from the *Dictionnaire de l'Académie*, of words such as 'plaisanterie', 'ridicule' and 'comique'.

One by one, meanwhile, the dramatic projects started to take shape. A list made on 9 June 1804 includes two 'drames à la manière de Shakespeare', one on the abortive landing of an *émigré* army at Quiberon (the cast includes William Pitt and Charles James Fox, 'homme estimable') and another on Bonaparte's assumption of imperial power. Among the comedies were to be a five-act *L'Homme du monde* 'a model of the man of the world in our own century', and *L'Homme qui craint d'être gouverné*, a three-act piece around the theme of an old man who suddenly refuses to let himself be guided any further by reason.

The idea which most tickled him was that of a satirical attack on the arbiters of contemporary dramatic taste, led of course by the egregious Geoffroy. As he told Louis Crozet, the outline (in part suggested by one of the critic's leading articles discussing a comedy by Alexis Piron) was dreamed up one hot, sleepless summer night as Stendhal lay meditating on the kind of Rousseau-esque figure who affects sensibility while actually possessing none. His play, to be called *Le Faux Métromane*, would vindicate true artists by exposing the critical establishment to just censure, thereby earning him the grateful applause of all those with any claims to real feeling and taste. It would be presented anonymously, as he told Crozet: if successful, he would declare his authorship after fifteen performances, and with the proceeds take off for Rennes to pay court to Victorine Mounier, whose father had been made prefect of the surrounding department.

Nothing came of *Le Faux Métromane* as originally conceived, but the notion of a play more specifically pillorying Geoffroy increasingly nagged at Stendhal's imagination. By the end of August 1804, he had arrived at a working title, based on the presumed reaction by its chief object of ridicule to the comedy itself, *Quelle Horreur: ou l'Ami du Despotisme Pervertisseur de l'Opinion Publique*. The central figure, named Letellier, was to be an intelligent man of low principles, envious of his more talented contemporaries and happiest when vilifying them in his newspaper column. 'My protagonist', wrote Stendhal:

> must be, as it seems to me, the anti-Voltaire, a man who has felt all the influence of Voltaire on his century, and the causes of such influence besides, and who desires to be equally influential in an entirely opposite sense . . . . his passions should be a source for the most comical incidents to take place around him, all of whicn ought to disclose small details of his character, such as, for example, his unhappiness at a play's success, a success which gives the lie to his notion of imperfectibility.

And so on, as it were, for almost thirty years, during which Stendhal chipped and scrapped, moulded and remoulded, never utterly convinced that the comic muse had abandoned him, if indeed she had ever been his companion from the outset. Relinquishing work on the play in 1806, he took it up once more in the summer of 1810, tinkered with it a little while in Moscow in 1812, set out a few key ideas after arriving in Milan four years later, listed a possible sequence of scenes in September 1821, and took a final swing at the enterprise in 1830, using a new title, *La Cheminée de Marbre*.

Supposing it had achieved completion, could the play ever have succeeded? Stendhal was scarcely incapable of managing swift, economical dramatic dialogue, and the few surviving sketches for *Letellier* (his usual name for the project) including a spirited opening scene in which the critic's reactionary meanness is shown by his refusal to pay a combative cab-driver holding out for his proper fare, might suggest that a career as a new Beaumarchais was in his grasp. Yet not all those patient mornings at the Bibliothèque Nationale and attentive evenings at the Comédie-Française would necessarily bring him that instinctive sense of dramatic momentum, awareness of true theatrical impact and gift for building episodes and characters likely to appeal to performers as well as to the audience, which are the hallmarks of a natural playwright.

There were to be other flirtations with the stage, even if Stendhal was never destined to travel quite as far down the road to disaster as his admirer Henry James, whose belief that he could make French boulevard theatre work for a London audience drove him to the spectacular catastrophe of *Guy Domville*, one of the most notorious miscalculations in the history of art. Doubtless because no single dramatic idea ever got beyond a rough draft, Stendhal could go on believing for ever in his own untested potential.

Ironically, it was creative powers of a different sort altogether to which *Letellier* and the other projects introduced him. In a sketch for a second scene, during which Letellier, in conversation with his wife, justifies his critical position while pouring scorn on Voltaire, whose *Zaïre* he has just seen performed, we can feel for the first time the full polemic vigour of Stendhal's prose. Madame Letellier, whose role in the exchange is merely that of a lively 'feed', asks him why he is not content, with all his success, to accept the prestigious and lucrative modern-languages professorship he has recently been offered. He answers:

> And you have the gall to propose such a position to Letellier? Look at what I have achieved. I have destroyed the *philosophes*. Everybody now appreciates the absurdity of those novels in dialogue which Voltaire called tragedies. Those crazy outbursts which pass in his plays for moments of passion touch no one but women and children, and you know that people are seldom affected by things which look ridiculous to others; as for those spoofs and frigid diatribes which make up the rest of his work, they've the misfortune not to make anyone laugh, and whatever can't create pity induces horror instead. The judgements of this great booby of letters have been obliterated by essays in a different literary style, masculine, vigorous, reinforced by a vast erudition. Such is the fate of philosophy's vainglorious patriarch. He lived only while there was nobody of a superior genius to his. Give me six months and I'll make sure he's no more spoken of than Ronsard.

It does not greatly matter that the whole nature of this speech, however striking its rhetoric, is essentially undramatic. What the twenty-one-year-old Stendhal demonstrates, albeit crudely, is the dawning of an extraordinary fictive gift for entering states of mind alien to his and exposing their inner workings by allowing them to speak without restraint, so that the reader is arrested, almost enchanted, by their fervour and persuasiveness. His vitality as an artist lies in compelling us to look beyond our instinctive respect for conviction and sincerity in others, to assess instead the quality of their beliefs themselves, and by doing so, to examine our powers of resistance to the assaults of folly, duplicity and easy answers.

Above all, these botches, fudges and stabs at the drama reveal their author's unquestioning confidence in his destiny as a writer. A tendency among certain commentators on Stendhal has been to view the great finished achievements of *Le Rouge et le Noir* and *La Chartreuse de Parme* as self-generated works without any but the sketchiest of perspectives in the novelist's earlier *oeuvre*. The importance of the whole inchoate heap of his '*Théâtre*' is as a testimony to his doggedness, to the fixity of his gaze on posterity and his belief in the enduring echo of a personal voice.

During September 1804, Henri Beyle took stock, for the first time seriously, of his monetary position. Attempts to persuade his close-fisted father to allow him greater financial independence had so far failed, but a monthly allowance of 200 livres was plainly not enough to encompass the full range of his expenses, from payments to the barber, the laundress and his landlady Mme Gruel, and an outlay of three livres thirteen sous on books, to his various debts to friends (the most obliging appears to have been Louis de Barral, owed a total of 106 livres). Ruin seemed to stare him in the face, and he wrote angrily: 'My father's unfeeling abandonment of me, as well as various features of my life, make me think that he can be nothing but a Tartuffe, whose single desire is for money.'

In this condition, how could he possibly set off for Rennes, to pay court to Victorine Mounier, still in view as a prospective bride? As luck would have it, she herself arrived in Paris with her brother Edouard, as part of the throng of visitors – among them Henri's uncle, Romain Gagnon – to witness the festivities for Napoleon's coronation. Neither the procession, which he watched outside the Café Français in the Rue Saint-Honoré, nor the political shift towards crowned despotism sanctified by the presence of the reluctant Pope Pius VII, especially enchanted Beyle. 'I reflected throughout the day upon such an evident alliance between assembled charlatans, on religion stooping to consecrate tyranny, and all this in the name of human happiness. I rinsed out my mouth by reading a little of Alfieri's prose.' The Italian dramatist, whose lines against tyrants in *Timoleone* he had admiringly copied out for Pauline, remained a lifelong, if continually moderated enthusiasm.

For Stendhal, the Emperor's coronation day was a case of 'how happy could I be with either, were tother dear charmer away', since at least some of the twenty-four hours were spent in the company of Adèle Rebuffel and her mother. Decidedly bucked by a conversation with Adèle during which he advised her to read Rousseau, Helvétius and Charles-Pinot Duclos' *Considérations sur les moeurs*, he was struck by the two or three moments of 'le naturel' she permitted herself with him, bursting into a little rhetorical flourish, in the privacy of his journal, which reads exactly like something from the eighteenth-century authors he had recommended.

When at last he saw Victorine, their exchange was merely one of frigid banalities. She looked taller and thinner than before, dressed as she was in a straw hat *à l'allemande*, tied with blue ribbons. Her brother received him politely but coldly, remarking, perhaps with a touch of irony, 'You've blossomed into a true Parisian'. Henri fancied he must have made something of an impact, with his smart jabot, cravat and waistcoat and his freshly barbered hair, and even though the visit lasted only a quarter of an hour, he sat down later to analyse thoroughly its every detail. For the first time he resorted to a device familiar to readers of *La Vie de Henry Brulard*, the 'battle plan' as he called it, with his penchant for applying military metaphor to love and sex, a pen-and-ink sketch map of the room in which the encounter took place, with the precise positions of those involved and dotted lines to represent their various movements.

By now he was going to the theatre almost every night and taking careful note of the great actors and actresses in their various roles. Mlle Contat was detestable in La Chaussée's *Le Préjugé à la mode*, one of those eighteenth-century comedies Stendhal had read as a boy in the country at Claix and which he felt had influenced his determination to become a dramatist. Duchesnois, in the title role of *Ariane*, was 'beautiful and superb, but too many of the verses were intoned chromatically'. Mlle Mars, on the other hand, grew steadily more perfect.

It was perhaps inevitable that Stendhal himself, at this degree of absorption with the drama, should want to try his hand at the business of theatrical declamation and acting. As early as June 1803 he had resolved, partly with the intention of impressing Adèle Rebuffel and her family, to get up a small number of roles to a professional standard, so that he could play them as brilliantly as Talma. His proposed tutor in the art was to be none other than the great Dugazon, whose acting classes took place every Monday, Wednesday and Friday at his apartment in the Hôtel du

Vigan in the Rue des Fossés-Montmartre, where Henri's cousin Martial Daru presented him on a December morning.

Born at Marseille in 1746, Jean-Baptiste-Henri Gourgaud had followed the standard French theatrical practice, familiar in our own century from such one-name celebrities as Mistinguett, Arletty and Fernandel, of adopting a single alias for his career as an entertainer. Known as Dugazon, he became one of the best-loved comic actors of the Ancien Régime, though it was his wife, Céline-Geneviève, who made the name more famous by her speciality in musical roles, so that 'la Dugazon' remained the generic term for a middle-aged woman in comedy and vaudeville throughout the nineteenth century.

Dugazon's personality, that of the disenchanted libertine who has seen and done it all, was calculated to appeal to a would-be man of the world like Henri Beyle, who confessed himself duly enchanted with the elderly actor. Other stars would now and then drop in on the classes at the Hôtel du Vigan, such as the tenor Louis Nourrit and Mlle Rolandeau, whose speciality was *opéra comique* and whose continuing encouragement led naturally to the typical Stendhalian confidence: 'when I've got new clothes and some money, I'll have her.'

This awareness of fresh sexual possibilities scarcely deterred Henri from his pursuit of Victorine Mounier. He spent several days preparing what he hoped would be a momentous letter to her, designed to reveal the true state of his heart and displaying as much of 'le naturel' as he could decently manage. To the journal meanwhile he poured out the hypothetical answer he would give Victorine if ever he were lucky enough to find himself at her feet and she were to ask him, 'Who are you?': 'In this soul, still somewhat sullied perhaps by certain faults, she would behold the noblest passions at their utmost, and a love for her sharing an empire with a love for glory, and very often overwhelming it.'

The letter, covering three large sheets of the finest-wove writing paper, was posted at seven o'clock in the evening of 13 January 1805, at a café in the Rue des Vieux-Augustins, after which Stendhal, feeling suitably bobbish, went out to dinner with Crozet and got himself wet through by falling into a gutter. Neither his declaration, nor Victorine's response supposing she offered any, has survived, and though her name recurs at various points in the journal of the ensuing year, the idea of her as a prospective Madame Beyle faded rapidly from view.

During the last days of 1805, Stendhal made a remarkable discovery. He had long been absorbed, as we have seen, in the serious study of philosophy, more especially of the works of Helvétius, Hobbes and Condillac. Out of such intensive reading he was able, as he felt, to evolve his own system, transmitted with his customary didactic enthusiasm in letters to Pauline and communicated to notebooks under the title *Filosofia Nuova*, recalling the *Scienza Nuova* of the eighteenth-century Neapolitan savant Giambattista Vico. Essentially – and indeed crucially for the development of his mature view of human impulse and motivation – this involved the centrality of a self, *le moi*, suffused with a yearning for happiness, *le bonheur*, and commanding the allegiance of the soul, which in turn rules the body and the understanding, rooted though each is in habit. Man is ruled by passion, by the search for happiness, ideas derive from feeling and imagination has no reality without desire.

Pompous and twaddling as much of the *Filosofia Nuova* appears, its author mercifully never abandoned his conviction in the sacred validity of passion and *la chasse au bonheur* which impels his characters to their most original deeds and utterances. Like other intelligent young men, however, he sought the easy answers that a rationalized philosophical system might offer, and found them, more neatly packaged than he himself could ever have contrived, in the *Eléments d'idéologie* published in 1801 by Antoine-Louis-Claude Destutt de Tracy. From a family of Scottish descent, Tracy, an aristocratic army officer who had been made a senator during Napoleon's consulate, had written a book to beguile a year's imprisonment in 1793–4, with the aim of consolidating on the work of Condillac and Cabanis in presenting moral and political concepts in the form of exact sciences, under the blanket term 'Idéologie' which he himself devised. His notion of interacting physical and social influences reduced to a clearly defined system linked the teaching of the later Enlightenment to those of nineteenth-century thinkers such as Saint-Simon and Marx, though the Idéologues themselves were subsequently regarded with merely indulgent interest as a quaint intellectual by-product of the Revolutionary era.

Going out in his slippers through the snow to buy Tracy's book and devouring it instantly, Stendhal was overwhelmed with its impact. Even if age and experience inevitably lessened the work's significance, the influence of *Eléments d'idéologie* remained permanent. Meeting the great *idéologue* himself in 1817, he was drawn into his circle in Paris during the 1820s, and though it is often stated that *De l'Amour*, cast as a kind of Tracian thesis, was ill-received by the philosopher, sour and disillusioned in old age, recent evidence, in the form of a letter to Beyle written in 1822, suggests that he rather enjoyed it, even if he evidently found the famous 'crystallization' theory hard to swallow.*

Stendhal's new philosophic enthusiasm was perfectly timed. His heart, rendered the more vulnerable by Victorine's neglect, seemed ready for a fresh engagement, and the exalting effect of his encounter with *Eléments d'idéologie* only heightened his susceptibility. The experience of regularly attending Dugazon's acting classes was not merely a matter of learning the mechanics of dramatic performance, but of discovering his own nature through the peculiar qualities of interpretation and expression he brought to the reading of each allotted role. 'If I have not *the must [sic] understanding soul*', he wrote, using English, according to his custom, as a species of talismanic secret language of intimacy, 'I have at least a soul all made of passion. One must be self-possessed in order to speak well, and one must perhaps possess one's soul, have an *understanding* of such a passion in order to write well.'

It was Dugazon's circle of pupils and theatrical acquaintances which presented Stendhal with the sentimental opportunity for which he had been waiting. His references to the acting lessons include several mentions of a personage named as Louason. She is one of those he intends to 'have', along with Mlle Rolandeau, once he can get hold of some more money. She takes note, he

* Tracy's own ideological chapter on Love was not published in French during his lifetime, but an Italian translation had recently been made by Giuseppe Compagnoni, which Stendhal evidently knew.

says, '*of my understanding*' and is '*toute à fait bonne fille avec moi*'. A day or two later, on 30 January 1805, we find him writing: 'I almost long to attach her to me, so as to cure me of my love for Victorine. With my little Louason I shall enjoy all the sweetness of happy love and gaiety until my departure for Grenoble; but for this she must have a soul.' With such vague imaginings began the earliest fully realized liaison of Stendhal's life, and one of the very few in which his passion was adequately recompensed.

Louason was the stage name of a young actress from Normandy, Jeanne-Françoise-Mélanie Guilbert, who, by the time she became Dugazon's pupil, had already begun her theatrical career and, at twenty-five, was a mother and a divorced wife. Running away from home in Caen, she fled to the arms of a merchant named Samson at Le Havre, became pregnant, escaped once more, this time to Paris, where she gave birth to a daughter. The child, for a second baptismal name, was christened Lodoïska, after the heroine of a popular novel of the age, Louvet du Coudray's *Les Amours du Chevalier de Faublas* (1787) subsequently turned into a highly successful opera by Luigi Cherubini. Given that the story features a runaway bride and a mother's need to survive so as to bring up her daughter adequately, the choice seems entirely apt.

Mélanie's obvious course, as an adolescent unmarried mother alone in the capital, would have been to find a protector, and her exceptional attractions, those of a tall, graceful figure and large blue eyes, made this very easy. Not long after arriving in Paris, she became the mistress of Alexandre-Joseph Paillet, a widower of fifty, who had made his fortune as a picture dealer in partnership with the husband of the celebrated portrait painter Elisabeth Vigée-Lebrun. It was evidently Paillet who suggested to Mélanie the possibility of a theatrical career and who introduced her to Claude Hochet, a handsome young journalist with whom she drifted into a love affair, but it was through her earliest professional drama teacher, none other than the great actress Mme Clairon, that she met her first husband, the Prussian diplomat Justus-Karl Grüner.

A man of varied talents – by the age of twenty-two he had published an essay on penal legislation and a novel entitled *Passion and Duty* – Grüner had arrived in Paris, ostensibly as part of the Prussian peace mission in 1802, but unofficially as a spy and informer. It is of course possible that his engagement and marriage to Mélanie the following year were in the nature of politic moves to entrench himself more firmly in Parisian life, but the basis of the match seems initially at least to have been naïve and sentimental, in keeping with the spirit of the age.

By the April of 1804 the young couple were applying for a divorce by mutual consent, with Grüner undertaking to pay Mélanie an annual pension of 650 livres and settling on her the inheritance of one sixth of his estate. He went on to become a fast-rising career diplomat, rewarded with a barony by the King of Prussia and appointed ambassador to Saxony and Switzerland, but dying after a long illness at Wiesbaden in 1820, aged only forty-three.

The house to which Mélanie and her daughter retreated after the divorce stood – and indeed still stands – on the corner of the Rue Neuve-des-Petits-Champs and Rue Sainte-Anne. Originally built in 1671 for the composer Jean-Baptiste Lully by Daniel Gittard, its elegantly pilastered façade is adorned, appropriately enough, with masks and musical instruments, and the semicircular windows of the actress's little *entresol* apartment over the gateway remain in place, though the interior has since been rebuilt.

It was here that Stendhal began to accompany Mélanie – or Louason as he first refers to her – from Dugazon's studio a few streets away. To begin with, their developing relationship was complicated by the presence of a tiresomely persistent German named Wagner, 'very limited in intelligence and rather stupid', who had the knack of always turning up when least wanted. Nevertheless, in a matter of days rather than weeks, Henri had fallen deeply under Mélanie's spell, conscious, what was more, that much of what he felt was unlike anything he had ever experienced before.

The impact of his new passion can be sensed in the gradual change in the tone and content of the journal. Though the record of theatrical impressions, books read and meetings with friends is still sustained, a fresh note of rhapsodic ecstasy breaks forth, partially influenced, no doubt, by Stendhal's enjoyment of such works as Mme de Staël's *Delphine* and of the *idéologue* Maine de Biran's *Influence de l'habitude sur la faculté de penser*, but far more obviously by his growing emotional involvement with Mélanie. On 9 February, apparently giddy with delight at Mlle Mars' performance in Regnard's *Les Folies amoureuses* – phrases such as 'la plus vive jouissance', 'cette impression enlevante', 'cette extrême gaieté' dot the page – he tried briefly to forget Louason, but ended by complaining: 'I'm tired of thinking and feeling, I've a perpetual headache, I'm tired of trying to amuse myself, it's the first time I've felt like this. My love has none of the tenderness I've felt towards Victorine, I haven't enough hope of that.'

What becomes clear is that Mélanie was being built into the airy construct of Stendhal's fantasy of himself as a successful playwright. The pedagogical instinct which inspired his letters to Pauline could now be turned towards Mlle Clairon's pupil, whom he would teach to connect the various dramatic representations of feeling with the general principles of philosophy, thus turning her into the greatest actress who ever lived. He summed up the desirable outcome in unusually precise English: 'a future young dramatic bard with a future young actress'.

He was still diffident as to the real impression he was currently making on her at Dugazon's classes, let alone anywhere else, but was even more anxious as to why exactly she was so distant towards him. At first he thought it was simply because she was having her period,* then, gnawed at by jealousy of Wagner, Martial Daru and other men in her circle, he supposed she might have contracted gonorrhoea. Yet he longed to make her his mistress, seeing her as the very incarnation of pleasure itself: 'all the genuine delights of love, detached from the sadness and gloom of this passion, all the reality of love.'

By 16 February their intimacy had deepened into kisses and shared confidences while the maid curled Mélanie's hair and she told Henri her life story as they sat by the fire.

* Stendhal refers to it as 'il marchese', apparently in connection with the red coats worn by marquesses.

> She was divine while telling me this story. I was sitting beside her, looking her full in the face, never missing any of its details, holding her hands in mine. She knew well enough the effect of her tender heart. There was just one point on which I might have reproached her, but what woman isn't something of a coquette? . . . . when she spoke of her father, she dabbed at her eyes once or twice, where there were no tears. I stole twenty kisses from her, at which she didn't greatly object; I think she loves me.

Henri, however, was no nearer the achievement of his hopes. The touches of melancholy and hypersensitivity he had noted in Mélanie's character were part of that essential vulnerability which hardly suited her to the combative toughness of life as a Parisian actress. This made her surround herself with male protectors, who had an irritating habit of showing up at the exact moment when her newest, most ardent suitor felt he might have pressed home a perfect opportunity. If the unwelcome disturber was not Agricol-Etienne de La Pierre de Châteauneuf, a hack writer from Avignon who had supplied the libretto for a patriotic opera by Lesueur on the story of Androcles and the lion, then it was the altogether more handsome and assiduous Joseph-Hilarion Blanc de Volx, a political economist with an interest in the theatre, and more particularly in Mélanie as the star of the plays he intended to write.

By the middle of March, Stendhal was beginning to despair: 'In the last analysis, I see that I may as well finish for good with Louason, but I love her too much to want this; either she or the circumstance must help me.' Neither was propitious. At Easter Mélanie went into the country near Melun, to stay with another of her elderly admirers, and a week or so after her return she announced to Henri that she was leaving once more, this time for her first major theatrical engagement, in Marseilles, where M. Beaussier, manager of the Grand-Théâtre, had contracted her for a year's salary of 6500 francs.

With the utmost coolness her lover made up his mind to accompany her at least as far as Lyons, or even to Marseilles itself, where he had his own affairs to attend to. The previous October, in a letter to Pauline, he had made the first of several references to a project devised by his friend Fortuné Mante for the pair of them to go into banking, and had since suggested to his sister that she ought to come to Paris and throw in her lot with them. Mante, amiable, honest and entirely devoted to Henri, had since been persuaded by his parents, from a *dauphinois* family well acquainted with the Beyles and the Gagnons, to enter as a junior partner in the business enterprise of their protégé Charles Meunier, now based in Marseilles. However, reluctant to quit Paris, he had returned to Grenoble, whence he sent a long and detailed account of an interview with Chérubin Beyle and Dr Gagnon, whom he attempted unsuccessfully to interest in making some sort of capital investment in the scheme. From the doctor's sardonic account of Chérubin's agricultural obsession it became clear that all his son-in-law's disposable income was tied up, and that even had anything been available, the two were hardly in favour of Henri's proposed venture.

What Mante's letter significantly underlined was the family's steadfast devotion to Henri, a loyalty which, given Fortuné's puzzled comparison between what his friend had told him and what he now heard for himself, the errant son and grandson scarcely deserved. Even the eternally unforgiven Zénaïde, the 'rapporteuse' of childhood, seemed devoted to her brother, while Dr Gagnon confided in Mante that he was convinced of Chérubin's passionate love for his son, which he was afraid of showing only because he wanted to maintain his authority over the boy. No response to this letter exists from Stendhal, though he can hardly have failed to reply, and he makes no mention of it in the journal. After all, it contained almost nothing he could have wanted to hear.

Nevertheless, having presumably escorted Mélanie as far as Lyons – his notes are entirely blank on this journey, except for a cryptic resolve in English '*To do the history of travel and that of the passion for M.*' – he returned, without much expectation of comfort or success, to Grenoble. The responses of both his father and grandfather were consistently discouraging. The banality in their predictions of financial disaster, their greed and meanness, the essential narrowness of their aspirations, finally disgusted him, and his reaction emphasizes the huge failure in sympathy and intuition which now divided them from him.

On 22 July, Stendhal set off in the diligence for Valence, on his way to Marseilles. It was the first time he had encountered the landscape of the Midi, among which his Gagnon ancestors had lived and worked, and even though the fragmented quality of his notes suggests a curious unwillingness to record his impressions, the sheer novelty of everything, the intense heat, the bald rocks and their Moorish-looking fortresses, the singing boatmen who carried them down the Rhône, the white, dusty houses at Avignon, the handsome, sturdy young porter who arranged their journey to Beaucaire, and the boy with heavy eyelids and fine eyelashes who looked like the self-portrait of the fifteen-year-old Raphael – the sudden pleasure of all these impressions was strengthened for Henri by his solitude, the first genuine solitude he had known for over a year. The whole of this passage of the journal, with its notes on colours, shapes and contrasts, lays bare a new kind of sensibility, by which the writer himself seems positively embarrassed: 'I break off my description, because I've observed that I'm wasting my memories, this sweet portion of existence. I should need fifty hours of work, with a burning sensitivity, flowing like an overwhelming river, to portray all I've felt . . . .' Oddly enough he says practically nothing, in the hundred pages which follow, about the city of Marseilles, in which he was to live for almost a year. The place held almost as little fascination for him as his job, which was essentially that of clerk and office boy for the firm of Meunier and Mante. This was not, as certain earlier writers on Stendhal have chosen to term it, a grocery business, but an agency for the buying and selling of spices, dyestuffs, drugs and colonial goods, employing Henri on errands to the customs offices and the stock exchange. Mante's mother had been instrumental in securing her son a share in the enterprise, if only because she felt he was doing little good by staying in Paris, but she was more seriously distressed to learn that 'M. Beylle' had been taken on as a junior.

'How can these people succeed in business from so weak a beginning?' she wrote angrily to Meunier. 'What do these banking projects signify without money, since one must be a millionaire to do anything in that line? This looks merely like young hotheads building castles in Spain, and what confidence could they possibly inspire?' As for Beyle, 'his father is rich enough to give his son the wherewithal, without sending him to you, I don't understand it. I have always said that M. Beyle was the cleverest man in Grenoble. How on earth could he have allowed his son to leave him and join with you?' Mme Mante, on whom Henri had actually called in on his way south, could hardly have known that his purpose in coming to Marseilles had very little indeed to do with pursuing a serious career in the import-export business.*

Mélanie had made her debut among the Marseillais in the role of Arménaïde in Voltaire's *Tancrède* on 30 May. A faithful account dispatched to Grenoble on the following day by Mante began by emphasizing the fact, apparently remarkable at the Grand-Théâtre, that she had been heard in silence, even though the stalls audience was worse than the riff-raff of the Paris boulevards and the first two tiers of boxes were thronged with prostitutes plying for custom. Fortuné was impressed with the clarity of her diction in comparison with that of the other actors, but implied that nervousness made her seem a little too breathless and over-inclined to exaggerate her gestures. Somewhat uncharitably, he added that whatever applause she received was most probably a tribute to her ability to silence the house, and that she was unlikely to sustain such a success at a third or fourth performance.

In an earlier letter to Henri she had voiced a characteristic defencelessness, and the querulous tone grew more shrill in her next. 'Does the profound melancholy I feel in the depths of my soul make itself felt in spite of me? I don't know, but I'm experiencing a terrible emptiness, I'm isolated in the midst of those around me, even those I love. Everything bothers me, wears me out, disgusts me, nothing can amuse me.' At least if he was with her, he could help her rehearse. Mante, for his part, was at pains to assure Henri that Mélanie was seriously in love with him: 'What goodness! what simplicity! If ever I were to marry, I should give half my money for such a character. Do you want me to put you into the same hotel? I'll ask her when next we meet.'

The hotel was the Pension Rambert in the Rue Sainte, and it

* The correct nineteenth-century English term for Meunier, Mante and Beyle in their commercial line was 'Italian warehousemen'.

was here that Stendhal and Mélanie were finally able to consummate their affair. The ecstatic opening of a letter to Pauline – 'I'm as happy as possible, as well as possible. . . . This is the truest happiness I ever felt in my life, ah how sweet it is!' – has been taken to indicate that the long-delayed event took place on the evening of 25 July 1805. The journal, however, is almost entirely mute, and a single note in English on 29 July, '*the evening till the midnight for ever*', is the only indication we have that the young couple, in a hot southern seaport noted (according to Mante at least) for the promiscuity of its inhabitants, lost no time in enjoying one another.

Writing home for more ties and shirts, which he needed to change twice a day in the sultry weather, Stendhal sought to recommend Mélanie to his sister and fondly envisaged them all living together in Paris, with Pauline married perhaps to Mante. He spoke tenderly of the actress's openness of character, her sadness, the hurts she received in early life, her delicate health and her despair at finding another soul like hers with whom to fall in love. As for Mante, was he not an excellent young man, with a suitable fortune, ready to spend his life close to his friend?

One August afternoon the lovers went out into the country east of Marseilles for a picnic, taking with them a brace of partridge, a roast pigeon, a pâté, a veal stew, some peaches and grapes and a bottle of claret. The letter Henri wrote to Pauline is beautifully precise on the landscape, with a castle embowered in chestnut woods, whose contrast with a nearby avenue of plane trees recalled 'a piece by Cimarosa in which this great master of the heart's emotions, among grand arias both sombre and terrible and in the midst of a sublime work, painting energetically all the horrors of vengeance, jealousy and unhappy love, has placed a charming gay little air accompanied by a bagpipe'. Mélanie and Henri went to a little inn to ask for refreshment, and gazed enchanted at a four-year-old boy lying asleep.

What Pauline was not told, in this small vignette of sensibility, was that her brother, that same afternoon, had been equally rapt by the sight of his mistress bathing in the nearby River Huveaune. There is nothing to suggest that she was naked, as Paul Arbelet and successive *stendhaliens* would have us assume, but the image fixed itself in Stendhal's memory, and when he came to assemble *Vie de Henry Brulard* it suddenly surfaced, in poignant connection with a painting of nude women frolicking in a stream, seen in the studio of his Grenoble drawing master, Joseph Le Roy.

By the autumn the edges of this idyllic existence were starting, however imperceptibly at first, to fray. Henri had soon enough discovered that he was not Mélanie's sole admirer in Marseilles. Besides a merchant named Baux, whom he jokingly refers to in English translation as 'Leases', there was Blanc de Volx's friend Joseph de Girard, and the sixty-year-old retired General Vicomte de Saint-Gervais, whose vanity and pedantry increasingly irritated him. Even the faithful Mante was becoming exasperating in the apparent limitations of his intelligence and narrowness of his sympathies, a test which most of Stendhal's intimates were almost invariably destined to fail in any case.

Henri despised himself, what was more, for having cynically considered the possibility of making a match with a fellow lodger at the Pension Rambert, Mme Cossonnier, a mature divorcee who had begun blatantly flirting with him. A series of character portraits written in tandem with Louis Crozet, now working as a civil engineer, and undertaken as part of Stendhal's youthful scheme for a systematic study of human nature in preparation for becoming a great writer, includes a malicious sketch of Cossonnier which underlines the coolness of its author's marital calculations. 'She is a chatterbox . . . vain to her fingers' ends . . . a backbiter greedy for small objects . . . . happiest when in a position that allows her to humiliate others . . . base in small matters . . . cold . . . dry' and so on. The merciless acidity of the author's assessment may have something to do with his growing mood of restlessness as he began to take stock of his position, of the people among whom he found himself and of the current quality of his ambitions.

At the end of January 1806 the Grand-Théâtre was forced to close its doors, a symptom of the weakening economic situation among the Marseillais under pressure from the allied naval blockade of French ports which had been imposed with the resumption of hostilities. A month later, together with Mme Cossonnier, Mélanie left for Paris. While Stendhal lingered in

Marseilles, she cast about for a fresh engagement, hinting that she might go as far as Naples 'in spite of my weak chest' and that he could follow her there. Evidently neither this letter nor its successor was answered with anything but the vaguest of promises to join her as soon as he could. By the time she took up her pen once more, on 10 June, he had returned to Grenoble. On this occasion she was more forthright and voluble than before in remonstrating with him over his neglect, and the document, an extended analysis of the state of their relationship, suggests that though she might not have been as responsive as Pauline to Henri's plans for her intellectual improvement, Mélanie was neither stupid nor lacking in refinement.

Essentially she was demanding some form of written commitment. 'I base my tranquillity on such a declaration, I give you tokens of the most sincere tenderness, of the tenderest attachment. I have offered you incontestable proof of this, and your sole response has been vague letters in which you declare that you love me always and that I shall see this to be so in a fortnight.' With remarkable shrewdness (her experience of men was a good deal more extensive than Henri's knowledge of women) she went on: 'You love me like a young man whose present conduct has not the slightest consequence for his future destiny, and whose only aim is to pass the time as little unpleasantly as possible.' Doubtless with a view to goading her lover into action, she told him it was Blanc de Volx who had engaged her for Naples at a salary of 5000 livres, and that she had asked for some time in which to ponder this offer.

The affair was not quite at an end. A kind of liaison survived through the summer months of 1806, when Stendhal came back to Paris. On 22 August he laconically notes that they were together for three hours in the Champs-Elysées, when she was cross and hardly said a word; on 2 September he writes absent-mindedly, 'Yesterday I slept with Mélanie'; and on the 30th he mentions getting home at a quarter past eight in the morning from spending the night with her. Yet the exhilaration, the Stendhalian sense of *bonheur*, have faded, and even a trip to the zoo with the Rebuffels seems to inspire him more genuinely. 'We looked at the bats, the monkeys, the she-elephant, but above all at a monkey with red stripes on its face and with hind quarters in brilliant colours, violet and red. Its prick a fiery red. Its spirit, the human expression in its eyes. I fed it pineapple drops. It trembled, its access of nerves.'

Mélanie Guilbert's later career followed a pattern more familiar in our own century than in an age when 'actress' was almost synonymous with 'whore'. In 1808 she acquired another protector, a politician named François Roger, who gained her a series of probationary appearances at the Comédie-Française under the new, more resonant stage name of Mademoiselle Sainte-Albe. The press was relatively kind to her in *Iphigénie*, *Andromaque* and *Zaïre*, but was forced to conclude that though well taught by Clairon, Mélanie's declamation was much better than her acting.

The following year she joined a French troupe at Kassel in Germany, and from there she went on to form part of another crew of Parisian actors in Russia. Her good fortune was to avoid being swept up in Napoleon's retreat from Moscow (during which almost the entire dramatic company was either killed or else died of starvation) for in 1810 she had married Nikolai Aleksandrovich Barkoff, counsellor of state to the Tsar. The pair separated soon enough, Mélanie returning to Paris in time to give birth to a daughter, Sophie, whom she brought back to Barkoff when hostilities between France and Russia temporarily ceased in 1814. After an agonizing period of illness, under the ministrations of a dubious doctor named Frappart, she died on 18 August 1828, at her apartment near the Madeleine. Her will, an extraordinary essay in rage, frustration, cynicism and black humour – 'if I wish my tomb to be covered with flowers, it is only so that its aspect may seem less sinister to the few persons likely to visit it' – took fifteen years to settle.

CHAPTER 4

THE GREEN HUNTSMAN

If, as Stendhal always claimed, he 'fell with Napoleon', it could equally be maintained that he rose alongside him. The popular image of the writer has always been that of a diehard Bonapartist, but the truth is naturally more ambiguous. While the Emperor was in power, Henri Beyle was no more conspicuously devoted to him than were all those others content to don the uniform of the Grande Armée or negotiate the tightly woven meshes of imperial bureaucracy in pursuit of a career. At several points throughout the surviving journals for the Consulate and Empire period Stendhal is openly critical of Napoleon, or at any rate doubtful of him, and a sense of Bonaparte's true significance, whether in the context of French politics or against a wider spectrum of Romantic hero-worship, never really dawns until after St Helena.

What Stendhal's papers during the years 1802–6 interestingly underline is the minimal impact on him, at that period, of contemporary political developments in Europe as France returned to war after the collapse of the Peace of Amiens. There is almost no indication, for instance, of the commercial pressures on the firm of Meunier and Mante created by allied blockade of French ports following the battle of Trafalgar in 1805, and hardly any significant mention of Napoleon, let alone of public affairs in France, even in the heavily censored form in which they were filtered through the press to ordinary citizens.

When Henri's involvement in the great business of the Empire ultimately began, it was not through his own initiative but via that of his solicitous family. Since leaving the army he had never lost touch with his cousin Pierre Daru, now effectively one of the most influential men in Europe as architect of the vast infrastructure underpinning the successes of Napoleon's army. The Marseilles venture had from the outset been looked at askance by Chérubin Beyle and Dr Gagnon, who evidently saw no possible lustre accruing to Henri as a minor functionary in a business house. During the last days of December 1805, the doctor sat down to write his grandson a long and carefully phrased letter, which reveals both a sharper awareness of the young man's true character than he was probably ready to acknowledge at that moment, and a genuine wish to leave no stone unturned in promoting his welfare.

Gagnon was doubtless right in accusing Henri of rushing to judgement on men and issues, and still more accurate in assessing his negative view of human behaviour. 'Your relationships with several people have inspired you with contempt, an altogether too universal disdain. It is a pleasure to discover honest souls and generous actions; as for you, my dear boy, it seems to me that you delight instead in unveiling perfidy and disgrace.' There was not much point, however, in recommending Stendhal to visit their distant cousin, a sister of M. Rebuffel, who was a nun in a convent at Castres, or in suggesting a more considerate approach to religious matters and a glance at Fénelon's treatise on the existence of God.

The central point at issue between them was Henri's apparent neglect of the Daru connection and all its practical uses. Why not, urged the old man, go back to Paris and take up the administrative post which the Minister, if applied to, was sure to offer his young cousin? By now Stendhal had taken Gagnon into his confidence regarding Mélanie (though he pretended her name was Henriette) and the doctor was charmingly optimistic about their future, as long as Chérubin's monthly allowance was properly used. 'The way is now open; if you should take it, you'll have a guaranteed independence, a home in Paris, and enough leisure to follow your taste for literature, the sciences and languages, and to look after whatever concerns you.'

When the letter arrived at Marseilles, Stendhal, who later scribbled on it '4 very reasonable pages', was busy reading

Molière's *L'Avare* and noted that once he had glanced over his grandfather's advice he could no longer concentrate on the play. Suddenly seized with passionate ambition, he started daydreaming of his possible happiness in the post of Auditor of the Council of State, the sort of job Daru would certainly be able to procure, and indeed later succeeded in finding for him. So powerful was this reverie that it drove all love for Mélanie out of his head.

The Daru scheme hung fire during the early months of 1806, and the Minister himself at first seemed unwilling to countenance any sort of favour towards Henri. A letter to Pauline speculated ruefully on the need to change shirts and cravats more often if any sort of decent impression was to be made on the influential cousin and his family. On 1 June, Stendhal wrote from Grenoble to Daru's younger brother, Martial, telling him somewhat disingenuously that he had left Marseilles under pressure from Dr Gagnon and Chérubin. 'Commerce humiliates my father: he will do nothing for a son who shakes up brandy bottles and everything in the world for a son whose name appears in the newspapers.' Enquiring as to whether Daru cared after all to do anything for him, he admitted to preferring an office job in Paris to a highly paid position two hundred leagues distant and looked back nostalgically to the life they had led as young subalterns at the Casa d'Adda in Milan. Though he was careful to tell Martial not to put himself out by asking favours from the Minister, the whole tone of Stendhal's address suggests that this is exactly what he was after.

The family had in any case been busy pulling every available string. Dr Gagnon's original application to Daru, summarized in a long letter to his grandson, was as fulsome in its praise of Henri and recommendations for his welfare as its author dared to be without ruining his case by overstatement. Romain Gagnon had preferred instead to write to Martial, in suitably unctuous terms. 'If Monsieur your brother will but show him the way, this young man, flattered by the guiding hand of genius, will move promptly towards his goal. Permit me, sir, to believe that your friendship will assist him.'

Throughout the later summer in Paris Stendhal hung around the Darus, waiting for something to turn up. His life, for the time being, resumed its earlier rhythms. He could start going again to the theatre, more especially to an Italian opera company which was giving *Il matrimonio segreto*, a work that ravished him as much as ever it had in Italy four years earlier. He settled down to read Hobbes and Montesquieu, and went out to Montmorency to look at Rousseau's hermitage in a park belonging to the composer Grétry, where he watched entranced as the sixteen-year-old boy who acted as their guide sought to attract the attention of a ten-year-old girl who followed with the keys, and the pair started acting up to each other like two adults. Stendhal's companions paid no attention: it was one of those innumerable moments when, by virtue of noticing such things, he felt himself alone, lacking common ground with those around him.

By the end of September Martial was preparing to set off for Germany, bearing the grandiose title of 'Inspecteur aux Revues de la Garde Impériale au Grand Quartier Impérial', in the wake of Napoleon's victorious army as it moved ever deeper into Bavaria and prepared to enter Prussia. On the 23rd Henri had been one of the witnesses of the contract for his marriage to Mlle Charlotte de Froidefond du Chatenay, and a week later was present at the wedding after spending the night with Mélanie Guilbert. At last, after another fortnight of uncertainty and occasional gloom as to his immediate prospects, he was able to tell Pauline on 12 October that he was setting off for Bamberg with Martial, who had arranged with his brother, the Minister, to take him along as a companion.

Leaving Paris on 16 October, they hurried towards Metz, thence onwards via Frankfurt and Würzburg to follow the Emperor into Berlin. Stendhal was unimpressed by the Prussian capital. The River Spree, as he told Pauline, looked like green oil, and the entire city was built on sand. As soon as you stepped off the pavement your foot sank in it up to the ankle. Nevertheless he could find it in himself to be moderately happy, since it was here that Pierre Daru was at last moved to acknowledge his *grenoblois* connection, and all the solicitous addresses the family had made him, by naming his cousin a provisional *Commissaire des guerres*, a type of military bureaucrat whose job was to obtain provisions and supplies for the army. Henri's base was to be at the town of Brunswick (Braunschweig) in northern Saxony, and the appointment was confirmed on 16 December.

Stendhal never really learned to love Germany and the Germans, just as he never bothered, despite taking lessons in it, to master their language. At first glance his two years in Brunswick appear simply a dry run for the kind of pseudo-exile he was to endure twenty years later as consul at Civitavecchia, without the relief of an equivalent Rome close by. In fact, as he must later have perceived, the whole experience was central to both his incarnations, as an administrator of considerable resourcefulness and efficiency, and as a literary artist. Memories, motifs and suggestions from these Brunswick days recur constantly in his fiction, and at least two of his finest unfinished stories, *Le Rose et le Vert* and *Mina de Vanghel*, bear the impress of tender feelings towards a German girl. The entire first portion of *Lucien Leuwen*, entitled *Le Chasseur Vert* after an inn Stendhal was in the habit of frequenting while in Brunswick, is steeped in recollection of his tedious hours as a young commissary in that town.

He wrote at the beginning of an uncompleted memoir from this period:

> Imagine a great muddy plain with islands of sand, sloping upwards to the north, and you will gain a general notion of this country, sixty leagues in diameter . . . it rains a lot. The roads are impracticable seven months of the year for their mud. There is no such thing as spring. One is amazed to see leaves in bud amid the cold air of winter. Never a hint of that velvet air so sweet to delicate chests, never any of those evenings when one lives for the pleasure of breathing a gentle atmosphere – twice only have I known that healthy air that follows a warm rain. The rarity of such weather is one of my principal complaints against this country.

Others included the boring two-hour wait for horses at the post-houses, the *Trinkgelt* or tip which had to be given to the postilions, and their tendency to stop halfway along the road in order to drink schnapps. There were the fat, savourless strawberries, the disgusting smell of boiled cabbage in the inns, the detestable wine and the stink of old sweat on the bedroom duvets. In the tiny rooms of the old wooden town houses the family gathered in a single noisome parlour, its overwhelming fug seasoned with pipe smoke and its walls covered with engravings and silhouette portraits.

Henri was charmed all the same by the German Christmas, when the houses were full of Nuremberg toys ('they're wonderful for the children and cost almost nothing') and 'pine trees hung with gilt paper and cakes and covered all over with little candle-ends' (Christmas trees were then unknown outside Germany and Scandinavia). The women, with their splendid arms and thighs, their magnificent hair and complexions, and the faint suggestion about them of a certain Hellenic grandeur, he thought the most beautiful he had ever seen: the men, on the other hand, were irredeemably ugly, barbarous and common. From a distance, a young mounted officer might look as handsome as Alexander the Great, but at close quarters he was just a big, stupid soldier.

Brunswick, where Stendhal garnered these mingled impressions of German provincial life, had been the burial place of the early medieval Emperor Henry the Lion, ancestor of the Guelph dynasty, one of whose branches became Electors of Hanover and ultimately Kings of Great Britain. Another branch, as Dukes of Brunswick-Lüneburg, had covered itself in glory during the various wars of the eighteenth century, and late Duke Karl Wilhelm Ferdinand had distinguished himself by a resolute stand against the progress of the French Revolution through the German states. Praised by Voltaire and Mirabeau as the very model of an enlightened sovereign, he had nevertheless been prepared to accept command of the allied army in Germany during the war with France, and it was from Brunswick that the counter-revolutionary powers published their manifesto. After the failure of the peace in 1803, the Duke took up arms once more, only to meet his death at the battle of Jena three years later – a fight, incidentally, which Stendhal claimed to have seen, though he was still in Paris when it took place on 14 October 1806. Karl Wilhelm's successor, Friedrich Wilhelm, never returned to the duchy and was himself killed at Waterloo. (He is the 'Brunswick's fated chieftain' of Byron's famous lines in *Childe Harold's Pilgrimage*.)

Napoleon, baldly declaring that 'the house of Brunswick has

ceased to reign', annexed its territories to the kingdom of Westphalia created for his brother Jérôme. Several of the chief courtiers and the Duke's family went into exile, though his sister Augusta Dorothea had been allowed to remain at her castle of Gandersheim, and the palaces and grander houses of Brunswick itself were quickly occupied by senior military personnel, including Martial Daru.

Stendhal's job as adjutant commissary was by its very nature unexciting and we can scarcely wonder that he hardly ever mentions it in his letters to Pauline. Though he seems to have carried out his duties more than adequately, the work made no extraordinary demands on him. For the time being Napoleon had pinned down his enemies, in the shape of Austria, Russia and Prussia, and the labour of finding billets for hard-pressed troops, transport for the wounded or forage for a cavalry brigade, all of which came within Henri's province, did not fall to his lot at this stage. If he worked hard, it was to impress the Darus, but as a bureaucrat he was naturally thorough and conscientious, so that within eighteen months he had been promoted to become a paymaster for the King of Westphalia and an assistant to the Prefect of the Ocker district (as in France, Napoleon's German empire was divided into river-named departments).

His marvellous adaptability and readiness to make the best of unpromising circumstances came to his aid in shaping a social life for himself in the context of a German provincial capital with more than a touch of polish and sophistication in its own right. He was not especially drawn to his French colleagues: the only one of them with whom he felt any affinity, a financial official named Brichard, was insufferably suspicious, and Stendhal had caught him trying to read his journal. A quarrel with Martial Daru took a month to make up. The Brunswickers, on the other hand, grew more and more congenial. French-speaking, in the manner of Ancien Régime German courts, they were entirely at their ease with the conquerors and evidently found the Napoleonic occupation rather pleasurable than otherwise.

Among those who had thrown in their lot with the new regime was Baron Friedrich Karl von Strombeck, Princess Augusta Dorothea's man of business and a firm friend, with the rest of his family, of the young adjutant commissary Beyle. Thirty years later, in his autobiography *Darstellungen aus meinem Leben*, he cast a nostalgic glance at the years of the French in Brunswick:

> Never was life more brilliant than during the occupation . . . At the castle as at the palace, balls and gala suppers succeeded one another. In the city the nobility outdid one another in their zeal to entertain the French authorities. Young women displayed their finest jewels. They seemed unaware that the French were their enemies, and to the latter's credit it must be said that they carried out their unpleasant task with the greatest humanity. Martial Daru was especially distinguished in this respect. I was far better acquainted, however, with his close relation, war commissary De Beyle, native of Grenoble. I may truly say that we became friends. He was in those days a young man schooled in the sciences, aged around twenty-six. Gifted with a thoroughly French vivacity, he possessed in addition a supreme cheerfulness. Almost every day he came to see me, accompanying me on my rides and spending several days as a guest at my country house.

Strombeck, for his part, was learned, cosmopolitan and intelligent enough to engage the attention of the volatile Henri Beyle, though the Frenchman's verdict on his German friend was no less exacting than usual in its detachment:

> . . . He has the air of an apothecary. A dull, heavy, slow character; some ideas however, although neither clear nor precise, on the matter of virtue and government. A good friend, a tender father, good son, good brother. Loving the arts, knowing a bit of astronomy, well educated, but lacking philosophical leaven and never collecting his ideas together. . . . Thirty-five years old and 12,000 francs in rents. His wife merely a mother, nothing more. Completely empty, sweet, virtuous, but dreadfully boring. As German as possible.

Strombeck admitted that he was secretly in love with his sister-in-law, Philippine von Bülow.

Through such a friendship Stendhal found his way easily into the most congenial circles and began to encounter a society and a set of values totally different from anything he had come across before. The tone of his journals and letters does not necessarily alter its customary devastating matter of factness in recording emotional and aesthetic reactions, but the accumulated detail underlines the sheer novelty of the Brunswick experience, however tedious and dissatisfying he fancied it at the time.

This was the first encounter with the fully evolved romantic sensibility of northern Europe, a strain of feeling with which he had so far had little first-hand acquaintance and whose rhetoric of spiritual exaltation and morbid sentimentality would never entirely convince him or claim him for its own. The central paradox of Stendhal's position within the cultural perspective of his age must always be defined by his rigorously selective sympathy with its cult of sensation. He had his hours of feeling, a great many indeed, but few of them could ever have been defined as especially Wordsworthian.

Here he was, nevertheless, in the world of Goethe's *Sorrows of Young Werther* and *Elective Affinities*, of Schiller's Plutarch-spouting bandits and amorous imbibers of poisoned lemonade, of poets who committed suicide and poets who went mad. The contrast with France, a country in which, with the honourable exception of André Chénier, the poetic impulse had lain neglected for almost two hundred years, and where the drama still plodded dutifully after the approved Aristotelian *règle*, could not have been more marked. Different also was the philosophy of sex. From nights with Mélanie Guilbert and venal banter with Madame Cossonnier in the Marseilles boarding house, let alone the opportunist pursuit of Adèle Rebuffel via the favours of her compliant mother, it was a planetary distance to a provincial town in lower Saxony, where infidelity was not viewed as the inevitable concomitant of marriage, where seduction was not mandatory for the establishment of a lover's credentials and where gallantry was not always coloured with sceptical calculations as to the durability of female virtue.

Stendhal received some inkling of this contrast in attitudes, between the French view of love as a kind of freebooting amusement, energizing life with the vitamins of pursuit and possession, and the German version of the same thing as a matter of yearning, heart-searching, noble suppression and sentimental heroism, when he and Strombeck, together with their friends, went exploring to Wolffenbüttel. Once the capital of a separate Brunswick duchy, the town was noted for possessing one of the great libraries of Europe, which Beyle later used when embarking on a history (unfinished) of the War of the Spanish Succession.

During the homeward journey, he had talked with Strombeck of Philippine von Bülow and his friend's secret ardour for her. On a carriage journey she had leant on Strombeck's shoulder, seeming to be asleep until the vehicle went over a bump in the road and she was thrown into his arms. When he hugged her, she moved quickly into the opposite corner of the coach. 'He does not think her altogether unseducible,' wrote Stendhal, 'but he is almost certain she would kill herself the morning after the crime.' To the Frenchman such a reaction clearly seemed as extraordinary as the Draconian punishments meted out to adulterers in the duchy of Brunswick: a married man found guilty of the offence received ten years in jail and at least one prominent courtier thus stigmatized had been sent into exile with only twenty-four hours' notice.

Just as bizarre was the fact that most of the Brunswickers appeared to marry for love rather than money. When, earlier that day, they had all been discussing Madame de Staël's recently published novel *Corinne*, and Stendhal had criticized the hero, Lord Oswald Neville, for waiting four years before declaring his passion for the heroine, Philippine's outraged answer was: 'But he was married!' A woman who had stayed up till three in the morning to finish *Corinne* but could still justify Lord Oswald's self-restraint simply by the fact that he was married would surely make her husband happy. Mystified, Henri later went to the tavern, fired twenty pistol shots, took the host's daughter to bed and came home to confide in the journal that the girl was 'the first German woman I ever saw who was totally exhausted after an orgasm. I made her passionate with my caresses; she was very frightened.'

The name of this tavern, on the edge of the town, was Der Grüne Jäger, The Green Huntsman, and its charm and convivial *Gemütlichkeit* were unforgettable. Afterwards, when he turned to the business of transforming and rearranging his Brunswick souvenirs into a fictional design, Stendhal specifically identified the place with a kind of Watteauesque amorous bandinage, a resort along the lines of an English pleasure garden. In *Lucien Leuwen* it becomes 'a delightful café situated a league and a half out of town . . . . Cafés of this sort among the woods, where music on wind instruments is generally played in the evenings and where one just drops in, are a German custom fortunately spreading throughout several towns in eastern France.' In his unfinished *Le Rose et le Vert*, Der Grüne Jäger figures as 'an English garden, famous for its old elms . . . . there, two or three times a week at five o'clock on a summer afternoon, all the girls and young women of the town meet to drink coffee in the open air'. The sound of the wind band, that German *Harmoniemusik* for which Mozart and Haydn wrote so expressively, ravishes 'hearts that are ripe for music and love' as it has in *Lucien Leuwen*, where 'nothing could be more absorbing, more in harmony with the sun setting behind the great forest trees'.

Stendhal used to go there with several of the friends who had accompanied him on the outing to Wolffenbüttel, such as the Strombecks, Philippine von Bülow and Fraulein von Oeynhausen, up whose skirts Henri once managed to slip a hand almost to the top of the thigh 'where the ebony starts to shade the lily'. They would be accompanied by another family, the wife and daughters of General August Heinrich Ernst von Griesheim, former military governor of Brunswick, who had gone into voluntary exile on the arrival of the French. The eldest of the three girls, Augusta, was married to Stendhal's friend Christian von Münchhausen, but it was with her sister Wilhelmine that he now fell seriously in love.

We know less about Mina von Griesheim than about any of Henri Beyle's other amorous enthusiasms except for Virginie Kubly, perhaps because he and she were seldom alone together and it is doubtful whether she was prepared, except very discreetly, to indulge him in his feelings for her. At that moment he probably did not understand them very well himself. When, in the autumn of 1807, he took stock of the events in his life between July and November of that year, he felt able to note that he was cured of his love for 'Minette' and was sleeping every three or four days 'for physical needs' with a certain Charlotte Knabelhüber, the mistress of a rich Dutchman. Yet it becomes obvious, in the broader perspective of Stendhal's life as an artist and of the emotional archive on which he was later to draw, that Minette's personality, her identity as an intelligent, sensitive, independent-minded girl whose background and upbringing placed her beyond reach of his automatic urge to effect a sexual conquest, made a profound, not to say eternal impression on him. Shadows of her haunt the pages of *De l'Amour* and the *Histoire de la Peinture en Italie*, and she features, thinly disguised, as the heroine in *Le Rose et le Vert* and another incomplete fictional sketch, *Mina de Vanghel*.

In the latter, Stendhal has left us a description which may or may not be accurate:

> Never had so much real superiority been seen to combine with such modesty. Through a sharp contrast, the energy and impulsiveness of her decisions were concealed under a countenance which still retained all the naive charm of childhood, a countenance never spoiled by the graver expression which announces the onset of reason. Reason, indeed, was never a deciding factor in her character.

A single likeness of Wilhelmine von Griesheim exists, in the piled coiffure and gophered frills of the 1820s. The slightest of smiles plays around the attractive mouth and serene eyes, though her life in truth had been marked by sadness when her fiancé, a Dutchman named De Heerdt, was killed in battle. She never married, outliving Stendhal by nearly twenty years and dying at the age of seventy-five in 1861.

Henri admired De Heerdt's cheerful good sense and enjoyed his anecdotes of life in Holland, but he found his constant attentiveness to Minette dfficult to take, if only because it was so unlike anything one ever came across in France, where 'such an overt preference would shock society and disrupt it. The Germans, less civilized, are much less concerned than we are with what disrupts society'. A week later De Heerdt's amorous solicitude had come to seem positively tiresome. 'In France the open manner with which he pays court to Minette would be the last word in indecency, absurdity and coarseness.'

Minette herself, however, had already been made aware of Henri's passion when she rallied him on his flirtation with her friend Fraulein von Treuenfels and he responded with an ardent declaration. There are hints in what he tells us of her behaviour and conversation that she was keeping her options open despite the presence of De Heerdt, but apart from a squeeze of the hand she granted no special favours to her French admirer.

He could always talk about her to Pauline, towards whom his letters were growing less pedagogical and more confiding, even if she must have been tempted to take with a pinch of salt his claim on 30 April that 'I have no more interest in Minette, this blonde and charming Minette, this northern soul, such as I never saw in France or Italy', when a month afterwards he followed a similar assertion with a long account of his emotional state after seeing her with De Heerdt for the first time. The cure was simple: a volume of Helvétius in the pocket, a gallop to the nearby 'English garden' named Richmond, and two hours alone on the lawn with the consolations of the *philosophe*.

Brunswick was beginning to bore him, if indeed it had ever been seriously interesting. Little of any real significance had happened during his two-year sojourn in Germany, and the nature of his work as war commissary and administrator of revenues for the Ocker department was of no special fascination. A batch of official correspondence from this period includes such items as an order for the loan of fifty rifles to a Westphalian regiment, a delivery note for 242 greatcoats and a message informing Daru that the second infantry regiment of the Polish-Italian brigade had been told not to take the cartridge cases and bandoliers from the Brunswick magazine. He had gone out shooting after hare, duck and deer, learned a good deal more English (from Professor Friedrich Emperius of the Collegium Carolinum, who had made him study Shakespeare's *Richard III*), climbed the Brocken apparently without knowing anything of its Faustian connections, crossed the bleak Lüneburg Heath on a trip to Hamburg, projected a history of the War of the Spanish Succession, and come to the conclusion that eating peas was a sovereign remedy against love.

By the autumn of 1808 he had started, or so he thought, to

understand the Germans. 'Their principal defect, in my eyes, is a lack of character. . . . What is more, reading the Bible has made them stupid and pompous. It has the same effect on the English. Their coldness is well explained by their diet: black bread, butter, milk and beer', though he was struck by the remarkable honesty of a nation which was in the habit of sending money through the post. An insufferable Teutonic seriousness overclouded all social intercourse, and nobody made jokes in case it might be thought they were showing off. As Henri told Pauline:

> four years ago, I was in Paris with a solitary pair of holed boots, without a fire in the depth of winter, and often without a candle. Here I am a somebody, getting plenty of letters in which the Germans address me as *Monseigneur*, and important Frenchmen call me *Monsieur l'intendant*; generals pay me visits; I receive solicitations, I write letters, get cross with my secretaries, go to formal dinners, ride a horse and read Shakespeare, but I was happier in Paris. . . . What delicious moments there were in the midst of that wretched existence! I was in a desert where, now and then, I found a spring; now I'm at a table covered with dishes, but I haven't the least appetite.

The order of release arrived on 11 November, and Stendhal hurried back to Paris, where he spent the first months of 1809 much as he had done during earlier sojourns in the capital, dropping in at the Vaudeville, where he picked up a pretty girl named Eliza, who gave him her address and invited him to call, eating ices at the Café de Foy, taking lessons in dancing and Spanish and improving the acquaintance gained in Brunswick with the music of Mozart, though he described the composer to Pauline as 'born for his art but a northern soul, more expert at depicting misfortune and the tranquillity produced by its absence than at portraying the raptures and graces which the sweet climate of the south permits to its inhabitants'. On 4 February he went to a performance of *Cosi fan tutte*, whose music he judged 'agreeable, but it's a comedy, and I only like Mozart when he expresses a sweet, dreamy melancholy'.

Apart from translating a few pages of *Don Quixote* as part of his Spanish lessons, Stendhal had written nothing of any significance in Paris, and only one letter survives from his regular correspondence with Pauline. In May of the previous year she had married François Périer-Lagrange, a *grenoblois* industrialist whose help Henri had invoked in connection with the Beyle family's country properties and the possible sale of the house at Claix. The superstition which ordains that May marriages are cursed with misfortune or unhappiness seems to have had some truth in it where Pauline and her husband were concerned. Never exactly liberal with his praise of others, Stendhal came to despise Périer-Lagrange, whom in any case he must have found it hard to forgive for depriving him of a beloved sister's allegiance.

Only later were the tender intimacy and confidence between brother and sister as letter-writers to dissipate. For the time being Henri could still trust Pauline to respond sympathetically to his anxieties, one of which was over the news that Adèle Rebuffel was due to arrive in Grenoble at the beginning of April, on her way to Italy. She too had recently married, and her husband, Alexandre Petiet, had been appointed intendant of the civil list at the court of Tuscany, now ruled by Napoleon's sister, Elisa Baciocchi. Though Stendhal claimed, in his customary emotion-salving English, '*I have much loved this woman; my love is intirely dead*', he was nonetheless eager for Pauline to do her honour on her visit, with perhaps a party or a trip to some local beauty spot, 'better something quite ordinary than nothing at all', as though his passion were not altogether dead and might thus vicariously be kept warm.

At the end of the letter, he added the postscript 'Employed by M. Count Daru, intendant general of the armies of Germany at imperial headquarters at Munich'. His second commissary posting was indeed with the French army invading Bavaria and striking at the very heart of the Austrian empire, the capital Vienna itself. The campaign was one of Napoleon's bloodiest and most bitterly contested, and for the first time Stendhal encountered the true reeking horror of warfare as he had never really faced it while a subaltern in Italy. His response to what he witnessed, however, was neither a conventional disgust nor necessarily a romantic compassion for victims and sufferers, though he was no stranger to horror and pity. What emerges most powerfully from his personal writings during the journey to Vienna is his command of a style which matches and dignifies its often harrowing themes by the clarity through which the author conveys what he sees to the reader. There is, in short, a strong sense that Stendhal the prose artist has arrived, and that the creator of these letters and journal entries is aiming at something more solid and outward-turning than the medium of 'private papers' seems initially to warrant.

Even the relatively unremarkable journey from Strasbourg to Stuttgart, with its notes on the price of post-horses in the grand duchy of Baden, the pleasure of a dish of fried potatoes and the sight of a pretty girl at a window, is given significance by such paragraphs as the following:

> After the storm, the evening was very beautiful, and the sky at sunset was magnificent for its purity and the perfect fading away of the beautiful red aurora it assumed. We sang in the carriage, or rather M. Cuny, who has a good voice, sang several Italian airs, among them the beautiful romance from Mozart's *Figaro* '*Voi che d'amore*' [Presumably Cherubino's famous '*Voi che sapete*'.] This air seems to me perfectly in harmony with everything I ever liked in Germany. It is still sweetness and softness united with something celestial, but a touching softness produced by passion, and not of the dull kind which inspires contempt. Time will doubtless alter my ideas, but everything I find pleasing in Germany always bears the stamp of Minette.

The speed with which Henri and his fellow commissaries, Cuny, Chatenay and Jacqueminot, bowled across Bavaria, the delights of landscape and mercurial weather and the sheer novelty of travelling buoyed up the spirits remarkably. 'This life enchants me,' he told Pauline, 'I'm at the very centre of my being.' The only difficulty lay in his perpetually edgy relationship with Pierre Daru, whom he joined at Ingolstadt. He noted ruefully:

> He'll never like me, there's something mutually resistant in our characters. He has only spoken to me seven or eight times, and always with a strongly emphasized exclamation. 'A scatterbrain! A scatterbrain like you! Stay away from there, a scatterbrain like you

would get into a fight with those people at once.' Last year he said, in some connection or other, 'Young men must be led with iron rods, that's the only way to get results from them.'

One by one the signs of war began to show themselves: a burnt bridge and three dead Austrian soldiers on the way to Landshut, where the city gate was riddled with bullet holes, helmets scattered across the fields and the little town of Neustadt devastated and empty. At Lambach Stendhal watched the progress of a fire engulfing the houses, but the genuine horror arrived at Ebersberg, where Marshal Masséna two days earlier had fought a tough action with the Austrians for control of a crucial bridge across the River Traun.

'As we started across the bridge,' wrote Stendhal:

> we found bodies of men and horses, about thirty of them still there; we had to throw a good number into the river, which was inordinately wide; in the middle, about four hundred paces downstream, a horse was standing, erect and motionless. Singular effect. The whole town of Ebersberg was still in flames, the street along which we passed was strewn with corpses, mostly French and almost all charred. Some were so badly burned that the human form of the skeleton was barely recognizable. In several places were piles of corpses; I examined their faces. On the bridge a worthy German, dead, his eyes open; German courage, fidelity and kindness were depicted on his face, which expressed only a slight touch of melancholy . . . . our carriage was obliged to run over these corpses disfigured by flames . . . . I confess that this whole thing made me sick.

The bodies in French uniform were those of wounded left in the town as Masséna's troops moved on across the bridge and dying at last when the pursuing Austrians had put the whole of Ebersberg to the torch. Stendhal's colleague Montbadon, who had found a hundred and fifty corpses still smoking in the castle, came across 'a very handsome dead officer; wishing to discover how he died, he took him by the hand; the officer's skin remained in his grasp. This handsome young man was killed in a fashion which did him little honour, by a bullet which hit him in the back and lodged in his heart.'

As fires blazed across the countryside through which the French moved on Vienna, Henri's earlier brio changed to a mood of sardonic disenchantment. Nobody, it seemed, could achieve anything in the army without being a pushy, brazen intriguer. Pierre Daru grew more and more bad-tempered, and he himself, as he told Pauline, had never sworn so often in his life before. Nor was he especially impressed by the conduct of his countrymen as an occupying force. In the hills behind Melk, above the Danube, as part of his commissariat duty, he searched a hamlet for eggs, and there 'plainly saw the character of the French. Everything that couldn't be carried off was smashed.'

His humour changed for the better when on 13 May the Emperor entered Vienna. Once again Martial Daru was able to show a ready goodwill towards his cousin Beyle by asking the Minister, now somewhat better disposed, whether he could keep Henri by his side, and received a speedy affirmative. 'So now I'm a Viennese for a year or two,' Stendhal wrote to Félix Faure, telling him that he had never felt so happy since Italy, though the city induced a curious sadness through its abundance of pretty women and his resultant bashfulness when it came to trying to charm them.

It was Milan all over again, the agreeable sophistication of a foreign metropolis, the easy availability of music and sex, and the pleasures of a cosmopolitan society. This was substantially the same Vienna that Mozart had known, the gossipy, promiscuous south German town, with flavours of Italian, Turk and Hungarian, with its fondness for coffee, satire and dancing, a place perfectly calculated to seduce, if not absolutely to corrupt, the young officer who had bounded all the way from Paris into its heady embrace.

The breathlessness of a letter dashed off to Pauline on 15 June 1809, says it all:

> Still not a moment to write. Work day and night. Riding, girls and divine music the remainder of the time. Alas, this remainder isn't very long. Despite all these reasons for not writing, I must congratulate you on your non-pregnancy ['ta non-grossesse']. Run, gallop, have a look at Milan, Genoa or Berne. Your chains will

come soon enough. I've never understood this mania for having children, pretty dolls who become frightful fools, unless strongly and originally educated, and who has the patience to offer them this education?

His imagination, fired by the sudden sense of possibilities held out to him by the siren city, took off into fantasizing about the future. He would travel Europe with a friend, Warsaw, Naples, Rome, Genoa – and Grenoble! 'But I haven't yet found the perfect happiness I've been seeking. I need a woman with an exalted soul, but they're all like novels – interesting up to the denouement and two days later you're astonished at having been interested in anything so common.'

Perhaps not surprisingly, he contracted syphilis, which prevented him from accompanying Martial to the battle of Wagram, Napoleon's costliest victory over the Austrians. Whether he picked up the disease in Vienna or along the route is not clear, since the fever and headaches described in the journal are symptoms more usually associated with a secondary phase. There was no cure for this or any other venereal infection, and though Stendhal was lucky enough not to be smitten by the worst manifestations of the tertiary stage of an illness which cut such a notorious swath through the field of nineteenth-century French literature, there seems little doubt that it contributed to the apoplexy which caused his death.

Jokingly he told Pauline that he had performed at least one good action in the campaign, by saving the lives of two German prisoners and two hundred merino sheep. His job nevertheless was one of those on which Napoleon's army, with its hyper-efficient infrastructure, needed to rely, and we must presume he was good at it, since during the late July of 1809 he was sent on a mission to Hungary,* and later was put in charge of operations for transporting food and uniforms down the Danube on barges from Linz.

* Henri Martineau (*Calendrier*) suggests that this was connected with Napoleon's offer to Prince Esterházy of the Hungarian throne but it seems more likely that Stendhal's errand was to buy horses for the army.

Nothing, however, distracted him from his Viennese pleasures. He watched the return of the Emperor Francis II to the capital in a shabby post carriage and marvelled at the people's enthusiasm for a sovereign so insignificant-looking. He attended Haydn's memorial service at the Schottenkirche, where the assembled musicians of the city, in the presence of the composer's family, three or four wretched little women in black, gave Mozart's *Requiem*, which Stendhal considered too noisy, though he acknowledged that he was beginning to understand *Don Giovanni*, being given almost every week in a German translation at the Theater An Der Wien.

His increasing absorption with Mozart was merely one aspect of an intense engagement with music and theatre of a kind which Paris, for all its grander, more cohesive cultural traditions, was unable to provide. Here he could choose, in seven months, among nearly forty operas and a wealth of excellent ballet performances which kindled the enthusiasm for dance he was subsequently to revive during his years in Milan after the fall of Napoleon.

In the *Souvenirs d'Egotisme* this nascent musical passion, to which his German and Austrian experience contributed so much, is put into sharper perspective. As with other aspects of his personality and emotions, the stimulus seems to have arisen from a conscious reaction to Chérubin Beyle's oppressive shadow. 'When I was ten, my father, who had all the prejudices of religion and aristocracy, vehemently forbade me to study music. At sixteen I learned successively to play the violin, to sing and to play the clarinet.' The act of filial rebellion is implicit in the juxtaposition and syntax of these two sentences. Music, like literature and politics, became a playground for Stendhal's subversiveness.

It was in this lively, crowded Viennese musical world that he indulged in a short liaison with a girl he refers to in his papers as 'Babet' but who figures as the most shadowy of presences. In a letter dated 4 September, Beyle speaks of having been prevented from taking advantage of her love for him by 'a small illness', mentioning also the embarrassment he has caused by sending her a lemon tree hung with fruit for her birthday. Discussing retrospective jealousy in *Henry Brulard*, he remembers how envious he became when she talked of a lover she had enjoyed ten years previously. In the summer of 1810 he looked forward to her possible arrival in Paris.

Otherwise all we can gather of 'Babet' is that her real name was probably Babette Rothe, adoptive member of a theatrical family based at the Theater An Der Wien, that she sang in operas by Paër and Cherubini, took the role of Servilia in Mozart's *La Clemenza di Tito*, and acted in plays by Kotzebue and Schikaneder, and that Stendhal fought, or prepared to fight, a duel over her with Colonel Jean-Baptiste-Victor Raindre of the horse artillery. Soon enough, however, she faded into the sentimental background as a more powerful attachment started taking shape, altogether stranger than any Beyle had formed before.

CHAPTER 5

SILENCIOUS HARRY AND LADY PALFY

During the latter part of 1805 Henri Beyle fell in love. Yet again the affair was unconsummated and yet again the object of his passion was never made fully aware of the ardour she inspired. The drama of his desire was created as it had been in the cases of Victorine Mounier, Adèle Rebuffel and, to a lesser extent, of Mina von Griesheim, with the help of the lover's energetic suppression of his feelings beneath the safety of the journal and the guaranteed confidentiality of his letters to Pauline. A certain zest was undeniably added by the fact that the woman in question was the wife of his patron, Pierre Daru, Minister for War.

Stendhal's exact contemporary, who had married Count Daru at the age of nineteen in 1802, Alexandrine-Thérèse Nardot was the daughter of a high-ranking civil servant from the district of Béarn in the Pyrenees. A portrait of her by Jacques-Louis David in the Musée Stendhal in Grenoble shows a plump, good-natured young woman with a maternal air which is likely to have appealed to the motherless Henri. Others besides were attracted by her friendliness and spontaneity. Napoleon, himself, in the habit of teasing Alexandrine for her piety, spoke of her as 'charming and full of good sense', while Tsar Alexander I of Russia, to whom she was presented while in Germany, praised her as 'a Frenchwoman of the most pleasing simplicity, of whom he retained the happiest recollections.'

Napoleon was right in singling out common sense as one of Alexandrine Daru's principal attributes, and it was this quality which she brought to her relationship with Henri. 'Cette fraîche cousine', as the *stendhalien* Henri Martineau calls her, offered genuine friendship and solicitude to the young man whom her husband still somewhat coldly and reluctantly patronized. The question of whether she actually encouraged his passion can never entirely be settled, by the very partiality of the evidence available. Almost nothing exists on her side, in the form of letters or other documents, let alone the testimony of independent witnesses, to indicate a thoroughgoing reciprocation. That her husband was generally complaisant as to the relationship is suggested by his failure to intervene (he could, if he had wished, have used his authority to separate the pair) as well as by his reference, in a letter of 1810, to a journey of Alexandrine's on which 'Beyle was her cavalier'.

Reliance on Stendhal's testimony assumes a need to sift carefully through those various moments at which, according to him, Mme Daru was on the brink of acknowledging a concealed passion and returning his love in an equal degree. Nobody can doubt the importance of an obsession which monopolized him for over two years and which provided the dominant motif for the journal entries of 1810 and early 1811. Yet, more than with Mélanie or Mina, the interest in Alexandrine was a preoccupation with the state of being in love, with the nature of the condition, rather than the kind of emotional attachment which takes for granted, or even necessarily requires, an answering tenderness in order to survive.

The morals of Napoleonic France were not underpinned by the sanctions of an established church, and the Emperor himself, having been frequently unfaithful to his first wife, Joséphine de Beauharnais, divorced her in 1810 for the sake of a politically advantageous match with the Habsburg princess, Marie-Louise. Even if the religious devoutness on which he rallied Countess Daru was likely to prevent her from granting Henri the last favour, a certain element of dalliance and flirtation was a flattering adjunct to her life as the consort of a successful civil servant, the strong right arm of Bonaparte the military campaigner. Alexandrine may not have encouraged Stendhal's attentions to her, but she certainly did little in the way of restricting the various opportunities for him to develop his amorous theme.

Theme essentially it was. Once again the text of the journal provides us with clues as to the character of this peculiarly one-sided relationship. What Stendhal seems to have been doing was to act out a love affair as though it were part of a novel. Mme la Comtesse Daru is not a specific prototype for Madame de Rênal, Madame de Chasteller, Gina di Sanseverina or any of the other married women with whom the Stendhalian hero, by the terms, as it were, of his agreement with the author, is bound to have an affair. None of these, however, could have existed without the foreshadowing dimension of Alexandrine Daru and what her husband's cousin, the young commissary-at-war, created from his obsession with the idea of loving her.

Not surprisingly, she appears in the journal under a variety of aliases, less for the sake of concealment or merely as a result of Stendhal's passion for codenames than because she is a creation in need of a working label. Elvire, Marie, Mme Z, Mme S, Mme R, Mme de Trautmand, Lady Palfy, Mme de Saint-Romain, Mme Delaitre, la dame du Val-de-Grâce, Lady Charlotte, are all variants of the same chimerical figure, who makes her first real appearance in the diary in an entry fitted out with a fictional title, *Journal du Kahlenberg et du Léopoldsberg (ou liaison du colonel L avec la princesse P)*. The date is 21 October 1809, and the setting is Vienna, where Mme Daru has recently arrived from Pressburg in Hungary. The whole scene has been devised as a romantic episode. 'Her first gesture was exactly what it would have been for anyone else. She stood up so that I could kiss her, but from lack of social experience I didn't dare to, and feebly shook her hand instead.' A passage of breathless dialogue follows, whose entirely trivial exchanges – 'Have you been there?' 'Yes, for a month.' 'When was that?' 'At the beginning' – are set out as a kind of dramatic stichomythia into which it is presumed we will read volumes as to the significance of what has been left unsaid.

In the next entry, for an unspecified day in November, the author goes yet further into the business of transmuting life into art. On the front of the notebook which this initiates, he has scribbled, in English, the title of what would seem to be an eighteenth-century *Bildungsroman* in the manner of *Tom Jones*, *Wilhelm Meister* or *Peregrine Pickle*: '*The life and sentiments of silencious Harry*'. Under this is written: 'The life and opinions. *Relations avec Mme la princesse P à Vienne*. The man perhaps, the memory little.' For this last enigma Victor del Litto, the journal's latest editor, on the basis of an English note made some six months afterwards, states that what Stendhal really meant to write was: 'The man perhaps, but the men very little', though even here the meaning is scarcely clear. A whole paragraph in the third person singular describing Henri's morning visit to the Countess simply reinforces the fictional illusion.

A day or two later Alexandrine had been transformed into 'la comtesse Triangi la cadette', as the pair of them set out to scramble up to the pavilions on the Kahlenberg, the mountain overlooking Grinzing of which their contemporary the poet Franz Grillparzer later wrote: 'If you have seen the country all around from its summit, then you will understand what I have written and what I am.' No similar intuitions were granted to Henri as he clambered after the adventurous Mme Daru across catwalks, up ladders and over terraces, but at least he was able, a few days afterwards, to make something out of her apparent indulgence when he dared to kiss her outstretched hand and squeeze her arm. Every motion of hers towards him, every utterance however banal, was now being recorded in the journal, less from the point of view of valuable evidence than as a continuing source of nurture for his fancied attachment.

Things were no different when, early in 1810, he returned to Paris and settled at the Hôtel d'Espagne in what is now the Rue Jacob, a few doors down the street from his friend Félix Faure. The friendly intimacy of his relationship with Comtesse Daru had a more practical aspect to it. Her husband, albeit grudgingly, was increasing in respect towards his young cousin, and Henri's prospects as a career civil servant had never looked so tempting.

The official position now in view was the highly attractive one of Auditeur du Conseil d'Etat. Despite its fundamentally despotic character, Napoleon's empire involved at least some semblance of government by consensus and debate, embodied by the fifty-strong Conseil d'Etat, whose subordinate staff included a number of *auditeurs* attached to each councillor in a secretarial capacity. Being an auditor opened the way to a variety of influential administrative posts, including prefectures of the departments and, eventually, membership of the council itself. Once an auditorship was secured, Stendhal, with an optimism not altogether naïve, could look forward to obtaining, with a little manipulation here and there, a series of jobs whose light duties, social cachet and generous salaries would allow him to make an advantageous marriage and at last to fulfil his ambition of being able to spend the rest of his life writing comedies.

Making plans to obtain his auditorship formed a constant theme in the letters he was now writing to Pauline. The problem, as always, was Chérubin Beyle, required to come down handsomely with funds so that his son, in the likelihood of success, would be able to flourish a style of living appropriate to his new position. The intensity of Stendhal's feelings over the whole business may in part be judged by the fact that two of the letters to his sister, those of 9 February and 28 April, are written almost entirely in the idiosyncratic English he employed to relieve emotional tension. 'My father writes to me,' he told her, 'that he will see with a great pleasure my not being appointed auditeur. He says that a man of great sense hearing of my suit for this place, had presented to him many good reasons for not being fond of it; after that many lines of nonsense.' Henri was of course convinced that this was merely a pretext for Chérubin's 'ruling passion viz covetousness'.

Stendhal, fortified by the news that his name, misrendered as 'Reile', was now being mentioned in connection with an auditorship, had no special wish to resume his duties as a commissary. Life in Paris was more than ever delightful, and day after day throughout the early months of 1810 the journal noted the various onrushes of unadulterated happiness. On 28 February, 'I've just seen *Figaro*, delicious appearance of Mlle Mars. Spring day, long bath, *Tom Jones*, happiness. Mars makes me rediscover my heart, which I'd supposed was dead'; on 2 March, 'at midnight I went to eat ices at the Café de Foy, and now I've come home *conscious of happiness* amid weather which is almost springlike.' Later he simply records, in English: '*A day full of happiness.*'

When not hanging around the Darus, he amused himself with Louis Crozet's friends Madame Rougier de la Bergerie and her daughters, Julie, Blanche and Amélie. Their father was a leading agronomist from Auxerre, author of, among other works, a history of ancient Gaulish farming practices and a long poem, *Les Georgiques françaises* (1804), which Madame de Staël, who had settled among the *auxerrois* according to the legal terms of her banishment from Paris, condemned as 'smelling of the dunghill'. Beyle and Crozet got into a joking habit of referring to the Rougier girls as 'these divine beauties', but to the former they were a good deal less interesting from a personal point of view than as sophisticated specimens of a bourgeois social type which Stendhal could anatomize with a future novelist's eye.

Ironically, it was the boredom engendered by 'les demoiselles de La Bergerie' which enabled Stendhal to observe them with due detachment. 'Not the least idea, not the smallest sentiment,' he complained to the journal after a particularly trying evening. 'We kept on talking like people doomed to sustain a conversation, listlessly developing the most trivial themes. When I left, I almost had an attack of indigestion from so much yawning.' Mme Rougier and her daughters made up in social experience whatever they lacked in ideas: their tact, as he quickly perceived, was 'not a tact of the *soul*, but of education, of experience'. If they had a soul, it was of that peculiarly French variety which made no distinction between baseness and refinement.

Paragraph by paragraph he took the evening to pieces, berating himself for his bashfulness, Crozet for his pedantic awkwardness and their friend Camille Basset, who had accompanied them (Stendhal invariably refers to him as Ouéhihé) for his mediocrity.

> The inane habit of remaining dignified ruined everything. In a village we'd have been seized by mad gaiety, in Germany we'd have been amused, in Italy voluptuousness would have flourished among us and made us follow its sweet laws. *French corruption* was so strong that the most charming of men attending this party would have come away envious rather than joyful.

Though he continued to lament the Rougiers' vacuousness every time he had occasion to mention them, and though they came to symbolize the dullness and trifling at which he began to fret after his first few months in Paris, Stendhal never altogether forgot the most agreeable of the three girls, Julie, who later that year married Louis-Florent-Xavier Gaulthier, receiver-general for the Yonne department. Over two decades later, when each was well into middle age, Beyle and Julie resumed their friendship in a correspondence remarkable on her side for an expressive eloquence which gave the lie to all his earlier accusations of banality and emptiness.

In between reading Malthus, Adam Smith and Arthur Young (whose *Travels In France* (1790) gave him an idea for a dramatized history of the French Revolution) Stendhal kept up his attentions to Countess Daru. He was present at David's studio when the painter, whom he assessed accurately enough as a pompous, small-minded, vain, unintelligent man, signed his portrait of her. Much was to be made of her shyness in not daring to confront Henri's adoring gaze while they stood together before the painting, but he was entirely candid with himself in identifying his role in their relationship as that of Beaumarchais' Chérubin to her Countess Almaviva.

The journal for these spring and summer months of 1810 takes on a monotonous repetitiveness deriving almost entirely from Stendhal's aimless, unfulfilled existence as Mme Daru's *cavaliere servente*, squiring her on walks, breakfasting with her, accompanying her to the court theatre at Saint-Cloud to hear Méhul's *Joseph* or Gnecco's *La prova d'un opera seria*, to eat ham in the park at Ermenonville, to dance attendance on her at an infinity of visits, drives and dinners, and always to be waiting on the notional moment when the assault might begin in earnest. Once again the military metaphor recommended itself, couched in the macaronic style (Italian was now being drafted into service as well as English) increasingly appropriate to the psychic confusions underlying the whole business. 'The chambers of the Palace were obscure, a kiss did can incomminciar the siege, and it would not have resembled that of Ciudad Rodrigo,* the news of which

* The Spanish fortress had fallen to a French army under Marshal Ney on 10 July. It was later successfully attacked by the Duke of Wellington.

pleased me this morning at the Tuileries; the first report of the cannon will probably decide everything *in the mine*.'

Of far greater moment where Stendhal was concerned were the continuing negotiations in favour of his auditorship. Whatever the complaints against Chérubin, this unloved parent had not, after all, been idle on his son's behalf. Supported by his rank as assistant mayor of Grenoble, he wrote to the relevant minister, the Duc de Massa, guaranteeing Henri's financial credit as the recipient of a regular income, according to documents signed by them both in 1808, and sending attestations to the young man's birth certificate, signed by, among others, the husband of that very Madame Pison du Galland whose cheek the infant Beyle had so peevishly bitten. Henri meanwhile had been busy working out a likely budget for his life as an auditor. Keeping up the right appearances would involve maintaining two servants, two horses, dinners at 2160 francs, suppers at 400, 2000 francs spent on clothes and 1500 on lodgings. The final and most telling entry in the calculation reads 'entertainments, books, girls – 3440 francs'.

On 3 August the longed-for letter arrived, addressed to Pierre Daru and countersigned 'The Minister Secretary of State'. Opening it, Henri read as follows: 'The Minister Secretary of State hastens to inform M. de Beyle that he has been named an auditor of the Council of State by decree of the 1st of this month. He has the honour to send M. de Beyle the official letters which were attached to his letter of the first of this month. Saint-Cloud, August 3rd 1810'. It must have seemed the apogee of his good fortune, and the addition of the particle 'de', to which he had no claim, surely added a flattering lustre to the moment. Full of a sense of its significance for his career, Stendhal promptly wrote down the exact time, twenty-two minutes past eleven in the evening, and then added his age in years, months and days, as if to convince himself of reality.

On the following day the letters of felicitation began to arrive. Daru, addressing him as 'mon cher Beyle', attached a copy of a note to the Duc de Bassano, Imperial *chef de Cabinet*, in which he described his cousin as 'well equipped to prepare reports with clarity, intelligence and precision' and asked that Henri's name be added to the Civil List. From the Countess (now being referred to as 'Lady Maria' and 'Lady Charlotte' in her English-novel avatar) the congratulations were somewhat too moderate for Stendhal's taste. A letter from Chérubin Beyle, whom he calls 'my bastard', included a present of twenty-five louis and a promise of 5000 francs from Dr Gagnon.

Yet, as a sudden reaction to his good luck, he felt profoundly unsatisfied. Having stopped tinkering with *Letellier*, which he had taken up again in Vienna, and sensing a temporary waning of interest in Alexandrine Daru, he fretted at the tedium of Paris in August and finally left the city to visit Louis Crozet at Plancy-sur-l'Aube. However loyal to his friends, Stendhal was completely ruthless in his assessment of their various shortcomings and in making demands on their attention which they could never have hoped to satisfy. Like many another writer, he kept up a litany of complaint, accusation and criticism throughout his personal papers, but the fact was that he could rely on the respectful solicitude of a compact circle of friends throughout his life. Few of them ever had occasion to confront the merciless acerbity with which, alone with pen and paper, he sat in judgement on them.

Crozet was among the small handful of Stendhal's acquaintances who actually retained his respect, if only because Beyle envied his sagacity, though judging him inferior in imagination and sensibility. An engineer by profession, he shared certain of his friend's literary interests, collaborated with him in 1805–6 on a series of psychological portraits of members of their immediate circle, and was taken into Stendhal's confidence as to the *Letellier* project. From comments in the journal regarding his mild, reasonable, easily satisfied nature, we can see that his real significance for Henri Beyle lay in being totally unlike him, a contrast summed up in the telling conclusion: 'I don't believe him capable of that elevation of feeling which makes Italy necessary for happiness.'

While at Plancy, Henri amused himself with sending a letter to Félix Faure with what he called 'advice on style', but which is actually a typical attempt at systematizing literature into a series of rules. Significant indeed is his answer to the question of where literature is best studied. 'In Helvétius, Hobbes and a little in

Burke,' to which he adds almost as an afterthought, 'and many applications are to be seen in Shakespeare, Cervantes and Molière.' Everything could, it seems, be reduced to five rules: 1. never describe what you have not seen; 2. the sublime, sympathy with a power we see as terrifying; 3. laughter; 4. the smile, a view of happiness; 5. study a passion in medical books, nature and the arts. Then look for confirmation of these points among poets and dramatists.

Such insistence on the primacy of philosophers over imaginative writers, and on the need to sift the creative impulse through the mesh of theory, says much about Stendhal's whole approach to the business of art. There can seldom have been a novelist who had so little overt interest in the process of fiction, a creative spirit with so little time for the fanciful, or an imaginative writer with such apparent disdain for others working in his own genre. What strengthens the individuality of his voice as a novelist is precisely the fact that his sources of inspiration and imitation are not, as they might be with anyone else, the narrative inventions of his contemporaries, but instead a whole variety of books on history, political economy and philosophical systems, biographies and autobiographies, and writings on travel. It is hard to imagine anyone other than Stendhal recommending a friend to embark on a study of literature with the works of Hobbes.

Not unconnected with this is a curious journal entry, dated 9 September 1810 and headed 'My tower', involving a whole set of specific measurements, a small sketch of the proposed building and a list of individual features, including a lightning conductor, a staircase and a marble fireplace, with the exact cost of each. Was this a genuine plan to erect a writer's retreat at Plancy, with the help of Crozet's practical skills as an engineer, bearing in mind that the tower forms a recurring feature in the Stendhalian world of symbols? Both Julien and Fabrice are imprisoned within towers, while in *Le Rose et le Vert* the young Duc de Montenotte wants to build a tower two hundred feet high, to immortalize his father's heroic charge at the battle of Heilsberg.

The project was never carried out, if only because Beyle was now swept headfirst into the new life created for him by his latest incarnation as a career civil servant. On 22 August he had been appointed to another post in addition to his auditorship, that of Inspector General of Imperial Crown Furniture. The job was neither an interesting one, nor in any way appropriate to his talents. Apart from approving the bills presented to the court by cabinet-makers and upholsterers, he had to compare trade prices and enter into amazingly pettifogging correspondence on such matters as whether the curtains at the Tuileries were of blue taffeta or embroidered muslin.

Though Stendhal had by now laid the foundations of the kind of life he wanted – or at any rate imagined himself to want – the experience of securing the auditorship and its concomitant status turned out to be a good deal more satisfying than the position itself, let alone the inspectorate, which required him to make frequent attendances at court, offering intimate glimpses of the great figures of the Empire from Napoleon and Marie-Louise downwards. His newest style of living involved much heavier expenses than those incurred while he was still a commissary, and his perpetual discontent now fretted itself over the need to obtain a title, the so-called *majorat de baron*, and the likelihood of being able to raise a loan to this end on the security of his father's estate.

Letters to Pauline during the autumn of 1810 worried away at the financial problem. Why would not Chérubin do as his son asked and take out a mortgage on one of his properties, either at Grenoble or the country estate at Claix? Surely Henri's career must count for something with his father. The sum in question, 6000 francs, was a mere bagatelle. Sour reflections of this kind, Stendhal thought, might lead Pauline to think that he was turning into an ambitious wretch with sunken, wrinkled cheeks and an envious eye.

Quite the contrary, he assured his sister, he was more chubby-cheeked than ever, and as a proof that he was not yet irretrievably hard-hearted and cynical, he told her of a recent incident involving Victorine Mounier, who had cropped up in conversation at dinner with an old Grenoble acquaintance, Amédée Pastoret. '*At the name of this once so beloved girl, all my sentiment were awackened.*' Learning from Pastoret that Victorine was going that very evening to a play at the Variétés, Stendhal hurried home to change, dashed to the theatre and managed to get a seat in the footmen's gallery at the top of the house.

> With the aid of an opera-glass I made out *the brother* at the back of a box, behind six women. I couldn't see her distinctly, but now and then, from some charming gesture, I imagined it must be the woman in the black spencer. A moment later, I thought it was probably the blue hat. I went quite blind with quizzing the box. Almost coming to blows in getting out of this elevated pit, I came downstairs to the first tiers, by dint of seducing three box-openers. There I got a seat only twenty paces from her. I didn't dare take it. I hope this shows my timidity, a real sensibility. She hasn't seen me for four years . . . my reason told me that, but as it isn't reason which governs love, I refused this seat in the first tier. There was only the one. I had to go up to the next level, where I quizzed her to distraction, over the folding panel of the box. Impossible, I couldn't make her out properly . . . . I want to see her, nevertheless.

Even Burke's *Reflections on the Sublime* could not effectively distract Stendhal from the corrosive gnawings of his ambition. For Pauline's benefit he painted a verbal picture of himself sitting in his new apartment, at 3 Rue Neuve-du-Luxembourg (now Rue Cambon, linking Rue Saint-Honoré to Rue de Rivoli) watching the sunset amid rain and storm clouds, abstractedly pulling a letter from her out of his desk drawer and weeping over it as he recognized an *alter ego* in her words, so exactly matching his own feelings. He looked up at the engravings on the wall beside him, *Leda's Bath* by Porporati after Correggio, and *The Divine Mozart*, a print bought in Vienna from the music publisher Artaria. 'Why didn't you come to Paris?' he wrote, 'I long too much to see you. Farewell, you whom I love most in all the world! Tears overcome me. Burn my letter.'

In this self-pitying state he entered 1811, apparently unloved, either by Alexandrine Daru or by any of the Rougier de La Bergerie girls. (Julie having recently married, his attentions had turned to her sister Blanche, whom he refers to as '*White*' and succinctly describes as 'fuckable'.) This condition of sexual limbo was not one in which Stendhal was likely to allow himself to remain for long. Since the summer of 1810 he had been writing to a young singer with the Italian troupe currently giving opera performances at the Odéon.* A pretty Jewish girl named Angéline Bereyter, she numbered among her *seconda* and *terza donna* roles that of Cherubino in *Le Nozze di Figaro*, a work Stendhal heard frequently during this period, and whose composer he identified with Angéline, nicknaming her 'Frau Mozart'.

We know almost nothing about Mademoiselle Bereyter except what Stendhal tells us in his journal, much of which was, as he confesses, not properly written up during the early months of 1811 through sheer laziness and because it was locked inside a small table of which he had lost the key. She had apparently consented to sleep with him on the evening of 29 January, having initially been put off by his small eyes and general air of stupidity. Thereafter the pair spent every night together, arguing periodically over the respective merits of French music, represented by Henri Berton and Etienne-Joseph Méhul, which she championed, and Henri's favourite 'Italians', Mozart and Cimarosa.

Evidently he was not in love with Angéline, or at any rate she failed to evoke the kind of feelings which Victorine Mounier was calculated to excite in him, but she was charming and kind, in the word's old-fashioned sense of 'sexually compliant', and write letters like an angel, none of which has come down to us. We must make what we please of his cryptic remark in English: '*I make that one or two every day, she five, six and sometimes neuf fois.*' Does this, indeed, refer to orgasms?

On the night of 20 March, they lay in each other's arms and listened to the cannon booming the tidings of the birth of a son to Napoleon and Marie-Louise. 'It is a grand and happy event,' wrote Stendhal with unusual bourgeois pomposity, yet in truth he was getting restless once more, eager to be off to Italy, Holland or Russia, anywhere rather than staying in Paris, bored by dinners at the Darus', by Martial especially, whose own recent promotion was making him insufferable, and by the city itself. 'This capital of the greatest empire of modern times is used up for me, I've become blasé with regard to its pleasures . . . . obviously I haven't

* Known at this time as 'Théâtre de l'Impératrice'.

the light, frivolous character necessary for enjoying Paris to the full.' In the Parisians themselves he beheld a surly, fretful, envious people, in a perpetual state of dissatisfaction. Pedestrians stared after carriages with expressions full of hatred. Even the pretty girls bore five or six wrinkles across their foreheads, traced by envy.

There was, of course, a place where this kind of niggling discontent was unknown, the abode of happiness itself, his adored Italy, to which Henri imagined Daru might send him as assistant to Martial, but though he scribbled on his new notebook the English words '*A tour trough* [sic] *some parts of Italy in the year 1811*', imitating a typical travel book title of the period, for the present the scheme hung fire. Meanwhile he immersed himself eagerly in anything with an Italian flavour, *Romeo and Juliet*, in which he commended Shakespeare's gift for Italianizing his characters, Patrick Brydone's *Tour Through Sicily and Malta* (1773) and the trio from Cimarosa's lofty neoclassical lyric drama, *Gli Orazi ed i Curiazi*, while he and Crozet, his proposed travelling companion, continued to lay plans for their journey.

Meanwhile they could make do with a jaunt into Normandy, taking along their friend Félix Faure. Stendhal's journal more or less gives up during these five days (29 April–3 May) but the narratives of both Crozet and Faure have survived, to give us a more obviously synoptic and matter-of-fact account of the three schoolfellows together for almost the last time in their lives. 'We travelled,' said Stendhal, 'with a rapidity worthy of the most advanced civilization', leaving Paris at four in the morning and covering the sixty miles to Rouen in twelve hours. In the old cathedral city they visited Corneille's birthplace and went to the theatre. At Le Havre the smell of tar reminded Henri of Marseilles and Mélanie, and set him wondering whether he was likely to fall in love again. They went out in a fishing boat through the fog 'in the direction of the Isle of Wight', and for an hour or so he was able to reflect on the ennobling marine influence on the local character, until one by one the three of them were gripped by seasickness, Crozet first, with dire consequences (he had been meditating on Shakespeare, escaping to America and being shipwrecked alongside some adored mistress) then Faure, and last of all Henri, whose stomach had finally turned at the sight of the fishermen's catch.

He had told Faure of yet another marriage project, this time with a certain Mlle Jenny Leschenault, but the return to Paris seems to have kindled anew his imagined passion for Alexandrine Daru. On 25 May he paid a visit to his cousins' newly acquired château of Bècheville, near Meulan in the Seine valley west of Paris. Pierre Daru had bought the estate from a banker named Biderman some two weeks previously, and his wife was now busy planting new shrubs, including *Josephina imperatricis*, *Hemitoma fruticosus*, *Diosma imbricata*, *Leptospermum juniperium* and *Gaultheria erecta*, ordered, with Beyle's help, from Baron Costaz, intendant of crown buildings and parks.

Beyle arrived at Bècheville in a state of nervous apprehension, resolved to throw all caution to the winds in declaring his love to the Countess. As so often, he saw the episode in military terms, heading his account of it in the journal 'History of the battle of the 31st May, 1811', talking about 'the army I commanded', 'the need to fight' and 'a sight of the enemy', and describing frankly his terror at the prospect of the undertaking now before him.

It was decided that he would stay for a week, and during the first few days he went on various walks and drives with Alexandrine, accompanied by her friend Madame Dubignon and by her children, to whom he told stories. The merest sign was to be taken as indicating her love for him. On the morning of Friday the 31st, when they were alone together, he found her pale, depressed and tired. Had she perhaps been crying? She told him that she had not slept properly since arriving there. Later she played her harp to him and sang a romance beginning 'Il est trop tard' into which she put striking expression.

> She had a passionate look about her, which I've rarely seen and which accords ill with her character. Her eyes were fixed, red and serious, her face pale and the movements of her head were brusque. She looked at me all the time. One of the verses, the last one I think, made me turn away, so obvious was its relevance to my situation.

Then she took him out for a walk in the garden.

Following a habit which he was to make excessive use of in *La Vie de Henry Brulard*, Stendhal drew a plan of their ramble, with the letters A to G corresponding to its key points. Barely were they out of the house than he began unburdening himself of his feelings. 'You have nothing but friendship for me,' he told the Countess, 'but I love you passionately'. Taking her by the hand, he tried to kiss her. Gently but firmly, she bade him not think of such things, and to see her simply as a cousin who had friendly feelings towards him.

We can only admire Alexandrine's coolly intelligent handling of the situation. She insisted on questioning Henri scrupulously as to the sincerity of his marital intentions towards Mlle Leschenault, while simultaneously deflecting his renewed efforts at eliciting some sort of amorous response. From her agitated manner, he remained absolutely convinced that she must have been prepared, with a little more prompting, to give him the answer he craved. On the Sunday, he left, fully persuaded that she returned his passion, and that evening promptly went to seek more palpable solace in the arms of Angéline Bereyter.

It is to this critical moment during the phantom affair, that the curious document entitled *Histoire d'une partie de ma vie* acts as a prelude. So preoccupied was Stendhal with the outcome of his intended declaration that in April he invoked the assistance of Louis Crozet in exorcizing his feelings by means of a detailed written analysis. Formerly it was thought that Crozet alone was responsible for this, but it now seems likely that the work, divided into three sections, is largely Stendhal's, dictated to his sympathetic confidant, who incorporated his own notes and interpretations.

The first part, headed *Consultation en faveur de la Duchesse de B*** pour Banti*, is an account of Madame Daru's current position in relation to her mother and husband, designed to answer the question of whether Banti (Beyle) should or should not have her. There follows a long account of her character, under various headings, 'Religion', 'Aptitude of her soul for passion', 'How does she take to happiness and misfortune?', 'Would she hold on to Banti for long?', 'Would she be jealous?', to which the appended comments are, perhaps inevitably, a series of favourable prognostications. In an ensuing section, 'la Duchesse' suddenly becomes 'Mme de Bérulle', and the whole history of the relationship is picked over from their first meeting in 1802.

The exercise concludes with an extended examination of Pierre Daru himself, essentially a brilliant biographical sketch, remarkably fair and dispassionate under the circumstances, and revealing, for the first time at any length, Stendhal's extraordinary gift for apprehending character within the detailed perspective of its social and historical formation. Nobody reading this 'caractère de Burrhus' can fail to be reminded of the fictional creations it so obviously foreshadows.

The summer was frittered away in continual attempts to interpret Alexandrine's behaviour as something more than cousinly kindness, in reading Hume's *History of England*, and in overhauling *Letellier*. His old Brunswick friend Friedrich Karl von Strombeck, now a magistrate at Celle, arrived for a visit, and Henri took him to Saint-Cloud to present him to the Emperor. Apart from the perpetual worry over finances, there was the problem of Pauline, whose marriage to François Périer-Lagrange was hardly the rustic idyll they had hoped for in settling at his little château of Thuellin, outside Grenoble. Sliding ever further into debt, Périer fatally justified the character for mediocrity his brother-in-law had given him, and Pauline, bored and fretful as before, had begun an affair with a certain Albert, about which Henri now cautioned her. 'Remind yourself, above all, of this great and immutable truth: all men are cold, mediocre and love to hurt those they believe to be happy.' In the same letter he warned her that her fondness for going about dressed as a man might well do at Paris, but would hardly answer among the *grenoblois*. He had had occasion, some years earlier, to caution her about such 'travestissements', though he could well have asked himself whether his own encouragement of her masculine independence had its share of influence.

Was Pauline a lesbian? The hypothesis has been convincingly advanced by André Doyon in his reconstruction of her long and singularly unhappy life. Her relationship with her old schoolfriend Sophie Boulot, who came to live at Thuellin during the last years of the Périers' marriage, seems to have been something of an *amitié amoureuse*, and none of her subsequent male liaisons was particularly serious. The notion of Pauline as her brother's alter ego may in part have been based on apprehensions of a shared sexual complexity.

At the end of August, Stendhal, despairing of getting anywhere with 'Lady Palfy', petitioned her husband, Pierre Daru, for leave of absence and set off at last for Milan. His companions in the diligence were a good deal more varied than the noisy, loutish collection of soldiers returning to join their Italian regiments he had feared to find. There were two women, a little cotton seller and a fat, greedy *bourgeoise* accompanied by her son. A Genoese, formerly in the Neapolitan navy, had been a prisoner of the English, and a pleasant-mannered Lombard, 'an epicurean, or at least in search of happiness like me', turned out to be a brother of General Lechi, with whose family Stendhal had lodged years before when a subaltern stationed at Brescia.

Giacomo Lechi's unforced charm revived Henri's latent Italophilia, increased when Scotti the Genoese started to sing. 'I felt the ferocity of my masculine way of thinking begin to evaporate, and tenderness enter my heart. My sentiments start to elaborate on a song which, following the dominant passion, gives pleasure to my soul; I couldn't elaborate like this on the verses of the finest French drama. Hence my love for music, my boredom with French theatre. . . . '

As they moved south, Stendhal's journal mirrored the phases of that conscious change taking place in his sensibilities, reanimated by the nearness of Italy and increasingly disenchanted with the provincialism of those French towns, Dijon, Auxonne, Dôle, through which they passed. Giacomo Lechi, in his role as the incarnation of Italian *joie de vivre*, became an ever more enchanting companion, and when he began speaking of 'the art of being happy', Henri felt that in ten years he had never met anybody more charming. His Italian discourse with Lechi was starting to give him the kind of vitalizing detachment his intellect always craved, and he saw their conversation, whatever its trifling anecdotal framework, as significant of something far more important. 'Until now, I rejoiced in the French Revolution, which brought with it such splendid institutions, even if slightly clouded by ensuing events. Only recently have I begun to think that it might have banished *allegria* [happiness] from Europe for at least another century. What M. Lechi said helped me to understand this.'

On 8 September 1811 Stendhal arrived in Milan. The effect on him of seeing once again this city which, more than any other place on earth, he associated with spiritual and emotional exaltation, was truly devastating, and for a day at least he took stock of what he was now and what he had been a decade earlier in relation to it. As usual, his powerfully associative sense of smell was a trigger for strong feelings. 'Should I say what has most moved me on arriving in Milan? It's a certain dunghill odour peculiar to these streets. That, more than anything, proves to me that I'm in Milan.'

His re-encounter with La Scala almost reduced him to tears. Piermarini's great theatre, he acknowledged, had a profound influence on his character, and was a symbol for him of that *arte di godere*, the art of enjoyment, which placed the Milanese two hundred years ahead of the Parisians. By degrees he began reconstructing his earlier Italian experience in a kind of rage at the missed opportunities of that crucial time. It was a period spent entirely without the solace of women, just when the grand climacteric of youthful ardour between seventeen and nineteen might have fulfilled his desire for happiness and rendered him attractive. Instead he had been nervous, proud and without a single friend who might have helped him to a mistress. The result was his present state of overdeveloped sensitivity, which gave him his obsessive eye for detail, but which made him, on the other hand, so diffident with women.

It was at this point that Stendhal took the fateful step of going to call on the one woman by whom his feelings had been deeply stirred as a lieutenant with the Army of Italy all those years ago. Angela Pietragrua, or 'Gina' as she was known, to whom her lover Louis Joinville had presented him in 1801, was now a ripe Italian matron in her late thirties, and Henri, seeing her once more, was delighted to find her statuesque beauty entirely unaltered.

What ensued, if it was hardly the romantic liaison for which he hoped, was an authentically Italian affair as far as Stendhal was concerned. From Gina's behaviour, it seems obvious that she had no serious emotional commitment to him, but that the chance of keeping him dangling by raising his hopes at one moment and dashing them the next was much too good to forgo. The eighteenth-century social fixture of the *cicisbeo*, the attendant lover tolerated by a complaisant husband, had not altogether been killed off by the changes wrought in Italian life by the arrival of the French and the new order under Bonaparte. Gina already had one such, together with a bona fide lover, the Venetian patrician Lodovico Widmann Rezzonico, an officer in the guard of the Viceroy Eugène de Beauharnais, Napoleon's stepson. The possibility of entertaining a third admirer on terms prescribed by her was no doubt irresistible, given the fact that her husband, though she could always invoke his jealousy as a convenient pretext, evidently played little significant part in her calculations.

Calculation, indeed, was what everything amounted to. Gina must have been in her element when, on 10 September, she was squired to the newly opened Brera gallery by Widmann, Beyle and the viceregal aide-de-camp Marco Migliorini.* That evening at La Scala her imperturbable calm simply increased Henri's gloom at the idea that he might in some way or other have made a fool of himself in her presence. As always, he felt lonely and in want of a friend, turning characteristically to his journal to exorcize pent-up emotion by trying without much success to analyse Gina's character.

On the following morning he made up his mind to declare his passion for her, as a condition for remaining in Milan. When he did so, she wept, they kissed, and began significantly to use the informal '*tu*', and with what, in retrospect, looks like a flawless sense of the dramatic, she cried, 'Leave, leave! I feel you must leave for the sake of my tranquillity. Tomorrow perhaps I shan't have the courage to tell you so.' When Stendhal objected that the

* The latter subsequently gave Stendhal a formula for maintaining a permanent erection. This involved rubbing the big toe of the right foot with a paste made of the ashes of a tarantula mixed with olive oil.

journey would make him unhappy, she rejoined, 'But you will have the certainty of being loved.'

Well aware of the risks he was taking – had she not, after all, simply laughed off the threats of a jealous admirer who had menaced her with a pistol? – Henri was nevertheless convinced that Gina might indeed love him, and was ready to shed tears at the thought of leaving her. What appears, from his account of it, to have been an increasingly moving performance on her part now took the form of a rhetorical appeal for self-restraint, whose implication was that everything was going too fast and that they must not lose their heads. Somewhat pathetically, after having been foiled in an attempt to kiss her on the thigh, he writes: 'I felt the presence of superior reason'. He wanted to weep with her, to die in her arms, so much did he admire her greatness of soul. We can only marvel at the resourcefulness with which she continually baulked him of the opportunity to do so.

The notion that Gina might simply be entertaining herself with his amorous pursuit occurred to Stendhal ten days later, when she failed to turn up at a German play currently showing at the Teatro Patriotico (later renamed, for obvious political reasons, Teatro Filodrammatico). It was simply another of the infinite ruses of this woman 'cunning past man's thought', in Shakespeare's phrase, designed to reduce her lover to the appropriate posture of submission when she should at last condescend to comply. The next day, as Gina well knew, was Stendhal's last before he was due to set off for Bologna. That morning she had fixed a rendezvous for a quarter to ten at the little church on the corner of Contrada dei Meravigli, where she lived. It was half an hour before she offered the agreed signal. 'After an extremely serious moral combat, in which I represented myself as unfortunate, almost desperate, she became mine at half past eleven.' In the small hours of 22 September, victorious as he fancied himself, Stendhal left Milan.

There is no indication at this point in his journal that he actually knew how much she was 'playing' him, or that he saw himself as entering into the spirit of some energetically contrived sport. Conquest was, as always, important to him, but at this stage he was not inclined to be cynical as regards Gina's behaviour.

Everything, or nearly everything, suggests that he was ready to credit her with a genuine sincerity.

By way of Cremona, which he found lonely and sad, Mantua, where he was plagued by vermin in the bed, and Modena, which he judged the cleanest and gayest of the smaller Italian towns, he arrived at Bologna, then as now one of the handsomest cities in northern Italy, greatly embellished by successive popes over the three centuries since its annexation to the States of the Church in 1506. Almost immediately Stendhal went to the opera, to see Stefano Pavesi's *Ser Marcantonio*, apparently founded on a true story, whose protagonist he seems actually to have met in Gina Pietragrua's box at La Scala. By the prima donna Marietta Marcolini he was enraptured, but found the theatre itself thoroughly provincial in its unadorned meanness and barely managed to keep awake during the performance.

It was while staying in Bologna that Stendhal conceived the initial idea for what would eventually become his first large-scale prose work, *L'Histoire de la Peinture en Italie*, published in 1817. An interest in the visual arts had never left him since his boyhood studies in Grenoble with Jay and Roy, and the recent involvement with the Musée Napoléon must inevitably have heightened his preoccupation with the classic traditions of Italian painting. Wandering among the churches and galleries of Bologna, he felt the need of some pictorial equivalent to the standard French literary guide of the period, Laharpe's *Lycée ou Cours de littérature*, the last of whose nineteen volumes had appeared in 1805, and considered his own sensibility uniquely adapted to the task.

From now on, his personal writings reveal a more obvious alertness than ever before to the prodigal wealth of fine painting and sculpture with which Italy surrounded him. At Bologna he revelled in the works of the great seventeenth-century Emilian school, though the Carraccis, pioneering exponents of the style, he found commonplace and lacking in grandeur. Guido Reni, on the other hand, moved him so profoundly that he began thinking of his beloved Mozart, and, by felicitous association, of Wilhelmine von Griesheim. What disappointed him about the city was the severe contrast presented by the grand exterior appearance of its palaces with the squalor of their apartments, and a notable absence of really attractive women. The sole exception was a pretty girl from Imola he met while looking at the gallery in Palazzo Marescalchi, and with whom, of course, he fancied he could have scored easily, given a little more time. 'My conversation with her . . . . made me suppose that one might find happiness at Bologna': the ultimate Stendhalian seal of approval had been set upon the place.

The first things he wanted to see when he reached Florence, on 26 September, were the house and tomb of the dramatist Vittorio Alfieri. The author of twenty-one tragedies and of an autobiography which offered a stylistic model for *La Vie de Henry Brulard*, Alfieri died in 1803, famous alike for the poetic power of his dramaturgy, which made him the leading Italian literary figure of his generation, and for the glamour of his love affair with Louise von Stolberg, Countess of Albany, estranged wife of Charles Edward Stuart, 'Bonnie Prince Charlie', whose failure in the abortive 1745 Jacobite coup against the Hanoverian King of England, George II, had driven him into gloomy alcoholism. While Stendhal disapproved of Alfieri's conservative politics, he seems always to have admired the dramatist's sternly voiced opposition to tyranny and never lost a fundamental regard for him as one of the first Italian authors he had studied in any depth. In the earliest version of the travel book he based on this 1811 journey, *Rome, Naples et Florence en 1817*, he included a long analysis of the Alfierian achievement, mostly lifted wholesale from an article in the *Edinburgh Review*,* but containing several of his own remarks. Concluding a paragraph on the tragedian's dramatic style, he adds: 'There is doubtless more eloquence and dignity in Alfieri's system: in that of Shakespeare there are all the charms of illusion. Many are the nights I have spent reading Shakespeare; I read Alfieri at night only when I am angry against tyrants.'

He could have fancied burial at the church of Santa Croce, where Alfieri lay alongside Machiavelli, Michelangelo and Gali-

* Number 30, January, 1810, reviewing Alfieri's autobiography. The plagiarism went undetected in the review of Stendhal's own work in November 1817, and was only picked up two years later by the reviewer of the *Histoire de la Peinture en Italie*.

leo, though its unadorned brick front (the present façade dates from 1871) reminded him of a farm. The sight of these tombs made a powerful impression on him. Even if he had been struck elsewhere by the theatrical potential of sculpture, this was the first occasion on which his rapidly maturing visual sensibility had responded to it in any depth. Still more significant for Stendhal was a further encounter with the genius of Antonio Canova, the greatest sculptor of the age, whose monument to Alfieri in Santa Croce had been paid for by the Countess of Albany herself.

He had first come across Canova's work two years earlier at the Augustinerkirche in Vienna, where the tomb of Archduchess Maria Christina (1793) made a lasting impact, but it was in Italy that he could acknowledge the sculptor's true status as the finest living exponent of an art which, along with painting, was almost dead among the modern Italians. Later he actually paralleled Canova's position in a moribund artistic culture with that of Alfieri. Both, he declared, were freaks, emerging quite by chance 'through the sheer vegetative strength which the soul of man possesses in this fine climate .... nothing resembles him, nothing approaches him.' Canova's skill, enhanced by the unintellectual physicality with which his images were realized, became a notable stick for Stendhal to use in belabouring the dry overrefinement of French artists in the coming decade.

Naturally enough the paintings gathered in Florence entranced him still more than those he had seen at Bologna. The canons of modern taste having altered so radically, we can scarcely be surprised if his most obsessive interest in Santa Croce concentrated not on the Giotto frescoes which nowadays monopolize the visitor's attention, or on Brunelleschi's Cappella Pazzi – neither artist rates a mention at this point in the journal – but on the four sibyls adorning the vaults of the Niccolini chapel, painted by the quite unremarkable seventeenth-century Tuscan artist Baldessare Francesconi *detto* Il Volterrano. His response, which he saw no reason to modify when the second version of *Rome, Naples et Florence* was published fifteen years later, was ecstatic. 'It's majestic, it's alive, it seems like nature in relief; one of them . . . has a grace which, joined with majesty, makes me fall in love with her at once.' Not for the first time he was reminded of Mina von Griesheim.

The excitement of reading this Italian journal derives from the sensation of an aesthetic in the making. Henri was learning not to muddle Guercino with Bronzino, to distinguish the Carraccis' apparently coarse tonal language from the softer vein of Guido Reni, and to speculate as to whether Rubens' strong reds might not be designed to help those with weak eyesight such as his own. The drama of his developing sensibilities dominated this Florentine autumn, yet he found himself lacking either in an adequate descriptive language to encompass the experience or in the detachment necessary to record it properly.

To complicate matters further, Adèle Rebuffel, at whom he had set his cap during the early days in Paris, was now here in Florence as Madame Alexandre Petiet. The idea of her presence, connected as it was with memories of what she had made him suffer, and of 'the pettiness of a cold heart', somewhat took the edge off Stendhal's Florentine enthusiasms. The effect of the city – and, it may as well be said, the effect of a prolonged absence from Gina Pietragrua – was nevertheless to reactivate that effervescent interest in the broad sweep of European culture, history and manners which makes Stendhal's civilized conversation with his readers some of the richest available among the writers of the last two hundred years. His ear catches that typical aspirate of the Tuscan accent which converts the hard 'c' into a guttural 'hh', he meditates on the essential sweetness of Virgil in comparison with Lucretius, he contemplates the beauty of a skeleton in the natural history museum, and supplies a sardonic analysis of a bad picture by Jacopo Ligozzi, before crystallizing everything into the image of a meandering river changing its course, a symbol of the way in which his character has altered and deepened in the last dozen years. 'The river is always drawn on down the same slope, but the nature of the terrain which determines its course has changed. Those truths which penetrate the spirit are the hills which redirect its flow.'

Moving on to Rome, Stendhal stayed with his cousin Martial Daru, now Superintendent of Crown Property at Rome, but this first sojourn in a city which twenty years afterwards he was to make so much his own produced nothing more than the observation in his journal that a veil of dreariness had been thrown over the place by Martial's tedious household, and a remark in a letter to Pauline that what had touched him most on his Italian journey was the birdsong in the Colosseum.

On the way to Naples he imagined a possible rendezvous with any one of various mistresses, including Alexandrine Daru, Angéline Bereyter and Mélanie Guilbert. As for Gina Pietragrua, he had realized, ever since reaching Bologna, that he must be in love with her. The symptoms were all there, the incessant tender reveries, the accelerated breathing and the painful wrench back to reality from such sweet reflexes. It was she who, after all, kept him here in Italy and filled him with longing to return at once to Milan. Climbing Vesuvius, where he found the names of the noted German critic and Shakespearian translator August Wilhelm Schlegel and of Madame de Staël in the visitors' book of the mountain hermitage, visiting the ruins of Pompeii and yawning through Spontini's *La Vestale* at the Teatro San Carlo, all were minor pleasures in comparison. A scarcely more effective diversion awaited him at Ancona, where he met up with Livia Bialowejska, the Italian wife of a Polish colonel whose acquaintance he had made in Brunswick four years earlier. The impression given by the journal is that she was not Gina Pietragrua but would have to do for the time being. Now a young widow, she had returned to the provincial tedium of Ancona and the problems created by her elderly father's affair with a housemaid, but her boredom, as Stendhal perceived it, simply made her more apathetic, for all his attempts to engage her with music and gallantry. The Abbate Cesarotti's Italian translation of Juvenal turned out, under the circumstances, to be far more stimulating.

It was a version by the same translator of James Macpherson's 'Ossian' poems which Stendhal began reading after his return to Milan at the end of October. These purported renderings of ancient Gaelic folk epic, named from their bardic author, which had excited contempt in Dr Johnson and ardent admiration in Napoleon, were among the most popular works of the earliest phase of Romanticism. On Stendhal, beyond his occasional use of the word 'ossianique' in connection with picturesque landscape, they made very little impression, further evidence that his personal Romantic enthusiasms was a highly selective affair.

The real romance of the moment was guaranteed by his re-encounter with Gina Pietragrua. He had come back with his memory full of tender, charming speeches, specially prepared for the occasion during his journey, but was unable at the crucial moment to articulate them. Gina's reception of him was a lethally skilful brew of provocative emotional nudges, little bursts of moral scruple, shameless self-dramatizing and that uniquely Italian fondness for scandalous intrigue with which she continually sought to clothe the affair. She had evidently taken the measure of her lover's susceptibility – he speaks to us of 'the continuous delight I experienced' and 'the mad vivacity which never left me day and night' – and was now playing upon it without mercy.

She had retired with her husband to a house in the country, near the town of Varese, north of Milan, and here Stendhal followed them. Gina's strategy appears so transparent that there is something positively pathetic in his willingness to fall victim to it. Having told him that their affair was suspected and that her maid had betrayed them, she contrived an appropriate *mise-en-scène* of put-offs, subterfuges and secret notes, whose genuineness even Henri began to suspect. The weather played its part, with wind and rain rattling the window as he consoled himself with Ossian, until Gina, having carefully avoided another meeting, announced that she was returning to Milan.

In the city she kept up the game, taking care to let her lover know that her husband had discovered their liaison and was jealous as all the devils in hell, but declaring herself ready to sacrifice everything to follow Henri to France. 'She seems too confident of the effect she produces on everyone around her,' he wrote, 'so far is she above other women that none of her friends can think of ignoring her. You might be unaware of her merit, but once you have appreciated it – since she seems to be the only one of her kind in Milan – you remain at her feet.'

The emotional intensity of his share in the relationship meant that he slept little and grew thinner. 'My sensibility is excited by drinking coffee, travelling, nights spent in carriages, and by sensations.' Gina's letter, brought to him by her handsome son, Antonio, whom she regularly used as a messenger, was calculated to fan the flame. It read:

> Just a line to tell you that a fatal combination of circumstances held me here till after eleven, but that I went to the rendezvous as soon as I could and found you already gone! Tomorrow at ten I hope to be more fortunate and to tell you how much I love you and how much I suffer for you. P.S. At six this evening I'll pass in front of the Café Sanquirico, near my new house, on the corner of Contrada del Bocchetto.

Whether the sentiments were authentic or not mattered less than the fact that she kept the appointment, and as Stendhal noted in English, '*she seemed to have pleasure. For my own account I made that two times, and for she three or four.*'

By now she seemed dazzling to him. Sitting alone with her in a little coffee shop, he marvelled at her brilliant eyes and her half-lit face, harmonious yet terrible in its supernatural beauty. It was as if she were a superior being who assumed beauty because it was a more effective disguise than any other, and who could read the very depths of your soul with her penetrating eyes. She must have made a sublime sibyl, concluded Henri, convinced that this was the most beautiful woman he had ever possessed. When he left Milan in November to return to France, it was with a full heart. The affair, orchestrated by Gina with such consummate skill, was by no means over.

CHAPTER 6

FALLING WITH NAPOLEON

The Italian jaunt had not gone unnoticed by Pierre Daru, whose genuine fatherly solicitude for his cousin was mixed with vexation at the young man's irresponsible caprices. From Breda in Holland the Minister wrote to Martial, apropos some letters for Beyle:

> he spoke to me of an absence of a few days on business, and as he can have none at such distance, I cannot imagine that he would conduct this sort of escapade without ascertaining whether or not it was convenient or whether he was needed elsewhere. I cannot suppose it fitting that he should have made such a mystery of it to me. This is a further example of his frivolity . . .

To the Countess, Daru was still more forthright:

> I thought Beyle had become a little more solid, but he has just demonstrated the sort of trifling behaviour appropriate to someone else entirely. After having spoken to me of a journey of a few days, for the sake of attending to business and visiting his relatives, he has set off, without telling anybody, without the least warning, and run away to Milan, Rome and Naples, spending twenty-four hours in each city, which has given rise to ridiculous conjectures, the most ridiculous of which is that this is all due to some singer or other. Liking comic opera is all very well, but a fondness for comediennes is scarcely in good taste. When one is anxious to succeed and obtain a responsible position, one ought to behave differently . . .

Stendhal returned to his desk in Paris to resume work on the laborious commission of checking the inventory and accounting for a new museum to be established in the palace of the Louvre and named the Musée Napoléon. Incorporating the paintings and sculptures first displayed there in 1791, it was under the supervision of Dominique-Vivant Denon, the artist and Egyptologist who had accompanied Napoleon to the Pyramids, and who was now required to submit to the Emperor a complete list of its holdings, drawn as they had been from royal collections of the deposed Bourbons. From the official correspondence between Denon, Pierre Daru, the minister responsible for overseeing the enterprise, and his successor, Jean-Baptiste Nompère de Champagny, Duc de Cadore, it is obvious that neither Napoleon nor his administrators appreciated or was even ready to acknowledge the magnitude of the task involved. As early as February 1810 Denon had warned an impatient Daru that the work would take far longer than initially envisaged, but eight months later a ministerial letter to Beyle, who had been provided with a team of clerks to help him with monitoring the museum's catalogue, budget and expenses, was peremptorily requesting four copies of a notional inventory.

The whole business was not much further advanced at the beginning of 1812, when Stendhal addressed a long memorandum to the Duc de Cadore on the museum's accounting system, detailing payments to staff, expenses in their accommodation and sums spent in the purchase of works of art. The document, set out with careful attention to clarity and a comprehensible ordering of the relevant facts, shows that Daru's confidence in his cousin's bureaucratic skills was fully justified, and interestingly foreshadows Stendhal's later incarnation as a French consular official.

More significant, in the context of his work at the Louvre, was the opportunity it afforded for renewing his acquaintance with the Italian painters who had made so powerful an impression on his sensibilities during the recent tour. However primitive his connoisseurship at this stage, a growing enthusiasm had prompted the purchase in Milan of the Jesuit critic Luigi Lanzi's *Storia pittorica dell'Italia dal risorgimento delle Belle Arti presso al fine del XVIII secolo* (1792) with some of whose judgements he was already able to take issue, and whom he now decided to translate, drawing up a proposal to send to a Parisian publisher. The purpose in view was not simply to raise money for another Italian trip, but to provide Stendhal with a basis for making his own assessments of the works of art he saw along the route. Like several of his other literary projects, the scheme was not realized at once, and when the book finally appeared as the *Histoire de la Peinture en Italie* in 1817, it was Stendhal based on Lanzi rather than a straightforward translation.

The early months of 1812, while he was still savouring the recollected pleasures of Italy and while he had money, sufficient leisure and a relatively congenial employment, gave him time to extend his art-historical reading and to pass on improving recommendations to Pauline. From Italy he had sent his 'chère amie' another of those ardently affectionate letters which suggest that he continued to see his sister as another part of himself, engaged in the same kind of cultural dialogue, responsive to the same beauty and stirred by comparable degrees of emotional intensity. 'Ah! my dear, how I've missed you in Italy! If it happens that somebody is left with only a heart and a shirt, they should sell the shirt so as to see the country around Lake Maggiore, Santa Croce at Florence, the Vatican at Rome and Vesuvius at Naples.' Why should they be separated for such long periods? Why didn't she come and stay at his fourth-floor apartment in Rue Neuve-du-Luxembourg? Yes, the Italian *canaille* was insufferable and the inns were foul, but this was a nation born for the arts, a people of excessive sensiblity.

While Pauline languished in the unwelcome domesticity of Thuellin (where her brother had visited her on his way back to Paris) Stendhal reluctantly assumed the pattern of existence so drastically interrupted by his re-encounter with Italy. As he told his sister, he was like a man who goes to a brilliant ball, lit by a thousand candles, adorned by women whose eyes are aflame with pleasure, and then has to go out into a thick fog and the mud of a rainy night, in which he staggers several times before tumbling into a cesspit.

The journal for this period collapses into a macaronic incoherence of French, English and Italian before petering out altogether with some notes for 23 April on ideal beauty in music and art. From a close reading of the various jottings, it becomes obvious that Italy, through its heady alloy of sexual and aesthetic delights, had traumatized Stendhal to a point at which the merest trifling reminiscence threatened to overpower him completely. A long, rambling sequence of notes for 5 March 1812, in which everything from Pierre Daru's displeasure on his return, the graces of Correggio, a taste for Fénelon as opposed to Rousseau, his sense that 'the love for Palfy is dying' and the frightening possibility that he might never marry, is jumbled together hugger-mugger, concludes with the words (in English): 'From the 15 aout 1811 till now I have been perfectly happy.' The image of this happiness and its sources were to dominate the remainder of his existence.

What might have made him still happier was some further development in the continuing affair of the *majorat*. Pauline was charged once more with sweetening Dr Gagnon and Chérubin Beyle, in order to raise the 5000 francs needed as security for the title of baron. When, however, Chérubin appeared to be conceding the point at last, his complaisance turned out to be a ruse whereby, while seeming to offer Henri a generous financial arrangement, he would not actually be forced to part with any money. In 1805 the house at Rue des Vieux-Jésuites had been sold and Chérubin moved to the new residence he had built on the corner of Rue de Bonne and Place Grenette. Henri Gagnon had already complained to his grandson of the folly of the enterprise, wondering 'where he has found the money to put up this detestable house, which is never likely to be finished or rented out', but the building, three floors, *entresol* and cellar, now became the principal bargaining counter in the transaction between Beyle *père et fils*.

By the terms of the agreement, made on 25 June 1812, Chérubin transferred the house to Henri (who always appears as 'Henry' in the document). The latter paid him in return the sum of 45,000 francs, borrowed from a Swiss banker, Benjamin Begue de Fort, guaranteeing, what was more, not to ask for any repayment from his father. Chérubin was to be allowed to spend his life in the house and Henri Beyle was to be answerable for all rates and service charges on the property. The most curious aspect of the whole contract is Stendhal's willing assent to such blatant paternal sponging, and Chérubin's corresponding meanness and chicanery, as though father and son knew exactly what roles they had to play in the ongoing drama of filial alienation and accepted them without demur.

All further question of the *majorat* and the expected title was soon shelved by the award, in July 1812, of a commission far more momentous than any Stendhal had so far undertaken as an imperial official. The collapse of Napoleon's alliance with Tsar Alexander I had led Bonaparte towards the most foolhardy and self-destructive episode of his career, the expedition of the Grande Armée into Russia, culminating in the disastrous retreat from Moscow during a preternaturally bitter autumn and winter, occasioning the Tsar's notorious boast that his two most powerful commanders were Generals January and February. Stendhal was not of a mind to be dawdling in Paris at such a time, making memoranda on curtain materials and velvet upholstery for the Department of Crown Furniture, let alone pursuing his labours over the Musée Napoléon inventory. Requesting permission from the Duc de Cadore to return to his old job as commissary, he was given two large portfolios and entrusted by the Empress Marie-Louise with a letter to her husband, then started off in his carriage through Germany to catch up with the army as it crossed Lithuania on the earliest victorious stage of the doomed enterprise.

What Stendhal now encountered was a form of warfare more desperate and relentless than any he had known, even on the blood-spattered road to Vienna in 1809. The Russian campaign was distinguished by the wastefulness and ferocity with which both sides flung themselves upon one another. As in Spain, where a similar insensate fury of resistance among the native population was being turned by Wellington's army to its advantage in sweeping the French from the Peninsula, the Russians confronted Napoleon with the kind of brute patriotism, a people's war, to which the limited egocentricity of his imperial vision was entirely unequal. His consequent failure, underlined by a characteristic inability to confront the facts of the débâcle, played its part in preparing Europe to embrace the likelihood of his downfall.

Catching up with the main force at Krasnoie, Stendhal saw his first serious action of the campaign at Smolensk, where, in the midst of the blazing city, with Russian shells falling to right and left, he watched Pierre Daru calmly supervising a party of grenadiers busy making sure their quarters did not catch fire before a long-delayed dinner. Barely arrived in Russia, he made up his mind to loathe everything around him, dreaming desperately of Milan and Italy. 'In this ocean of barbarity,' he told Félix Faure:

> there is not one sound which touches my soul: Everything here is coarse, filthy, stinking physically and morally. I've found only a moderate pleasure in having some music played to me on a little out-of-tune piano by a creature with as much feeling for music as I have for the mass. Ambition means nothing to me anymore, the finest military decoration would scarcely compensate for the mire into which I'm plunged.

Tormented by fantasies of happiness involving Angela Pietragrua, the music of Cimarosa and the chance to write books, he began speculating gloomily on his future. So as to avoid the banality of a Parisian desk job, he was tempted to ask for the sub-prefecture of Rome. 'I wouldn't hesitate to do so if I was sure of dying at forty. This is a sin against Beylism, the result of the execrable moral education we have received. We're like orange trees springing up, purely as a result of their germination, in the middle of a frozen pool in Iceland.'

On 14 September he arrived in Moscow, preparing, along with the rest of the army, to enjoy the hard-won conquest, only to discover that the city's governor, Count Fyodor Vassilievitch Rostopchin, had ordered it to be set alight, freeing all the prisoners from the jails and giving each a torch for the purpose. As fires broke out around the capital, the French fell to looting the various palaces originally chosen for billeting the officers. While Stendhal's drunken servant staggered to the carriage laden with tablecloths, bottles of wine and a violin, his master, momentarily softening towards Dr Gagnon's favourite author, prigged a volume of Voltaire, 'the one entitled *Facéties*'. According to Prosper Mérimée, Henri's friends later taxed him with having thus broken up a fine set, and he acknowledged a suitable remorse, though subsequently during the retreat he stole part of an edition of Lord Chesterfield's letters from one of Rostopchin's country houses.

> We left the city, lit up by the finest fire in the world, forming an immense pyramid which, like the prayers of the faithful, had its base on earth and its apex in heaven. The moon appeared above the fire. It was a splendid spectacle, but it would have been better to be alone, or else surrounded by intelligent people in order to enjoy it. What has spoilt the Russian campaign for me is to have taken part in it with the sort of people who would have disparaged the Colosseum and the Bay of Naples.

Through sheer boredom Henri resumed *Letellier* and fell to lecturing Félix Faure, in a letter signed 'Favier, Capitaine', on the importance of happiness as a central tenet of *le Beylisme*. While the Grande Armée dawdled aimlessly around the fringes of Moscow, Marshal Prince Mikhail Ilarionovich Kutuzov led the Russian army southwards to recuperate in the fertile countryside of Kaluga and wait for hunger and the northern winter to have weakened and worn down the foreigners before striking back at the rearguard of their inevitable retreat. 'I hope, trusting in God and in the courage of the army,' he told his officers, 'that they will pay for all the absurdities they have perpetrated and will leave our holy soil in disgrace.'

For Bonaparte's battalions the worst was yet to come. Ominous signs of what they might expect from the Russian peasantry and the pursuing Cossacks were noted in the diary of Boris von Uexküll, a Baltic baron who rode as an ensign in the Tsar's Garde à Cheval. In one village 'I saw a French prisoner sold to the peasants for twenty rubles; they baptized him with boiling tar and impaled him alive on a piece of pointed iron.' In another, soldiers looting a manor house had broken open the cellar and got drunk on its choice wines. 'The peasants of the neighbourhood, having waited for a favourable moment, shut them in and then, as a token of their meritorious action, cut off their noses.'

By the first days of October, the grip of a premature winter had tightened on the country. Napoleon's typical rodomontade, in a bulletin declaring that 'the Army is in the best mood in the world; it has an excess of everything and is being wonderfully well favoured by the weather'*, was eloquently contradicted by the facts, expressed with magnanimous compassion by Uexküll:

> The horrors we're surrounded by make mankind tremble and move the coldest and most cruel of men. Imagine a whole army in rout, in the most frightful disorder, feeding on horseflesh and God knows what, fleeing and attacking during the nights, deprived of rest and clothing, and you will have a feeble idea of what has become of Bonaparte's redoubtable army.

Plagued by the dullness of his companions, Stendhal busied himself with his official duty of trying to obtain provisions for the famished force struggling westwards towards Smolensk. His letters, intercepted by the Russians and unpublished until the present century, are entirely candid as to the miracles expected of him. Where, in a countryside pillaged by the troops of both sides, was he to find the 100,000 quintals of grain, oats and beef demanded by the commissariat of the reserve force? The task, as he told Pauline, was merely a spur towards working harder so that one day he might see his beloved Italy again. 'The more I advance, the more ambition disgusts me. It's simply putting one's happiness in the hands of others. If one has a soul, it's so easy to give it agreeable passions, and apply oneself, for the rest of the time to the enjoyment of the arts.'

A letter in Italian to Angéline Bereyter, telling her that he hoped to be home by February, ended in the Moscow archives, but Henri's thoughts, during these days, had strayed towards an earlier attachment. Mélanie Guilbert was by now Madame de Barkoff, and while in Moscow he had wandered about the burning city seeking news of her. A harpist named Fécel told him that a few days before the army's arrival, she and her husband, 'an ugly little man, very jealous', had fled to St Petersburg. She was pregnant but there was a possibility that she might return to

* Reading Livy in 1832, Stendhal compared his propagandistic untruthfulncss to that of a Grande Armée bulletin, recalling that: 'Napoleon declared it necessary to hide any truth unfavourable to France and that it was the act of a bad citizen to proclaim it.'

France. If so, Stendhal wrote to her lawyer's clerk in Paris, she could make use of his apartment in Rue Neuve-du-Luxembourg and added directions to the concierge to open it up. Was he perhaps hoping for a renewal of the affair? Mélanie, as we have seen, did indeed return to France for her daughter's birth, and was briefly reunited with her solicitous ex-lover.

With appalling loss of men, horses and munitions, the army reached Smolensk on 2 November, Beyle himself accompanying a convoy of fifteen hundred wounded. At one ticklish moment the wagons came up against a detachment of Russians reinforced by local peasants; rather than fall into such hands the French officers resolved to form a tight square and die where they stood. Each man made a bundle of his least valued effects to jettison at the first sign of attack, distributed money among the servants and helped to drink the remaining supply of looted wine. Setting out on foot beside their carriages through the thickest of fogs, they failed to encounter the expected onslaught, but the halts they made were so many that Stendhal was able to almost to finish the volume of Madame du Deffand's letters he had brought along to beguile the time.

Night after night they scrambled together their bivouacs of dry branches and lit their camp-fires. 'You wouldn't recognize us, my dear cousin,' Henri told Alexandrine Daru, 'we're enough to make anybody afraid. We look like our lackeys.' The main problem for everyone was the simple lack of provisions. He rejoiced in finding a few potatoes and a bit of damp bread, and the memory of his hunger never left him: years afterwards he told Prosper Mérimée that he could still recall with pleasure the piece of suet which, somewhere along the snowbound road, he had purchased for the immense sum of twenty francs. Not surprisingly he was always proud of the fact that it was his efforts as commissary which gave the army, encamped at Orcha, west of Smolensk, the only square meal its men had eaten in a month since leaving Moscow.

On 27 November, Napoleon, having watched his force of over half a million men shrink to almost a quarter of its strength, made a last desperate assault on the pursuing Russians at Borisov. The costly triumph at Borodino now found its ironic reverse in a battle which sent the remnants of the Grande Armée in headlong flight across the River Beresina, losing most of its artillery and scattering its Muscovite loot as it ran. Stendhal himself watched an entire brigade, two thousand men and five generals recognizable by their braided hats, routed by five Cossacks. Imprudently taking off one of his boots, he himself was forced to flee, clutching it in one hand, but turning to watch the only two men who dared to face the charging lancers, a gendarme named Menneval, and a conscript who shot Menneval's horse by mistake while trying to fire at the Cossacks. Later Stendhal was deputed to report the incident to the Emperor himself, whose silent rage expressed itself in his fiddling with one of the iron handles used to turn the window shutters of the room in which he gave audience. When, on his orders, they sought out Menneval to congratulate him on his bravery, the gendarme was discovered hiding, apparently afraid that he was going to be shot for cowardice.

It was one of Stendhal's fellow *auditeurs*, named Bergognié, who praised his coolness under fire during the terrible crossing of the Beresina. Sharpened perhaps by a profound contempt for the officers with whom he served, the old courage which had accompanied Henri in his boyhood duel with 'Odruas Kambin' at Grenoble distinguished his conduct throughout the Russian campaign, and there is no reason whatever to doubt the evidence constantly offered by his letters home of an extraordinary inner toughness and buoyancy which enabled him to survive where others languished.

His feelings with regard to Napoleon's management of the campaign are more difficult to judge; a possibility that his letters might fall into the wrong hands made him reticent on the subject even to Pauline and such close friends as Félix Faure. On 5 December 1812 the Emperor took the fateful decision to return to Paris ahead of his army, ostensibly to quell an attempted coup fuelled by rumours of his death. Refusing to acknowledge the significance of the Russian débâcle, he persistently maintained that victory was really his throughout the expedition and blamed disaster on everything from the freakish weather conditions and the reduced stamina of Norman cavalry horses to the curiously perishable contingent of Bavarian troops – on everything, that is, except his own miscalculations.

With laconic magnanimity towards his master, Stendhal wrote to Pauline from Wilna: 'I'm very well, my dear. I've often thought of you on the long road here from Moscow, lasting fifty days. I've lost everything except the clothes I stand up in. What is nicer is that I'm thin. I had many physical pains and no moral pleasure; but all this is forgotten and I am ready to begin again in the service of his Majesty.' It may be that he expected something more substantial than mere nodding recognition of his not undistinguished part in one of the most dramatic episodes in Bonaparte's reign. Nothing arrived in the way of reward, neither the coveted post of prefect nor even a medal, while the title of Baron de Beyle, notwithstanding Chérubin's canny property transaction, was as far off as ever. His return from Russia was to the same aimless, foot-tapping Parisian existence which had confronted him on his homecoming from Milan. What saddened him most was that at some stage during the retreat from Moscow he had lost the notebook containing the journal kept during his year in Brunswick in 1806-7 and the account of his passion for Mina von Griesheim. Together with this went the whole of the first draft of the *Histoire de la Peinture en Italie* and with it, as he now feared, all interest in the scheme itself.

His sudden state of cold passionlessness horrified him. What was the object of life if not to be in love? As a refuge from the emotional void which threatened, he turned once again to *Letellier* and to the close study of comic dramatists and their mechanisms for inducing laughter. Detached theoretical analysis could at least stave off the tedium of waiting for something in the nature of strong sensation to turn up. 'La passion viendra.' In the meanwhile he endured, with gritted teeth, what he saw as a species of moral death, in which not even old masters in the Louvre and memories of Gina Pietragrua could excite him.

All this may sound as though Stendhal was beginning to turn into an orthodox romantic, but the complexity of his viewpoint, both as a creative artist and as a critic, makes it impossible for us, here or elsewhere, to ticket him so easily. That he perceived dramatic neoclassicism as a spent force in the French theatre is clear from his comments on a performance of *Hamlet*, or rather of Jean-François Ducis' Gallicized version of the tragedy, which he saw at the Comédie-Française on 18 March, with the great Talma in the title role. 'I've no longer any feeling for French tragedy,' he wrote:

> this matter of representing tragic events bores me. . . . Hamlet is, excuse me, an oaf.* His enemy has to menace him before he can resolve to kill him. There's nothing beautiful here save for the moment when, raising the dagger over his mother, he asks his father's ghost what he must do. A young man beside me let out little gasps of admiration. Me, I just yawned.

Love offered him nothing in the way of distracting novelty. The *tendresse* for Countess Daru was revived for want of anything better, as a sentimental equivalent of the inevitable *Letellier*. Some diversion was perhaps offered by his meeting once more with Mélanie Guilbert, just arrived in Paris, whom he found almost as entrancing as in the old days in Marseilles. Life was made no sweeter, however, when the news reached Henri Beyle, Auditor of the Council of State, that he was not after all to be appointed to the coveted post of prefect. He had not especially wanted a French prefecture while there was a chance of an Italian equivalent, and even this was not quite so desirable as an appointment as master of requests, which would surely lead to the exalted office of crown intendant at Florence or Rome. Yet there was real mortification at seeing his fellow auditors Bergognié, Cochelet and Pastoret promoted while he received nothing. With the absorption of a naturalist describing the habits of some bird or insect, Stendhal watched and noted the development of his various feelings and fell briefly into the habit of pigeon-holing them under various headings in his journal. Under 'Chagrin d'ambition' on 19 March he recorded: 'If I have nothing, it is not through lack of merit or seniority, but because somebody [presumably Daru] wanted to subdue my pride and see how I swallowed the pill. In response to this, be cheerful with this person; when I can no

* Some modern equivalent of Stendhal's original 'couillon' seems more appropriate here – 'jerk, 'prat' or, aptest of all, 'pillock'.

longer hope for anything, then my pique will be over and done with in a couple of days.'

Still clinging to a rag or two of hope regarding the chimerical prefecture, he looked forward to a proposed visit from Pauline, whose boredom with her marriage to Périer-Lagrange was making her eager to travel, a desire which earned Stendhal's enthusiastic approval. He had evidently come round to her fondness for male disguise, and told her that in any case a woman of twenty-seven had a right to enjoy herself without having to bother with idle gossip.

Within a day or two of writing to Pauline he received the unwelcome order to resume his auditor's duties with the army in Germany, as Napoleon prepared to take on the regrouped alliance between Austria, Russia and Prussia. At Bautzen in Saxony he watched with sardonic detachment his first and only pitched battle, some of whose details later found their way into the Waterloo chapter of *La Chartreuse de Parme*:

> From midday until three o'clock we saw everything it is possible to see of a battle, namely nothing. The pleasure consists in being stirred somewhat by the certainty that out there something is happening which you know to be terrifying. The majestic noise of cannon-fire contributes a good deal to the effect, being entirely in harmony with the impression. If cannon produced a sharp, high-pitched whistle it would not be nearly so exciting. I've no doubt the sound of a whistle might be terrifying, but not half so fine as that of a cannon.

As Marshals Macdonald and Oudinot hammered it out with the Russians under pouring rain, Stendhal ran into Edouard Mounier, who entertained him with salty Voltairean anecdotes, told with inimitable spirit, as they sheltered from the downpour in a nearby hovel before venturing out once more to get a better view of the action.

Fighting continued for the next few days, and Beyle himself was involved in a ticklish episode when the wagon train he accompanied to Görlitz was surprised and nearly captured by a troop of Cossacks. His written report of this exists, signed 'De Beyle, auditeur', but he was also ordered to brief the Emperor in person, one of the only two occasions on which they met. Since the matter was entirely one of military routine, Stendhal left no record of the encounter, though a draft dedication of his *Histoire de la Peinture en Italie* is from 'the soldier you buttonholed at Görlitz'.

It was typical of the ironies governing his professional life both before and after Napoleon's fall that promotion should now arrive in a form which left Stendhal wholly indifferent. After lunch one afternoon his cousin Daru announced, with the air of somebody handing out a considerable favour, that Henri was to be made intendant of the Silesian town of Sagan. Since the Minister had already quelled the objections of one of the other auditors, who had asked for 'active employment' and been told to expect nothing until a treaty was signed, Beyle accepted without demur and set off for his seven weeks' reign in the little town, later to become the capital of a small principality belonging to the Talleyrand family.

On arrival he made a list of the civic notables, Monsieur André, the Duchess of Courland's man of business, Baroness Litwitz, 'an amiable woman, apparently aged thirty, that's to say forty-eight', legal councillor Friedlitz, a hypochondriac of fifty, Peter Heinrich Raabe, a printer who issued a special newspaper, the *Sagansches Wochenblatt*, for the local peasantry. It was hardly as sophisticated a milieu as Brunswick's and Stendhal was prepared to find it intolerably dull, but he made the best he could out of an unpromising situation. He borrowed a piano and found a local music master who could play Mozart on it. He read the books lent him by the Duke of Courland's librarian (which he probably never returned), Tacitus in translation and Roland's *Lettres écrites de Suisse, d'Italie de Sicile et de Malte*. There is even the possibility that he fathered an illegitimate daughter, who turns up in a document of 1833, aged twenty, as Christiane Beil, the only known instance of the name in the Sagan district. Was her mother the mysterious '*sister of my –* ' in an English note in the journal for 20 June?

Or perhaps not, since a long letter to Félix Faure on 16 July records that 'since I have no feelings of tenderness here, girls fill me with horror'. In any case he had already succumbed to one of those unspecified epidemic 'fevers' which swept across Napoleonic Europe in the wake of war. Four hundred people had died already that summer, and Stendhal was writing to Faure in one of the lucid intervals between successive bouts of delirium. Presumably he applied for sick leave, since ten days later he was at Dresden for a month-long convalescence before returning to Paris by way of Metz and Verdun, still so racked with illness that he could scarcely make ten lines of a note to Pauline asking her to send him more sheets and towels.

His lingering sickness offered the ideal pretext for a journey southwards, and he had no trouble in obtaining the necessary permission from his head of department, the Duc de Cadore. Once again he turned towards Milan, following the French shore of Lake Geneva in a fragile cabriolet, which nearly came to grief in the driving rain as they rattled across Lombardy. The fever continued to grip him, though it may simply have been nervous emotion which made him spill a cup of coffee with cream over his new pair of grey trousers as he sat in the Caffè Nuovo.

The destined happiness with Angela Pietragrua, with whom he instinctively resumed his affair, was perfect enough for Stendhal not to need a written outlet for his feelings. She was spending the last of the summer in *villeggiatura* in Monza, and when he caught sight of her at the end of the avenue leading to her house, his happiness reached such a pitch that he no longer felt able to write anything down. To describe what he felt would merely diminish it. He could only note that though there was nothing like the heady intoxication of a first encounter after years of absence, as when they met in 1811, their love had entered a calmer second phase, with a greater intimacy, confidence and naturalness between them.

Work, whether on the history of painting or on *Letellier,* was impossible, but 'only in this happy state can I read with any profit, increasing my stock of ideas, or rather correcting my ideas and drawing closer to the truth. This latter, in the study of mankind, is like a painting covered over with whitewash; some of the whitewash continues to peel off, and thus I approach the desired truth.' Rereading this and other passages later, Stendhal added the footnote: 'I was wrong, I ought to have got on with the *Histoire de la Peinture*. A little work was the only thing lacking to my happiness in 1813.'

On 21 September, in the villa at Monza, the pair made love as they had on the same day, at an almost identical hour, two years previously. Henri remembered because he had written it on his braces, a curious habit which, in one form or another, stayed with him for life. Yet even in the sweetness of a confidently renewed passion he could not stop himself from meditating on the differences in attitude between them, on the nature of his existence and its ultimate purpose. Slowly but perceptibly his sense of focus and direction as a writer gathered strength, and after one of his continual visits to the Brera gallery he posed himself the significant question: 'Is it your business to live or to describe your life?' The notebooks began gradually to dissolve into fragments, rough jottings and scattered epigrams, like the preparatory sketches for a novel.

Gina was as exuberantly scheming as ever, and Henri entered willingly into the assignation game. 'The first window as you come from Via dei Martiri, wide open at half past eight, the hour when I pass your door, will mean that you can come out at ten o'clock; half open, at eleven; half open with a cloth hanging from the window, at noon; wide open, with a cloth, half past nine, and wide open with two towels, one o'clock.' He had come to understand why Italians needed this world of theatrical intrigue: it was because, as he believed, natural expression came too easily to them and they required instead a sense of difficulty, the challenge of an amorous problem to be solved by portraying love with exaggerated refinement. Wonderful lovers though they might be, they preferred wit to passion.

It must have become obvious to Stendhal, as the Milanese autumn drew on, that he could no longer stay in Italy with impunity while the Empire itself was starting to collapse. With Wellington pushing home his victories in Spain and after the crushing defeat administered by the Allies on the French at Leipzig, Beyle's return to Paris at the end of November was, to say the least, prudent. So too was his request for exemption from military service, on the basis of his record in the Russian and Austrian campaigns and the efficient discharge of his intendant's duties at Sagan. The petition was calculated to secure him enough leisure to settle back easily into the role of comic dramatist he was still keen to realize, but no sooner was it granted, on Christmas Eve 1813, than two days later, coming home from dinner with Annette Questienne, his friend Louis de Barral's mistress, Henri was horrified to receive a letter from the Ministry of the Interior, ordering him to return forthwith to Grenoble.

The fact was that as France prepared to receive the first wave of Allied assault on her defences, frontier cities such as the Dauphiné's capital needed to be hustled into something like a state of military preparedness. Beyle's job was to assist Marshal Comte de Saint-Vallier to coordinate operations in the Grenoble area, and though initially there was a flicker of hope that the order might after all have been a false alarm, he at length followed Saint-Vallier out of Paris on 31 December.

With him went Pauline and her husband, François Périer-Lagrange, who had at last arrived on the long-meditated Parisian visit and were now to be swept unceremoniously homewards to the engulfing dreariness of Cularo, 'this headquarters of pettiness'. Stendhal, lodging with his father, now regularly referred to as '*my bastard*', felt not the slightest twinge of sentiment at re-establishing himself in the town from which he had been so willing an exile. The single relief from provincial boredom was afforded by Sophie Boulon, Pauline's former schoolfriend and perhaps at this time her lover, with whom they went on an outing to Claix.

Henri distinctly warmed to Sophie, whom he later introduced into *Le Rouge et le Noir* as Madame Derville, the all-too shrewd confidant of Madame de Rênal.

> From the moment Madame Derville arrived, she seemed to Julien to be his friend. He hastened to show her the prospect visible from the end of the new path under the great walnut trees: it equalled, if indeed it did not surpass, the most wonderful views Switzerland and the Italian lakes can offer. By climbing the steep slope which starts a few paces further on, you soon come to lofty precipices fringed by oak woods, pushing forwards almost to the edge of the river. It was to the summits of those rocks, falling to the water, that Julien, happy, free and, what was more, king of his castle, led

these two friends, delighting in their wonder at the sublimity of the view. 'For me,' said Madame Derville, 'it's like Mozart's music.'

Another figure drafted into fictional service from these Grenoble days was Baron Jean-Joseph Fourier, a noted mathematician and, in his official capacity as Prefect of the Isère district, an insufferable pedant and chatterbox, who wore down the patience even of the good-humoured Comte de Saint-Vallier. In *Lucien Leuwen* Fourier is paraded before us as Monsieur Boucaut de Seranville, Prefect of Calvados, an early-nineteenth-century Vicar of Bray, who, having written a score of liberal articles in 1829, has now become a pillar of public order under Louis-Philippe, and is gleefully trounced by Lucien during a corrupt Norman election. In sketching the character, a choleric dandy standing firmly on his official dignity, Stendhal can be detected indulging the pleasure of a long-delayed revenge.

It was not merely the inherent pointlessness of shoring up one sector of the French frontier as the Allied armies poured across another which made life at Grenoble so dreary. The 'nervous fever' from which Henri had suffered periodically since his return from Russia now broke out once more, and Saint-Vallier had to ask for another auditor, pointing out nevertheless that M. de Beyle had served him well and deserved favourable consideration from the government. In the same letter the Marshal, noting that during an engagement at Echelles eighty-two conscripts had thrown down their arms, ominously protests: 'Please believe, Monseigneur, that we shall do all that is humanly possible in His Majesty's service.' No wonder Stendhal, in his own aggrieved request to the Duc de Cadore for a recall to Paris, felt the need to declare: 'I have given proof of my zeal.'

His illness marched in step with the Empire's imminent ruin. By the middle of March 1814, the Dauphiné was overrun with Austrian and Russian troops, Croats and Kalmucks whose atrocities among the peasantry were reported to Saint-Vallier in the florid style customary among Imperial officials, by Beyle and his fellow auditor Delamarre. 'In order that the present tragedy can become something entirely Shakespearian,' Henri told Pauline, 'the King of Naples [Joachim Murat] has apparently run mad. He goes from Bologna to Ferrara and Ferrara to Bologna without stopping and weeps at every opportunity. He's the buffoon of the tragedy.' The Pope was at Savona, the Cossacks were at Lyons, and three days after Stendhal arrived in Paris on 27 March, the Russians had taken Montmartre. Amid a silent, uncomprehending crowd, he and Louis Crozet watched the Empress Marie-Louise leaving the city with her son, the little King of Rome, before the two friends hurried to the Louvre for a last look at its looted treasures as they were wrapped up and (in several but by no means all cases) restored to their original owners.

Crozet describes a curiously moving little episode which took place when they ran into Vivant Denon, accompanied by his secretary. Denon asked Henri whether he had come to the Louvre on official business.

'No, I came to pay a final visit to the paintings. I went into the office and gave an art-lover's advice.'

'In that case I shan't listen to you,' answered Denon. 'I like you and hold you in high regard, but I shan't listen to you. If you had come with a message from the Duc de Cadore. . . .'

Henri answered with some heat: 'No, no, I come at nobody's request, I merely offered advice as an artist, as an art-lover. . . . If only the beautiful *Madonna della Seggiola** might be saved . . . The Empress has gone to Rambouillet. Well, the *Madonna* might be sent to her: the work involved is nothing, and there would at least be some advantage in it.'

'You're right,' answered Denon, 'but I cannot act without official orders, and besides, what's the point of a little measure like that? Do you want me to risk looking a fool by sending *one painting* to Rambouillet? After holding me back for two months the Duc de Cadore comes to me at the last moment . . . What's more, you haven't been sent by him. . . . Hasn't he said anything to you about the museum?'

'He has told me to include my inventory.'

'Well, I'm going to close the Museum and that's the end of it. I wish you a good evening.'

* A painting by Raphael, nowadays known as the *Madonna della Sedia*, from the Grandducal collection in the Pitti Palace in Florence.

This exchange, one of the very few Stendhalian conversations to be recorded verbatim, is not without its significance, both as the first occasion on which we catch the writer referring to himself as an artist, and as evidence of his real attachment to the paintings of which he was both cataloguer and historian. Both the dissolution of the Imperial collection and the fickle delight of the Parisian crowd as the Allied troops entered the city were omens of Stendhal's own material débâcle. He was never to recover either his respectable official position (the two consulships with which the July Monarchy fobbed him off were hardly a valid equivalent) or the relative financial stability on which he had counted during his years as a bureaucrat. At a stroke, as it were, most, if not all, of the Napoleonic machine was dismantled by senatorial acts passed on 1 April 1814, and with this process went the auditorship, the job as commissary and the post of inspector of crown furnishings.

We can hardly blame 'M. Henri de Beyle' for hurrying to acknowledge his adherence to the acts, let alone for the abject letters written to the Comte de Blacas asking to be retained in the court almanac of the newly restored Louis XVIII, at least as an honorary inspector, so as not to endure the shame of being swept aside completely. Others closer to him were invited to speak on his behalf. A curious note was addressed to Edouard Mounier as 'Monsieur le baron', in an awkward mixture of facetious pseudo-intimacy and pompous formality, asking to bear witness to his meritorious conduct and to that of a certain *émigré* Captain Beyle, 'who won the cross of Saint-Louis and . . . . was my uncle'. Since this is the first and last time a paternal uncle appears on the scene, we must assume that he was one of Henri's opportune fictions.

Potentially more useful was his acquaintance with the wife of the new Minister of Police, Jacques-Claude Beugnot, who now offered him the post of 'Directeur de l'approvisionnement de réserve de Paris'. Many years later Stendhal recalled:

> I asked for nothing, and was in an admirable position to accept. I replied in such a way as to discourage M. Beugnot, a man with vanity enough for two Frenchmen; he must have been extremely

> shocked. The person who eventually took up this position retired after four or five years, tired of earning money and apparently without stealing any of it. My extreme contempt for the Bourbons – for me they were the scum of the earth – made me leave Paris a few days after having declined M. Beugnot's obliging proposal.

Countess Beugnot's lover was Henri's friend Louis Pépin de Bellisle, whom her influence eventually created master of requests. A cheerful, strong-willed woman in her forties, the Countess acted as another of those mother-substitutes, like Madame Rebuffel or Alexandrine Daru, with whom Stendhal always felt at ease. He regretted never having been in love with her. 'What a pleasure it would have been to converse intimately with somebody of her social standing.' Instead he began to grow interested in her twenty-six-year-old daughter Clémentine, married to a general in the army, but it was ten years before mutual attraction developed into a serious relationship.

Had Beugnot's agents been keeping an eye on him? What purports to be a police report, dated 31 May 1814, describes him as:

> a stout lad, born at Grenoble, aged 31, lodging at Rue Neuve-du Luxembourg no 3. . . . He goes frequently to the theatre and always lives with some actress or other. When not absent on business, he works four or five hours a day on making historical extracts and notes of his journeys. As a copyist he uses a shady type named Bougeol. He lived for a long while with an actress from the Opéra-Buffa, with whom he has apparently broken up. . . . He always eats at the Café de Foy and dines at the Frères Provençaux. He buys many books and comes home at midnight.

If at first the authenticity of these details seems a little sinister, the reader can take comfort from the fact that the report was written, probably as a joke, by no less person than Stendhal himself.

His hopes of an Italian consular post in Naples or Florence were dashed almost in the same instant as those expectations of a barony he had naïvely hoped to realize at last in the earliest creation of peers by the new King. Yet as the world of material certainties crumbled around him and the chances of raising funds and foiling creditors grew ever more bleak, Stendhal, with his usual courage and singlemindedness, sought solace in writing and, more significantly, finishing a book. This time it was not the umpteenth stab at *Letellier*, or indeed anything connected with his lifelong reveries of dramatic success. What emerged from the limbo of apparent failure was one of the oddest, least auspicious débuts of a great author in the annals of literature.

The volume in hand was eventually to appear in January 1815 under the cumbersome label of *Lettres écrites à Vienne en Autriche sur le célèbre compositeur Haydn, suivies d'une Vie de Mozart et de Considérations sur Métastase et l'état présent de la musique en France et en Italie*. We now know it by the more manageable title of its second edition, published in 1817 as *Vies de Haydn, de Mozart et de Métastase*. Translated into several languages (the first English version also appeared in 1817) it has nevertheless remained among Stendhal's least read and least respected works, though hindsight enables us to catch, amid the tissue of shameless plagiarisms, an occasional glimpse of the characteristic Stendhalian persona in all its sublimely mendacious authoritativeness.

The book's first and longest section consists of a series of epistles, ostensibly addressed by the author from Vienna to an unnamed friend and presenting an account of the life and works of Joseph Haydn, whose funeral Stendhal had witnessed in 1809, the year in which the twenty-two letters purport to have been written. There follows a short life of Mozart 'translated from the German by M. Schlichtegroll', and the work concludes with a 'Letter on the present state of music in Italy' as a footnote to two studies of the highly influential eighteenth-century theatre poet Pietro Metastasio, whose texts were set by everybody from Handel and Vivaldi to Schubert and Beethoven.

A closer inspection of what seems on the surface to be merely a little anthology of Beyle's musical enthusiasms (with more than a few references to Cimarosa along the way) has since disclosed the degree to which Stendhal was indebted to a whole range of literary and musicological sources. The Metastasio letters, for example, rely heavily on an essay in the critical satire *La frusta letteraria* (The Literary Scourge) published in periodical form in 1763 by the Piedmontese writer and friend of Dr Johnson,

Giuseppe Baretti, as well as incorporating elements from the works of Jean-Louis Simond de Sismondi and the Président de Brosses. For his Mozart biography, Beyle adapted a life of the composer by G. Winckler which had originally appeared in the *Magasin Encyclopédique* of 1801.

Most glaring and notorious of all Stendhal's plagiarisms were those underpinning the letters on Haydn. Besides making use of passages from a recently published musical dictionary, he was now seeking to pass off as his own the work of Haydn's friend Giuseppe Carpani, whose *Le Haydine ovvero Lettere sulla vita e le opere del celebre maestro Giuseppe Haydn* (1812) was an important early attempt at assessing the career of the great Austrian master. Stendhal can scarcely have imagined that his theft would go undetected, but when its full extent was disclosed in an angry and spirited pair of letters sent by Carpani to the Paris newspaper *Le Constitutionnel* in 1815, supported by a declaration from several distinguished Viennese musicians including Antonio Salieri and Haydn's pupil Marianna von Kurzbeck, the response was anything but a grovelling apology. As with all his published works, Beyle had availed himself of a pseudonym, one of over two hundred in his amazing repertoire of aliases, and *Haydn, Mozart & Metastasio* had appeared under the authorship of a certain 'Louis Alexandre César Bombet'. Posing as Bombet's brother Hector, writing from Rouen on behalf of the author 'at present in London, very old, gouty and little occupied with music', the impenitent thief insolently challenged Carpani to place any thirty pages of his *Haydine* side by side with the *Lettres sur Haydn* and let the public judge, as well as recommending him to take a few lessons from Bombet in the matter of style.

The controversy never entirely died down. As late as 1824, Carpani was threatening to unveil the identity of Bombet as a certain Enrico Beyle of Grenoble. As for Stendhal, he half acknowledged the plagiarism in the course of compiling the memoir entitled *Souvenirs d'Egotisme*, where he recorded that 'in 1814, when he was making up his mind on the Bourbons, he had two or three dark days. So as to make them pass more quickly, he hired a copyist and dictated a corrected translation of the lives of Haydn, Mozart and Metastasio, based on an Italian work.' Yet just before he died, he told Quérard, compiler of the dictionary *Supercheries Littéraires dévoilées* (Literary Hoaxes Unveiled) that he had committed the deception solely because Didot, the publisher, had told him that no one would read a book advertised as 'translated from the Italian'. In any case, could a pseudonymous writer actually count as a plagiarist? 'M. Beyle, being at Vienna in 1809, had been present at Haydn's interment; he studied the works of this great composer and wished to make him better known in Paris. M. Beyle had purchased many of Haydn's autographs and several of his articles of furniture.'

There is no evidence that M. Beyle had done any such thing. The nearest he ever came to Haydn outside Vienna was hearing Victorine Mounier practising a piano reduction of the composer's symphonies at Grenoble in the spring of 1802. That chauvinist isolationism which has characterized French musical life from Lully to our own day meant that Haydn, though revered throughout civilized Europe, was still hardly known in France. Thus it must at first seem strange that Stendhal, with his avowed lack of interest in any music not involving the human voice, should choose to celebrate the genius of a composer who, until the late twentieth century, was chiefly famous for his instrumental works.

Stendhaliens of all sorts have leaned over backwards to vindicate the author of the *Vies de Haydn, de Mozart et de Métastase* and to suggest, plausibly enough, that this curious ragbag was a proving ground for various significant themes, most notably the duel of classic and romantic providing the polemic foundation of *Racine et Shakespeare*, which he was to develop in later years. Most interesting in relation to Stendhal's own concerns is the blatantly pedagogical thrust of the 'Opus bombeticum', as he jokingly called it. Diffident as he might have seemed among the *habitués* of a fashionable salon or in the presence of a handsome woman, he never had any doubts as to an initial impetus and the direction of his energies once the pen was in his hand. All too conscious of the smugness and parochialism of contemporary French culture, he seems to have been consciously trying to teach his insular compatriots to look outwards, as he himself had done with such eagerness, and embrace the music and poetry of Italy and the

Austro-German tradition. Clearly he wanted both to share his musical enthusiasms and to apprise his French readers of an artistic world with which hardly any of them were familiar. Metastasio was not widely read in France, which, until the famous 'Guerre des bouffons' between the supporters of Gluck and Piccinni in the 1770s, had largely ignored the Italian lyric stage in favour of its own dogmatic approach to the evolution of a native operatic style. Haydn and Mozart, in spite of the fact that each had written works expressly tailored to the requirements of Parisian taste, remained largely unplayed by French musicians. The tone of Stendhal's book is, not surprisingly, that of someone engaged in telling us what we are unlikely to know, and it was a tone which the writer was to adopt without the least hesitation in several of his most important non-fictional works.

Whatever funds Beyle might have hoped to raise on the strength of an eventual publication of *Haydn, Mozart & Metastasio*, they were not of the substance likely to bail him out of his mounting financial difficulties. The apparatus of comfortable living must now be disposed of by the former *auditeur du Conseil d'Etat*, with his carriage and furniture going for 6000 francs, and appeals must be made to the family in the shape of his uncle Romain as administrator of the late Dr Gagnon's estate, his father, who might be prevailed upon to sell the mortgaged house in Grenoble, and Pauline, who, together with her husband, could perhaps supply a small annuity. In the end it was the first of these who provided him with the means of survival, a little income of 1600 francs from his grandfather's trust fund, a sum nevertheless wholly inadequate to the needs of somebody accustomed to spending 10,000 francs 'supporting the character of a gentleman' as his English contemporaries would have put it, in the fashionable world of Napoleonic Paris.

Not merely was it impractical for him to stay in the capital: he was plainly an unwelcome figure amid the throng of those jostling to make their peace with the Bourbons. There was no question of him becoming, as yet, a doctrinaire Bonapartist, sulking in all the romantic glamour of defeat, and he might easily have followed his friends Félix Faure and Louis Crozet down the respectable career paths opened up to them by the Restoration. His statement in *Souvenirs d'Egotisme* that he turned down Beugnot's job offer because of an inexpressible contempt for the newly reinstated royal family needs to be taken with a pinch of salt. It was the kind of thing he could easily declare in 1832 but was less likely to invoke as a genuine motive in 1814.

At some time during these summer months, while he was dictating *Haydn, Mozart & Metastasio* to a copyist, going periodically to the theatre and making a little retrospective love to Mélanie Guilbert de Barkoff, Stendhal made a pencilled breakdown of his current situation, one of those thinking-aloud processes whereby he could arrive at a quick solution to a current problem. 'I fully perceive,' he wrote, 'that it's possible to live in Paris in a fourth-floor room with one clean set of clothes, a woman who comes in each day to brush them, and my admission tickets to the Théâtre Français or the Odéon, which I love. Vanity and self-respect, however, are opposed to such a life. . . . Therefore I must leave Paris . . . . Paris has bored me for a long time, and I love Italy, where with 6000 francs and two dinners a month at the Ambassador's residence, I shall be respected.'

And Italy – momentously – it was to be.

CHAPTER 7

AMONG THE ROMANTICS

There was obviously no serious debate in Stendhal's mind as to where in Italy he would end up. His imagination fastened with predictable eagerness on Milan, and it was there, on 10 August 1814, that he arrived to begin what was to prove one of the most significant epochs of his life, in which he could most easily find the freedom to be the unique human organism that he was, and in which his receptivity to impressions and ideas was at its sharpest. At this instant Milan fixed him as her own, and even if he never lost his essentially French apprehension of the world around him, he became, more than many another of his countrymen, an Italian among Italians, the 'Arrigo Beyle, Milanese' claimed for him by his self-designed epitaph.

Almost as soon as he arrived, however, having crossed the Mont-Cenis pass and stopped at Turin to catch a performance of Pietro Generali's opera *La Contessa di Colle Erboso*, which remained a favourite of his, Henri was forced to leave Milan as a result of police surveillance of Angela Pietragrua, with whom he had instinctively resumed his affair. Reluctant to compromise her through too close an association, he retired discreetly westwards to Genoa to visit his friend Fabio Pallavicini, a young aristocrat whose mother had a house at Recco on the Riviera di Levante.

Pallavicini, at the tender age of eleven, had been present at the fateful dinner in Genoa in 1805 when Napoleon informed the Empress Joséphine that he was going to divorce her. On her fainting at the announcement, it was left to the boy, as page-in-waiting, to help the disgruntled Emperor to lift her on to a sofa and attempt to bring her around. He was subsequently rewarded with a civil service post on the Council of Regency by her successor, Marie-Louise, but had since, like so many others, returned home to wait on the progress of events.

During the last days of the Genoese Republic, his mother, the beautiful Marchesa Teresa, had held liberal political salons in her palace in Piazza San Domenico, where the guests took part in amateur performances of Alfieri's tragedies and the latest Parisian comedies. When the senate intervened to stop the plays, the Marchesa, with her friend and fellow hostess Anna Pieri Brignole, petitioned the government on behalf of an individual citizen's right to enjoy 'the liberty which everybody has and ought to have within their own house'. No doubt such a spirited rejoinder appealed to Stendhal, who had met her in Paris in the autumn of 1810, and now told his sister Pauline that 'Madame P. has had the extreme kindness to invite all the pretty women of her acquaintance to show me around the neighbourhood'.

If the company of these sirens ultimately proved rather dull, the visual enchantments of Recco and its seashore made a strong impression on him, so much so that several years afterwards he used the original record of it made for his journal as the basis of a passage in the style of a magazine article (in this case the English periodical *The Eclectic Review*) evoking one of his trips along the coast amid the idyllic Riviera landscape of small villages nestling amid fertile terraced fields and vineyards. The holiday atmosphere of donkey-rides, village fireworks and a *festa* in honour of the Virgin contrasted sharply with Stendhal's awareness of his own predicament. How much he would rather be like the young Italians, joyously unconscious of anything beyond their immediate existence! 'History, for them, is no more than the dates of accession and death of popes and kings; they have never had the misfortune to fall in love with mankind. They firmly believe that in a hundred years everything will be as it was a hundred years previously, and this fortunate mistake kills any spiritual concern over such matters.'

One of the most fascinating things he had so far written in its powerful indications of a more grown-up, less peremptory and demanding view of the world, the passage carries us with him to the edge of the shore, where, against a newly darkened sky, he watches the moon rise and feels himself immersed within a profound meditative serenity, deeper, despite its sombreness, than anything the Italians can ever have encountered. 'They know nothing of what it means to spend one's life without loving, to lead a wandering existence, shifting from town to town every fortnight, sacrificing all the emotions of youth to what is, or what one believes to be, a noble cause: all this is like mythology for them. They lack that experience of misfortune which will heighten the pleasure of their own happiness.'

Gazing at the Mediterranean he plunges headlong into a reverie on its emblematic significance in the shared culture of Europe, and listening to the jubilant popping and banging of the fireworks, he turns, through unstated but obvious association, to consider Marshal Ney's recent execution, and the terrible artistic aptness implicit both in this sordid conclusion to a glorious career and in Napoleon's defeat at Waterloo. Despotism has been restored, and Europe's only salvation a century hence will be America, whose 'sons of liberty will destroy in two or three campaigns, if they choose, the greatest power exercised by tyranny'. But it grows late, the moon shines still more brightly, he only has his knife with him, and the local peasantry, taking him for a rich *signore*, will not hesitate to hurl him into the sea, so he had best go home. When he gets back to Recco, the village is still making merry, the women whisk him into dancing the *monferrina*, and he does not get to bed till after supper in the small hours.

The interest of this Recco meditation, entitled *Rivages de la mer* and included among materials for a projected sequel to *Rome, Naples et Florence en 1817*, to be known as *L'Italie en 1818*, lies in its marked Romantic tone. Standing alone on the moonlit beach, musing on everything from love and mischance to the future fate of nations and the malign influence of Christianity, Stendhal becomes the Byronic loner, the Rousseauesque *promeneur solitaire*, in what is essentially a prose rhapsody of a kind which could hardly be described as typical of its author. The sudden perception of his own danger at the end strikes a note of comic self-awareness, as though he were embarrassed by his solemnity and knew that its resonances were not authentically Stendhalian. There are certain other passages in a similar style scattered through the novels – see, for example, the closing pages of *Armance* – yet, sensitive and affecting as these are, they scarcely constitute a dossier for the author as one of the great torchbearers of Romanticism. Absorbed though he later grew in the fervent polemic of the Italian Romantics, and important as his *Racine et Shakespeare* would become in enlarging the debate among his countrymen, Stendhal's ego was not that of a Wordsworth or a Goethe and he was never destined to enlist unreservedly beneath the fashionable colours of the hour, so that *Rivages de la mer* is significant as much for what it did not lead to as for the intriguing possibilities for stylistic development the whole passage carries with it.

Beyle's gracious recompense for the Marchese Pallavicini's hospitality at Recco was to ask Pauline to arrange the dispatch to Genoa of fifty peach trees from a Lyons nursery while he himself sailed south to Leghorn. He was beginning to notice, in the course of his travels, the congenial cheapness of Italy in comparison to France. Seven or eight pairs of trousers, an exercise book, an eight-volume Alfieri and the cost of a theatre ticket all came at prices which easily persuaded him that he was right to seek refuge here from the tiresome financial exigencies of Paris and Grenoble. In Tuscany, what was more, he sensed a lifting of the spirits, created as so often by a lack of immediate social obligations. He had now resumed work on the projected *Histoire de la Peinture en Italie*, whose genesis had been a translation of Lanzi's survey, and in Florence, where he arrived on 23 September, after spending a day wandering around Pisa in the pouring rain, he amused himself with sketching out thirteen versions of an opening for the work.

By mid October he was back in Milan and sending word to Gina Pietragrua, still on *villeggiatura*, of his return. Had she after all sent him away for sheer convenience, as opposed to the official pretext of political suspicion? A letter to his friend Countess Beugnot rather suggests that the Pietragrua's stratagem was motivated by a simple desire to stop her friends from tattling too perilously about the affair. From this point onwards the relationship embarked on its final phase, in which all Stendhal's powers of self-realization would one by one be summoned into play, and the ending of the liaison acted as a prelude to a far more intense experience of what it meant to be Milanese, let alone Italian, at this crucial moment, than any Stendhal had known on his previous visits to the city.

The lovers met again at a little church (he does not say which) and walked to the pretty porticoed cemetery next to the ramparts on the city's eastern side, behind Santa Maria della Passione. Gina lost no time in telling Henri that since he had failed to write to her during the whole fortnight he was at Genoa, everything must be over between them. Understandably he was not convinced, the more so because she offered him a rendezvous for noon the next day at his lodging in Contrada Belgiojoso. How pretty she looked under her black veil! She told him he was the one she loved best, but that he did nothing to deserve it, and that by next spring he would have grown bored and be on his way back to France.

Such blatant coquetry had its destined effect. Henri now fell totally beneath Gina's spell, writing of himself in English as '*being crossed in love*', '*mad by love*', '*I am loving*'. Ironically, passion acted as a species of vitamin to creativity, and he plunged more keenly than ever into the *Histoire de la Peinture*, completing the first volume, reading Humboldt's travels, Burke on the sublime, Reynolds's *Discourses* and the works of the English aesthetician Richard Payne Knight, as well as polishing his style with the aid of Montesquieu's *L'Esprit des lois*, of which he cynically observed that it was as useful to tyrants as to the people.

He was writing regularly to Pauline, giving her advice on reading and character development as in the old days, and on 14 January 1815 he ended his letter with the words: 'Ah! my dearest, what terrible news I've learned from the newspaper they've just brought me! The death of Mme Daru! She was, after all, the best friend I had in the world. I can write no more. Farewell.' It was true. Alexandrine, his beloved Lady Palfy of earlier days, had died aged only thirty-two from what was probably puerperal fever following the birth of a daughter. The anguished account of her last moments sent to Beyle by her husband the ex-minister ought to have convinced the sceptical cousin that his former employer was capable of genuine affection and tenderness of heart.

> You well knew the admirable wife I lost, but you never saw her at the moment when I was overtaken by singular and unforeseen

> events; she acquired a fresh title to my tenderness through the equanimity with which she contemplated the disappearance of all those advantages I owed to earlier circumstances. The most just spirit, the most steady character, the sweetest feelings, all these are lost to me.

In the midst of his grief Daru was kind enough to add: 'I am all too aware of the regrets you will feel towards my dear Alexandrine. She would surely have been delighted to busy herself with the affair over which you solicited her intervention.' Neither Stendhal's address to the Countess, presumably seeking her help in finding a job*, nor the condolence note he must have written to her husband, has survived.

The letter to Pauline was dispatched from Turin, where Gina had sent him, this time on a pretext of her husband's jealousy. 'Madame Simonetta', as he called her in his journal, was up to her old tricks, yet he resisted her injunction to return to France, and dawdled resolutely for a fortnight in the Piedmontese capital before coming back to Milan at the end of January. Madame Daru's death, as he later told Pauline, may have dissuaded him from heading for Paris, but this last, most passionate engagement with the Pietragrua kept him more securely in Italy, at the very moment when Napoleon was making landfall from Elba and the Hundred Days began on 1 March 1815. It was Gina who apparently forbade him at last to endanger himself through too direct an involvement in what seemed at first like a suddenly favourable shift in political affairs. His excuse to Pauline was that he had no wish to run up any further Parisian debts. 'The avarice of this tender father,' he declared, evoking the eternal spectre of Chérubin, 'will prevent me marrying and wearing a prefect's uniform.'

This apart, Stendhal's financial situation was now considerably improved as a result of investing his grandfather's legacy of 16,000 francs with the help of M. Ennemond Hélie of Grenoble. The modest income, even if it hardly guaranteed the elegant

* According to Stendhal (*Souvenirs d'Egotisme*) she had told him in 1814, 'without this accursed invasion you would have been prefect of a great city'.

lifestyle he had enjoyed as an auditor under the Empire, would at least allow him to live independently in Italy for the next six years. Doubtless too it contributed towards bolstering his elation as he was drawn ever deeper into Gina's toils. '*From the 1 February till now. 29th May, happy by love*,' he wrote in English, and in early July they set off separately for Padua, where 'Mme Simonetta' insisted that they stay in separate hotels. Henri's aim was to discover whether living in Venice might not after all be more advantageous to him than remaining at Milan. He liked the atmosphere of greater social relaxation in these cities of the Veneto, though at Padua, even if women frequented the cafés and society stayed up till two in the morning, there was a danger of too much gossip.

The rhythms of life in the old university town were nevertheless intoxicating to him. 'Here enjoyment is king, every countenance beams, everyone smiles, jokes and talks in loud voices,' he later wrote. 'The people to whom yesterday I presented my letters of introduction are by now old friends; such openness of heart is remarkable in Italy.' Every night he went out to supper (at three in the morning, he tells us, with Gina presumably accompanying him) to the Café Pedrocchi, later famous as a hotbed of political intrique against the Habsburg government and nowadays, along with the Café Greco in Rome and Venice's Café Florian (both holding Stendhalian associations) designated as a national monument.

From his hotel, the Croce di Malta, he went to call on the aged castrato Gasparo Pacchierotti, then living in venerable retirement in a palace surrounded by a delightful garden. Born near Ancona in 1740, he had become one of the greatest singing artists of the later eighteenth century, ravishing the ears of musical Londoners in the 1780s, meeting Haydn, Fanny Burney and William Beckford, who grew quite obsessed with his brilliance, and taking part in the première of Paisiello's *I giochi d'Agrigento* in 1792, the opera which opened the Teatro della Fenice at Venice. The English melomane Lord Mount Edgcumbe recalled Pacchierotti as 'a worthy, good man, modest and diffident even to a fault . . . unpresuming in his manners, grateful and attached to all his numerous friends and patrons'. He was affable towards Stendhal, who found him 'full of youthful fire' and claimed that he learned more about music in six visits to the old man than he could ever glean from books. 'C'est l'âme qui parle à l'âme.'

If, as he claimed, Beyle left Padua with tears in his eyes,* a first encounter with Venice made no such impression on him. One of the saddest facts which those who love both Stendhal and Venice have to confront is the writer's apparent failure to respond in any worthwhile measure to the sorceries of La Serenissima. The city that had ravished Goethe and was soon to claim Byron for her own left Henri Beyle, while not absolutely cold, decidedly lukewarm. If any proof were needed that though parts of him functioned in Romantic mode, others emphatically did not, then this curious lacuna of sensibility surely offers it. Significantly the Venetian sections included in the 1817 version of *Rome, Naples et Florence* are omitted in the revision of 1826, and their tone is mostly one of time-marking boredom, interspersed with a short disquisition on Goldoni, a mention of a performance of Rossini's *Tancredi*, and an account of a certain momentous encounter which in fact took place in a box at La Scala, Milan.

It is possible that something of his relative indifference to Venice was connected in part with his view of the place as a symbol of Napoleon's defeat. In spite of the brilliance of its colours in sea and sky, and the pleasures afforded by the Café Florian in Piazza San Marco, the city as an expression of everything he most valued in cultivated living left him somewhat depressed. On a moonlit gondola ride from the recently created public gardens at the lagoon's edge, past the Riva degli Schiavoni to the Piazzetta, he cursed Bonaparte for having finally sacrificed the city to the Austrians and shrewdly foresaw the devastating effect this would have on its economy. 'Venice used to be more civilized than London and Paris. Now there are fifty thousand poor people here. They are offering Palazzo Vendramin on the Grand Canal for a thousand louis. It cost twenty-five thousand to build and was still worth ten in 1794.'

He seems nevertheless to have seriously considered the possibility of living in Venice, since the agreeable rhythms of its social

* Though he also refers to it (Journal, p.938) as 'the sad hole'.

life, evidently allowing a freer intercourse between men and women than was possible in Milan, were exactly what suited his present needs. There had to be, on the other hand, a tighter control of his budget, especially as Gina was starting to make demands over and above the 3000 francs he had provided for the trip. However much he was enjoying himself – and his mistress, as he succinctly notes in the English words 'I have had her' – the overall sense of pleasure was numbed by the news now arriving from France. For it was here in Venice, seated at one of Florian's tables, that he read the news of the surrender of Paris after the battle of Waterloo on 18 July, and sardonically altered Francis I's famous words after his defeat at Pavia, 'tout est perdu fors l'honneur' – 'all is lost save honour' – to 'tout est perdu même l'honneur' – 'all is lost, even honour'. Angrily he drew the picture of a candle-snuffer in his journal, to signify the imminent destiny of France under repressive legitimism.

It was soon after Henri and Gina got back to Milan on 12 August 1815 that the crucial episode took place which made him open his eyes at last to the true nature of their relationship and the full extent of her deviousness. Years later, in somewhat garbled fashion, Stendhal told his friend Prosper Mérimée what had happened. Gina, he claimed, had only allowed him to see her once every ten days or so, making the rendezvous at a cheap inn where the chambermaid was handsomely bribed to show him upstairs. One day the maid, knowing what the Pietragrua was up to and that other admirers besides Beyle were being given the entrée, took pity on him for whatever reason, and told him he was being regularly deceived. To prove it, she hid him in a closet from which, with a strong sense of the situation's absurdity, he was able to spy on Gina in the throes of lovemaking with one of his rivals. Finally the indignity became insufferable, he burst open the door and she fell on her knees to beg forgiveness. 'I was stupefied,' he told Mérimée, 'I couldn't think straight. I was borne down by an intolerable burden, powerless to take account of what I honestly felt. It's the worst of evils because it drains you of all energy. Afterwards, somewhat recovered from such oppressive weakness, I was singularly curious to know about her other infidelities and got her to tell me all the details. This had a terrible effect on me, but I gained a certain physical pleasure from imagining her in all the situations she described.'

The personal papers are eloquent by their virtual silence on this semi-farcical incident, the sort of thing which might well have been represented in some French erotic engraving of the eighteenth century, with the unnamed rival hastily buttoning his breeches, the guilty mistress clutching the edges of her flimsy peignoir and the shadowy figures of the baffled lover and the knowing chambermaid at one side. A disgruntled 'full of superlatives and empty of thought' appears in the journal entry of 4 September, followed immediately by 'weeping'. On 15 October he solemnly notes that love has been killed, and the next day records in English '*a great battle*', which took place after they had visited the Brera together with Gina's husband, but offers no precise details.

A last straw was presumably her attempt, at the end of December, to blackmail him. Stendhal's note on a letter from her using the all-too familiar ploy of blaming him for the break-up she herself had brought about through her infinite deviousness, records: 'On 22 December, I fancy, in the presence of Count Bolognini . . . . she told me she would denounce me to the police. Since this disgraceful threat, I have not seen her again.' Six months later, when he wrote this, he had entered that pleasing post-amorous condition well summarized by the Italian saying 'se tu non mi vuoi bene, non mi meriti' – 'if you don't love me, you don't deserve me' – pronouncing of 'Lady Simonetta' that 'her loss is immense, she will endure it for ever'.

Without the dimension of Gina, and transfigured by that sudden clarity of vision which the end of a love affair always induces, Stendhal's life in Milan now assumed an entirely different character and array of purposes. His sensibilities had leisure, for a significant interval, to absorb the cultural ferment of a city which, whatever the new Austrian government might do, still strove to hang on to the freedom and sophistication it had enjoyed in the halcyon decades of Verri, Parini and Beccaria immediately before the French Revolution and Napoleon's invasion. Taking whatever chances were offered by La Scala, with its succession of operatic premières and thrilling ballet performances under the direction of

Salvatore Viganò, the age's most imaginative choreographer, and by the Brera, where Beyle's aesthetic, for better or worse, corrected itself through direct encounters with the artists he was currently surveying in his *Histoire de la Peinture en Italie*, he began understanding more precisely the nature of his emotional response to art as a correlative to his experiences of love and friendship. The grand passion had still not overtaken him, but there is no suggestion that in 1816, so recently deluded, he felt much immediate need for its onset. In May of that year he returned to Grenoble for a six-week visit. Chérubin Beyle had grown more sympathetic to his son aged thirty-three than he was when the boy Henri belittled him with scorn and loathing twenty years earlier. He was still 'the bastard' or 'the Jesuit', and even though the city had made him its deputy mayor*, he was unlikely to go to his grave with much in the way of material support for the character of a prosperous bourgeois. The house he had built ten years earlier on the corner of Rue de Bonne and Place Grenette was being let or sold off storey by storey, while Chérubin, its real owner despite the terms of his crafty arrangement made during the abortive *majorat* scheme, hung on to the second floor.

While in France, Henri wrote to the faithful Louis Crozet, addressing him, in the game of pseudonyms, as 'M. Seyssins' (from a village near Grenoble) sending instructions as to the preparation of the *Histoire de la Peinture* for the press. The publisher, as with the recently issued *Haydn, Mozart & Metastasio*, was Didot *l'aîné*, and a two-volume edition was envisaged, with four plates by the engraver Landon, including one of the celebrated *Last Supper* by Leonardo da Vinci in the Milanese convent of Santa Maria delle Grazie. The book was to be priced as highly as possible, with advertisements placed in Belgian and Swiss newspapers. Though the journal seems to indicate that he had completed the entire work by February, further chapters on Roman art were added the following year, and it was only announced for publication in August 1817.

The same journal entry which speaks of 'having finished the

* The title, as given in Henri Martineau's *Calendrier de Stendhal* (1950), is 'adjoint faisant fonction de maire'.

History' mentions the fact that Stendhal was undergoing medical treatment involving regular letting of blood. Presumably what troubled him was a recurrence of the syphilis-related illnesses which had plagued him ever since his arrival in Paris in 1800, and which are mentioned in the detailed medical history he set out for his Milanese doctor, surviving in an Italian version in the library at Grenoble. Here he records his weight as ninety-four kilos, a severe pox caught in Vienna in 1809, something referred to as 'une grande peine morale' in December 1814, which he cured by drinking coffee and plentiful helpings of zabaglione, and the onset of a fever in January 1815 which is indicated as the cause of his journey to Padua and Venice 'for a change of air'. Further alarming symptoms, sweating, breathlessness, pains in the side, palpitations and heavy salivation, were treated by the routine mercury cure used for syphilitic sufferers, which in this case seems to have done little good.

Later sections of this medical autobiography take a more personal, indeed a more positively Stendhalian tone. He has, the doctor is told, 'always used and abused coffee, and his nervous sensibility appears excited to the point of morbidity. His pulse, always very strong, shows that we are dealing with a proud and robust organism.' His retreat to Italy after Napoleon's fall was 'in order not to experience too great a heartbreak'. When he receives agreeable visits or news his nervous pains in the arm disappear: 'boring people, on the other hand, increase his suffering forthwith'.

The doctor, presumably Giovanni Fossati, whom Beyle had met among Gina Pietragrua's admirers, sensibly prescribed a diet low on meat, high on vegetables, a quarter of a bottle of wine daily, one black coffee and two or three cups of cherry-stalk tisane. His further recommendation of daily doses of sarsaparilla, the dried root of the Jamaican *smilax officinalis*, echoed a similar treatment for syphilis administered eight years earlier by the eminent Anthelme Richerand, professor of surgical pathology at the Hôpital Saint-Louis in Paris. Having diagnosed certain growths at the base of Stendhal's penis as syphilitic, Richerand had prescribed two dozen frictions with Neapolitan mercury ointment, abstinence from coffee, strong drink and women, a regular mouthwash of vinegar and water, and a pint of sarsaparilla per day. 'This treatment, followed with care for six weeks will destroy the excrescences and cause the slow fever recurring each evening to disappear.'

The Milan to which Stendhal returned in midsummer of 1816 might scarcely have been the same city, so completely did his engagement with the place alter its direction. By a series of fortunate accidents he found himself removed from a position on the margins of Milanese life, an inconsiderable expatriate seeking to establish himself as a man of letters, to the very centre of what was at that moment the most exhilarating intellectual milieu in the whole of Europe, a place where the battles between theorists, polemicists and practical critics were no mere parochial skirmishes but genuine struggles for liberty in the most sinister climate of political oppression the modern world had hitherto experienced. For the first time Stendhal could confront the reality of art as a form of subversion, could face the challenge of partisan issues, could breathe a literary air more intoxicating by far, in its combativeness and danger, than anything he had encountered in Paris.

The collapse of Napoleonic hegemony in 1814 had been a bitter blow to the hopes of many young Italians who, even if they chafed at the heavy-handed interference of the French government machine, nevertheless saw it as a harbinger of progress in the shape of rational reform and a measure of secularization. In its place came the new orthodoxy of restored despotism, no longer personified by the benevolent sovereigns of the Ancien Régime, beguiling boredom with enlightened political and fiscal experiment, but represented instead by their largely inglorious and intellectually dim successors, creeping back into the recovered territories in a spirit which mingled obscurantism and vindictiveness with a perpetually nervous apprehension lest the seed sown by the Army of Italy, by Eugène de Beauharnais, Joachim Murat and Elisa Baciocchi in the name of their Emperor, should turn out after all to be dragon's teeth.

For leadership the kings and princes looked towards Austria, the dominant power in Italy for the next fifty years, to whose ruling Habsburg family they were all connected by ancestry or marriage, and which, under the guidance of Prince Metternich, set an unforgettable example in the exercise of ruthlessly centralized autocracy. Milan was now the capital of the imperial province of Lombardy, under the rule of civil and military governors, and every aspect of life among its citizens was monitored for potential dissidence. As the hold of censorship and surveillance tightened, it was natural enough that the intelligentsia, its numbers drawn substantially from among young aristocrats and the professional classes, should turn outwards, looking beyond Lombardy's frontiers for liberating inspirations.

Their redeemers – at least as it then seemed – were the Romantics of northern Europe, of Germany, England and France. Romanticism had come late to Italy, whose literary idiom, during the last decades of the eighteenth century, adhered more naturally to a sinewy, clean-limbed neoclassicism than to the gloom and vapours of the Gothic spirit world or to sentimental rhapsodizing amid wild nature. By 1814, however, the allure of the new sensibilty was pervasive and irresistible, and soon inevitably took on a more localized significance as the metaphor for the kind of political dissent which could not be expressed via the straightforward rhetoric of meetings, posters, oratory and pamphleteering. Add to this a mounting concern among writers and critics with the range of expressive possibilities manifested by literary Italian, as well as with its autonomous validity as a language, and we can begin to feel the pulse of a cultural volatility which Italy had not known since the sixteenth century.

Milan, both as a city which had visibly benefited from Napoleonic expansion and as the first major halt (Turin and Genoa hardly counted in this respect) on the foreigner's descent from the Alps into Italy proper, was ideally cast as epicentre in such an upheaval. The Lombard aristocracy, most enlightened and cosmopolite of the Italian peninsula, had sent its sons to Russia, Germany and France during the years of the Empire, and a whole network of contacts had thus been established with the prominent literati of Europe, centred upon the numinous figure of Madame de Staël in her Swiss refuge of Coppet on Lake Geneva. It was from Coppet indeed that the man who was to forge Stendhal's principal link with the world of Milanese Romanticism came home later that same summer of 1816, intoxicated with the international sophistication of De Staël's guest list, which had included Henry Brougham, the English liberal politician, Arnail-François de Jaucourt, Talleyrand's fellow envoy at the Congress of Vienna, the Polish Princess Jablonowska Walewska, and Matthew Gregory Lewis, author of the scandalously successful Gothic romance *The Monk*.

Their Italian fellow visitor was no less distinguished. Ludovico Arborio Gattinara di Breme was born in 1787, the son of a Piedmontese diplomat now consoling himself for the loss of his post as Interior Minister for the Kingdom of Italy with the philanthropic management of his estates in the valleys of the Lomellina, promoting scientific agriculture, vaccination and Lancastrian schools.* The education of his brilliant son was entrusted to the illustrious polymath Tommaso Valperga di Caluso, and at the age of nineteen Ludovico was made an *abbate* (a title given to young men of good family, permitted to perform priestly functions but not necessarily bound to an absolute celibacy). His connections were a decided advantage, securing for him the office of Court Almoner to the Viceroy, Eugène de Beauharnais, and the deputy governorship of the Corps of Pages, though his refusal, in 1813, of the bishopric of Cremona, ostensibly on a spiritual technicality, was more likely due to his increasing unease within a life of single blessedness.

Di Breme's penchant for romantic friendships with women – he was devoted, for example, to Prince Charles Edward Stuart's widow Louise von Stolberg, Countess of Albany, and was suspected by the poet Ugo Foscolo of being 'spiritually enamoured' of the Viceroy's wife, Princess Amalia of Bavaria – blossomed into a fully fledged passion for Countess Anna Porro Lambertenghi, whose sudden death (which he was suspected of causing) drove him into an intense religious crisis.

The healing process was supplied through a ferocious engagement with the new currents of Romanticism unlocked by the

* Schools using the pupil-teacher method for rapid learning on a system devised by Joseph Lancaster (1778–1838) and evidently much admired by Stendhal himself.

peace (however numbing this might have been in other respects) which now descended upon Europe. Though his two tragedies, *Ida* and *Ernestina*, were both pronounced failures, his literary-political essays and pamphlets, such as the *Grand Commentaire* (1817), a distillation of his liberal credo, and the *Postille*, or footnotes, written in the same year and designed as a riposte to Carlo Giuseppe Londonio's *Cenni critici sulla poesia romantica*, placed him at the forefront of the polemic battle line drawn up by the young Milanese *enragés*.

Di Breme's personal appeal was magnetic. Jean-Charles-Léonard Simond de Sismondi, the great Swiss historian, normally so severe in his judgements, described him as 'one of the men most clearly designed to do honour to his country in its moment of rebirth, to serve his fellow citizens, to enlighten them, to be associated with all the triumphs of the common cause, of liberty, morality and virtue . . . .' and the breadth and loyalty of his circle of friends offered further testimony to this notion of indwelling greatness poised to fulfil its promise. In Milan he was surrounded by the sharpest talents among the new generation, including the critic Pietro Borsieri, the poets Giovanni Berchet and Silvio Pellico and the future revolutionary hero Federico Confalonieri, as well as seeking the friendship of more established figures such as Vincenzo Monti, a poet whose talent and charm excused his Vicar-of-Bray-like leaps from one political bandwagon to the next.

Stendhal was introduced to Ludovico di Breme at some moment during the late summer of 1816. The mutual friend who brought them together was probably Carlo Guasco, a lawyer from Turin who seems to have spent much of his short life in Milan, keeping close links with liberal circles. From here it was a short step to an invitation to call on Di Breme in his box at La Scala, the usual social rendezvous for noble Milanese during the opera season, which in those days seems to have begun well before 'Sant'Ambrogio' (11 December, Saint Ambrose's Day) its customary inauguration from the mid-nineteenth century onwards.

How friendly they were can never exactly be gauged. Even allowing for Henri's tendency to exaggerate the significance of his more illustrious connections, it is worth pointing out that Di Breme was noted for the warmth and intensity with which he entered on even the most fleeting relationship. The Frenchman must have felt flattered indeed by the notice of somebody from an altogether different order of beings from those he had mixed with in the company of Angelina Pietragrua. However it was, he now became, for the first time in his life, the member of a distinguished coterie, a group of volatile creative spirits sensitive to the latest shifts in Romantic aesthetics and eagerly receptive of foreign ideas, not to speak of foreigners themselves.

The latter now descended on Milan in droves, generally having taken in a visit to Mme de Staël on their way through Switzerland, and Di Breme was unfailingly hospitable to them. Silvio Pellico told a friend that 'the *abbate*' had become 'a martyr, after his journey to Coppet, to his infinite acquaintance among the English, who besiege him either by letter or else in person.' Sismondi drily reported to the Countess of Albany that 'the swarm of English, whose flight into Italy we foretold, is now on the move'. So we can hardly be surprised that Stendhal should have wanted to make the most of whatever opportunities were thrown in his way through links with Di Breme and his brilliant circle, or at his excited reference, in a letter to Crozet on 28 September, to 'the luckiest chance in the world' which had brought him 'the acquaintance of *four or five Englishmen of the first rank and understanding*'.

Who these Englishmen were remains a mystery, though one of them must almost certainly have been Henry Brougham, among the most influential figures in the cultural and political landscape of early-nineteenth-century Britain. His visit to Italy in 1816 was an interlude in an astonishing career as a radical parliamentarian, lawyer, educationalist, journalist and social reformer*, but none of his biographers makes more than a passing reference to this European tour or suggests any direct connection with Stendhal. That the pair undoubtedly met, however, is implied by Brougham's inclusion in the list, set out in *Souvenirs d'Egotisme*, of those

* He was, among his other incarnations, founder of London University and Lord Chancellor during the Reform crisis of 1832.

in whom the author had instantly recognized greatness (the others were Napoleon, Byron, Canova, Rossini and Monti). According to the same work, they talked about suicide, Brougham disapproving of it because of the impertinent curiosity it would arouse among motive-hunting journalists.

If it really was Brougham who introduced Stendhal to the *Edinburgh Review*, then he performed a service of permanent value. The literary magazine, which the Whig politician himself had helped to found in 1802, was a leader of contemporary European liberal opinion, and its original critiques and extensive articles made it the equivalent in reputation of the *New York Review of Books* in our own day. There was nothing remotely comparable in France for sheer authority of critical impact. The effect on Stendhal was clearly devastating, the more so since this was his first important encounter both with Romanticism as a theoretical concept and with a literary tradition and analytical method which maintained an almost total independence from continental trends.

In the same letter to Crozet he acknowledged that most of the general ideas of any substance discussed in the *Histoire de la Peinture* were based on hints from the *Edinburgh Review*. 'Half of what we ourselves admire has been overturned in England.* We know nothing of their development since 1790, and they, without bothering overmuch with the Continent, have followed their own judgements.' He claims also to have tried reading the Tory-directed *Quarterly Review*, but to have found it flat in comparison. 'In a word, for the last two months a revolution has taken place in my ideas. I have met seven or eight people of distinction, both in rank and intelligence. My vanity has been flattered. They have delighted in my chatter. This has robbed me of my usual timidity towards those I esteem great men.'

His enthusiasm echoed through later correspondence with Crozet. Francis Jeffrey's article on Byron's Oriental tales, in *Edinburgh Review* No 45, was avidly seized upon as a riposte to

* It is no doubt necessary to point out that despite its provenance and authorship, the *Edinburgh Review* was nearly always referred to by European writers as English rather than Scotch.

the Teutonic nationalist obfuscations of Mme de Staël's eminent but more than somewhat ludicrous protégé August Wilhelm Schlegel, about whom Di Breme had many an amusing anecdote to retail. 'Eat one meal less so as to read at any rate some numbers of the *Edinburgh Review* . . . . In a word, don't buy any other book.'

By the time he wrote these words, Stendhal had achieved his major success in Milanese literary society, and one upon which he would capitalize unscrupulously for the rest of his life. 'I have dined,' he told Crozet, 'with a handsome and charming young man, his face an eighteen-year-old's, even though he is twenty-eight, with the profile of an angel . . . When he enters an English drawing room, all the women leave at once. He is the greatest living poet, Lord Byron.'

Byron's arrival in Milan on 12 October 1816 was the inevitable sequel to a sojourn on Lake Geneva, together with Percy Bysshe Shelley and his wife Mary Godwin, which had also involved a series of visits across the water to Mme de Staël. He had come abroad in the wake of his notorious separation from Annabella Milbanke, an episode which had set the seal both on his reputation as the sort of Romantic *monstre sacré* who, like Napoleon, existed to fulfil the desires and fantasies of his era, and on his fame as a poet, already prodigious in England and now acknowledged throughout Europe.

His companion on the southward journey from Switzerland was John Cam Hobhouse, the man who had acted as a go-between with Lady Byron during the breakdown of the marriage and who piqued himself on being her husband's most trusted friend. During their stay in Milan, lasting almost a month, Byron and Hobhouse visited the cathedral and the Ambrosian Library, where the poet managed to secure a lock of Lucrezia Borgia's hair, and admired Guercino's *Abraham Dismissing Hagar* in the Brera. The presence of this tremendous celebrity in the city was clearly a source of great excitement to Di Breme and his circle, who at once drew him into the sociable world of La Scala, where, as Byron told Thomas Moore, 'all society in Milan is carried on . . . . they have private boxes, where they play cards, or talk, or anything else; but (except at the Casino) there are no open houses, or balls &c &c.'

This was not strictly fair. Di Breme had indeed first made himself known to Byron and Hobhouse in their box, where the latter appraised him as:

> a young man about thirty, wears his dark hair combed upright, which gives him a wildness of expression not unlike that of Alfieri. He is, on the whole, one of the most attractive men I ever saw . . . He spoke with a certain degree of point on every subject, delivering his apothegms [sic] and ironies in the gravest tone and air, which made him quite irresistible.

A few days later Di Breme gave a grand dinner at his palace, Casa Roma, for 'a large party of young men', with Byron as the lion of the occasion. To a friend in Turin he described his chief guest as 'gloriosissimo successore dei Classicisti', a phrase which seems rather oddly applied to one of the more flamboyant icons of European Romanticism, unless Di Breme actually knew how much Byron longed to be thought of as the heir to Alexander Pope and the Augustan wits of early-eighteenth-century England.

The other guests included Vincenzo Monti, Silvio Pellico, Pietro Borsieri, Giovanni Berchet, the Genoese patron of letters Gian Carlo Di Negro, and '*il dottissimo* Hobhouse' who noted in his diary the presence of 'a M. de Beyle, one of Napoleon's secretaries. Unfortunately, I had hardly a word with him.' The excellent dinner was enlivened by the behaviour of Monti, who started haranguing the company on the virtues of ancient literature, a signal for the younger Italians to begin teasing and winding him up, apparently very easy to do. Afterwards they adjourned to the theatre, where Hobhouse rallied Monti on his reluctance 'to sing the liberties of Italy' and Byron compared the old man to the portrait of Garrick.

A few days later, in Di Breme's box, they met Stendhal again (this time Hobhouse wrote him down as 'secretary of Napoleon's Cabinet'), who told them stories of the retreat from Moscow and anecdotes concerning Napoleon and those connected with him. He spoke of the Emperor's despondency and mental confusion as the army left Russia, of Murat sitting up in bed weeping when his master left him to take over as commander-in-chief, of the inscription Ney's wife had set on the Marshal's tomb after his execution – 'Trente-cinq ans de gloire, un jour d'erreur' – and been made to expunge by the police. He told them about the Emperor Francis of Austria's passion for sealing wax and 'employ in painting eyes at the bottom of ladies' chamber-pots, to which he gave a *regard fripon*'. He talked of the terrible dysentery that had seized the army at Königsberg, 'about 45,000 men who were half the day at stool . . . bedevilled by the extreme cold. The Prince Major-General Berthier, having pulled down his breeches for his occasions, could not button them again. Exelmans, who pulled off a glove to do it, lost the use of one of his fingers instantly'. He spoke of having heard the Marquis de Sade calling from his asylum window at Charenton, and of Napoleon's habit, while working in his study, of making love to the ladies of his court in order to assure himself of their husband's loyalty.

'I have every reason to think that Beyle is a trustworthy person,' wrote Hobhouse, adding with the characteristic censoriousness of somebody whose own ambivalent sexuality was kept firmly suppressed, 'However, he has a cruel way of talking, and looks, and is, a sensualist.' The fact was that nearly everything Stendhal told them was either second or third-hand gossip, or else an outright lie. It seems likely that, as one modern Byron authority has suggested, Beyle's head was turned by his association with this distinguished company and that he felt an understadable need to project himself a little more emphatically in order to remain on equal terms with them. In no time at all, therefore, the Intendant du Mobilier de la Couronne, who met his Emperor on two occasions only, was transformed into an imperial secretary 'in waiting on Napoleon on the Russian expedition' and in an advantageous position to comment on his behaviour.

Not long afterwards Stendhal was once more directly involved with Byron and Hobhouse in the most dramatic episode attending their stay in Milan. When Byron originally set out from England, he had brought with him as a personal physician Dr John William Polidori, a young man of Italian parentage with whom he amicably parted company in Switzerland after the hotheaded

Polidori had got into various unspecified 'scrapes'. Arriving in Milan, the doctor soon made friends with Di Breme, whom he praised for his charity, studiousness and warmth of character, and several members of his coterie, including Pietro Borsieri, 'a man of great mental digestive power and memory, superficially read', Carlo Guasco, praised for his 'vision and talents' and 'De Beyle', described as 'a fat, lascivious man'. He was present too at the Casa Roma dinner on 17 October.

On the evening of the 19th, while standing in the pit at La Scala, he quarrelled with an Austrian officer who churlishly declined to remove his cap, large enough to block Polidori's view of the stage. He was summarily hauled off to the guardroom attached to the theatre, where in a few minutes Byron, Hobhouse, Di Breme and Guasco, alerted by Borsieri, who had witnessed the episode, came down from the boxes and attempted to reason with the offended officer. The latter, according to Hobhouse, treated the Italians with contempt but civilly accepted Byron's guarantee for Polidori's reappearance at the guardroom next morning. Attempts to soften official outrage at the affront were unavailing – Byron's letters suggest that he was seriously concerned by the incident – and Polidori was given notice by the government to leave Milan forthwith. He and Di Breme exchanged affectionate farewells ('when parting from him, I wept like a child in his arms') before the young rebel, 'not a bad fellow, but . . . more likely to incur diseases than cure them' as Byron said, went south to Arezzo to look up his father's family.

Stendhal had also been present that night in the guardroom, and his fertile ingenuity, wasting nothing in the way of recollected experience, was later to make much of what he heard and saw, both on this occasion and throughout Byron's stay in Milan. When the first version of *Rome, Naples et Florence* appeared in September 1817, some account of a meeting with the poet was duly included, set, for some reason, in Venice at the Teatro della Fenice, featuring a rhapsodic account of the 'figure céleste' and 'beaux yeux' of 'le joli homme de génie', gleefully hinting at the scandal surrounding his marriage, mentioning his scholarly aptness in learning languages, and ending 'in his place, I should pass myself off as having died, and begin a new life as Mr Smith, merchant of Lima'. We must make what we can of the fact that this episode is omitted from the 1826 version of the book.

Byron eventually secured a copy of *Rome, Naples et Florence* and on 29 May 1823 sent Stendhal a letter from Genoa to thank him for so flattering a mention, but taking issue with a denigrating reference to Sir Walter Scott in the French writer's recently published *Racine et Shakespeare*. The letter is a curious one, couched in what at first seems a decidedly un-Byronic style, but one which is obviously meant to make it easier to read for someone whose first language is not English. Since the manuscript original has never been traced, and the writer fulsomely describes Beyle as 'one of whose good opinion I was really ambitious', the sceptical reader is tempted towards the intriguing possibility that Stendhal might have connived at a Byronian forgery. The extensive rejoinder he composed could well, if viewed in this light, have been intended to demonstrate the admirable consistency of his own liberal stance, invoking as it does Scott's high regard for royalty and acceptance of a title as suitable reasons for disapproving of him.

There is no hard evidence, however, with which to catch Stendhal in quite so blatant an act as that of faking Byron. Once the latter had died, he was content merely to elaborate on their former association and to place himself in a far closer relationship to the poet than had actually been the case during October 1816. On Byron's death in 1824, one of those who rushed into print with a biography was Anne Louise Swanton Belloc, an Irishwoman married and settled in France and earning her living as a translator of children's books. Asking Stendhal for any stray recollections, she was given in reply an extended memoir, which took the whole issue a crucial stage further. The meeting in the box was now relocated at La Scala, that evening's opera was identified as Johann Simon Mayr's *Elena*, which had indeed been one of the 1816 season's successes, and Stendhal admitted that he had 'implored M. di Breme to introduce me' after having gazed in admiration at Byron's beautiful eyes as he listened to the music.

Some mention of the great banquet follows, during which, says Stendhal, Monti delighted Byron by reciting a canto of a poem on the death of a fellow writer, Luigi Mascheroni. Stendhal goes on to offer what many of the noble lord's more detached admirers would regard as an extremely shrewd assessment of the essential flaws in his character, traits to which others besides a little fat French nobody, met on one or two occasions during a short stay in Milan, would draw attention. The distinction Beyle makes is fundamentally the same as that so memorably enshrined in Goethe's judgement on Byron 'only as a poet is he a man: once he starts thinking he becomes a child'. Fired by enthusiasm, he matched his genius with lofty sentiments, but at more prosaic moments he was vain, fearful of looking ridiculous, ready to compromise so as to win approval and not altogether free of that cant he so vehemently attacked in his satires. Added to these faults was an inordinate pride in his ancestry. 'One point which struck the Italians,' says Stendhal, 'was that this great poet plainly thought it far more important to be a descendant of those Norman Byrons who followed William the Conqueror to England than to be the author of *Parisina* and *Lara*.'

Six years after his Byronic reminiscences for Anne Swanton Belloc, Stendhal refurbished the material for an article, *Lord Byron en Italie*, published in English in *The Foreign Literary Gazette*, reprinted in *The Mirror* (a sort of *Reader's Digest* of the age) and subsequently added to John Galt's catchpenny life of the poet published in 1830. To his earlier memorial he now added material from an essay sent to his cousin Romain Colomb in 1829, but the final printed version showed him to still greater advantage. Whereas in the study written for Colomb's perusal he presented himself as a shy, susceptible 'man of sensibility' ready to dissolve into tears and kiss the beautiful poet's hand, in *Lord Byron en Italie* he became the man whom the noble lord most wanted to meet, 'a stranger who had performed the celebrated campaign of Moscow'. The pair were represented as meeting often thereafter, discussing such topics as Rousseau, Henri IV's execution of the Duc de Biron, and the charms of Milanese women seen passing the doors of La Scala after the performance.

Surely the most indignant reader of the 1830 article in its position as an appendix to Galt's biography was the man in whose company Byron had visited Milan in 1816, John Cam Hobhouse. The book itself was bad enough, a sneering depiction of the poet's personality and career by a Tory hack whose only genuine talent, as the author of such brilliant Scotch genre novels as *The Entail* and *Annals of the Parish*, was now harnessed to the business of belittling the Whig peer, enemy of legitimism and champion of liberty. To find tacked onto the back of this farrago a Byron portrait purporting to be by 'M. Stendhal, a gentleman of literary celebrity in France', in Galt's phrase, was more than Hobhouse could stomach, and he now sat down to tear the offending article to pieces.

Point by point he demolished all semblance of authenticity in the account. There was no such person as 'M. Stendhal', merely 'a certain M. de Beyle' whose 'two trumpery volumes containing his supposed adventures in Italy .... have not procured him "literary celebrity" in either France or England'. Everything, it seemed, was wrong with his facts. Byron was not at Milan in 1817, the two men were not first introduced at the opera, Byron never walked arm in arm with Stendhal and was not lodging in an obscure quarter of the city to which his newly acquired French acquaintance used to walk him home through 'a multitude of intricate, suspicious-looking streets'. As for Beyle's description of the circumstances surrounding Polidori's arrest, Hobhouse systematically shoots this down as melodramatic moonshine.

Does any of this really matter? Hobhouse's objections were never published: some years later he scribbled on the manuscript with enigmatic gloom: 'I wrote all this at a time when I thought the subject of much more importance than I now know it to be.' The three states of Stendhal's Byron record – the Belloc memoir, the letter to Colomb and *Lord Byron en Italie* – have been reprinted on various occasions, and the spirit, if not the factual essence of it, has been used to feed the voluminous central current of Byron studies. The whole Stendhal–Byron issue has merely served to polarize those intense, all-or-nothing loyalties which both writers apparently inspire. *Stendhaliens* will not allow you to call Henri Beyle a fibber, which in this case he unquestionably was, and Byronists refuse to acknowledge the implicit significance and literary interest attaching to Stendhal's cavalier treatment of their hero's Milanese sojourn.

Both positions miss the point – besides which, one is always inclined to doubt the good sense of people for whom those they admire as artists must be held morally infallible as human beings. The fact is that Stendhal, having lied to Byron *in propria persona* was not going to pass up the opportunity of lying *about* him after his death. Attempts at picking holes in Stendhal's testimony, of the sort made in 1830 by Hobhouse and a century later by the doyenne of Byron studies, Doris Langley Moore, merely reinforce the impression that Beyle the romancing *romancier* has somehow delivered a more authentic portrait in its finished effect than most biographers could have contrived with the accumulation of carefully checked detail. Nobody animated by a genuine interest in Byron, reading Stendhal's three sketches, can fail to admire their acute penetration of the flaws which made Byron's character interesting to his contemporaries. His typically aristocratic, uniquely English horror of appearing too much the poet as opposed to the Regency man of the world, and the evident importance he attached to his rank and ancestry, are noted as perceptively as that fondness for music which, for whatever reason, he was at pains to conceal in public, or his pleasure in an attractive woman.

If these are works of fiction, then their fictive process is Stendhalian, which renders it rather different from that of contemporaries like Scott, Jane Austen and Balzac. The author has not imagined a meeting with Byron – that reality is both advantageous and immutable – but has perceived at once the essentially plastic, protean quality of its outlines in response to the changing demands made upon it by his imagination. This is 'Stendhal's Byron', no less true in its author's realignment of the facts surrounding their meeting than the original as sketched for us by Thomas Moore, Edward Trelawny or any other of the poet's memorialists. A novelist well beyond the confines of his novels, Stendhal has as much right as any other distinguished practitioner of the genre to do as he sees fit with the materials offered him by experience and vicissitude: we can scarcely blame him for declining to pass up so remarkable an opportunity as this one.

An ironic postscript to the whole episode may be added here. On 15 August 1820, only four years after Byron's visit to Milan, Ludovico di Breme died of a lingering consumption, whose details, including the exact number of blood driblets expelled by his most recent coughing fit, were gruesomely recounted in a letter to Silvio Pellico. Stendhal, in the 1830 Byron article, pays him an affectionate tribute, as:

> a young man of considerable tallness and very thin, already suffering from the chest complaint which was to send him to his grave. . . . His slender, sad face was like those of marble statues to be found on Italian tombs of the eleventh century. I seem to see him yet, mounting the immense staircase in the sombre and magnificent palace of which his father had given him the use.

For various reasons (see p. 238) Stendhal, during the period of the *abbate's* last illness, had fallen foul of the illustrious Milanese literary circle, and in a letter dated 30 August 1820, accused them somewhat implausibly of being jealous of his success with the *Histoire de la Peinture*, published three years earlier. 'The abbé de Breme, their leader,' he wrote, 'has recently died of frustration at being nothing and from a flux of the lungs.' His cynical identification of a partial cause of Di Breme's death was not altogether wrong. It was widely believed that his suffering had been exacerbated by a controversy over a crotchety polemic essay, 'On the Present Literature of Italy', which had appeared as a follow-up to an edition of Byron's *Childe Harold's Pilgrimage*, published in 1818. This not merely made light of the current Romantic-versus-Classic controversy, but entirely failed to mention the Italian Romantic's leading campaigner, Di Breme himself. The essay's real author was the notoriously edgy and quarrelsome Italian poet Ugo Foscolo, then living in Surrey*, who had written it at the request of an English occasional man of letters keen to pass himself off as an expert. This *soi-disant* critic, egged on by Byron (maliciously content to ignore the honours done him by his erstwhile Milanese host) and only too pleased to wound Di Breme's *amour propre* still further, was none other than John Cam Hobhouse.

* His house at East Molesey was called Digamma Cottage, alluding to his Greek parentage and his translations from the classics.

CHAPTER 8

LE ROMAN DE METILDE

For the whole of January and February 1817 Stendhal was looking at paintings in Rome and Naples while working on the closing chapters of the *Histoire de la Peinture en Italie*. Neither the journals and marginal jottings nor the extant correspondence, chiefly concerned during this period with instructions to the long-suffering Louis Crozet as to preparing the text for the press, say much about the trip. We know Henri caught cold looking at Raphael's Stanze in the Vatican, that at Naples he attended an indifferent performance of a bad opera, Pietro Carlo Guglielmi's *Paolo e Virginia* at the Teatro dei Fiorentini, and that in the same city he met and talked with an American merchant, George Alexander Otis of Boston, 'very likeable and kindly, full of worldly wisdom and rare intelligence'.

Otherwise the impressions gleaned during this two-month southern tour were to be mingled with recollections of his 1811 journey to form a substantial early portion of *Rome, Naples et Florence en 1817*, published in September of this year. Now Stendhal could watch other restored regimes, Papal and Bourbon, in action and judge them beneath an unsparing but always alert gaze. In Rome's Teatro Valle he read the police regulations with grim amusement:

> a hundred strokes, instantly administered on the permanent scaffold in Piazza Navona . . . . for the spectator who takes another's place; *five years in the galleys* [author's italics] for anyone raising his voice against the attendant distributing the seats . . . . I shall copy down this police ordinance to justify myself against accusations of too much contempt for ecclesiastical government.

Nevertheless he early came to admire the upright and honest papal chief minister Ercole, Cardinal Consalvi, whom he praised as 'simple, reasonable, obliging; and, to end with a great characteristic, almost incredible in France, he is no hypocrite', later exclaiming 'Good God! why hasn't England a minister like this?'

Though he claims, in both versions of *Rome, Naples et Florence*, to have attended the opening of the new San Carlo opera house in Naples on 12 January 1817, Beyle had arrived in the city twelve days later, but seems thereafter to have spent almost every evening in the magnificently appointed theatre, with its gilt and silvered stucco decoration, its blue satin-upholstered boxes and the clock above the proscenium arch which told the time *à la française* as opposed to the old Italian way of counting the hours from the preceding evening's Angelus. He admired the French dancer Louis Duport, heard without much pleasure Rossini's *Otello* (the role of Desdemona was sung by the composer's mistress and later first wife, Isabella Colbran) and fretted at the petty snobbery and pomposity with which the establishment was managed:

> You wander through the corridors; the most pompous of titles inscribed on the box doors admonish you, in large characters, that you are but a mere citizen. You walk in with your hat on your head: some hero of Tolentino* pursues you. La Conti enchants you with her dancing and you want to applaud: the King's presence prevents you. You try to get a nobleman, festooned with orders, whose chamberlain's key has got entangled with your watch chain, to move from your seat in the parterre: mutterings of 'lack of respect'. Bored by all this ceremony, you leave and call for your carriage: the six horses of some princess or other are stopping the way, so you must wait and catch cold.

If Naples was not quite a city of the heart in the same exalted degree as Milan, Stendhal, like all other travellers at this time, was entranced by the beauty of a place which, 'despite its three hundred and forty thousand inhabitants, is like a country house in the midst of a fine landscape'. The celebrated Neapolitan *lazza-*

* An ironic allusion to the defeat by the Austrians of a Neapolitan army under Joachim Murat at Tolentino in 1815.

roni, the half-naked rag-tag-and-bobtail mob of beggars and loafers which amused the tourists, were somewhat shocking to him at first, but, as he soon realized, they were rascals from poverty rather than from naturally bad disposition.

In April, a month after his return from Milan, Henri set off for Grenoble. He never returned to his native city with an especially good grace, but under the present circumstances he could scarcely have stayed away. On 14 December 1816 his brother-in-law François Périer-Lagrange had been found dead in the bedroom of an inn at La Tour du Pin, north-west of Grenoble. There was a strong likelihood that he had committed suicide as the result of general failure, whether as a landowner (he had bought a small estate at Thuellin, in the Rhône valley) as a financial speculator or as a husband. Stendhal had never much cared for François and was unlikely to have viewed his departure with special regret. Theoretically Pauline was now free, a widow who could indulge her freaks of cross-dressing to her heart's content and wander where she wished in pursuit of happiness at her brother's side. As things transpired, her husband left hideous complications behind him, and what now ensued was a sordid chronicle of provincial litigation between Pauline and various disappointed creditors, worthy of forming an episode in Balzac's *La Comédie Humaine*.

From Grenoble, Stendhal went on to Paris, presumably to oversee the final stages of preparing the *Histoire de la Peinture en Italie* for the press. For at least a year Louis Crozet had been kept busy with fragments of the text, whether as copy editor and proofreader or as critic, fact checker and go-between with the publisher, Pierre Didot the elder, and the engraver, Charles-Paul Landon. The meticulous attention to detail shown in Stendhal's correspondence foreshadows his dealings as a consul with his browbeaten subordinates. In a single letter, written to Crozet on 16 June 1816, he raps out orders as to the page distribution between the two volumes, the running titles, the cost of Landon's engravings, the first advertisement for the book, the cover price and the advance publicity outside France.

Crozet himself had had something to say on the subject of the work's overall style and tone, and his perceptions were not always likely to please Henri Beyle. Reading a first bundle of manuscript in late January 1816, he observed:

> Your lively remarks don't just scratch, they bite. Excellent, no doubt, for us and you, bad for the common herd, cruel and dangerous for those in authority over this herd. . . . When Dominique [Stendhal's favourite pseudonym among his intimates] wants to disguise his thoughts, a savage irony becomes visible at once, in the most striking fashion. In the light of this, it seems hardly surprising that all our pensioned historians and writers on politics and manners should so completely have emasculated their thoughts, facts and observations that their works are empty, utterly empty.

The experience of coping, not merely with the technical operation of getting the *Histoire de la Peinture* into print, but with Stendhal's creative labour pains in connection with a work to which he attached such enormous significance, was probably more than Crozet could bear, and it certainly represented the severest test the friendship ever made on his devotion. It may indeed have been this which effectively dampened the intimacy between them, but it is just as likely to have been Crozet's recent marriage to a cousin, Praxède Payan. Stendhal's bachelor loneliness made him easily resentful of his friends' disposition to marry. 'Ask the charming Praxède,' he wrote a month or so before the wedding on 21 December 1816, 'not to rob me altogether of your heart. I have lost four fifths of *Happy's by his wife*.' '*Happy*' was of course Félix Faure, from whom Henri, ostensibly for political reasons, would at length become determinedly alienated. He never lost Crozet's friendship, but their correspondence more or less dried up after the publication of the *Histoire de la Peinture*, and this seems to be yet another example of Stendhal wringing a relationship to the last drop before throwing it aside as irrelevant to his immediate demands.

Crozet's fears as to the possible reception of the *Histoire* were not unfounded. The political mood of the restored Bourbon regime, whatever the benign disposition of its fat, jolly figurehead, Louis XVIII, had hardened after Waterloo, as a wave of reaction swept across France. One minor but interesting manifestation of this desire to return to the *status quo ante* was the official revival of the old-fangled orthography in which endings in 'ais' or 'ait' were changed to 'ois' or 'oit'. Writing to Crozet from Rome in January 1817, Stendhal raged against such pedantic absurdity as 'the thing which makes me most sick at heart'.

When the book was finally announced, on 2 August 1817, its author was merely a set of initials, 'M.B.A.A.', which have been taken to signify 'Monsieur Beyle Ancien Auditeur', though Stendhal was happy to confuse matters a little further by sending out complimentary copies signed 'B.A. Aubertin'. The volumes were dedicated, for motives which do little credit to his political integrity, to 'the greatest of living sovereigns' – not, as we might at first suppose, Napoleon, but Tsar Alexander I of Russia, from whom the author may perhaps have expected something in the way of an emolument along the lines of the traditional purse of guineas handed out by patrons in the previous century, or even a small job at the court of St Petersburg.

More significant than this in Stendhalian terms is the epigram which appears in the second of the work's two volumes. In a letter to Crozet in 1816, Stendhal had explained the practical reasons for a dedication to '*his northern Majesty*', basically deriving from a panic-stricken reaction to the possibility that 'the Jesuit', as he called his father, might live to a great old age and baulk him of an inheritance. 'If the old jesuit goes till 82,' he wrote in English, 'I prefer to go as a professor in Russia.' He went on to specify 'in lapidary style and lettering, on the page following the title, these words: "*To the happy few*". It has been my plan for the past two years. It explains the whole book. I dedicate the work to sensitive souls. People like Mgr. Z [Pierre Daru] won't understand it at all, and it will be hateful to them.'

The phrase 'the happy few', used here for the first time in Stendhal's works, but more familiar to modern readers in its place as the epigram for *La Chartreuse de Parme*, has traditionally been derived from Henry V's famous Agincourt speech in the fourth act of Shakespeare's eponymous play, in which the king invokes the concept of 'We few, we happy few, we band of brothers'. It was the French critic Paul Hazard who discovered, however, a more likely provenance in the second chapter of Oliver Goldsmith's *The Vicar of Wakefield*, where the engagingly naïve Doctor

Primrose admits to having published some tracts on monogamy 'which, as they never sold, I have the consolation of thinking are read only by the happy *Few*'. The novel was a particular favourite of Stendhal's: it figures in the list of English books he asked Pauline to send him at Marseilles in the autumn of 1805, he later claimed to have learned English from getting its opening pages by heart, and he was to make playful use of it on the title pages of the three manuscript volumes of *La Vie de Henry Brulard* – 'roman imité du *Vicaire de Wakefield* surtout pour la pureté des sentiments' et cetera – both to bamboozle the police and to baffle the reader's expectations as to the kind of work concealed within.

Who were, or are, 'the happy few'? Stendhalians, more specifically French *stendhaliens*, tend to use the term as the ultimate accolade of honourable service to Beyle's cause in the pages of *Stendhal Club* or of a learned monograph published by Editions du Grand Chêne. Beyle himself clearly intended the sort of reader who would grasp at once, without a need for plodding explication, the spirit and thrust of his writing, and whose temper, vision and sympathy were essentially in tune with his own. In this context, the word 'happy' is as strong a signifier as 'few'. Each plainly represents a call into the dark by the solitary pursuer of *le bonheur*, whose only real ally, when friends consistently failed to meet his expectations, was the notional kindred spirit brought into being by the books themselves.

The work now submitted to the judgement of the happy few was, and has remained, among the least accessible of Stendhal's achievements. The *Histoire de la Peinture en Italie* has never been popular, either with writers on Stendhal or with aestheticians chronicling the shifts in nineteenth-century artistic taste which led to the evolution of those criteria by which we now assess Italian medieval and Renaissance painting. The nature of the book itself is inherently frustrating. Originally projected as an elaboration of Luigi Antonio Lanzi's *Storia pittorica*, it was to have been developed, with the aid of a host of different sources including Giorgio Vasari's famous *Lives*, the works of Giuseppe Bossi and Giovanni Bellori, and the aesthetic studies of Richard Payne Knight and Johann Winckelmann, into a full-scale history, encompassing all the major Italian schools and ending with an assessment of the contemporary scene as represented by the sculptor Canova and the painter Andrea Appiani.

There was no likelihood that so entirely orthodox a project would ever have been completed by someone as wedded as Henri Beyle to the principle of not having to do things in the manner approved and followed by everyone else. It does not require much deep searching among his works to perceive that for a man with his boasted passion for 'la logique', and what some might feel was a typically French enthusiasm for pigeon-holing ideas and systematizing observations, he was among the most maddeningly inconsistent, crotchet-ridden of writers, uninterested, for long stretches of a book, in form, relevance or proportion, and guided solely by an unswerving conviction in the validity of whatever intellectual or emotional imperative happened to be dominant at the moment of writing. The three major works of his earliest phase as a published author, the *Histoire*, the travel book (which of course is not really that at all) *Rome, Naples et Florence en 1817* and *De l'Amour*, a creation of such weird, lonely singularity that it becomes hard to assign it to the nineteenth century, let alone to 1822, are all in this highly personal, fragmented form, developments from the journal-keeping of the previous decade which he now significantly abandoned.

What the purchaser of the *Histoire de la Peinture en Italie* acquired was a highly selective account of Florentine painting, culminating in studies of Leonardo and Michelangelo, interspersed with Stendhal's own, often calculatedly subversive comments on Italian political and socio-historical trends, comparative culture among modern European nations, the relationship of aesthetics to society, and the achievements of Napoleon Bonaparte, a figure whose potential for glamour among European liberals had vastly increased since his exile to St Helena, and with whom Stendhal was now starting to explore an interesting affinity.

Stendhal always claimed that he had lost the dozen volumes of his original version of Lanzi's *Storia*, dictated to a Parisian copyist named Fougeol, while in Russia during the campaign of 1812. What in fact seems to have happened was that Fougeol, on Stendhal's return, was able to make a second copy from his earlier manuscripts, but that the author, instead of publishing the straight translation as it stood, chose to take the first part of the work as an armature on which to build his own book, a mixture of direct plagiarism in the manner of *Haydn, Mozart & Metastasio*, discourses on the nature of ideal beauty, modern or antique, and essays on individual artists in which the most conspicuous feature was the meticulously wrought style over whose precision he repeatedly badgered Crozet.

To claim, as certain of Stendhal's biographers have done, that the *Histoire* is not authentic Beyle, simply because so much of it derives from other men's labours, is unfair to the author and his intentions. Even if this is not a history of painting pure and simple, even if its *raison d'être* is more obviously that of a cultural manifesto, powerfully influenced by Stendhal's sensitivity to the interlocking currents of literature and politics in post-Napolenoic Milan, he has arresting observations to make on the art and civilization he discusses, and the sheer unconventionality of the work, let alone the impact of its subliminal messages, excited several of his more perceptive contemporary readers.

If, for example, he was not the earliest to grasp the significance of Masaccio as a genius whose brief career marked a *terminus post quem* in the history of painting, he was surely the first to assert it so incontrovertibly, in his twentieth chapter. On Michelangelo he is, to put it at its feeblest, convincing because he has immersed himself in the aesthetic process he so movingly describes in Chapter CLIII, documenting, as though on film, the evolution of sensibility to the point at which it can adequately apprehend the full potency of the Sistine frescoes. We arrive in Rome uncertain of what to see and in danger of admiring what we do not actually enjoy: he tells us therefore to go and look at Raphael's scenes from the story of Psyche in the Villa Farnesina as a preparation for appreciating fresco, then, after two or three visits here, to inspect Annibale Carracci's paintings on the walls of Palazzo Farnese, and after that, to test our resilience by sampling the work of the immensely admired eighteenth-century painter Anton Raffael Mengs in the Papyrus Room of the Vatican Library.

'If this ceiling, in all its limpidity and mannered grace, gives you more pleasure than the Carracci gallery, you should halt, for such a preference is not founded on any spiritual difference, but on your own defective vision. A fortnight later, you can return to Raphael's Stanze.' Only after a month of cultural saturation in Rome, trying to acclimatize your northern soul to the Italian instinct for seeing, will you be ready to raise your eyes to the Sistine ceiling. And it is at this point that Stendhal invokes the personal connection with the work of art itself which validates the book and makes its more pedestrian pages worth enduring. 'Greek sculpture,' he declares:

> never tried to produce terrifying effects: there were too many misfortunes in the real life surrounding it. Nothing in the whole domain of art, therefore, can be compared to the figure of the Supreme Being creating the first man out of the void. Attitude, drawing, drapery, everything is striking, and the soul becomes stirred by impressions to which the eye is unaccustomed. When, during our unhappy retreat from Russia, we suddenly awoke in the midst of a dark night to the sound of persistent cannon fire, seeming closer every moment, every faculty was concentrated upon the heart, for we were face to face with destiny; heedless of petty cares, we prepared to engage with fatality on behalf of our own lives. The sight of Michelangelo's paintings revived in me this half-forgotten sensation. Noble souls are self-sufficient, while others are frightened and run mad.

Not merely is such a paragraph worth volumes of scholastic outpouring, the kind of reaction to art which we remember when all the minute enquiry into iconography and documentation has faded into footnotes, but there is something magnificent in the implied concept of Stendhal measuring his greatness against that of Michelangelo and not necessarily finding it wanting. He may indeed have had scant sensitivity to colour, composition or any of the other purely technical aspects of painting, yet he had grasped the essential truth that art speaks through emulation, challenging us to match its responses with our own, and, at its best, knowing us for what we are. He perceived the nature of those bonds and dispositions, love, despotism, religion, politeness, which shape the demands a society makes on its artists, and he refused to divorce creativity from the traditions, racial, climatic, spiritual and political, nurturing its development and inspiring its reactions. Though we should be going too far in hailing such a diffuse, ill-regulated work as the *Histoire de la Peinture en Italie* as a major document in modern cultural history, its position as a distinguished forerunner of Burckhardt or Berenson (though the latter poured scorn on Stendhal's visual criteria) is secure, and the book drew its share of discerning admirers, Baudelaire and Delacroix among them, during the first half of the nineteenth century.

Its initial reception, however, was hardly the triumph for which the author had hoped. One of Stendhal's most endearing qualities was a certain unquenchable innocence, a naïveté which transcended the cynical air of the man of the world which had so dismayed the buttoned-up Hobhouse in Di Breme's box at La Scala. He seems genuinely to have believed that the 'opiskile' (opuscule) as he jokingly referred to the book, would make his reputation among the European intelligentsia, and it is safe to presume that had this indeed been the case, further volumes might have appeared in due course. Though he had told Crozet that he could not be bothered, at the age of thirty-four, to spend time which might be devoted to *Letellier* on preparing new instalments of the *Histoire*, he took care to include in the printed prospectus an indication that 'the three final volumes will appear directly' and sketched out a more detailed announcement to be placed at the end of the published work. As it turned out, the remaining sections, covering Venice, Rome, Lombardy and Bologna, were only preserved, after his death, through the good offices of his cousin Romain Colomb, and made public in 1932 by Henri Martineau as *Ecoles italiennes de la peinture*.

Only two reviews appeared in Parisian newspapers during the six months following publication. The first, on 23 September 1817, in *Le Moniteur Universel*, was by Louis Crozet, praising the author as an 'enemy of servile imitation' who 'desires the artist to search for the ideal of beauty within his own soul', extolling the book for being 'rich in observations, fresh thoughts and inspired guesses', but having the good sense to single out such faults as his friend's tendency to skip from one idea to the next without adequate transition and his penchant for unseasonable jokes. The other, in the *Journal des Débats* for 6 March 1818, and purporting to be by the journalist and police spy Joseph Lingay, was probably the work of Stendhal himself. After a mealy-mouthed eulogy of Louis XVIII, 'Lingay' settles down to the business of singling out the work's particular merits, emphasizing the distinction of the chapters on the antique ideal of beauty, and pointing out that the *Histoire de la Peinture* 'contains very few phrases which one might suppose to have seen anywhere else. . . .' He draws attention to the singular qualities of the writer's style and claims that the book is being widely read and discussed. Was Stendhal also the only begetter of the apparently solemn riposte to this review which appeared in the *Débats* three days later, accusing him of 'insulting the principles of sound politics and outraging the maxims of the healthiest morality', of casting aspersions on King Francis I and of referring to Antinous in terms of such revolting perversion 'that we should blush in transcribing the relevant quotation'? Even if he had not read *The Critic*, he had certainly mastered all the techniques of Sheridan's Mr Puff.

Otherwise the critical silence was unnerving. Paul Arbelet, in his essay on the book's sources, is doubtless correct in claiming that those who might have been expected to take an interest in it either failed to grasp the novelty of Stendhal's ideas or, more likely still, had never bothered to open either of the two volumes. Some readers, however, took it seriously from the outset. We know, for instance, that it was studied by Alphonse Rabbe, the golden boy of early French Romanticism whose career of brilliant literary promise foundered in syphilitic horrors, and by Stendhal's former colleague in the preparation of the Louvre inventory for Napoleon, Vivant Denon. Another who gave it the minutest attention was the distinguished figure of Alexandre Lenoir, whose Musée des Monuments français was based on the collection of sculpture he had succeeded in rescuing from the iconoclastic fury of the Revolution. The conclusion of his manuscript annotations to a passionate amateur, a virtuoso in description, who had published his personal journal under 'a title calculated to provoke curiosity'. Stendhal's critical judgements, thought Lenoir, were the feeblest part of the book, interesting, lively, but useless to artists, even if the Leonardo and Michelangelo sections were admirable. With great shrewdness he suggested that it should really be called *Voyage en Italie suivi de quelques observations sur les arts*.

It was to be over a year before the critical approval Beyle most sought was given him in the pages of the *Edinburgh Review*. The importance of finding a London publisher for both the *Histoire* and for his forthcoming *Rome, Naples et Florence* was paramount, and he had requested Didot, his publisher, to dispatch copies of the former to the *Edinburgh Review* to Richard Payne Knight, on whom he had drawn extensively for his aesthetic chapters, to Byron and Hobhouse and to the editor of the Whig newspaper *The Morning Chronicle*. Further copies were of course to go to everyone of consequence in France, from Talma, Benjamin Constant and Madame de Staël to Destutt de Tracy and Pierre Daru. Ten were destined for 'the ministers and grand official of H.M. the Emperor Alexander at Petersburg (Take the names from the 1817 Almanack)' and two for 'M. Albert Gallatin, Ambassador of the United States, one for M. Jefferson, the second for Col. Monroe, now President'. Do these American copies survive?

Some possibility of an English edition, under the auspices of the Fleet Street bookseller Dessurne, may have prompted Stendhal's first visit to London, in the late summer of 1817. Regrettably nothing authentically his own on this English trip has survived (though the *Souvenirs d'Egotisme* conflate memories of it with an account of a later journey) but a manuscript account supposedly the work of his travelling companion Jean-Joseph-Marie Schmidt van Dorselaer was perhaps written by Beyle himself. The pair, accompanied by their friend Edward Edwards, whom they referred to as 'Brandy', arrived in London on 3 August and stayed for approximately a fortnight at the Tavistock Hotel in Covent Garden. They admired, as so many nineteenth-century foreign visitors tended to, the breadth of the streets, the handsomeness of the shop windows and the insouciant freedom of apparently respectable Englishwomen, so scantily clad at the theatres and in polite society (Schmidt notes 'the breasts of honest girls shaking like jelly'). Unimpressed by St Paul's, Westminster Abbey, the Tower and the Stock Exchange, they considered walking the streets the greatest pleasure London could afford, and thought

Oxford Street at nine o'clock in the evening a thousand times superior to Paris.

At Dolly's Beefsteak House near Newgate they dined most agreeably for three shillings and sixpence, plus sixpence for the waiter, washing everything down, 'pour faire l'expérience d'un dîner tout à fait à l'anglaise', with four cups of tea. 'We have never been better fed, digesting the whole dinner as if it were a cup of coffee.' From the five-shilling gallery of the King's Theatre in the Haymarket, they could have seen Mozart's *Don Giovanni*, going down to the pit at half price for the last two acts, but it was so stuffy in the theatre that they preferred to take a walk and eat ices, casting appreciative glances at the tall Englishwomen stalking purposefully past them. The next day they dined with a Mr Macklin, among ugly ladies, one of whom, an actress at the Surrey Theatre, spread her legs wide enough to suggest that she might not refuse 'a voluptuous proposition'. The men stayed half an hour over their wine and then went up in a procession to make water on the roof.

They approved of the lack of overt militarism, illustrated by people's reluctance to call the Strand Bridge by its new name of Waterloo Bridge, and by the relative absence of sentries: Paris in comparison looked as if in a perpetual state of siege. Their friend Edwards was assiduous in interpreting various aspects of English life and character, such as the national unwillingness to use wheeled transport where two feet would suffice, and the universal horror of having to enter into conversation with strangers, represented in the 'tristes cafés' by the habit of boxing off the tables, familiar to us from Dickensian coffee-room scenes.

The women never ceased to absorb the travellers. Puzzled by the appearance of something yellow in a glass jar and still mystified after being told that it was 'calf-foot jelly', they were even more amazed when 'two young ladies, very well bred, who were in the shop with their mother, came rapidly forward to tell us with a kindly air: "C'été de la dgelée de piaï de vôo."' Surely young women in France, especially upon a matter of gastronomy, would never have spoken thus to two men. Crossing Blackfriars Bridge, they were accosted by a girl who addressed them in French. 'Volez-vôo fôter moa?' she said. Schmidt himself picked up a whore in the opera foyer during the interval of another *Don Giovanni* performance, and started the business in a cab on the way to Soho Square. Though she insisted that the coachman was not to get more than a shilling, she took care to extract what she called her 'compliment', in the shape of a pound note. Watching her soaping 'les parties peccantes', he was reminded of a mare being groomed. When she offered him a lift back to the Haymarket afterwards he refused. Henri Beyle was still at the theatre, enchanted by the music, and only left at past one o'clock, out of pity for Schmidt, who, having sauntered back after his adventure, was falling asleep.

What they had presumably discussed with Dessurne was the book with which Stendhal quickly followed up the *Histoire de la Peinture en Italie*, a collection of Italian travel notes based partly on his own journals and partly on a charivari of episodes and observations, to be entitled *Rome, Naples et Florence en 1817*. His Paris publisher for this was Adrien Egron, with whom his agreement stipulated a print run of five hundred copies and proofs to be corrected by Beyle himself, over which, as it later transpired, he was surprisingly inefficient. The total cost to the author went above 900 francs, but although Egron showed no mercy in pressing him for the various sums due and refused to advertise, he assured Stendhal that the book would sell. 'Everything which isn't reasonable sells,' he added with decidedly Stendhalian dryness.

He was correct in his predictions. Coming out in mid-September, *Rome, Naples et Florence en 1817* rapidly sold out, Egron cannily taking care to raise the cover price of the final copies. One rather surprised potential purchaser was Pierre Daru, whose astonishment at being asked for forty francs by the bookseller Delauney was compounded by the discovery that his cousin was the author. '"Is it possible?" he exclaimed, raising his eyes to heaven? "This boy, ignorant as a carp!"' A second French edition appeared almost simultaneously in London, but expert opinion has still not made up its mind on which of the two was the actual original.

Egron had been concerned to warn Stendhal of the likely danger in which the book's contents might place him with the authorities. Writing on 19 June, soon after the first portions of the text were delivered, he assured him that he would devote all his attention to publishing the work.

> On your part, please have the goodness to re-read the manuscript with care, so as to avoid proof corrections, which cost a lot and do harm to the elegance of the production. I beg you, above all, to take the trouble to read everything over very carefully, so as to remove anything which might cause legal difficulties. I wish at all costs to avoid problems with the authorities, and shall not hesitate to point out any passage which seems to me to go beyond liberal bounds.

Stendhal was obviously taking a calculated risk, and though the book was not widely reviewed, and the censors seem wholly to have ignored it, at least one critic immediately divined its essentially political subtext, more freely emphasized, by the very nature of the work, than had been possible in the *Histoire de la Peinture*. An anonymous contributor to *L'Ambigu*, a periodical directed at the French *émigré* community in London (perhaps the editor Jean-Gabriel Peltier, who serialized extracts in four successive issues) noting that the arts, especially music, formed the basis of the author's remarks on Italy, went on to underline the extreme partiality of his reflections on 'the great reign, the great epoch, that is to say, on the benefits which Bonaparte, hero and object of the author's admiration, conferred, or might have conferred, on this superb country so favoured by nature. . . .'

Not for nothing had the author proudly labelled himself 'officier de cavalerie' on a title page signed 'M. de Stendhal'. This was the first appearance of the alias under which all the major works by which he is best known were subsequently to appear, but it was only one of the myriad names beneath which Henri Beyle concealed his identity, not merely as a public literary persona, but as an intimate correspondent or as a writer to himself in journal entries and marginal jottings. Stendhal enthusiasts amuse themselves by listing them – the writer Paul Léautaud managed to scramble together over two hundred – and the catalogue stretching out before us, Florisse, La Borde, Condotti, Jules Pardessus, Baron Pataut, Anastase de Serpière, Durand-

Robet, Old Hummums, William Crocodile and the rest, offers the bizarrest of testimonies to the catholicity of Beyle's monivorous interests and to his irrepressible sense of life as a game in which the rules are continually being redrawn.

Psycho-biography and the various concerns of different writers on Stendhal the literary artist have inevitably concentrated on this obsessive preoccupation with disguise and onomastic masquerade as an indicator of his absorption with the nature of himself, the eternally fascinating 'moi stendhalien'. Given his increasing sense of alienation from the legitimist *status quo* of Europe after Waterloo, it is enough to emphasize the purely practical motives for this amazing gallery of pseudonyms. In his posthumous sketch *H.B.*, Mérimée points out that the habit had been acquired during the days of the Empire, when Fouché's police were everywhere, and Beyle was afterwards convinced that his 'gigantic espionage' had retained its hidden powers.

> He never wrote a letter without signing it with an assumed name: César Bombet, Cotonet etc. He dated his letters 'Abeille' as opposed to 'Civitavecchia', and often began them with such phrases as 'I have received your raw silks and put them into store while awaiting embarkation'. All his friends had their noms de guerre, and he never referred to them in any other way. Nobody knew exactly what people he met, what books he had written, what travels he made.

The appeal of such subterfuges lay not merely in the perpetual glamour which exists for a writer in being on the other side, the hunted, the proscribed, the *mal vu*, the opposite of everything which subscribes to established values and received wisdom as embodied by the throne, the church and the family. Stendhal was not religious, never seriously supported the restored Bourbons and remained unconvinced that his own family life had been anything other than dismally frustrating. His fondness for baptizing his friends anew and putting on an entire shopful of different hats for himself went deeper than this, and would certainly have revealed itself without the various *raisons d'être* afforded by unwelcome political surveillance. Crozet became Seyssins, Faure's forename, Félix, was anglicized into Happy, Alexandrine Daru was Lady Palfy, Mérimée himself, from the title of one of his books, got changed to Clara and Henri Beyle turned himself into Dominique, because each was in a sense his re-invention, in terms of that insistently enigmatic view of life that at length enabled Stendhal to make a suitably honourable surrender to the fictional medium. The shamanistic use of English, his holy tongue of secrecy, in his private writings, mysterious in its sudden apparitions and disappearances, is but another example of this urge to transform general reality into his own apprehension of the truth.

As for 'Stendhal', its choice was perhaps dictated by the fact that the original 'Stendal' (no 'h'), a small cathedral town in the Altmark district of Hanover, which he may or may not have visited during his Brunswick year, was the birthplace of Johann Joachim Winckelmann, the aesthetician on whom Beyle had drawn for the *Histoire de la Peinture* while simultaneously setting out to challenge his sentimentally Germanic notions of idealized Hellenism that had so powerfully influenced European taste in the preceding decades. M. de Stendhal could now appear as the anti-Winckelmann, the cicerone of the modern, among divas and dancers, gossip and politics, in contrast to insipid rhapsodies in galleries full of cold marbles with broken noses and dismembered torsos. Not for nothing is the point of departure in *Rome, Naples et Florence en 1817* made a German city, Berlin, from which the narrator slips away like a naughty child.

Truanting and contrariness are the book's keynotes. As with the *Histoire*, what you see is not what you get. Ostensibly this is another volume in the, by then, well-established tradition of 'Notes from Italy' exemplified in French by the Président de Brosses, deservedly admired for his cynical candour, or Joseph-Jérôme Lalande, and in English by travellers such as Charles Burney, Hester Lynch Piozzi (Mrs Thrale) and Henry Swinburne. In fact what we embark upon is something which tells us a good deal more about the author than it does about the places and objects of local curiosity among which he finds himself. The presence of the 1811 journal is powerfully marked, the sense of direct emotional engagement with a living Italy is never far away, and even more than in Byron's *Childe Harold's Pilgrimage*, that classic exemplar of Romantic ego-tourism, the element of narrative autobiography conditions Stendhal's presentation of his material. The drama played out here is that of his increasing absorption with an Italy of the Italians, modern, immediate, answering through its theatres and cafés, its banter and flirtation, an intimate spiritual demand.

The title, apparently wished upon Stendhal by the publisher but not one he saw fit to change except by knocking the cumbersome '*en 1817*' off the end when it was revised nine years later, is a complete misnomer. There are indeed Roman, Neapolitan and Florentine passages, but over half the entries in this elaborately contrived travel diary describe other scenes entirely, laid at Milan, Bologna, Venice, Capua, in the Euganean Hills, Rimini, Ferrara and elsewhere. There are long, vigorously conducted digressions on the state of the Italian language, the plays of Vittorio Alfieri and the character of polite society in contemporary Paris (both the latter substantially cribbed from articles in the *Edinburgh Review*). An extensive section on 'l'Italie morale' allows Stendhal, against the entirely fictitious background of a pleasure trip to Villa Melzi on Lake Como, to discuss, in the most penetrating detail, the realities of modern Italian political experience and the impact of the Napoleonic invasion of Lombardy. Besides demonstrating his unparalleled gift for rapid sketching of essential outlines, this extraordinary passage, a detachable study in its own right, insists on the primacy of politics in any serious examination of modern Italian life by a non-Italian. In a single paragraph he brings before us the eighteenth-century Milan of the Austro-Lombard enlightenment, Prince Belgiojoso 'gorged on gold in the service of Austria' sprinkling twenty pounds of powder on his hair each day, the satirist Giuseppe Parini mocking him in *Il Mattino*, Beccaria and Verri illuminating Europe with their intelligence, the castrato Marchesi ravishing every heart, women decked out with portraits of him on their bracelets and shoe buckles, and 'every hateful passion . . . . excluded, almost no vanity, and since the nobles were good folk in those days, the people shared their happiness'. Yet, as Stendhal says, 'moral Italy is an unknown country; travellers only ever looked for the fine arts and were unable to see that masterpieces derive from the heart'.

This last point perfectly demonstrates the singularity of *Rome, Naples et Florence*, in both its versions, within the context of the rapidly developing genre of travel literature. The author is not content to play the polite cicerone among ruins and ridottos, in the manner of some rococo Grand Tourist, nor, despite the determinedly autobiographical stance of the narrator, is he especially concerned to maintain a heavily empathetic relationship with his surroundings. What his book again and again insists on is the immediate fact of contemporary Italy as a problem created rather than solved by recent political events. The critic in *L'Ambigu* was entirely correct in viewing Bonaparte as the unitary clue to a work so characteristically impatient of the decorum prescribed by its genre.

While Byron, as we have seen, appreciated it sufficiently to pen Stendhal an admiring letter, other readers were either more reserved in their approach or else decidedly impatient with the author's way of dressing up facts and occasionally inventing them so as to suit his purposes. Among these was Ludovico di Breme's friend Louise von Stolberg, Countess of Albany, the Prussian noblewoman whose marriage, at the age of twenty, to the seedy, drunken Prince Charles Edward Stuart, Pretender to the throne of Great Britain, led predictably to a rancorous separation. Her widely publicized love affair with the dramatist Alfieri gave her additional notoriety, as did a later liaison with the accomplished young portrait painter François-Xavier Fabre. Stendhal was naturally curious as to this elderly exotic, holding court among artists and poets in her Florentine palace, but her reaction to his remarks on Alfieri was one of disgust. In her copy of *Rome, Naples et Florence* she began pencilling comments: 'Stupid lie', 'Nonsense', 'Implausible platitude', 'Not true'. Beside his observation that the poet's 'scorn or rather hatred' for France, 'the heroic nation which unveiled his heart, cannot find terms strong enough', she scribbled contemptuously: 'For a nation which could not even free itself!'

Another who reacted sternly, though less peevishly, was Stendhal's friend Adolphe de Mareste. 'The author will find me severe,' he wrote in his letter of critical appraisal, 'but I shall not spare him from any of my sensations.' Coming straight to the point, he accused the book of lacking truthfulness, a curious defect in a work whose author prided himself on adhering to 'le naturel'. Stendhal's principal fault was to arrive in the various Italian towns and cities with his opinions on each of them already formed.

> He reminds me of my friend Henri Beyle who, sitting down in the Tuileries after a fork supper and amid the horrors of a laborious digestive process, seriously persuades himself that the young people walking about in front of him are all bored to death, and are there not to see but to be seen in public. The real boredom, however, is within the soul of Dominique himself . . .

Mareste, with a frankness which Beyle evidently respected, went on to arraign him of snobbery ('ducomanie') of spending too much time discussing music and singers, of being unjust towards Rome and Florence themselves, and of making a botched job of the book's ending, an inadequate imitation, as he saw it, of the style of the Duc de Saint-Simon.

This final thrust is the only one on which Mareste can be faulted as a shrewd critic of *Rome, Naples et Florence*. Stendhal's last words are a cry of defiance, a challenge to the plodding bourgeois world he has come home to ('Frankfurt' is a thinly disguised Paris), a rallying call to his heart, an image of Henri Beyle *contra mundum*, and the final confirmation of his symbiotic relationship with Italy.

> It is the spirit which has gained from this. My moral old age has been pushed back ten years. I have felt the possibility of a fresh happiness. All my inner resilience has been nourished and fortified: I feel rejuvenated. Dull people can do nothing against me: now I know a land where I can breathe that celestial air whose very existence they deny: against them I am iron.

The friend whose candour was so much valued had become Stendhal's chief correspondent, 'for sagacity, experience, knowledge of the world, and with the necessary character to use them properly . . . . one of the most remarkable men I ever met'.

Asthmatic and myopic, Adolphe de Mareste had divided his childhood between Grenoble and Turin, where his father was an officer in the Sardinian royal guard, but it was only on the eve of the Restoration in 1814 that he and Beyle seem to have met. Two years afterwards Mareste became a French citizen and began a successful career in the *Préfecture de police*. Rich, cultivated and enjoying a wide circle of friends in Paris, he was also socially ambitious, contracting what proved to be an unfortunate marriage to the daughter of a prosperous Genevan banker, a wife whom most of his acquaintances seem to have found insufferable and to whom he was consistently unfaithful. On Stendhal's return to France in 1821 the friends became inseparable, only falling out in an absurd squabble over a mistress, which colours the description of Mareste in *Souvenirs d'Egotisme* as an avaricious snob, married to 'a complete idiot, tall and pretty enough if only she had a nose worth speaking of'.

Mareste now replaced Pauline as the epistolary alter ego. Not merely had the 'cara sorella' outlived her usefulness as Henri's soulmate, but, as a querulous, impoverished widow, she hardly formed a desirable companion for her brother in the Milanese world to which he brought her back with him in the November of 1817. 'I have sought out and found an apartment for my sister; I have introduced her into society; she has already made three good friends,' he baldly tells Mareste, and that, apart from a few cursory references and a single (though extremely lively) letter, is more or less all we hear of her in his writings henceforth. If the protective warmth, intimacy and encouragement had all evaporated, this was perhaps because, like many others whom Stendhal initially held close to his heart, she had not turned into the model *beyliste* of his imagination.

For all her limited financial resources, Pauline was somehow able to take a box for the winter season at La Scala, and Henri now regaled Mareste with the delights of the ballet, at that time perhaps the best in Europe. Ever since his Viennese days in 1809, dance had fascinated him, and now he could renew his appreciation of the amazing talents of Salvatore Viganò, whose *Gli Uomini di Prometeo* he had seen five years earlier while at the height of his passion for Angelina Pietragrua. In *Rome, Naples et*

Florence he had extolled him for his imagination, 'like that of Shakespeare, whose name he perhaps does not know', and on 9 February 1818 he began a sort of open letter to the great dancer on the subject of an *Otello* ballet which he had lauded to Mareste as 'archi-sublime', but which proved too powerful and action-packed for the Milanese audience. Suggesting that in the last act Desdemona should express 'sinister presentiments to two of her ladies-in-waiting', he added that it might not come amiss were she to call for her harp and play 'Voi che sapete' from *Le nozze di Figaro*, since 'at this point we need an air by Mozart, the composer who best expresses sombre melancholy'. Could not ballet be used, what was more, to express the idea that the handkerchief was given to Othello's mother by a fairy? And why was the play's first act rejected purely through deference to the dramatic unities?

The last part of the unfinished epistle shows Stendhal moving ever closer in spirit to the Romantic enthusiasm which now began to grip the young Italians of his Milanese circle, and which he himself, as a lifelong Shakespearian, was to develop in his most noteworthy contribution to the Classic–Romantic debate, *Racine et Shakespeare*. 'Otherwise, Monsieur, I believe that with Canova and Rossini you are one of the glories of modern Italy . . . What fine things you might take from Shakespeare! For example a *Cymbeline* ballet, Iachimo coming out of the trunk in the middle of the night and contemplating the sleeping Imogen, the sublime simplicity of the two youngsters burying . . .' Here, alas, the manuscript breaks off.

Viganò became a living icon for the Italian Romantics, lauded by the critic Ermes Visconti in a series of articles on Romantic theory in the shortlived but powerfully influential periodical *Il Conciliatore*, first issued in 1818, but rapidly wound up the following year by the Austrian government censors, nervous of its robust polemic and general eagerness for innovation. Various of Stendhal's Milanese acquaintances, Ludovico di Breme, Silvio Pellico, Pietro Borsieri and Giovanni Rasori, gathered together to produce what was essentially an Italian equivalent, in intellectual scope, character and tone, of the *Edinburgh Review*, whose early numbers they had so much admired. There had been nothing like it in Italy since the Verri brothers, Pietro and Alessandro, had captured the attention of the enlightened Milanese in the 1760s with their journal *Il Caffè*. The thrust of *Il Conciliatore* was not merely literary; its appeal was to an educated readership prepared to challenge the deadening culture of acquiescence which kept the Habsburg regime in being, conscious as the editors were of Italy's political and intellectual fragmentation and overall provincialism, and ready also to steep themselves in the fresh currents of aesthetic sensibility now arriving from northern Europe.

Stendhal's approach to the magazine was characteristically ambiguous. In a letter to Mareste, dated 11 December 1818, he asks: 'Do you read the *Conciliatore*? No, first because it's stupid, second because it's liberal', but goes on to recommend Visconti's six articles under the general heading *Idee elementari sulla poesia romantica*, now regarded as among the key documents of Italian Romanticism during the age heralding the appearance of Manzoni and Leopardi as its most distinguished avatars. Beyle's deepening associations with the *Conciliatore* circle both fuelled his interest in the new mode of sensibility and encouraged him to believe that he might himself contribute something to an increasingly lively field of debate.

Throughout 1818 and 1819 the Romantic–Classic issue set the Milanese, cultivated or unlettered, at each other's throats. The Austrian police looked on darkly as 'romantic' became either an insult or a plaudit in the name-calling between conservatives and liberal innovators. Rossini, apparently, was an ultra-romantic, opera buffa was romantic because it was funny, the arcades of the Archbishop's palace were romantic because they were modern and useful for sheltering from the rain, and right-wing *Gazzetta di Milano* blasted as romantic the notion put forward by Angelo Cossa in his *Progetto di alcune riforme nell I.R. Teatro alla Scala* of introducing ballets on local customs and Italian themes. Even the witty dialect poet Carlo Porta, himself much admired by Stendhal, joined the squabblers with his scabrous little firecracker *El Romanticismo*.

Stendhal's own attempts to weigh into the controversy are a synthesis of his earlier theatrical interests, centring on the writing of successful modern comedy embodied by the perennial *Letellier* project, and his growing intimacy with idiomatic Italian, more especially with the 'lingua della minga', that very Milanese dialect in which Porta himself wrote and in which all classes of society took pains to speak in preference to the pure Tuscan, generally considered vulgar and ill-bred. The whole problem of dialect versus standard Italian, still a living issue today, had been vigorously canvassed in *Rome, Naples et Florence*, where, appropriately enough, one of the Florentine sections is given over to some lively reflections on the linguistic strait-jacket of standard literary Tuscan as opposed to the energy of local vernaculars. Stendhal chooses to illustrate this with Tommaso Grossi's poem *La Prineide*, a satire on the murder of Count Prina, the severe Napoleonic finance minister who was beaten to death in 1814 by an angry Milanese mob armed with umbrellas. He grasped the essential truth, nevertheless, that a unitary language, simple, beautiful, unclogged with pedantry, constituted an inestimable weapon in the hands of liberal intellectuals and politicians against the power of the 'ultras', as the French referred to the conservative legitimists of Europe after 1815. When the distinguished figure of Vincenzo Monti chose to take up the cause in his *Proposta di alcune correzioni ed aggiunte al Vocabolario della Crusca*, a polite attack on the provincial stuffiness of the official Tuscan dictionary, it was enthusiastically greeted by the Lombard intelligentsia – Silvio Pellico spoke of 'il desiderato volume' – and Stendhal was determined not to be left out.

His contribution to the linguistic debate came in the form of a pamphlet, *Des périls de la langue italienne*, written during February and March of 1818 as a response to the first part of Monti's *Proposta*. Its thrust was essentially towards the familiar accusation that Monti, well known for his accommodations with the political *status quo*, did not go far enough in lashing the lexicographers. 'The age of *mezzo termine* [half measures],' Stendhal magisterially pronounces, 'is over. No peace is possible between young people who will accept nothing but demonstrable truths as their rule of conduct, and old pedants who, swollen with pride merely for having the stupidity to spend eight or ten years of their lives reading thousands of dusty, stupid volumes, advance their authority.' Presumably with the encouragement of his friends Giuseppe Vismara and Giuseppe Compagnoni (the latter had recently translated Destutt de Tracy's *Eléments d'idéologie* into Italian) he added further chapters suggesting the need for a new universal national dictionary drawing on the wisdom of a commission from the various states and regions of Italy.

The pamphlet, originally called *Petit mot d'un barbare sur le beau livre de Monti* and swiftly translated under its new title by Vismara, was alas never published. At the last moment, for whatever reason, Stendhal seems to have drawn back from direct involvement in this aspect of the continuing critical skirmishes among the bookshops and salons of Milan, though this did not prevent him from turning instead to the general theme of Romanticism as the topic for a further polemic essay. Two years earlier, in September 1816, he had begun, presumably with the idea of sending it to the Milanese periodical *Lo Spettatore*, a short article on the dramatic unities, entitled *Sur le Romanticisme*. Now he took up the cudgels again, this time to wage war with the conservative Carlo Giuseppe Londonio, whose *Cenni critici sulla poesia romantica* savaged the new style on those very grounds of dogmatism and monotony which initially provoked the rejection of formal Neoclassicism by the young *enragés* gathering in Di Breme's box at La Scala.

It was Di Breme's studies of Byron's dashing Oriental verse tale *The Giaour*, published in the January and February numbers of *Lo Spettatore* and sounding a rallying bugle for the Romantic cohorts, which evidently fired Stendhal to produce *'Qu'est-ce que le romanticisme?' dit M. Londonio*, attacking the hallowed canons of French classical drama and roundly accusing Racine of servile grovelling to a despotic government. The tone of a passage like the following perhaps explains why this in its turn remained unpublished during Stendhal's Milanese years, and why the Austrian police should have regarded him as fundamentally unsound.

> Racine worked under Louis XIV for an audience half worn out by Richelieu's despotism. All enlightened people know what Richelieu did to strike at literature by founding the Académie Francaise. This prince of despots invented a dozen different powerful devices for draining from the French the ancient energy of the Gauls and

> covering with flowers the chains with which he loaded them. The depiction of great events and grand passions was forbidden to the tragedians, yet it is Racine, the poet of an effeminate court, a slave who adores his chains, whom pedantry seeks to impose on all the nations, instead of allowing Italians to write Italian tragedy, the English to compose English tragedy and the Germans to make German tragedy.

Stendhal's final stab at a critical essay on Romanticism within an Italian context can only be reconstructed from passages in his letters and notes. In *Racine et Shakespeare*, written and published from the relative safety of Paris, but powered by at least some of the residual dynamic derived from his involvement with the Milanese intellectual world, he mentions a pamphlet entitled *Del Romanticismo nelle Arti* which he had apparently issued in Florence in 1819. Copies of this have not yet come to light, but the hypothetical reconstruction effected by Pierre Martino in 1922 makes fascinating reading. Its generalizations, however absurdly inaccurate, are essentially Stendhalian. Only Henri Beyle, detesting the Englishness of the English yet needing all they could furnish him with in the way of ideas, opinions and books, could claim, in the age of Byron, Shelley, Keats and Wordworth, that there was no such thing as English Romanticism, and only Henri Beyle would have the critical shrewdness to hail Samuel Johnson, of whom he had not read that much, as 'le père du romanticisme'.

What all this cultural pamphleteering suggests is that Stendhal must have felt himself becoming more and more a part of the Milanese scene, the true 'Arrigo Beyle, Milanese' of his projected epitaph. At the time of Byron's visit he may well have been, as certain writers like to claim, a negligible figure among the choice spirits thronging the corridors of La Scala, but two years later, with several proven friendships among them, he could no longer be discounted, and it is easy to imagine that had *Il Conciliatore* not been summarily closed down in 1819, he might have been admitted to its distinguished roster of contributors. Not for nothing does he represent himself in *Des périls de la langue italienne* as a native Italian, a case of the wish being father to the thought, which, in the case of Stendhal's energetic imagination, embodied a special kind of reality.

There were other reasons than those offered by the agreeable rhythms of Milanese society why Stendhal should have cherished the city. Even if its populace, ungrateful for the benefits of French rule, had battered and stabbed the austerely efficient Prina to death in a fury of *ombrellate*, the place represented the benign aspects of Napoleonic government, whose imprint on it as an administrative capital, one of the chief urban models for the Empire, can still be felt today. Thus it became increasingly difficult for him, as for many others in Italy of that period, not to think of what might have happened to the country if Napoleon were still in power. Bonaparte was a despot, like the restored Ferdinand of Naples, Pope Pius VII or the Duke of Modena, but at least his despotism, unlike theirs, had been visionary, rational and creative.

Beyle's views on the more positive features of Napoleon's achievement were not necessarily shared by his Milanese circle. With good reason he suspected the so-called liberal nobility of Lombardy and Piedmont of seeking merely to establish a sort of patriotic oligarchy, and detected a certain element of sour grapes in their snobbish detestation of the man who had not done them the honour they felt was deserved. Had not Ludovico di Breme, reviewing Madame de Staël's *Considérations sur les principaux évènements de la Révolution française* for the *Conciliatore*, described the Emperor as 'this immortal criminal'?

It was the appearance of this very work, published in 1818 following Madame de Staël's death, which stung Stendhal into embarking on an appropriate riposte. After initially admiring her first novel, *Delphine*, he had swiftly grown disillusioned with its wildly exaggerated style, later calling the book 'stilted, boring, atrocious'. *Corinne*, despite making him yawn, evidently created a better impression, since he took certain hints from it for the *Histoire de la Peinture*, but in general he seems to have found her manner pompous and overblown. Fearing lest her *Considérations* should come out at the same time as the *Histoire*, he wrote to Crozet in 1816:

> This poor woman, who at bottom lacks ideas and wit enough to make an impact in print, though she has enough of both for the purposes of scandal, is likely indeed to need some sort of scandal to make the right kind of effect. She has talked *of going to America after this book*, which will be published as soon as she leaves Paris for Coppet.

When he eventually got hold of the book, Stendhal was outraged by its mixture of childish absurdity with outright slander, and sat down at once to tear its pretensions to pieces. He doubtless intended his comments for an early number of the *Conciliatore*, since he sent them with a covering note to an unnamed acquaintance, probably Silvio Pellico, asking him to 'add the necessary touches which may have escaped my notice, and cut out anything which seemes to you to be false'. Though here also he failed to make the necessary leap into print, the exercise sent him back to the idea of writing a life of Napoleon, a project which his conversations with Byron and Hobhouse in 1816 may well have helped to inspire.

His method, typically at this early stage in his career as a writer with a realistic chance of getting read, was to begin with a translation and then work outwards towards a personal intervention. In this case it was an article in the *Edinburgh Review* for December 1816, which had ended a notice of the naval surgeon William Warden's *Letters From Saint Helena* with a detailed account of Napoleon's career. To this Stendhal added passages from other books, such as Hobhouse's personal memoir of his stay in Paris during the Hundred Days, and was strengthened in his overall purpose by meeting the heroic Bonapartist doctor Giovanni Rasori, who had been arrested and flung in jail at Mantua in 1814 for publishing a seditious proclamation.

Suitably impressed by Rasori's firmness of character both during and after his imprisonment, Stendhal placed him alongside Canova, Byron, Rossini and Napoleon himself in his personal pantheon. On his manuscript, in reference to the Emperor, he noted: 'It is a duty for those of us who know this great man to leave a portrait of him for posterity, so that the Humes of the future cannot lie' (referring to the philosopher David Hume's

Tory-biased history of England during the reign of Charles I). He then added, in English: 'After seeing a great man, the 21 March 1818.' Rasori was described admiringly for Mareste's benefit: 'Poor as Job, lively as a chaffinch and as great as Voltaire . . . a doctor and inventor, as well as being a poet and writer of the first rank. . . . Astonishing conversation; face ravaged but superb, the face on a cameo.'

Whatever the influence of his conversations with Rasori, soon forced by the Austrian police to leave Lombardy, Stendhal shortly laid the *Vie de Napoléon* aside. A historical biography was obviously not what he really wanted to write, even if his talents in this direction had been sensitively appraised by the critic Pietro Borsieri, to whom he submitted part of the work in progress. While detecting his stylistic debt to Montesquieu, Borsieri seized, like others before and since, on Stendhal's inveterate tendency to assume that the reader would understand his thought processes without needing to have them set out in clear, logical sequence, as well as criticizing his over-willingness to concentrate on Bonaparte the despot and military commander rather than on the man himself. There was, he felt, too much circumstantial anecdote, and he was inclined in any case to disagree with the writer's idea that the Emperor was politically inept, destroying with the pen what he had built up with the sword. It was no doubt as a partial result of judgements like this from sympathetic acquaintances that Stendhal gave up the project. By the time he returned to it seventeen years later, Napoleon's significance in relation to his own view of the world had deepened so radically that he needed to embark on an entirely new version of the biography.

In addition to all these botched jobs, half-finished drafts and literary fits and starts which marked Stendhal's curiously rudderless creativity throughout 1818, there was the intriguing possibility of a sequel to *Rome, Naples et Florence*. Entitled *L'Italie en 1818*, it was to be a symbolic rebuttal of the charge of flippancy which he felt had been levelled against him by the *Edinburgh Review*, whose comparatively short article on the earlier book, appearing in November 1817, had seriously disappointed him by its failure to grasp the underlying seriousness of his intentions. The letter prepared but not finally sent to the periodical's editor,

Francis Jeffrey, was a model of aggrieved integrity, dealing point by point with several of the anonymous critic's more charmless responses to those sections of the book, such as the essay on the Italian language, on which the author evidently prided himself. It hammered home the crucial difference between his own approach, that of a commentator on the state of modern Italy in the wake of Napoleonic hegemony, and the style of a work such as Francis Eustace's *A Tour Through Italy*, the standard guide for English travellers and a byword for the dreariest pieties on the subject of art and architecture.

Even if, as Beyle claimed, England was loathed, not simply in Italy but throughout Europe, for having defeated Napoleon and restored tyranny, it was surely pique rather than political altruism which now spurred him to concentrate his attack on the English in the draft manuscripts of the projected sequel, an extended series of fragments which amount almost to an entire book. Remaining unpublished until the present century, *L'Italie en 1818* is, by the very nature of its inspiring animus, a more absorbing demonstration of its author's astonishing catholicity of intellectual interests than the finished work it was intended to vindicate. A whole section is devoted to plans for a constitution for the Papal States, with a bicameral system, trial by jury and Lancastrian schools (all, by no particular irony, English concepts), there are passages on Milanese bookshops and the freedom of the press, and various free-ranging disquisitions on Italian society, portraying it as essentially enslaved and forcibly trivialized in its interests, between the rise of Spanish power in the sixteenth century under Philip II, 'ce prince exécrable', and the arrival of the liberator Napoleon.

Yet another fling at Madame de Staël as 'always recognizably the daughter of a parvenu, with her blind respect for the nobility to which her family could never attain' is balanced by Stendhal's laudatory comments on Ugo Foscolo's romantic epistolary novel *Ultime Lettere di Jacopo Ortis* and the sculptures of Thorwaldsen and Canova. As for the writer himself, he prefaces a long section on Italian women, their love of flattery, their horror of teasing, their fondness for novelty and storytelling, the need to be clear and energetic in your dealings with them, by a self-portrait, intended to supply the missing image of the narrator in *Rome, Naples et Florence*. This is, indeed, the Henri Beyle we know. 'The great evil of my life is boredom. My head is a magic lantern; I amuse myself with those images, foolish or tender, which my imagination offers me. . . . My pet aversions are obviously vulgarity and affectation. Only two things anger me: Popery and the lack of liberty, both which I hold to be the source of all crimes.'

Yet again and again, in the midst of this lively Stendhalian charivari, he forces us to confront the ineluctable fact of an ascendant England, and the presence of its natives, joyless, arrogant interlopers, as a distasteful reality of the modern Italian scene. How, he asks, both directly and by implication, can England in its present political condition possibly set itself up as the champion of constitutional government? The very day of the battle of Waterloo spelled the end of English liberty, and it was then that the nobility and the rich merchants signed an offensive alliance against the working classes and the poor. With a certain relish, Stendhal foresaw a growing controversy over franchise reform, and suggested that sixty years thence England would either be a kingdom united under an aristocratic establishment living at the expense of the workers, or else a republic under a president like the United States of America. The country, whatever its power, was now on the brink of revolution, and it was perhaps this, together with 'the ferocious cruelty of the lower orders, nourished on Bible-reading and Hebrew massacres', which prompted many Englishmen to buy property in France.

Whatever his ambiguous motives for castigating the English, Stendhal displayed a remarkable shrewdness in his assessment of current political realities, striking at the heart of certain problems connected with class, national temperament and legislative hypocrisy which continue to bedevil English life to this day. As regards his own era, he understood just how deeply England was currently loathed in Europe for its part in substituting a timid, cruel, unimaginative despotism for the rule of Napoleon, 'who, without knowing it, sowed the seeds of liberty'.

Throughout the early months of 1818, Stendhal was busy pursuing his advantages in Milanese society, especially in the salon of Salvatore Viganò's daughter Elena, known as Nina, a talented pianist and singer, and a creature whose surrender to passion made her envied and resented by other women. Henri described her to Mareste as:

> brio, wit, coquetry incarnate. I've been going there for a month now, and listen to her singing each evening. She has the true soul of an artist . . . All the ladies of Milan detest her, because she has the gift of gathering together fifteen men every evening and forty on Fridays, a talent absolutely unknown here, where one woman is always afraid that another will rob her of her lover.

Henri became used to dropping in on Nina Viganò at eleven in the evening and staying until two, savouring the easy *naturel* of the Italian social life he so enjoyed, and not feeling he had to do anything more than fall back onto the sofa and delight in the company and conversation around him. 'Treat her like my sister,' Stendhal told Mareste when Nina went to Paris (his friend seems to have obliged as handsomely as possible) and his whole tone in writing of her suggests that she had been quickly cast in the role of successor to Pauline, as the kind of lively female confidante for whom Stendhal always felt a need.

Though she was easily made jealous by his attentions to the young Countess Luigia Cassera, he never thought to offer love to Nina, and in everything he writes about her, initially at least, there is a sense of respectful distance, created perhaps by his awareness of her past, rich in admirers for whom she had sacrificed comfort and security. She told her guests enchanting anecdotes of old Venice (still in her twenties, she can hardly have known the city in its last days as capital of the Serene Republic) and, according to her mood, regaled them with Venetian airs or else certain arias full of passion composed for her some time ago by the Neapolitan composer Michele Carafa, greatly admired by Rossini, who jokingly said of him that 'he committed the sin of having been born my contemporary'.

It was in this flattering ambience of Milanese drawing rooms that in the March of 1818 Stendhal fell in love more drastically than at any other time before or afterwards. The experience, lasting approximately three years, may be said to have both shattered and recreated him, so that the Henri Beyle of the two succeeding decades was in a certain sense, definable only in the most banal terms of middle age and deeper shades of seriousness and cynicism, a different man. He never achieved the wished-for fulfilment of his passion, nor did it offer him much in the way of immediate happiness, but the inspiring image of the woman he loved became that of a tutelar muse, and it is paradoxically to her pride and ultimate coldness towards him that we owe so much of what we now admire as 'Stendhal.'

She was, it need hardly be said, a Milanese, born Elena Maria Metilde Viscontini, the daughter of a rich banker and landowner, Carlo Viscontini, and his Mantuan cousin, Luigia Marliani. When Beyle met her she was twenty-eight, a mother of two sons and separated from her husband, a Polish army officer seventeen years her senior, whom she had married in 1808. Jan Dembowski, member of the Polish legion which fought for the Directory and eventually formed part of Napoleon's army, had distinguished himself by his bravery and intelligence as an officer, and in 1810 was awarded the title of Baron by the Emperor. His marriage to Metilde Viscontini was consummated as hastily as it was solemnized, by the birth of a son, Carlo, nine months later. A second boy, Ercole, was born in 1812.

How scrupulous was the fidelity of either husband or wife in the relatively loose moral climate of the Empire is a questionable issue. Dembowski was away campaigning or on official business for long periods, and it is possible that Metilde conducted affairs with the poet Ugo Foscolo and with Giuseppe Pecchio, a Milanese lawyer who was later to write for the *Conciliatore* and, more significantly where she was concerned, to become involved in the Carbonarist movement, whose activities brought its adherents into fatal conflict with the Habsburg government in 1821. Whatever the truth, she was friendly with both men, attracted to each by, among other features, a shared Italian patriotism which would send each at different times into foreign exile.

It was this patriotic loyalty which may have contributed to the break-up of her marriage. After Napoleon's first fall in 1814, Dembowski had written offering his services to the Austrians, who showed no interest in accepting them. Very soon afterwards, for whatever reason, Metilde, having obtained 'a convention of separation' lasting eighteen months, left for Switzerland with her younger son, Ercole, while Carlo remained with the family. A letter from the Swiss chargé d'affaires at Milan hints not merely at the lovelessness of the marriage, but states that Dembowski, 'hard and unsympathetic', maltreated her before the pair parted by mutual agreement.

Metilde's precipitate retreat to Berne made her instantly suspect to the Austrians, though certain well-placed connections among her family and friends, including the Russian Grand Duchess Anna Feodorovna, who had left her husband to settle in Switzerland, brought their good offices to bear with the Milanese military governor, Count Bubna von Littitz. There was always the danger that Dembowski would try to abduct little Ercole, and in June 1816 this is exactly what happened. When Metilde slipped back to Milan to see Carlo off to a new school, her irate husband, claiming that he had forbidden her to return except for the purpose of meeting him in person, found his way into her parents' house and snatched Ercole from her arms. Only through Bubna's intervention was the boy returned to her.

Metilde evidently viewed the military governor's presence as essential to her security thereafter, whatever her patriotic antipathy to the regime, but was able to assure Foscolo that Dembowski was at any rate staying clear of the children. By March 1818 she was telling the Grand Duchess's Swiss lover, Rudolph Abraham Schiferli, that she had secured a separation for life, guaranteed by law, whose terms allowed her to see Ercole twice a week. For this reason alone she preferred to remain in Milan, though behind her remark that the city was not what it used to be from the point of view of amusements, we can perhaps detect a certain resentment of a society in which not all doors were open to her any longer. Her friends, however enchanted with her, never lost sight of the complexity and edginess which lent additional fascination to Metilde's character. Baron Sigismondo Trechi wrote to Foscolo:

> She is more beautiful, more original than ever and maybe the only one of our ladies who, in a different context, might rival the candid

> and artless English with her physical and moral attractions. The Dembowski is good-natured, she converses well, with great vivacity, but she has too many angles in her forms to be really gracious.

The date of Stendhal's first visit to Metilde Viscontini Dembowski*, 4 March 1818, at her house in Piazza delle Galline, was engraved on his memory ever afterwards. In *Vie de Henry Brulard* he calls it 'the beginning of a great musical phrase', and if by this is understood the intense exaltation of love, then the significance of this description becomes clear. It was not, as some of his earlier attachments had unquestionably been, a fancied passion induced by a sense that he ought to be in love. He honestly was deeply, defencelessly smitten with this haughty, reserved, somewhat unscrupulous woman, her life already marked by the sophistications of adverse experience, in a way which makes her seem, inexplicably, more grown-up than the thirty-five-year-old Henri Beyle. As usual he shared almost nothing of the experience with his correspondents. There was really only one at this stage, Mareste, with whom his epistolary exchanges discussed politics and the various operas and ballets on show at La Scala. Otherwise we plot the course of his obsession – it was not an affair, since Metilde never answered his love and grew increasingly embarrassed by it – through the various, often impenetrably cryptic jottings made in the books he read. What, for example, was the '*Bataille et défaite du 29 mars 1818 on Me's bancks*' noted in a copy of the *Histoire de la Peinture*? What is '*The My*' referred to in the margin of a volume of Montesquieu, and what exactly does '*M. joue Othello*' imply?

Pauline Beyle meanwhile had fallen ill, and Stendhal had to take her back to Grenoble, where the legal tussles over Périer-Lagrange's estate were nearing a judgement at last. Another distraction was offered in the summer by a trip to the Brianza region of northern Lombardy in the company of his friend

* The correct Polish form – Dembowska – has never been used by previous writers on Stendhal. Since contemporary Italian documents always use her husband's (masculine) surname, in such approximations as Dumbrowski and Dambowski, I see no reason to alter this convention.

Giuseppe Vismara, but Metilde was patently with him in his thoughts, however distant he might be from her. For the biographer the most exasperating aspect of the whole relationship, given its wider implications, is that it remains almost impossible to reconstruct in any but the most fragmentary form. We know, for instance, that something momentous took place on 30 September in Via del Giardino – the distracted lover never forgot the date or the time, '9 h. 32 mi.', keeping it as part of a calendar of Metildean anniversaries – but we have no way of discovering what this 'greatest event of his life' actually was, let alone the precise nature of the '*Affaire de San Francisco against bash*' (these last two words are in English, the latter apparently short for 'bashfulness') noted on 4 October.

That day he wrote her a letter, not all of which survives, telling her how unhappy he was, how he loved her more as each day passed, and reproaching her with no longer offering him the friendship she formerly showed. 'One really striking part of my love,' he told her, 'is my gaucherie when I'm with you, which I can't overcome and which makes me angry with myself. I'm strong until I reach your drawing room and then, as soon as I see you, I start trembling. No other woman has inspired this feeling in me for ages.' Somewhat pointlessly, since Metilde spoke and wrote excellent French, he began translating his earlier remarks into Italian, then told her he was leaving the next day for La Tremezzina on Lake Como, so as to try and forget her. 'My principal concern has been to find ways of seeing you without appearing imprudent. I love you even more when distant from you than when in your presence. From far away you seem well-disposed towards me, but your presence destroys these sweet illusions.'

A month-long autumnal *villeggiatura* on the delightful shore of Como's western arm was scarcely an uncongenial distraction. 'I have a charming room,' Beyle told Mareste, 'separated from the lake only by a road eight feet wide, where each day I see pass some fifty people from the society spread out among the hundred villas ornamenting this delicious valley.' He could look at the two or three good pictures and a Canova statue in the Villa Sommariva, and in the evenings become cheerfully absorbed into the lively, musical, 'foutante' company along the lakeside.

In its remaining section, his long letter to Mareste encapsulates that exuberant internationalism which overtook Europe once the end of the Napoleonic wars allowed people to travel, initiating a cosmopolitan society disdaining frontiers, passports or loudly asserted nationalism, which flourished continuously until the Great War of 1914–18 destroyed it altogether. Stendhal's pleasure in ballooning across the social landscape of Lombardy must have derived in part from that agreeable sense of weightless confidence and cheaply bought smartness the expatriate always receives from a temporary absorption into the life of gossip and intrigue animating the borrowed world he inhabits. None of this, however, or Benjamin Constant's pamphlet on the elections to the French Chamber of Deputies, or Thomas Moore's entertaining skit on the new wave of British tourists, *The Fudge Family In Paris*, or the début of the promising young Sicilian composer Giovanni Pacini, or a possible visit to Italy by Tsar Alexander of Russia, could wrench his thoughts away from Metilde.

Milan was suddenly unbearable without her presence. He returned to the city only to leave it again because she had gone to stay with a cousin at Sannazaro in southern Lombardy. Stendhal himself went north to Varese, then as now the incarnation of provincialism, hoping perhaps that this self-exile among 'les bons bourgeois' who discussed the price of corn and the health of their horses would make him more desired by the woman he loved. His passion had now reached its most imploring phase, and he was writing to her in terms of ardent desperation he had seldom if ever used before. Surely, he says, there will be a letter waiting for him when he gets back to Milan:

> for I can count on you having enough humanity not to refuse me a line or two, scribbled so nonchalantly by you, yet so precious and consoling to a heart in despair. You should be too certain of your absolute power over me to pause for an instant in the vain fear of seeming to encourage my passion by replying. I know myself; I shall love you for the rest of my life; nothing you do will ever change the idea which strikes upon my soul, the idea that I am

made for the happiness of being loved by you, or the contempt which this gives me for any other sort of happiness. . . .

His total absorption in the grand business of loving made work impossible. The logbook of this consuming desire can be read through the marginal scribbles he made during the winter of 1818–19. 'From 22nd December to 7th January I have written nothing *by love*, *by* health and through a wish *of making* dialogues instead of prose.' 'I love her too much to work.' 'Today *I am too in L.* to be able to work.' '*I am without witt* and very tender.' To agitate him yet further came the suspicion that the Austrian police were reading his letters from Mareste, so that it became necessary to use friends in Turin and Novara as a cover. Worse still, the military governor of Grenoble had suspended the 900 francs half pay to which he was entitled as an ex-assistant commissary officer, purely because he had been unable to present himself in the city on a certain day each month. Stendhal's sole consolations were playing cards with Nina Viganò and visits to La Scala, where 'Rossini has written a duet in his *Armida* which will give you an erection for ten days'.

When, on 12 May 1819, Metilde left Milan, the situation became intolerable. She had gone on a journey into Tuscany to visit her two sons, currently at a boarding school to which General Dembowski had sent them, run by the teaching order of the Scolopi – short for 'Scuole Pie' – a Jansenist group whose educational record was generally respected. The college was situated, for obvious reasons, in one of the loneliest, most inaccessible towns in the Grand Duke's domains, the ancient Etruscan stronghold of Volterra, perched on a windswept ridge overlooking the bleak landscape of the Maremma stretching westwards to the sea.

To this sombre place, famous for its monumental alabaster and a kind of biscuit known as 'dead men's bones', whose Medici fortress was now the most notorious of grandducal prisons and whose cyclopean ramparts still preserved the stone lions set there by Etruscan masons, Stendhal came in pursuit of Metilde. The expedition was a circuitous one. For eight days he remained at Genoa, going thence by sea to Porto Venere and Leghorn and arriving at Volterra in the early afternoon of 3 June. His idea, which must have seemed as astonishing to Metilde as it does to us, was to appear in disguise, his face concealed by a pair of green spectacles. By one of those singular coincidences which love seems to ordain, Metilde was the first person he saw, on her way home to dine after visiting the college. Apparently she did not recognize him, but that same evening, just as he was taking off his glasses, she happened to pass by.

The next day a similar encounter took place outside the Porta a Selci, beside the fortress, where Metilde delighted to walk in the meadow beyond the walls, a stretch of grass and olive trees still existing today. Stendhal, in his long, self-extenuating letter to her, swore that his presence was entirely fortuitous, and pointed out that as soon as he saw her coming he fell into conversation with a young man who happened to be there, before hurrying away to the ramparts on the other side of the town to look at the sea.

Complicating the issue was the presence of a certain Signor Giorgi, with whom Beyle immediately suspected some sort of attachment. He was pardonably surprised when at last Metilde agreed to meet him at the college, on condition that he would say absolutely nothing about his love. A letter she had already sent him was a sufficient indication of her coldness, beginning as it did with a formal 'Monsieur'. Wounded by her seeming cruelty, he endured the interview and left, 'wanting to hate you and not finding any hate at all in my heart'.

Ludicrous as the journey to Volterra must have appeared, Stendhal could nevertheless find it in him to say that a prosaic person would never have attempted it, firstly because of the expense and secondly because the inns were so bad. He was right of course: there was something splendidly quixotic in trailing the beloved across Italy for the sake of the smallest pledge of answered passion, but the woman he dared, in one of his more frantic paragraphs, to address as 'divine Metilde', remained impenetrable and unimpressed.

He retreated to Florence, to the solace of the Uffizi and nocturnal rendezvous on the Ponte Santa Trinità, to catch the breezes cooling the torrid summer city, with two young Englishwomen he met in the Cascine each evening. From here he sent a short, dignified letter to Metilde, asking her to write to him at Bologna, where he arrived on 22 July, convinced that she had gone to the nearby spa of Porretta, only to discover a letter waiting at his inn informing him that his father was dead.

There was no reason why Henri should feel any sort of grief at the news that Chérubin Beyle, his 'Jesuit', the loathed and despised paterfamilias of the Grenoble childhood, had at last gone out of the world. As adults they had grown no closer to one another, and there had been none of that reappraisal which allows parent and child, with the advantage of distance, to renew their relationship on a less emotional, more generously appreciative basis. The shadow and the grudge would always remain, to be utilized in Stendhal's ambiguous portrayal of various fictional fathers, and his constant invocation of the theme of surrogate paternity for his heroes.

Nothing interested him about Chérubin's death except the will, which he interpreted as 'a sort of manifesto against this poor Henri'. His brother-in-law, Zénaïde's husband, Alexandre Mallein, was to have all the movable property, while he himself would end up, after the various debts had been paid, with about 7000 francs, not much but enough to make it worth asking Mareste whether he thought it advisable for him to stay in Milan or move to Paris.

From Grenoble, whither he had returned at once to help settle the estate (almost the only asset remaining from Chérubin's house in the Rue Bonne was the contents of the cesspit) Stendhal wrote again to Metilde, angrily depicting the ruin of his paternal hopes effected by his father's malign improvidence. 'Everything which the deepest, most implacable, most calculated hatred could contrive against a son, I have experienced from my father. This is all dressed up in the finest hypocrisy: I am an heir and have apparently no excuse to complain.' Nevertheless he foresaw prolonged litigation and a tedious involvement in clearing loans and payments still outstanding. Just how immense these were became all too soon apparent.

After a short trip to Paris he came home to Milan in the autumn of 1819. Even if he met with a cool reception from Metilde, there was the perennial consolation of La Scala, now playing host to Gioacchino Rossini, who had swiftly established himself as the most admired operatic master of his generation. Stendhal's thoughts, turning as they did on his current financial problems, were much exercised by Rossini's success in making and keeping hold of money. He noted interestingly that the twenty-eight-year-old composer planned to cease work at thirty, an ambition not actually achieved for another decade, after the creation of *Guillaume Tell*.

His new opera for La Scala was *Bianca e Faliero*, first produced on 26 December. Five days before this, Stendhal had told Mareste that 'I'm spending my evenings with Rossini and Monti; all things considered, I prefer extraordinary to ordinary men', and mentioned that he was dining with the composer, whom he admired for his ability to create without knowing how he achieved his effects, something he had found equally worthy of praise in Byron's work. As regards his music, however, Beyle was still doubtful. The critical enthusiasm which later inspired a complete study of the man and his work had not yet altogether seized hold, and we find him noting, on 11 December: 'Rossini's music is pretty and sometimes beautiful, but never, never sublime. He puts in too many details; his music lacks simplicity; it seems that basically he is afraid of being bored. Through the effect of this mass of detail, he can make himself perfectly understood by vulgar listeners.'

Perhaps the least noteworthy year of Stendhal's life in terms of either experience or achievement, the whole of 1820 saw him obsessed by his passion for Metilde. Notes here and there among his books and papers emphasize the continuing hopelessness of the attachment. '*Very in love and very melancholy*', he wrote in a copy of *Haydn, Mozart & Metastasio*. '*Seen her in the chamber, the window open by moonlight*', he scribbled in Madame de Staël's *Considérations*. The emotional stress began to affect his health. Two years earlier he had plotted a graph indicating the gradual weakening of the effect of his mercury treatment for syphilis, the increase of angina pectoris, but a corresponding decline in 'suffering of the soul'. Now the suffering had grown, and to the list of physical ailments he could add gout and the recrudescence of his blenorrhagia.

But who was the woman with whom, on 8 February, he told Mareste he was in love and who had apparently given him the mucus discharge in question? Metilde of course can be ruled out – Stendhal was lucky to see her about once a fortnight, and their intimacy was never more than conversational – but solace had been offered meanwhile by others, including a certain 'Luisina', perhaps Countess Cassera, to whom his notes refer in the previous November. He was continuing to visit Nina Viganò, and on 15 February they both attended the gala inaugural ball of the Casin di San Paolo, a society for rich Milanese merchants, which had begun its existence as a bowling club called the Società del Giardino.

Its new premises at Palazzo Spinola in Via di San Paolo had been magnificently decorated with new ceiling frescoes and mock marble made of painted papier mâché. Over eight hundred tickets were sold for the occasion, and some one and a half thousand guests included the grander Milanese families such as the Melzi, Visconti and Borromeo, and the statutory sprinkling of English nobility, Lady Kinnaird, Lady Oxford and others. Among the company was Metilde Dembowski's protector, Count Bubna, whose presence testified to his unusual popularity even among the Italian patriots. Stendhal, who wrote up the evening for the second version of *Rome, Naples et Florence*, was entranced by the beauty of the Englishwomen. 'An unequalled freshness and a childlike happiness animates their fine features, showing no trace of fear and seeming to promise beforehand a recognition of an absolute master in whatever man they love.' Such a submission, however, could only induce boredom. One glance at the flirtatious eyes of the Italians, on the other hand, assured him that they were total strangers to this feeling. 'Caprice keeps watch to drive away the monster.' Yet whatever their zeal in pursuing and sustaining amorous liaisons, the Italians, Stendhal noted, thought dancing too much like hard work, and left it to the blond, red-faced Austrian officers and the foreign guests.

The ball at the Casin di San Paolo was in some sense a swansong for the relatively peaceful coexistence of the Milanese with their

Austrian rulers, as well as for the government's comparatively benign approach towards its subjects. Modern travellers in Italy will be familiar with the time-honoured practice of fly-posting government notices and political proclamations on the walls of houses and public buildings, and the nineteenth-century visitor to any Italian town was always conscious of these edicts and rescripts around him, with their stern black upper-case headlines under the badge of the ruling house. On 29 August 1820 the citizens of Milan could read the 'notification' issued by the Imperial and Royal Government, signed by the Viceroy's chief minister, Count Strassoldo, warning against the developing influence of the secret society known as the Carbonari and threatening its associates with arrest and trial for high treason. The relevant extracts from the penal code were attached as a chilling reminder of the appropriate punishments.

The Carbonari, literally 'charcoal-burners', were members of a revolutionary secret society, the Carboneria, vague in its specific aims but strongly inspired by a general nostalgia for the Napoleonic era, when ambitious and talented young Italians of whatever class might pursue a worthwhile career in the armed forces or the various branches of the civil service, and when thought and expression were not subjected to the kind of Draconian controls imposed by the restored monarchies. Taking root in Naples, the movement gained an equally firm hold among the younger nobility and professional classes of Milan, Turin and Genoa, where a series of abortive revolutionary attempts during 1821 were punished by the Habsburg and Sardinian authorities with an unexampled severity, establishing the hostile terms on which governors and governed (at least among the educated classes) henceforth viewed one another and setting a precedent adhered to by rulers elsewhere in Italy during the Risorgimento.

Even if Stendhal had no exact knowledge of the Carboneria and its aims, it is most unlikely that he would not have sensed something of the rising political tensions in the Milanese circles he frequented. Almost all his acquaintances, Vismara, Pellico, Rasori, Romagnosi, the various contributors to the recently suppressed *Conciliatore*, even Metilde Viscontini Dembowski herself, had some kind of subversive association, and several of them were directly implicated in the terrible events which now ensued.

It was the bitterest of ironies which decreed that as well as being suspect to the Austrian police for his links with Milanese liberals, Stendhal should now be looked at askance by the liberals themselves. According to a worried letter he sent Mareste on 23 July, a rumour had been gathering in the city that he was a French government agent. Certain of his former friends had begun avoiding him and a general curiosity had arisen as to what he, as a Frenchman, was doing there in the first place. 'Milanese good humour will never be able to understand my philosophical life and the fact that I can live better here on five thousand francs than at Paris on twelve.' The news that he had been barred from a particular circle because others might leave as soon as he came in was, he said, 'the profoundest blow I ever received in my life'.

In a subsequent letter, Stendhal tells Mareste in English that suspicion has been cast on him '*by the husband of my object*'. This has traditionally been accepted as a covert reference to the Austrian police, on the basis of his calm, fifteen years later, to have adored 'a woman named *mille ans* [Milan]'. The interpretation seems a little too labyrinthine, even among the winding stairs and secret passageways of Stendhalian cryptography, and we need surely look no further for the original calumniator than the husband himself, General Dembowski, who must by now, in the scandalmongering world of Milan, have heard something about this Beyle paying addresses to his wife.

There is also a possibility – and until documentary proof appears, it must always remain only a possibility – that Stendhal was actually working for some secret service arm of the French government. In the light of this, it is worth considering how many of his journeys outside Milan, apart from the madcap pursuit of Metilde to Volterra, were made purely for pleasure. What, for instance, was the exact purpose of his week at Bologna in the March of 1820, and were his two visits to Varese simply along the lines of a country weekend?

The intriguing suggestion has been made, most notably in a short biography published in 1955 by Claude Boncompain and François Vermale, subtitled *La double vie de Henri Beyle*, that he was in fact employed as a spy on the slighted consort of King George IV, the notorious Caroline of Brunswick, then living beside Lake Como. A French police inspector, writing to Stendhal's old schoolfriend Edouard Mounier, now Director-General of Police, told him that the former interior minister, Decazes, now appointed ambassador to London, was taking with him a number of documents he thought might interest the King, including reports from 'a secret agent Monsieur Decazes retained at Milan to keep watch on the Queen'.

As the political atmosphere grew more fretful during the early months of 1821, Stendhal nevertheless seems to have tried to carry on as if nothing serious were happening, going to the opera to hear Maria Teresa Belloc, 'horribly ugly but probably at present the finest singing actress in Italy', and steeping himself with ferocious enthusiasm in the romances of Sir Walter Scott, *Waverley*, *The Abbot* and *The Bride of Lammermoor*, regretting that the novelist had never chosen medieval Italy as his theme. 'He might have come across the first steps made by the human soul towards freedom. Instead of the egotistical heroics of an absurd feudalism, he might have been able to depict everything which the human soul could achieve at that time on behalf of others.' What could he not have done with the life of Cola di Rienzi or the exile of Cosimo de' Medici, considered Stendhal?

He would return again and again to Scott as a major literary figure of the age, whose work taught younger novelists their craft and broadened the serious scope of contemporary fiction. Though Stendhal never properly grasped the political ambiguity inherent in works like *Rob Roy* and *Redgauntlet*, and continually berated their author as a lackey of Tory reaction in the age of Canning and Castlereagh (so much so, indeed, that Byron was later at pains to set him right) he absorbed that sense of historical imperatives with which the Waverley novels so successfully surround the motivation of their characters, and, perhaps more significantly, cast his protagonists, especially such figures as Fabrice del Dongo and Clelia Conti, in an unmistakably Scott-like mould.

It was now Beyle's own turn to be seized by great historical events – or rather, events which might have proved momentous if those seeking to bring them about had managed the business more competently. His letters to Adolphe de Mareste during the early spring of 1821 are in places almost incoherent with nervous apprehensions of secrecy unmasked, and the magic English now becomes the frantic cypher-language of somebody suspecting a police spy in the movement of every shadow. After a last sentimental ten days on Lake Como (perhaps watching Queen Caroline?) Henri faced the reality of 'il distacco amaro', the bitter separation – bitterest, surely, of his whole life – from Milan, Metilde and everything which had given meaning and solace to his existence for nearly seven years. On 13 June 1821 he left Italy, as it seemed for ever.

Anything was better than having to reflect on this terrible exile from a place to which he saw himself as belonging more truly, through an adoptive sympathy, than to his perpetually despised 'Cularo', his native Grenoble. On the way northwards into Italian Switzerland, the very sound of whose toponyms, Airolo, Bellinzona, Lugano, caused him to tremble as he wrote them ten years later in the *Souvenirs d'Egotisme*, he kept melancholy introspection at bay by conversing with the postilions of his carriage, canvassing their views on the price of wine. He would have wanted, he says, to cross the St Gotthard pass on horseback, so that he could at least enjoy the distraction of falling down a precipice, but the courier who accompanied him discouraged the idea on account of its being bad for business. 'Well, I can't walk,' said Stendhal, 'as I have the pox', an announcement which made the guide curse all the way across the mountain.

What his acquaintance made of his Milanese débâcle we can tell only through a concerned letter which Louis Crozet wrote to Adolphe de Mareste on 31 October 1820. Amid much justifiable headshaking over their friend's obstinacy and foolhardiness, Crozet observes that: 'it would have been preferable if Henri had followed his friends' advice and not tried to sink his reputation in attempts at acquiring a character for haughtiness and lofty manners, but the evil has been done, and I really do not see how we can apply a remedy to it.' The tendency of Crozet's letter reflects the feeling among Stendhal's intimate circle that he had only himself to blame for his current difficulty. Mareste was urged to write to their Italian intermediary and old schoolfellow, the Torinese astronomer Giovanni Plana, persuading him to tell Beyle to cut his losses and retire gracefully, assuming no job was available in Paris, to 'a modest country house in the Dauphiné', where he could settle down to serious writing.

If only it were that simple! Crozet perhaps knew little or nothing of the significance of Metilde Dembowski in any calculation for future happiness Stendhal might make. Her own fortunes, unconnected any longer with his, were about to take their most unwelcome turn. In the summer of 1821 the projected insurrection by the Carbonari was brought nearer reality when three Milanese noblemen, Federico Confalonieri, Giorgio Pallavicino and Metilde's cousin Gaetano de Castillia, journeyed to Turin to try to persuade Prince Charles Albert, head of the Carignan branch of the house of Savoy and heir to the Piedmontese throne, to lead an army of invasion into Lombardy. Characteristically, as his behaviour revealed twenty-seven years later when faced with the threat of Austrian military intervention (he became known as 'il Re tentenna', 'the wobbly King') the Prince quickly stepped aside from the challenge once Metternich, who had of course got wind of the plot, sent troops into Piedmont.

The nobles and their supporters, gathered once more in Milan, were quickly arrested by the efficient, well-briefed Habsburg police. Among several of the more illustrious Lombard Carbonari there seems to have been a combination of considerable naïveté with an understandable desire to limit individual damage, which encouraged them freely to name most of the others involved in the conspiracy and various people only marginally connected with it. Thus another of Metilde's cousins, Bianca Mojon Milesi, a member of the Carboneria almost since its foundation, was arrested on suspicion of having conducted a clandestine correspondence with the plotters and forced to flee into Switzerland. Gaetano de Castillia's brother, Carlo, had meanwhile denounced most of the inner ring, including Giuseppe Pecchio and Giuseppe Vismara.

It was not long before Stendhal's name was mentioned among those linked with the abortive uprising. The egregious Confalonieri, whose subsequent execution turned him quickly into a protomartyr of the Risorgimento, hastened to label 'a certain De Bell, a Frenchman' as a very dangerous person. At his trial, the assessor Giulio Pagani noted:

> Debel, native of Grenoble in France, known as an irreligious man, revolutionary, liberal, enemy of legitimism. He is the author of the work, suppressed through our efforts, *L'Histoire de la Peinture en Italie*. . . . He is no longer here now, and is thought to have returned to his native country in 1820.

The long shadow of Austrian police suspicion, assisted by a reserve of detailed information and a network of spies, dogged Stendhal for the rest of his life. He was never allowed to return for any length of time to Milan, and his consular career during the last decade of his life was hampered by the irremovable slurs of liberalism and subversion which the Carbonaris' denunciations merely confirmed. Perhaps by reason of this, few of his former Italian circle maintained contact with him after he left Lombardy: Vismara, for instance, though he arrived in Paris two years later as Italian teacher to an Irish countess whose man of business he afterwards became, was forced to hide for a time from the Bourbon police, identified as 'a criminal of the first order', and seems to have made no effort whatever to get in touch with his erstwhile companion on the jaunt into Brianza.

With extraordinary courage Metilde Dembowski herself faced her interrogators in the form of a special commission assembled on Christmas Eve, 1822. Another of the names on the list Carlo de Castillia had given to the authorities, she had scorned escape and was now subjected to a battery of detailed questions on her associations with the conspirators. Her cunning in the provision of one evasive answer after another was severely tested by the five-hour inquisition, and she was placed under surveillance and subjected to a house-search, following which a further grilling took place. This time her friendship with Count Bubna von Littitz proved invaluable, since, alerted to her plight, he was able to invoke the technicality of her position as the former wife of a serving officer and declare that the civil jurisdiction had no power over her. All confiscated documents were returned, and she spent the remaining few years of her life quietly in Milan. When she died of consumption in 1825, aged only thirty-five, Confalonieri's sister Teresa, whose husband, Alexandre Andryane, had been among the Carbonarists sent to fester in the notorious Moravian fortress of Spielberg, wrote: 'An incomparable friend was my hope, my consolation . . . . and I lost her only a few days since! I saw Metilde Dembowski die, that angelic woman who united within her all the perfections of an adorable sensibility with the energy which makes the most sublime actions possible.'

That Metilde really was a Stendhalian muse is proved by the book which the writer's affair with her most directly inspired. *De l'Amour*, published in August 1822 by the Parisian firm of Mongie, is without question one of the most singular productions of its epoch and, we may say, of the nineteenth century in general. Stendhal had begun writing his analytical treatise on love in the throes of the relationship itself, and carried it to a conclusion on his return to France, during the terrible period of depression occasioned by hankerings for an unattainable Milan and an equally unreachable Metilde. Its composition carried him through into the summer of 1822, which he spent correcting the galleys at Montmorency, where he rented a room, or at Bonneuil-sur-Marne as the guest of his old friend Comtesse Beugnot.

At first glance *De l'Amour* appears to be a perfectly orthodox essay of the kind familiar to French readers in such celebrated incarnations as Descartes' *De la méthode* or Pinot Duclos' *Considérations sur les moeurs*, a work much admired by Stendhal. Its chapter headings purport to be topic-related: 'Concerning Modesty', 'Concerning Female Courage', 'Concerning Wounded Vanity' and so on, and it is neatly split into two books, one of them largely theoretical, the other examining the practice of love in various foreign countries, adducing historical evidence from medieval Provence and the Islamic world and featuring observations on women's education and the phenomenology of marriage.

The act of reading the book lays bare an essentially Beylian dichotomy between the *mise-en-scène* and the performance. As with the *Histoire de la Peinture en Italie*, the apparatus is an illusion, even more delightfully inspired in its efforts to deceive because

Stendhal himself is not fully in control of the deception. It is not just us, the interested readers, whom he tries initially to convince with his air of authority, of having, as it were, been there, seen this, done that: he is always fascinatingly in the process of attempting to convince himself that his enquiring spirit can effectively detach him from the rawness and vulnerability of passion, and of discovering simultaneously that it cannot.

In short, *De l'Amour* enacts a significant tension between the two most important areas of Stendhal's personality, between the Frenchman he unavoidably was and the Italian a large part of him aspired in some sense to be. The apostle of 'la lo-gique', the disciple of Destutt de Tracy, with his systems, parallels and categories, is seen trying frantically to hang on, by way of codifying and analysis, to an essentially uncontrollable emotion that both embarrasses him with the absurdities he perpetrates under its incalculable influence, and at the same time reassures him that, unlike most of his countrymen, he is at least capable of spontaneous feeling *à l'italienne*.

Stendhal's observations on love are not necessarily new or original. Despite its four prefaces, its plethora of digressions, its author's habit (shared with Coleridge – if only the two of them had met!) of thinking aloud and insisting that we follow him up and down all the alleys and zigzags of allusion, comparison, epigram, quotation and cross-reference, till we grasp the point, *De l'Amour* is valued by many readers as one of his most accessible works for the opportunity it offers to acknowledge the truth, in every outline, of a familiar amatory experience.

The most celebrated example of such authenticity, an example no writer on Stendhal can afford to ignore, if only because so many others have sedulously picked it over in all its various aspects, is the so-called 'Salzburg Bough'. Recalling a visit to a salt mine near Salzburg during his war service in Austria, the writer uses the image of a branch thrown down the shaft of an abandoned working and taken out again after three months, now covered to its smallest twig with a shining crust of crystals. 'What I have termed crystallization is a mental process, drawing from every occurrence fresh proofs of the loved one's perfection.' Stendhalians have tended to treat this idea of crystallization as if it were something so totally novel and profound that the writer himself could be considered its creator. One might suppose from this that none of them had ever been deeply in love: the remarkable feature of Stendhal's treatment of this theme is not the perfectly commonplace experience itself, but the power of his chosen metaphor, sublimely developed in an appendix to the book, itself entitled 'The Salzburg Bough' and in essence a short story, perhaps the most perfectly designed of all the writer's few essays in shorter forms.

Why *De l'Amour* remained Stendhal's favourite among his works was surely because it enshrined such an extraordinary commitment of his entire personality to the business of examining the quality of an emotion he was actually in the process of experiencing. For this biographer at least, it is the book to which readers who have tried and failed with the 'dry' fiction of *Le Rouge et le Noir* and *La Chartreuse de Parme* should turn if they want to discover what it is about the man and the artist that allures Stendhalians and keeps them loyal. More than any other book, it is its author, Beyle himself, incessantly curious, spontaneously epigrammatic, imaginative, humane and vulnerable, his ideas especially as regards the status and intellectual capacity of women formulated with an articulate freedom which he already perceived as likely to be alien and incomprehensible to his contemporaries. 'Between 1822 and 1833,' he wrote, 'my book only found seventeen readers; in its twenty years' existence, I doubt if it has been properly understood by more than a hundred enquiring minds.' It has taken a good deal longer for *De l'Amour* to reach the audience it deserves.

In an attempt to make *De l'Amour* 'go', Stendhal drafted two puffing articles (neither of which was published) one a dialogue between an old man and a young reader of the book, the other a favourable recension of the two volumes. At the end of the second article a note in English on its final paragraph reads '*Said by M. Hazlitt*'. The correspondences and coincidental similarities between Stendhal's work and William Hazlitt's *Liber Amoris*, the fictionalized account published in 1823 of his hopeless passion for his landlord's daughter, have often been noted, and the two writers, with similar political views and a shared enthusiasm for

Napoleon, were destined at last to meet, when the Englishman arrived in Paris in the autumn of 1824. Each reviewed the paintings exhibited in that year's Salon, Hazlitt in the *Morning Chronicle* and Stendhal in a series of *feuilletons* for *Le Journal de Paris*, and Beyle gave his new acquaintance valuable hints as to what he should seek out during his Italian tour. Years afterwards, in his *Mémoires d'un touriste*, Stendhal adduced the authority of '*Hazlitt homme d'esprit, anglais et misanthrope*'. For his part Hazlitt took with him across the Alps a certain 'charming little work entitled *De l'Amour*' by 'my friend Mr Beyle'. Had they ever discussed their common experience of blighted passion? Alas, there is no evidence for this, or for any other meeting between two such obviously kindred spirits.

CHAPTER 9

A CHUBBY MEPHISTOPHELES

It was not in Italy alone that secret societies, sworn to act against oppressive governments, gathered and flourished during 1820 and 1821. Restoration France during these years saw a gradual increase in liberal discontent, whether among nostalgic veterans of the former Imperial army, restive students, Protestant industrialists or dissident lawyers. There was even an attempt at establishing a French chapter, or at least its equivalent, of the Carbonari, known as the Charbonnerie, each of whose members was expected to provide a gun and twenty-five cartridges.

Symptomatic of growing disenchantment with a monarchy whose reactionary stance seemed to harden with each successive year, these movements, whatever their failures in action, polarized sympathies and fuelled that political turbulence which characterized nineteenth-century France from the fall of Napoleon to the establishment of the Third Republic and beyond. Stendhal was returning to a country profoundly ill at ease with itself, ruled by an ultra-royalist government largely composed of mediocrities (though headed by a shrewd, capable manipulator in the person of the Comte de Villèle) prepared to consolidate its power by severe press censorship and ruthless parliamentary fixing in the newly constituted Chamber of Deputies.

The Paris in which much of the more virulent opposition to Villèle's government was concentrated, and where the thirty-eight-year-old Stendhal now settled at the Hôtel de Bruxelles in Rue de Richelieu, was still a small city, its core largely medieval and without any of the sweeping arterial thoroughfares with which it was to be stamped three or four decades later, the metropolitan grandeur contributing so extensively to its modern romantic image. The undoubted attraction of Parisian life during the Restoration and the July Monarchy of Louis-Philippe, lay in its social cohesiveness and the fact that most of its leading cultural figures were able without difficulty to make one another's acquaintance. What bound them still further was an increasing sense of political alienation, at first from the government of the day and later, under Louis-Philippe, from the aspirations of the new bourgeoisie. Slowly the foundations were being laid for that cynicism and disdain with which Parisian writers, artists and intellectuals have ever since confronted the more banal rhythms and pulses of ordinary life. The romantic ideal of the creator at odds with the world, his attitudes and opinions justified by his singularity and otherness, if not actually born among the disenchanted literati of Restoration Paris, was indubitably nurtured by their collective scorn for the broken promises and repressive violations of trust perpetrated under the seemingly benevolent rule of the last three kings of France.

It was some time before Stendhal, one of the most outstanding exemplars of such ingrained antipathy to the *status quo*, was able to find himself a niche within this established world of Parisian writing and publishing. The loss of Milan and Metilde was an enduring trauma, and his mental state on returning to the French capital may be gauged from the apparently serious resolve he formed, however briefly, of assassinating King Louis XVIII. He had almost no money, very few friends, and no present prospect of employment.

To begin with, the pattern of his existence was one of crashing dullness, made worse on Sundays, which by their very nature he detested. On these days he would wander disconsolately into the Tuileries and stroll under the chestnut trees, solacing himself with recollections of Metilde Dembowski. Each morning he went to the café with Adolphe de Mareste, his fellow lodger at the Hôtel de Bruxelles. For nine years it was always the same Café de Rouen, further down Rue de Richelieu, and for nine years the regularity of the assignation was uninterrupted. In the cynical, half-angry character sketch Stendhal gives of his friend in *Souvenirs d'Egotisme*, written after the relationship had somewhat cooled, he captures for us the exact nature of their mutual sympathy. 'My good sense stopped me from allowing myself to be run away with by poetic illusion. My gaiety, because I could be lively, or at any rate acquire the art of seeming so, distracted him from his habitual savage gloom and his terrible fear of losing money.'

The two subjects they never discussed were literature and love. Stendhal's passion for Metilde, he sardonically reflected, had at least kept him chaste throughout the first six or seven months of 1821, but in August there was an attempt to alter this unhappy state of affairs, devised by Mareste, the lawyer Nicolas-Rémy Lolot and a friend whom Beyle calls 'Poitevin', otherwise unidentified. The three had arranged 'une délicieuse partie de filles' at the home of Lolot's former mistress, Mme Petit, to whom the sexually athletic advocate had lent money to open a brothel.

The four men arrived at the house in Rue de Cadran (now Rue Léopold Bellan) off Rue Montmartre, at eight o'clock, and were given a most elegant fourth-floor room, with iced champagne, warm punch and the services of a girl named Alexandrine, about seventeen or eighteen years of age, whose beautiful dark eyes reminded Stendhal of Titian's *Venus of Urbino* in the Uffizi at Florence. Mareste, having offered her a glass of champagne which she refused, retired with her at once, while Mme Petit presented the others with two 'not bad-looking' consolations.

After a while Mareste, now slightly pale, came back into the room. 'She's yours, Beyle. All honour to the new arrival!' cried his friends. Accepting the challenge, Stendhal found Alexandrine stretched out on the bed, a little tired, now looking more like Titian's Venus than ever. 'Let's just talk for ten minutes,' said she, 'I shall soon recover my youthful fire.' He thought her utterly adorable, without the merest touch of *libertinage* apart from a certain hint of 'folly, or passion, if you like' with which her eyes now and then were full.

Perhaps visited by that spasmodic bashfulness which never altogether abandoned him in his dealings with women, Henri was suddenly incapable of an adequate performance, and suggested masturbation as a substitute. When he quit the field and Lolot arrived to have the situation explained to him by an astonished

Alexandrine, they could hear his laughter echoing through three rooms, and when the others were told what had happened they burst into a peal of guffaws that went on for twenty minutes and sent Poitevin rolling about on the carpet. 'Alexandrine's ingenuous astonishment was hilarious; it was the first time anyone had failed with the poor child.'

Whatever the cause – and Stendhal claimed it was because he was suddenly struck with memoires of Metilde – he passed with his friends henceforth for what he calls a 'babilan', a word derived from an Italian term, *babilano*, meaning 'a platonic lover by nature's decree' and originating with a certain Babilano Pallavicino whose marriage had been annulled on the grounds of his impotence. The word, discovered during Stendhal's reading among Italian travel writings of De Brosses and Lalande, apparently gained general acceptance within his circle of friends. As for the episode itself, this seems to have endeared him to his companions and consolidated his friendship with Lolot:

> the only Frenchman with whom I'd willingly spend a fortnight at his country house, the most open-hearted, honest, least witty and least educated man I know, but in his two talents, for winning money without ever playing the stockmarket, and for making the acquaintance of whatever woman he happens to notice in the street or at the theatre, quite inimitable, especially in the second of these things.

An experience which completely effaced his fiasco at Mme Petit's took place when, halfway through October, Stendhal paid his second visit to England. Already bored by Paris, he set out for London in search of a cure for the spleen. 'I needed to put a hill between me and the sight of Milan cathedral. Shakespeare's plays and the actor Kean (pronounced *Kine*) were the very thing'. His later recollections of the trip became hopelessly entangled with memories of the 1817 visit, but it seems likely that once again the irrepressible Lolot and Mareste suggested an English jaunt to cheer up their all too easily desponding friend.

Shakespeare was not currently playing at either of the London 'patent houses', the theatres licensed by the 1737 act to present stage plays, so they had to make do with a performance of Goldsmith's *She Stoops to Conquer* at the Haymarket, in which Stendhal was delighted by the facial contortions of the actor playing Marlowe. When three weeks later he managed to see Kean as Othello at Drury Lane, he was almost crushed to death in the customary stampede for tickets, though the long wait beforehand brought happy reminders of his youthful stage-struck days in the Paris of Dugazon and Duchesnois.

Once he got to his stall seat and his anger at the jostling crowd in the box-office passageway had died down, he was able to revel in Kean's interpretation of the Moor, understanding at once how much of the actor's erratic genius arose from the essential fact that he was not a gentleman, and at the same time marvelling at the way in which the English seemed to have a completely different language of gesture for expressing their deepest emotions.

With his lifelong passion for trees, which he claimed as another motive for his English journey, he found solace at Richmond, climbing to the top of the hill to gaze across the fields from the famous terrace, so often used as a vantage point by painters of the period. Inevitably the vista recalled the mountain slopes around Como, Cadenabbia, the Brianza, the *sacro monte* of Varese, but the intense green was that of England and Stendhal was never insensitive to its particular visual enchantment.

Within these Richmond shades he sat reading the *Memoirs of the Life of Colonel Hutchinson*, the biography written by Lucy Hutchinson in 1670 in vindication of her husband, a Parliamentarian soldier who had signed King Charles I's death warrant. Published for the first time in 1806, the work had easily established itself as a minor classic, distinguished by the grave beauty of its prose style and the noble singlemindedness with which its author, consciously working against the political grain of Restoration England, sought to justify her subject's life and aims. It has been pointed out that the *Memoirs*, which ten years later Stendhal could still speak of as 'one of my favourite books', had a pervasive influence on *La Chartreuse de Parme*, both in a general military and political context, and maybe also in the steadfastness, intelligence and energy of Lucy Hutchinson herself as one of the models for Gina Sanseverina. More personally, its appeal to Beyle himself must inevitably have lain in the sense of an unflinching integrity sharpened by being on the losing side, and in that ambiguous fascination which the sober vigour of puritan England so often exerted upon him.

It was while reading Lucy Hutchinson on the terrace at Richmond one day that he heard a voice calling 'Mister Bell!' and recognized Sir Francis Burdett, the radical member of parliament and champion of political reform, whom he had met in Milan in the company of the gadabout socialite Lady Jersey. Surprised that Stendhal had not seen her during his stay in England, Burdett was equally astonished that he had not looked up any of his other English acquaintances, such as Hobhouse and Brougham, let alone been to dine at Holland House, *de rigueur* for any foreign visitor with literary pretensions and liberal sympathies. It was only during his third visit five years later that Stendhal seems to have started pushing these social advantages to the full. Though on this occasion Burdett introduced him to the delights of a journey back to London by boat along the Thames, he was apparently incapable of comprehending the Frenchman's reluctance to look for good company when he might have found it so easily.

Mareste and Lolot, always on the lookout for girls, drew him into an arrangement they had made with their hired English valet to find them some amusement at a brothel in Westminster Bridge Road, Lambeth (near the present Waterloo Station). The area was decidedly louche, the sort of place where, Stendhal feared, they could easily have been beaten up by sailors, but the ladies themselves, young, timid and pale, with lovely chestnut hair, turned out to be very dainty and particular, having already made difficulties with the valet over the price of providing morning tea if the gentlemen stopped the night.

The tiny house, with equally minute articles of furniture, had a miniature garden of which the girls were inordinately proud, containing the laundry copper and a vat for brewing beer. 'Let's get out of here!' said the disgusted Lolot. Henri, more humanely, felt touched by the neatness of everything, however small and shabby. Even though he shared his friends' fear of getting murdered and made no secret of it to his hostesses, who were duly put out, he started to feel at ease, 'as if I'd been among dear friends whom I saw again after having been away for a year'.

To heighten their nervousness still further, none of the bedroom doors locked properly. From the floor above, Lolot called down to him: 'If someone's murdering you, just shout out!' and Stendhal's young companion, Miss Appleby, was surprised to see him take out pistols and a knife and put them on top of the commode. She was modest enough, however, to insist on snuffing out the candle before they commenced. So charmed was he by such gestures that he readily consented to return next day, looking forward to the agreeable, quiet evening '*full of snugness*' which awaited him. This time he and Lolot brought bottles of claret and some champagne, the popping of whose corks delighted the girls, 'though their expressions of pleasure were decently subdued'. He thought for a moment of asking Miss Appleby to Paris – she told him she would live off apples (was there a pun lurking here which Stendhal failed to pick up?) and cost him nothing – but the memory of having to look after Pauline at Milan, that 'oyster so tediously clinging to the hull of my ship', soon enough deterred him from the scheme.

His visits to the humble little establishment in the Westminster Bridge Road had worked the necessary magic of dislocation and detachment which, if it did not cure him of anguished longing for Italy and Italian love (he neither needed nor desired a cure) at any rate served to reconcile him with his situation and palliate the effects of his loneliness. One of the most stimulating and imaginative of modern writers on Stendhal, Philippe Berthier, suggests convincingly that the presentation of this episode in *Souvenirs d'Egotisme* has a certain legendary dimension. The crossing of the bridge, the mysterious cab ride through the half-built suburbs, the brothel which turns out to be a doll's house, the 'Gulliverization' of the Frenchmen into giants among their Lilliputian hostesses, the childlike nature of their entertainment, the absence of adult menace embodied by the simple fact that they were not murdered during the night, the otherworldly paleness of the girls, benign goddesses of Fate living off propitiatory offerings in the shape of wine and cold meats brought by their guests – there is no reason to doubt any of these details themselves, but life's tendency to make accommodations with art easily transmutes them into something more like the elements of a mythical redemption.

If it saved Stendhal's sanity, the trip to London failed to mitigate his distaste for English attitudes and his fundamental suspicion of English social and political institutions. He saw what many of his European contemporaries were reluctant or unable to see, and what England itself has only been willing to address in the closing decades of our own century, that genuine political liberty was a carefully nurtured illusion, that the object of British government was to sustain privileges rather than rights, and that grinding devotion to hard work and an obsession with the maintenance and the successful passage of rigid class barriers were the chimeras which distracted this 'most obtuse and barbarous people in the whole world' from achieving real freedom.

None of these shrewd realizations, let alone his entirely justifiable view of the English as incapable of finding real happiness, clouded his mature admiration of the country's literary culture or in any way lessened his enduring interest in the manners and value-system of Outre-Manche. The ability of Stendhal's intelligence to free itself from the least hint of emotional compromise made him a total stranger to that ignorant chauvinism with which cultivated Frenchmen have so often amply repaid England's xenophobic scorn. Now, what is more, he was to be drawn yet closer into the world of English letters through his newest incarnation, that of a periodical journalist.

No account of the London literary scene during the early nineteenth century can ignore the immense significance of the magazines and reviews which sprang up with mushroom rapidity in the wake of the *Edinburgh* and the *Quarterly*, and often in direct imitation of their style. By the early 1820s a kind of circulation war, in the manner of our modern newspapers, had developed between the leading contenders in the field, and there were plenty of smaller ventures ready to pitch into the fray. Publishing was becoming increasingly competitive, and it would not be long before the tradition of serial fiction, which was to engross the efforts of almost every major British novelist of the mid-century, was established through the house magazines of firms such as Bentley and Frazer.

Nobody seems quite certain as to how Stendhal began his fruitful association with English magazines, but it is probable that the first editorial contacts were made after his return to Paris in the autumn of 1821. On earlier visits from Italy he had frequented the English reading room opened in Rue Vivienne by the enterprising Giovanni Antonio Galignani, an Italian from Brescia whose quick perception of the profit to be made from supplying books and newspapers in their own language to the British travellers now pouring into France soon made him the principal foreign-language publisher on the Continent. His newspaper, *Galignani's English Messenger*, founded in 1814, exists today as the *International Herald Tribune*, and the Librairie Galignani, now in Rue de Rivoli, is owned by W.H. Smith.

It was at Galignani's 'cabinet de lecture', with a pleasant garden attached, that Stendhal could read the latest editions of British magazines, and where he presumbably made the acquaintance of Thomas Colley Grattan and William Henry Curran, members of a lively Parisian circle of Irish expatriates and each of them connected with an English review, either as commissioning editor or as editor-in-chief. Grattan (no relation to his more famous contemporary, the politician and orator Henry Grattan) subsequently tried and failed as a dramatist, became more successful as a travel writer, and ended his career as a much esteemed British consul in Boston. While in France he founded *The Paris Monthly Review of British & Continental Literature, by A Society of English Gentlemen*, which would soon be taken over by Galignani himself, no stranger to magazine publishing.

Curran, son of the great Irish judge John Philpot Curran, acted as a Parisian agent for the London publisher Henry Colburn, who had bought *The New Monthly Magazine* in 1821 and appointed the poet Thomas Campbell as its editor, with the indefatigable journalist Cyrus Redding, formerly at *Galignani's English Messenger*, as his assistant. The paper, in its new incarnation, was intended by Colburn as a deliberate challenge to more heavyweight fare such as *Blackwood's Magazine*, and the presence of a Paris correspondent was taken by certain of its critics as a distinct sign of frivolity, enhanced by the bantering irony of his particular tone.

Knowing his English audience as he did, Stendhal was ideally equipped for the job of providing a series of lively, sharply focused articles, dealing critically and dispassionately with every aspect of contemporary Parisian cultural and political life. There was evidently no great degree of editorial interference, and the tone of his pieces is as freely waspish and subversive as we might imagine. The effectiveness of these articles, some of them extended periodical essays in the form he so admired in reading the *Edinburgh Review*, others merely brief recensions and notes, owes much to that inimitable stylistic terseness which, as we have seen, was evolved during his period as a Napoleonic bureaucrat. Yet the practical experience of journalism could only consolidate this idiom, and it is impossible to read these pithy, acerbic pieces without hearing the voice of the novelist in the making.

Unfortunately, in almost every case where the magazine articles are concerned, that voice arrives at second hand, via an English translation, since practically none of Stendhal's copy survives in the original French. Even in such a guise, it becomes clear at once that he was naturally suited to the journalistic medium. We can only regret that the opportunity for him to try out his talents, to fly a few of his favourite kites, set out his pet theories and formulate an axiom or two, in the presence of a reading public should not have arrived many years earlier.

The subject matter of his articles was often literary, but he was soon able to give them a more obviously social and political slant when in 1824 he joined the *London Magazine*. This was a periodical which in its heyday three years previously had included Hazlitt, Lamb, De Quincey and Leigh Hunt among its contributors. When its brilliant editor, John Scott, was killed in a duel, the printers appointed Henry Southern, formerly of *The Retrospective Review*, as his successor, but the circulation forthwith began falling. Southern's relations with his authors were decidedly unreliable and Stendhal wisely kept a foot in the door at the *New Monthly Magazine*, to which he later returned. His contributions to the *London*, forming a regular series from December 1824 onwards, nevertheless rank as his most sustained and consistent journalistic achievement.

During this period, in addition to articles on the Vagrancy Act, railways, acupuncture and the Metropolitan Tithe Question, a translation of Pindar's tenth Nemean ode and a memoir of Liston the comedian, the *London's* dwindling readership could enjoy the witty and urbane sequence of essays entitled 'Letters From Paris by Grimm's Grandson' – who was of course Stendhal, reporting on the newest topics of intelligent conversation in the French capital.

In these he could be devastatingly funny, particularly as a reviewer of the latest literary success. When in March 1825 the Vicomte D'Arlincourt published his novel *L'Etrangère*, a farrago of romantic medievalism clearly calculated to appeal to the fashionable taste for things feudal and baronial, Stendhal made gleeful mincemeat of the work and its author. Starting his piece with the words 'M. d'Arlincourt is a young man remarkable for a handsome person, considerable wealth and boundless absurdity', he went on to retail a series of anecdotes designed to expose the writer's ludicrous vanity and pomposity, as a prelude to a hilarious summary of the novel's plot and the information that D'Arlincourt was known as 'le vicomte inversif' from his habit of inverting the syntax of his sentences. None of this, however, seems to have prevented Vincenzo Bellini from using the book as the basis of his earliest operatic success, *La Straniera*, which Stendhal himself was later to hear performed on his return to Italy.

The translator of the *London Magazine* articles was Sarah Austin, the remarkably gifted and energetic wife of a noted English jurist for whose professional failure as an overscrupulous barrister she compensated with her literary work. Beyle, having taken issue with his supposed 'Mister Translator*' over certain of the

* The letter, dated 10 September 1825, was first published (in part) by Sarah Austin's granddaughter, the noted Italophile Janet Ross. On it Austin has scribbled: 'From M. de Beyle alias Baron de Stendhal.' It is unsigned, dispatched as if from Orléans, and has the characteristically bamboozling conclusion: 'My wife is well. Edgard sends you a kiss', which must have mystified the recipient.

English renderings, finally guessed that she must be a woman on the grounds that she was too innocent to understand 'those things which the world takes as read' and pressed Colburn to employ somebody else, a man for preference, to do the job: the publisher stayed loyal to Austin, and she and Stendhal eventually met in London in 1826. Of his *Paris Monthly Review* translator, we know only that the man's name was Bartholomew Stritch, and that Stendhal thought him 'impassive and sad, perfectly honest, a victim of the aristocracy because he was Irish and a lawyer, yet always maintaining as a matter of personal honour the prejudices sown and cultivated in English heads by this same aristocracy'.

For too long these English versions of Stendhal's magazine essays, the nearest that we possess, in many cases, to their lost originals, lay neglected by scholars, critics and biographers, and until the appearance, from 1980 onwards, of an authoritative modern edition, Stendhalians were content to make do with translations prepared for French journals of the period, which recycled British review articles. In his apparent unwillingness to disclose an identity, the author may simply have been following the common practice of the day by remaining anonymous, but it has been suggested that more was at stake even than the well-established Beylian tradition of aliases, pseudonyms and disappearing acts.

In fact, to several of the most eminent French scholars, the very nature of his journalism has seemed like the most outrageous betrayal. In an extraordinary article published in 1950, by way of an introduction to some unpublished correspondence with Colburn's Parisian agent, a tirade which at its least restrained reads like a parody of the worst sort of defensive Gallic chauvinism was unleashed by the otherwise rational and painstaking scholar François Michel. Reiterating an earlier claim made by Pierre Martino in connection with *Racine et Shakespeare* that there was a conspiracy among English magazines 'to contest the intellectual hegemony of France and to ruin the final vestiges of its influence in England', he accuses Stendhal of sacrificing his patriotism to literary and political prejudices, of cowardice and duplicity. With a grandiloquence for which only the original French provides an appropriate vehicle, he concludes 'that same pen which taught

English readers that the French people were incapable of demonstrating the slightest moral courage, a few years later would write the *Rouge* and the *Chartreuse*, whose lustre beyond our borders is hardly rivalled by that of a few dusty *Reviews*'.

There is no evidence for this preposterous vision of Stendhal maliciously setting out to trash the national *gloire*. His stance was always a critical one, even with regard to people and works of art he particularly admired, and we should scarcely expect to find him indulging in a bland public-relations exercise on behalf of Restoration France, so many aspects of which were repugnant to him. Like any other capable journalist, he had gauged both the tone of the papers for which he wrote and, no doubt, the quality of their readership, and it is in this light that his periodical labours, whether in the form of extended essays, or as brief notices of the kind which appeared in the *New Monthly*'s 'Historical Papers' section, should be evaluated.

Far from being a cowardly sell-out to an Albion super-perfidious in its dastardly defeat of Bonaparte, Stendhal's dusty reviews, judged more seriously, can be seen as an entirely valid personal comment on a culture which had entered a phase of serious vulnerability and confusion. France's 'intellectual hegemony' had died with the Revolution and the generation with which it regained ascendancy over Europe, that of Balzac, Hugo, Mérimée and Musset, of Gautier, Dumas and George Sand, was still young and barely tested. With the major exception of Lamartine and the minor exceptions of Béranger and Marceline Desbordes-Valmore, poetry (for which Stendhal in any case had little or no taste) was moribund, while the drama, however nervously twitching in the direction of full-blooded Romanticism, still seemed uncertain of its aims. The number of distinguished novels produced in France between the publication of *Les Liaisons Dangereuses* in 1782 and Stendhal's own *Le Rouge et le Noir* in 1830 can almost be told on the fingers of one hand.

Through the mesh of unsparing judgements on the fads and foibles of Beyle's Parisian contemporaries, we can glimpse a cultural constituency in the crucial process of regrouping, and begin to feel that the vital modernity of a Berlioz or a Delacroix is not, after all, that far off. The crucial element in this recovery was the very same that enabled Stendhal to gather essential copy for his articles themselves. Ever since the fall of the Ancien Régime, the unique institution of the salon, the drawing room in which the hostess or the host, not necessarily themselves people of talent or intellect, would draw together the brightness and wittiest spirits of the day, had gone into serious decline. Under the Restoration, partly as a result of the need for the politically divided segments of metropolitan upper and middle-class society to rally their various sympathizers, these remarkable concentrations of brilliance and originality underwent a spectacular revival. Everyone from liberal duchesses and exiled foreign idealists to the wives of royalist bureaucrats and fashionable philosophers, from the widow of the chemist Lavoisier and Madame de Staël's daughter to the painters Elisabeth Vigée-Lebrun and Baron Gérard or the purveyor of Gothic fantasy fiction Charles Nodier, kept open house on at least one evening or afternoon each week for the makers, the dreamers or the coruscating conversationalists, hailing from anywhere between Paris and St Petersburg, London and Lisbon.

The greatest irony of Stendhal's professional life was that it should have been here, in the drawing rooms of despised Paris rather than in the society of his beloved Milan, that he consolidated his reputation as a literary artist, that he found the earliest genuinely appreciative public for his works, and became identified for the first time as an arresting personality, someone to be recalled and memorialized even at his most infuriating. The hosts and guests through a whole range of differently complexioned salons never forgot him, and it was in this social context that he forged several of the deeper, more enduring friendships of his middle age.

The house where he was perhaps the most often to be seen was number 1, Rue Chabanais, a street running north out of Rue Neuve des Petits Champs, not far from his new lodgings at Hôtel des Lillois, in Rue de Richelieu. It was here that every Sunday the painter and art critic Etienne-Jean Delécluze, inhabitant of the archetypal Parisian *grenier* or attic storey, received company of a kind representing the cream of that rising generation of artistic, scientific and political talent which, for better or worse, was to give nineteenth-century France its most sharply etched identity.

Delécluze was one of those singular figures regularly produced by a sophisticated culture, whose awareness of their own creative limitations, combined with a lack of envy or pomposity, makes them willing to accept the role of enablers and minglers rather than jostle for recognition as artistic personalities in their own right. Two years older than Stendhal, he had trained and practised as a painter, but boasted an additional gift for writing which in 1822 had earned him the coveted post of art critic on the conservative *Journal des Débats*. Here, against the background of fierce controversy generated by paintings such as Géricault's *Le Radeau de la Méduse* and Delacroix's *Massacre de Scio*, he exercised a prudent moderation, sympathetic towards the classicists (he was the pupil, friend and distinguished biographer of David) but capable of appreciating real merit in the younger Romantics. He never married – which explains why, with one occasional exception, the *habitués* of his *grenier* were exclusively male – but fell hopelessly in love with Amélie Cyvoct, the young niece of Juliette Récamier, most famous of the royalist salon hostesses and a kind of surrogate elder sister to the lovestruck Delécluze. The passion was alas never reciprocated by Amélie.

Stendhal's first contact with Delécluze was in connection with the *Histoire de la Peinture en Italie*. The critic had wanted to review the book for *Le Lycée français*, but the magazine folded after its fifth issue, just as he was preparing his article. One Sunday in February 1822, Stendhal was taken, presumably by the ubiquitous Mareste, to Rue Chabanais at two o'clock in the afternoon.

> It was at this inconvenient hour that he used to receive company. You had to climb 95 stairs, because he had his drawing class on the sixth floor of a house belonging to him and his sisters. . . . From his little windows you could merely glimpse a forest of chimneys covered in black plaster. For me it was one of the ugliest of views, but the four small rooms in which M. Delécluze lived were decorated with engravings and curious and pleasing objects d'art.

Around a small fire sat eight or ten men talking about everything under the sun. Stendhal was struck, not just by their liveliness and good sense, and by Delécluze's supreme tact in subtly manoeuvring the conversation so that everybody had a chance to speak, but by a sense of a special, unforgettable atmosphere which he could find nowhere else, and which, quite correctly, he identified as being uniquely French. In England the occasion would have been bogged down with snobbish deference to rank and title, in Germany the air would have been thick with transcendental metaphysics. 'Only in the land of Voltaire, Molière and Courier is such a society possible.'

Paul-Louis Courier, the political theorist who was also a successful winemaker, and several of whose ideas powerfully influenced Stendhal, was probably present on that first afternoon in February. The other guests are not identified, and the *Souvenirs d'Egotisme* tantalizingly comes to a halt soon after the passage quoted above, but some of the company can at least be guessed at. Sooner or later on these Sunday visits to Rue Chabanais, he would meet Jean-Jacques Ampère, son of the great physicist, a writer for the liberal newspaper *Le Globe* and a noted teacher at the Collège de France, Albert Stapfer, translator of Goethe's *Faust*, the dramatist and politician Charles de Rémusat, and the botanist Adrien de Jussieu, 'long de taille, long de tête, long de visage'. Another regular visitor was Delécluze's brother-in-law, Emmanuel-Louis-Nicolas Viollet-le-Duc, whose interest in historic buildings was passed on to his son Eugène-Emmanuel, famous as a Gothicizing architect and overzealous restorer of medieval churches and castles.

On the host himself, Stendhal, once alone with pen and paper, was as always unrestrained by considerations of friendship or gratitude. Delécluze, he tells us, is:

> a character in the mould of the worthy Vicar of Wakefield. It needs the half-tones of a Goldsmith or an Addison to give you a notion of him. To begin with, he is extremely ugly and, rarely for Paris, he has an ignoble, low countenance, but is well made and fairly tall. He has all the pettiness of a bourgeois. If he buys a dozen handkerchiefs at 36 francs from the corner shop, two hours later he will think these same handkerchiefs a rarity and that their equals can scarcely be found throughout the city.

Delécluze's own verdict on Beyle would probably not have surprised him, and for shrewdness and precision his testimony counts as among the most valuable from a period when Stendhal was starting to be recognized as a literary figure. The critic-painter's journal evokes for us a whole series of lively vignettes, seasoned with his own, not always admiring comments. At one moment Stendhal figures as the intellectual Mephistopheles to a Faustian Mareste, filling his head with devilish nonsense in favour of Romanticism, at another pontificating, during a poetry reading, on the inherent tedium of verse, then suddenly tongue-tied like a schoolboy when it came to discussing the poem's ideas, Beyle the iconoclast, Beyle the arguer in the teeth of reason, enemy of that very logic whose defender he claimed to be, hurling his paradoxes and generalizations to and fro in a deliberate attempt to churn up the waters of debate if ever they threatened to grow too limpid.

For all their intimacy, the friendship between the two was never intense, and their accounts of one another possess a curiously deliberate remoteness, Stendhal writing about Delécluze as if he were an old man and the latter dissecting Stendhal with the sort of fascinated distaste an anthropologist might show when confronted with an entirely novel yet at the same time repugnant manifestation of humanity. Yet even though sometimes driven to distraction by Beyle's conversational sabotage, Delécluze clearly recognized a singular personality. One Sunday in 1827, when the assembly in Rue Chabanais had been locked into a particularly knotty discussion on the ideas of the right-wing ideologue Xavier De Maistre, he tried afterwards to write down the various interventions in the form of a Socratic dialogue, extending this to some words with another guest, an Alsatian named Meynier, in the corner of the room while the controversy was still in progress.

The subject of their talk was that 'homme singulier . . . M. Beyle'. Meynier confessed himself staggered by Stendhal's mixture of ignorance and assurance, was amazed to discover that anyone so clearly unacquainted with either England or Germany had actually visited both those countries. Delécluze drily concluded that with people like him around, you understood why the Jesuits existed; if they really knew their business, they would have sent more like Beyle out into the world. The two men could nevertheless praise his honesty and openness. 'He's a good enemy and it's a pleasure to do battle with him.' Warmly praising his artistic enthusiasms as 'natural and sincere', Delécluze claimed to have a better opinion of him than he held himself, and made what was doubtless an entirely accurate judgement in saying that the atmosphere of the Paris salons, by making him nervous and edgy, merely exposed the pretentiousness and brutality of Beyle's discourse. His obsession with appearing mathematically precise was a mere absurdity, displayed at its most risible in *De l'Amour*, where Delécluze had rallied him on the possibility that the book might have been bound up in the wrong order. Nobody knew how he lived, he had few friends and Delécluze's own attempts at befriending him had been rebuffed.

Nevertheless he respected this independence, and, as a witness to his regard, on a visit to Rome in the winter of 1823–4, he undertook a detailed character portrait which seems, to this biographer at least, more consistently revealing of the paradoxes of Stendhal's personality than the much more frequently quoted *H.B.* by their mutual friend Mérimée. 'Fat, short, stocky, vivacious' with curly hair and bright eyes, Beyle appears, in Delécluze's remarkably perceptive and beautifully penned sketch, a kind of existentialist *avant la lettre*, devoted to physical and intellectual pleasures, but letting his soul sleep.

> He loves the arts, the sciences, women and the whole of nature as a sort of toy designed to distract him: every time he senses that one of these things might make a deep impression on him, he turns his desires, his feelings, his eyes, towards an object which can engage his attention and give a different direction to his longings. Gravity and seriousness are displeasing to him . . . . friendship bores him because it is a serious matter; and of all his thoughts, the one which wearies him most is that there was a yesterday and that there will be a tomorrow.

Delécluze recalls Stendhal's blazing eyes as he contrasted their different backgrounds and personalities, the one brought up in an atmosphere of love and sweetness, easily achieving his ambitions, the other perpetually scarred by a sense of his father's coldness and of the deception that had tricked him of his rightful portion in life. 'Suddenly, as though to avoid a discussion which threatened to grow too serious, he turned down a Roman street and we never saw him for the rest of the day.'

He was at his best, thought Delécluze, with intelligent men whom he did not know well enough to adopt his more habitual pose of cynicism. With women he put on too many airs, probably because he was worried that being too fat made him lack the confidence which a more naturally elegant figure would have given. The vigour and clarity of his intelligence compensated for the unaccountable gaps in his thinking. 'It is like a bullet hole in a flag. The flag keeps on flying, but through part of it you can glimpse the sky beyond.'

Admiring Stendhal's scrupulous personal honesty, which made him such excellent company, Delécluze identifies very clearly for us what he perceived as the writer's principal dilemma at that moment. 'Stendhal himself,' he says:

> is the slave of our language to a far greater degree than he supposes. In his writings he appears prudish and affected, because the French language is timid, and the nature of Stendhal's talent is frank, brusque and fearless. He resembles one of those men of strong character with a black beard but a thin voice. In a word, there is a disparity between his ideas and his style. It is tiresome that Stendhal should not have been born in an age and a country where language would have served him better, or at any rate that at the present time in which we live he should have so invincible an aversion to work. He will be among those who, like certain painters, make a few sketches and leave two or three imperfect studies which inspire us to exclaim 'What a pity this man never took work seriously!'

Delécluze's apprehension of his friend as someone essentially reluctant to encourage intimacy was not purely grounded in a personal regret. There can be no doubt that Stendhal's understanding of friendship had radically altered as he approached middle age, and that he was now far more guarded, wary and sceptical in his relationship than he had been as a boy in Grenoble, as a young man jaunting up and down Napoleonic Europe, or even as an expatriate in Milan. His typical bachelor horror of being alienated from his married friends by their wives had made him suspicious, as noted earlier, even of someone like Louis Crozet.

> His wife has taken him away from me for several years, jealous of our friendship. What a pity! What a superior being M. Crozet would have been had he lived in Paris. Marriage, and provincial life especially, age a man astoundingly, the intelligence grows lazy, and any movement of the brain, through its sheer rarity, becomes painful, and eventually impossible.

It was probably true that Praxède Crozet, in the manner of many careful wives, wanted to sweep her husband's life clean of unrespectable acquaintance, but the judgement is unfair on Crozet himself, who had at least stayed loyal to Stendhal. If friendship with Henri Beyle was only half the pleasure it might have been, there were plenty of people prepared to run the risk of trying to get to know him better. One of these, introduced to him by Delécluze one Sunday in March 1825, was a young man who, within the limits of his chosen genres, the short story and the novella, was to become one of the mid-century's most admired literary practitioners, a writer whose work bears the obvious imprint of Stendhal's influence.

The son of a painter, Prosper Mérimée first made his mark in the Rue Chabanais circle when he read aloud two of his little closet dramas published as *Théâtre de Clara Gazul*. Stendhal puffed these in the *London Magazine* the following July ('Clara' became a nickname for Mérimée) and the pair meanwhile became the greatest of friends. Almost all the older man's letters to the younger were subsequently destroyed, but Mérimée's frequently scabrous bulletins of gossip, meant to beguile a tedious hour in Civitavecchia, survive to show how well attuned he was to Beyle's needs as a correspondent.

Together they travelled through France, to Laon and into the Auvergne, and when Mérimée visited Italy in 1839 they made journeys to Naples and Paestum. It was Mérimée who recommended a subtitle for *Armance*, 'ou le faubourg Saint-Germain', who asked Victor Hugo for tickets so that he could take his friend to that most notorious of all theatrical first nights, the première of Hernani on 25 February 1830, and who made the ideal boon companion at the Café de la Rotonde, where the pair could meet up with kindred souls such as Alfred de Musset and Eugène Delacroix, and share in the general mood of political cynicism which would overtake the artistic world of the 1830s after the July Revolution and the accession of Louis-Philippe.

The gap in age between Beyle and Mérimée was nearly twenty years, and it was no doubt flattering to the former to find himself readily accepted by the latter as a mentor and confessor. Such a relationship, however, did nothing to soften Stendhal's judgement. In the *Souvenirs d'Egotisme* he remembered meeting 'this poor young man in a grey overcoat, so ugly, with his retroussé nose', who had 'an impertinent and extremely unpleasing air about him. His small expressionless eyes always had the same look in them, and it was a nasty look'. Even conceding that Mérimée had since become one of his best friends, he was still, five years later, 'not too sure of his heart'. By the time they set off on their 1839 Neapolitan jaunt, Henri could note sourly in a copy of his *Promenades dans Rome* that 'the frightful vanity of Academus [his nickname for Mérimée] spoils this trip to Naples'.

Another young man encountered among the salon-goers, and though somewhat more doubtful of Stendhal's manner and attitudes, always willingly responsive to the fascinating contrariness of his personality, was the naturalist Victor Jacquemont, one of those golden boys with whom everyone of either sex falls a little and innocuously in love, and whose abundant promise dooms them to an early death. Born in 1801, he belonged to a distinguished family from the lesser nobility in Artois, and his father, Frédéric-François-Venceslas Jacquemont de Moreau, had originally been ordained as a priest before gaining a certain mournful celebrity through his involvement in a plot against Napoleon.

Hostility to Bonapartism was the single flaw – we might almost say, the necessary flaw – which Stendhal could identify in Victor's otherwise engaging character. Amid the severity of his judgements in *Souvenirs d'Egotisme*, his verdict on Jacquemont, soon to die at the age of thirty-one from a fever at Bombay after an epic tour of India, stands out in its generous admiration. After setting his friend's voyage to the East in the context of a journey which was 'really the only door which vanity left open to truth', he admits that he may be wrong after all about the younger man's lack of logic and resulting misanthropy. 'Victor seems to me a person of the greatest distinction. I view him rather as a connoisseur (forgive me this word) might perceive the makings of a fine horse in a four-month-old foal with unsteady legs.'

Jacquemont, who jokingly addressed Stendhal as 'le Baron' and seized on the nickname 'Jemoi' – 'I-me' – to encapsulate the Beylian ego, was a shrewd, unsparing critic of the writer's work. He understood from the outset that whereas the social animal might be gauche, timid and vulnerable under the bantering, combative exterior, the author and artist, singleminded in his resolve to say what needed saying, respected the frankness of criticism uncompromised by envy or malice. That personal courage Stendhal had shown in his duel with Odruas Kambin or during the ardours of the Russian campaign was an invaluable attribute on battlefields of another sort altogether.

If they had not already met at the house of the louche and slightly sinister journalist and police spy Joseph Lingay, the two were perhaps introduced at a salon with obvious and important associations for Stendal. At number 35, Rue d'Anjou, lived the son and daughter-in-law of the great *idéologue* Destutt de Tracy himself, a friend and mentor of the Jacquemont family, with whom Beyle had at last made contact in 1817, when the philosopher had come in person to his hotel in Place Favart to acknowledge a complimentary copy of the *Histoire de la Peinture*. Naturally enough, the younger man was profoundly flattered, to the point of feeling that his manifest admiration must inevitably have compromised him in Tracy's eyes, but the connection, once made, proved a useful one, and Stendhal, on his return to Paris, found himself a welcome visitor at the house in Rue d'Anjou.

Here Tracy, a handsome figure in black, used to stand in front of the fireplace, shifting from one foot to the other:

> with a habit of talking which was completely the opposite to his manner as a writer. His conversation was all neat, elegant perceptions: he was as horrified by an emphatic word as by an oath, and

> he wrote like a country mayor. The energetic directness which I seem to have cultivated in those days can scarcely have pleased him. I had huge black whiskers . . . . this look of an Italian butcher never quite seemed to agree with someone who had formerly been a colonel in the days of Louis XVI.

Destutt de Tracy's son, Victor, a liberal deputy for the Allier district, who Stendhal tells us was known as Barre de Fer – iron bar – for his extreme bravery, was married to a lively Englishwoman, a Cheshire girl from Stockport named Sarah Newton, whose father had moved to Normandy during the Revolution to manage a cotton mill at Dreux. Her first husband was an officer of dragoons, killed on the way to Waterloo, but Victor de Tracy, whom she married in 1816, was a loving stepfather to her two small daughters.

Sarah Newton de Tracy was yet another of those adoptive sisters whom Henri in the latter part of his life picked up as successors to Pauline. In the salon over which she presided as hostess with her sympathetic, intelligent mother-in-law, Victor Jacquemont was honoured as a family friend. Always attracted to good-looking men, Stendhal was additionally drawn to Jacquemont by the obvious candour with which he responded to the challenge of works such as *De l'Amour* and *Rome, Naples et Florence*. An entire letter of Victor's is devoted to a critique of the newly written 'Salzburg Bough' section of the former work, with trenchant criticism of the author's tendency to interpose himself unnecessarily between reader and subject and a recommendation to suppress certain passages 'at the expense of your writer's self-esteem, to the advantage of clarity'. A subsequent critique of a new preface to *Haydn, Mozart & Metastasio* was still more incisive. Jacquemont told 'Monsieur le Baron' that it really belonged in *Rome, Naples et Florence*, that it was too long, that most of it had been said already, and that his friend was simply a liar in making such effusive eulogies of the conversation to be found in Parisian salons. 'I believe you have lied in good faith,' he conceded, 'you have painted things as you would wish them to be.'

Victor Jacquemont's favourite nickname for Stendhal, 'Jemoi', which others of their mutual acquaintance soon adopted, neatly acknowledged the significance of the Beylian ego. Reading his letters, it is hard not to see him, along with certain other male associates like Mérimée, besides such widely differing inspirations as Metilde Dembowski and Gina Pietragrua, as one of those who, in some sense, turned Stendhal into a novelist. Critical reaction of this kind, which Beyle respected for its honesty, must have encouraged him to confront the unique nature of his gifts at their most effective. Added to which, Jacquemont himself was something of a Stendhalian hero incarnate, with the adventurous dash of a Fabrice del Dongo and the allure of an up-to-date young man in the Lucien Leuwen mode. While Victor, wryly amused though he was by the less guarded aspects of his friend's character, drew readily on the other's cosmopolitanism in literature and art in order to feed his own burgeoning cultural appetites, Stendhal for his part willingly acknowledged the restraining influence of Jacquemont's forthrightness. He was in the habit of interleaving copies of his books with comments on the work in question: one such copy of *De l'Amour* contains a reference to Victor as 'Candide Judex', in another he pays him a still more impressive tribute. 'In looking over the different prefaces for *De l'Amour*, I think what a waste of time! Victor Ja. rendered me a valuable service in forbidding me to talk about myself in public.'

Yet if he was not to speak openly of himself, what was left for 'Jemoi'? The salons undoubtedly fed his self-regard by encouraging him to support the character of a maverick, the kite-flyer and coat-trailer par excellence, and their assembled wits and talents were more than merely amused by what Delécluze neatly describes as 'the conflict of reveries and realities knocking against one another, which made Beyle the most incoherent of men'. In a drawing room like that of the Marquis de La Fayette, aged hero of the American War of Independence, who lived down the street from the Tracys and for whom, as the Plutarchan hero whose principal interest lay in goosing pretty girls, Stendhal maintained an ambiguous admiration, he was always made welcome, but, as he himself observes, only up to a point. It cannot have been especially flattering to the other guests, here or elsewhere, to listen to Stendhal, having skimmed the cream of their conversation, triumphantly announcing with the words 'Mon article est fait!' that he had gathered enough copy to turn into another piece for the *London Magazine* or the *Paris Monthly Review*.

On some of the livelier spirits in Restoration Paris he made a decidedly poor impression. Among these was Mary Clarke (known after her marriage as Madame Mohl) one of those literary figures whose talents, not in themselves creative, are for befriending all the celebrities of the age and sealing these friendships with wonderfully witty, astutely slanted correspondence. Born in 1793, the daughter of a Scotch mother and an Irish father, she spent most of her very long life in France, sharing intensely, either at first or second hand, in the political and social upheavals of her age, and maintaining a salon at which she received everyone from Renan and Turgenev to George Eliot and Mrs Gaskell.

At the house of Mme Cabanis, widow of the physiologist Pierre-Jean-Georges Cabanis, Destutt de Tracy's fellow *idéologue*, Beyle had met the critic and scholar Claude-Charles Fauriel, whose relationship with Mary Clarke was to turn into a serious, long-standing liaison. A friend of young Italian writers like Alessandro Manzoni and Giovanni Berchet, as well as acting in the capacity of mentor to several of Stendhal's acquaintances, including Jean-Jacques Ampère and the historian Augustin Thierry*, Fauriel never quite justified his own promise with the great work everyone might have expected from him. Stendhal nevertheless singles him out for praise as 'together with M. Mérimée and myself, the sole example known to me of non-charlatanism among those in the writing business'.

What would surely have developed into a solid, worthwhile friendship was thwarted by Mary Clarke, to whose drawing room Fauriel sought to introduce Henri Beyle soon after the latter's return to Paris in 1821. 'In a year or two,' Stendhal tells us, 'Mlle Clark quarrelled with me . . . . after which I stopped seeing her.' No love was lost between the two. In his memoirs of the period he describes her as 'a little shrew, half hunchbacked . . . an Englishwoman, lively, I must admit, but with a wit like

* Author of a popular account of the Norman Conquest of England. Stendhal believed he had gone blind through too much masturbation at boarding school.

Chamois horns, hard, dry and twisted'. As for Mary, when she heard that Stendhal was busy over 'a book on old ballads' which was in fact *De l'Amour*, she begged Fauriel not to help him. 'I'm horrified at the thought of his beastly paws being laid on such a subject. He is just like the harpies, with the gift of spoiling everything he touches.' She was probably right in warning Fauriel that 'you are a man he enjoys exploiting', though Stendhal was fulsome in his thanks for the assistance the savant had provided by furnishing him with the details of courtly love in medieval Provence and with translations of Arabic poetry.*

The cause of the quarrel, according to Stendhal, was a silly remark he made after the death of Fauriel's mistress Mme de Condorcet, widow of the famous philosopher guillotined in 1793. Commenting on her humiliating legacy to him of 1200 francs a year, the sort of sum she might have left to a servant, Beyle observed: 'When you have to deal with a princess or a woman who is too rich, you should beat her or else love dies away.' Piously shocked by a remark which those who knew Stendhal better would simply have shrugged off, Fauriel repeated it to Mary, who sent Augustin Thierry's Jesuitical brother Amédée to reprove him. Fauriel took her part, and Stendhal was never afterwards forgiven by her circle, who, he claimed, considered him a monster of immorality.

His alertness to the prevailing artistic trends which engrossed the various salons had begun to revive an enthusiasm first kindled several years before among Ludovico Di Breme's circle in Milan. One of the more obvious ironies of the Restoration lay in what it conspicuously failed to replace from the world devastated by the Revolution and Empire. The sacred principles of French literary classicism, grounded in the marmoreal perfections of the alexandrine line with its inevitable caesura, were now being undermined by the belated advent of Romanticism among French poets and artists, appropriately tinged as this was with a perceptible dash of subversive politics.

Stendhal, whatever the fundamental ambiguity of his position

* Including the tragic tale of Weddah and Om El Bonain, which the poet James Thomson 'B.V.', one of the earliest British Stendhalians, turned into a verse narrative.

as a creative spirit conditioned by early contact with the tastes and styles of the Englightenment, was bound to be excited by any contact with a movement which, by implication at least, flew in the face of *bien-pensant* legitimist sentiment and which was championed by several of the more promising younger men who visited Delécluze, La Fayette and the Tracys, such as Charles de Rémusat, who married La Fayette's granddaughter and whose perfumed elegance made an ambiguous impression on Stendhal, and Prosper Mérimée himself, whose *Théâtre de Clara Gazul* constituted a deliberately anti-classical statement, dealing as it did with realistically evoked contexts of comparatively recent history, using prose as the dialogue medium. Their journalistic mouthpiece was the newly founded newspaper *Le Globe*, with which Stendhal initially tried to ingratiate himself through a puff in the *London Magazine's* December 1824 issue, and in whose pages he managed to publish an article on Roman puppets, as well as the letter he had received from Lord Byron.

His principal link with the *Globe* seems to have been through the journalist Prosper Duvergier de Hauranne, later described by Rémusat as 'a servile, rather dull disciple of Stendhal's school, a dilettante of Romanticism who cared for nothing else'. By degrees, however, Beyle grew wary of the puritanism and pomposity of the youthful *globistes*, comparing them to the Roundheads in the English Civil War. 'Grave, haters of mirth, pedantic a little; often obscure in their reasonsings, which they conduct with all the fervour of thorough-paced dialecticians . . . *logic* is what they want most.' They were, he decided, 'young men who are sincere in search of truth, but unluckily have got weak heads and warm hearts . . . None of them is yet celebrated; but in my opinion, many of them will become so.'

The paper's editor and founder Paul-François Dubois never forgave these patronizing remarks, and years later set down in writing what is probably the most vitriolic of all contemporary portraits of Stendhal, its sting sharpened by the indubitable accuracy of its criticisms, however maliciously phrased.

> M. de Stendhal (Beyle) occupied the entire day in wasting and perverting his various natural gifts in an effort to astonish and

> surprise. A fat personage, round both of form and countenance, affecting the negligent air of a marquis, but remaining nonetheless more like the heavy German baron whose name he assumed. A sad apostle of materialism, grimacing with laughter at everything in the way of affection, elevated sentiment, holy ideas of God and duty, breathless in the pursuit of pleasures which he derided in the act of enjoying, dishonouring the arts in sweeping away their foundation in the ideal. A sort of chubby Mephistopheles whose publications annoyed me, and whose fitful conversation, picked up that morning from some book or other, poured out each evening in pretentious witticisms . . . . affecting to wear the livery of M. de Tracy's logic and forming an artistic metaphysic from the works of Helvétius, baffling the reader either in the guise of an old whitehaired dilettante, or as a young and brilliant nobleman burning up the roads of Italy with the swiftest of coachmen in the lightest of carriages. And every evening, through the gloom, you'd meet him with an umbrella under his arm, in galoshes, hurrying along the street to pay court to the Marquis de LaFayette and the Comte de Tracy – or to sound off his opinions in the foyer of the Vaudeville.

The chubby Mephistopheles was nevertheless ready to prove himself in the very cause for which the restless young lions of Paris were now starting to rally to the *Globe*. On 29 July 1822 another liberal newspaper, *Le Constitutionnel*, announced the arrival at the Théâtre de la Porte Saint-Martin of a troupe of English actors, led by their manager, a Mr Penley. 'Certain persons,' noted the paper, 'may find it strange that in Paris we should be offered such productions from abroad. Literature and the fine arts form a republic which must take to its bosom all the peoples of the earth. . . . Is not France, besides, richly enough endowed not to fear any comparison?'

Two days later, the first performance by the venturesome company, a production of Shakespeare's *Othello*, took place amid scenes of appalling uproar, while the next, on 2 August, was effectively halted by an affray between the audience and the police. One by one the papers weighed in, the *Constitutionnel* rather surprisingly lauding the patriotic motives of the noisy audience and the other liberal prints vindicating the demonstration on similar grounds of purity of intention, while conservative 'ultra' journals like *Le Moniteur* and *Le Drapeau blanc* supported the English actors. Penley's troupe meanwhile had prudently retreated from the Porte Saint-Martin to a small theatre in Rue Chantereine, where it offered subscription performances of Shakespeare and the standard London repertoire of eighteenth-century comedy to thin houses of the discerning and the curious, before packing its traps for home at the end of October.

The effect of this Anglo-Saxon intrusion on the classic serenities of the Parisian theatrical scene was not nearly as devastating as the advent, a few years afterwards, of the artistically far superior company led by Charles Kemble and Harriet Smithson (whom Hector Berlioz made the muse of his *Symphonie Fantastique* and later disastrously married). By then the tide of French Romanticism was at the flood and a degree of Anglomania was *de rigueur*. At present, however, England was viewed as the ignoble spoiler of Napoleonic glory and the principal architect of restored legitimist rule in Europe under the political will of a Castlereagh or a Canning.

Though the concept of 'journalistic responsibility' may well be a contradiction in terms, Stendhal undoubtedly felt a degree of responsibility to his English readers, and was keen to present an exact account of what had happened, whether in the *New Monthly Magazine* or the *Paris Monthly Review*. To the former, almost as soon as he joined its contributors, he sent a detailed description of the performances as he claimed to have witnessed them, while for the latter he wrote two articles, one in the form of a dialogue between an academician and a romantic, contrasting the British and French attitudes to drama, the other developing some of his long-held ideas on the nature of laughter, a theme at which his speculative intelligence had worked continuously since his earliest close reading of Molière and the first attempts at writing comedy.

In producing these two critical essays Stendhal must have perceived that they were leading him on towards the far broader, more significant field of Romanticism in general. The roughly sketched beginning he made in Milan in 1816 on an article examining the unities of French classical theatre, and a similar attempt two years later to produce a riposte to an Italian critic's objections to the new aesthetic, were taken up once more and given a sharper topical focus in a third critical philippic, *Ce que c'est que le romanticisme* (the affirmative reversal of the earlier interrogative *Qu'est-ce que* undoubtedly makes its point) which was added to the two published magazine pieces and issued in March 1828 as a pamphlet under the title *Racine et Shakespeare*.

Brief as it was, this polemical flourish on behalf of Romanticism earned its share of critical attention in the French and English press. The *Drapeau blanc* shrewdly pinpointed the author's lack of real feeling for poetry as the reason for his advocacy of prose drama, the *Journal de Paris* described him as 'fighting without breastplate or shield, in the manner of certain heroes of antiquity', but the *London Magazine*, to which he was not yet a contributor, loftily declared that 'readers already familiar with this author's earlier productions may suppose that he has nothing serious to say on the subject'. Stendhal himself presumably wrote the puff which appeared in the *New Monthly Magazine*, praising the third chapter as 'probably the most original and piquant part of this publication'.

Among those who read the pamphlet was the writer and politician Alphonse de Lamartine, the most distinguished French poet of his generation and a great friend of Adolphe de Mareste, to whom he wrote in warm but always judicious appreciation of Stendhal's achievement. 'He has spoken the words we were about to say; he has rendered clear and palpable what was merely a confused perception on the part of all right-thinking people.' Praising Beyle's ideas, 'as ingenious as they are profound and true', he nevertheless recommended him to observe a fundamental distinction between concept and expression in the age's romantic tendency. 'Classic in utterance, romantic in ideas – this, in my opinion, is how things should be.'

This was of course Lamartine's own approach to poetry, which Stendhal was soon to analyse, with extraordinary critical boldness and acumen, in two of the 'Grimm's Grandson' letters of 1825, written around the time (13 April) when Mareste introduced him and Victor Jacquemont to the poet. While Jacquemont beheld in the thirty-four-year-old Lamartine a figure of genuinely simple integrity and a dignified, unaffected physical presence, Stendhal, relentless as always towards anyone with the merest taint of political conformity and perhaps a trifle jealous of the other's literary success, dismissed him as ridiculous and empty-headed. In a year or two he was to be afforded a magnificent opportunity to revise this unjust verdict completely.

By the moment of this encounter, two years after the publication of the *Racine et Shakespeare* pamphlet, the Romantic debate among the Parisians had intensified and Beyle himself had broadened his acquaintance with the salons of the capital. Politics no longer dictated the entire extent of the division between pro and anti-Romantic, since the younger royalist writers such as Charles Nodier and (at this stage) Victor Hugo were fervent in their appeal to the new spirit against the stuffiness of the academic establishment. A solemn meeting of the Académie Française on 24 April 1824, though grudgingly admitting the term 'romantique' 'as currently understood' to the latest edition of its official dictionary, unleashed the sacred national thunders against the whole horrid innovation conveyed by a single word. Its mouthpiece was Louis-Simon Auger, a reactionary *apparatchik* despised by the liberals for having been a Bourbon appointee with no real claim to literary eminence. Having contemptuously dismissed the dramatic achievements of Shakespeare, Goethe and Lope de Vega as symptomatic of what he called 'German Romanticism', this ex-lawyer turned a withering forensic fire on his own countrymen, adherents of 'a bastard Romanticism, with neither the same energy, the same daring or the same excuses', lacking regulation and focus.

The speech was loudly applauded, as was the rather more sinister warning issued a few months afterwards, during a prize-giving ceremony at the Sorbonne, by the university's chancellor, the Comte de Frayssinous, Bishop of Hermopolis *in partibus infidelium*, to 'the youth confided to our charge to keep itself constantly on guard against the invasion of bad taste'. Opinions like these were calculated to fan the flames of a gathering opposition, spearheaded by the *Globe*, which was, as it were, provoked into existence by the execrations of anti-Romanticism. Once more the liberal and conservative banners were hoisted by the opposing sides and the battle was now joined on a far wider front than had formerly been afforded by a small Parisian theatre and a not especially distinguished troupe of jobbing English actors.

The cue for Stendhal to take down his *Racine et Shakespeare* brochure from the shelf and redeliver it to a keenly excited readership was obvious. Through Mareste he lost no time in canvassing the bookseller Ladvocat as to the possibility of a short reply to Auger's Academy address, but it was not until March 1825 that the second version of the work came out. This time he had to some extent made sure of his public by giving a reading at one of Delécluze's Sunday afternoon gatherings. Having warmed up the audience with some of his treasury of well-spiced anecdotes (including one about a parrot notorious for its foul language, presented to the King's sister-in-law, the Duchess de Berry, by a well-meaning missionary) Henri launched into his presentation, to general applause. Even if Delécluze was somewhat cynical as to the new book's rather too slavish cultivation of liberal opinion (he noted the pained smile on Paul-Louis Courier's face when a flattering reference was made to him) he could generously acknowledge, in looking back on those years, the significance of the second *Racine et Shakespeare* as a crucial influence on the rising literary generation. Like practically everything Stendhal wrote, it made him little money, but his name was now one to reckon with among all the Parisian readers who mattered.

Racine et Shakespeare II is a very different book – we may as well say an altogether different book – from its predecessor. The pamphlet is essentially an assemblage of those ideas with which Stendhal enjoyed challenging the intellectual wakefulness of his salon acquaintances, alternately gripped or exasperated by the indiscriminate outpouring. With little in the way of order or discipline in its sequence of arguments, the opuscule gathers what strength it has from the combative absoluteness of the writer's unmistakable voice in declarations such as the celebrated opening of Chapter III:

> Romanticism is the art of presenting to the various nations the literary works which, given the current state of their habits and beliefs, are susceptible of offering the fullest possible pleasure.

> Classicism, on the contrary, presents them with the literature which gave the greatest possible pleasure to their great-grandparents.

By 1825 the original had been subsumed, almost without trace, into a short book consisting of ten letters between a Romantic and an adherent of Classicism. As ever with Stendhal, the title was a blind, more so, indeed, than in the 1823 version, where at least some attempt was made to engage with the controversial issue of Shakespeare's effect on contemporary audiences. We know how much Beyle, imbued with an early passion for Corneille, disliked Racine the dramatic artist and deeply despised him as an establishment lackey at Louis XIV's court. Neither writer is really the beast in view in *Racine et Shakespeare II*, and it is not even, in any consistent sense, the response to Auger's Academy address which the subtitle claims.

What we discover instead is a typically subversive publication, in which the fires of its author's wit and irony, exercised in the name of modern prose drama as opposed to the traditional rhymed-verse mode, are trained upon the political *status quo*, embodied not just by attitudes but by institutions. Rather than Racine himself, it is the Racinian age of unexampled fawning and flattery exercised in the promotion of King Louis' greater glory which is used to arraign the modern reality of a stultifying, tyrannical conservatism. An apparently bland observation, for instance, that 'unknown to most men, habit exercises a despotic power over their imaginations', ushers in a telling allusion to King Ferdinand of Naples's abhorrence of men without powdered hair, because of his association of a natural coiffure with the terrors of the French Revolution, in which his sister-in-law, Marie-Antoinette, had been guillotined.

It is Stendhal's gift for focusing on anecdotal detail of this kind which beguiles us as it beguiled the young Romantics who seized avidly on the messages of dissent communicated in none too coded a fashion by his critical text. Ironically the change he sought in the approach to drama never came about in any significant sense during his lifetime. A type of modern prose drama, canvassing the significant issues of the day, only found its way onto the Parisian stage with the advent of literary naturalism and the concomitant shifts in acting style during the latter part of the nineteenth century. Romantic tragedy, whether deliberately repossessing the alexandrine couplet, as in Hugo's plays, or making the highly effective use of prose employed by Alexandre Dumas in *Henri III et sa cour* or Alfred de Musset in *Lorenzaccio*, stuck firmly to historical themes. Even Musset is constrained to set his comedies of sexual intrigue in a kind of Ancien Régime fantasy bubble inspired by *marivaudage* and Fragonard paintings.

Though his book may not have met with precisely the kind of success he would have wanted, *Racine et Shakespeare*, in its modified form, played a notable part in making Stendhal's name known throughout literary Paris. The pamphlet format evidently appealed to him, and in November 1825 he struck again, on an entirely different but quite as important contemporary issue, in his essay *D'un nouveau complot contre les Industriels*.

The increasing pace of industrialization in France, though it never properly gathered momentum until after the July Revolution of 1830, was a cause for either rejoicing or alarm among the liberal intelligentsia of Stendhal's circle. There were those on the one hand who believed inevitably that a booming commercial and industrial economy would bring with it the social blessings of prosperity, and cynics in the opposing camp who saw the whole impetus of trade and manufacture as one merely calculated to promote the worst sort of callous exploitation, philistinism and vulgarity.

Stendhal belonged in the latter party. Political economy had interested him since he started reading Adam Smith's *The Wealth of Nations* in 1802, and his curiosity led him on to study the work of Ricardo, Malthus and Mill. The whole subject, however, was simultaneously repugnant to that 'aristocratic' side of his character which could relish the novels of Sir Walter Scott and turn up its nose at the English as chief promoters of the hideous new gospel of money grubbing. Was there not something inherently contemptible in the commercial arts of peacetime to those who had lived through the chivalric era of Napoleon?

We should also recall the influence on Stendhal's whole attitude to the industrial issue of the fact that he had very little money of his own. His small private income needed reinforcement from what he picked up as a journalist, and this was hardly enough to maintain him in more than the fundamental decencies of a genteel existence and a scatter of *menus plaisirs*. Almost everybody he knew either earned more than he did, or else was in the happy position of enjoying the fruits of inherited wealth and properly administered finances.

Envy and resentment undoubtedly played their part here, as did a corresponding desire, by no means uncommon among writers uneasy over their economic status, to avoid all reference to money in his works. With Stendhal money is not, as so often with his friend Balzac, the ultimate definer and motivator. Even when mentioned in the novels, it does not offer an essential dynamic for the plot. Part of the pleasure of a book like *La Chartreuse de Parme*, for example, must always derive from the absence of any but the most trifling knowledge of its characters' financial affairs.

Thus he was not likely to view with much favour a project widely discussed among the circles in which he moved for establishing a magazine to promote the ideals of the proto-socialist Henri de Saint-Simon, who had died during the summer of 1825, leaving an ardent band of disciples. Member of a junior branch of the family which produced the famous memorialist of Louis XIV's court in its final phase (among Stendhal's favourite authors) Saint-Simon was imbued with a desire to reorganize contemporary society by bringing together bankers, industrialists, merchants and farmers in a single 'industrial' party. Its activities, concentrated on redistributing capital among those with genuine ability and divided between committees of 'invention', 'examination' and 'execution', were contrasted with the inaction of the traditional executive formed of nobility, clergy, lawyers and landholders. The gradual amelioration of conditions among the poor which this projected reform was designed to bring about received greater moral sanction, as far as Saint-Simon was concerned, from the inculcation of a new kind of Christianity, based not on authority and hierarchy but on messages of love and social harmony.

The trouble, as Stendhal and others perceived it, with this gospel of progress under the banner of Christian renewal was that it laid far too much stress on industry as a socio-political force.

When the noted *globiste* Cerclet arrived one Sunday at Delécluze's with the prospectus for a new Saint-Simonian journal, to be entitled *Le Producteur*, Beyle, according to their host, 'made a dreadful grimace, took his hat and left in the midst of universal laughter provoked by his horror of political economy'. A further glance at the document, the work of Saint-Simon's loyal adherent Léon Halévy, would indeed have confirmed his worst fears. After proposing work and peace as the two principal facilitators of liberty and happiness, it went on to address three distinct but equally significant sectors of society, intellectuals, workers and artists, with the idea of uniting their labours in 'a great moral action', in the name of what Halévy loosely calls 'la production'.

Stendhal's horror at such idealistic consecration of industry as an all-important focus of social and creative energy may be imagined. He could scarcely have received with anything but sardonic distaste statements such as: 'the exclusive reign of the imagination has passed away. . . . Thus the arts risk losing their importance for ever, and far from directing the march of civilization, they must no longer be ranged among society's needs.' When *Le Producteur*, with Cerclet as its editor-in-chief, published its first issue, on 1 October 1825, this peremptory redirection of the arts towards a clearly defined social goal was evidently one of the theoretical pillars on which the whole enterprise rested. Even if he felt able to refer to the journal in fairly respectful terms within the pages of the *London Magazine*, Stendhal was not going to allow its industrial evangelizing to pass without comment, and two months later, impertinently making use of *Le Producteur*'s own publisher, Sautelet, he unleashed his assault.

D'un nouveau complot contre les industriels is not a title which renders easily into English. The term *industriel* was used vaguely enough by the Saint-Simonians to mean just about anybody whom they judged to be 'useful', from a carpenter or a baker to a farmer or a travelling salesman. Stendhal remains patently sceptical of such value-judgements, and his pamphlet, magisterial in its deployment of irony, is one of the earliest noteworthy challenges thrown down to what soon became a favourite nineteenth-century cliché, that exaggerated notion of dignity and importance (Oscar

Wilde's Lady Bracknell scoffingly talks of 'the purple of commerce') attached to people involved in manufacturing industry.

One by one, with a devastating clarity, Stendhal pulls apart these pretentions. Conceding that industry supplies an economic basis for political change and scientific enquiry, and that a certain degree of freedom is needed for the *industriel* to prosper, he nevertheless dismisses the arrogant claim that the recent acquisition of independence by the South American republics or the Polar explorations of Sir John Parry are due solely to commercial forces. If Saint-Simon's criterion of 'usefulness' is strictly applied, then 'la classe pensante' is liable to set an entirely different interpretation on it, rating a soldier, a skilful doctor or a lawyer who defends the innocent without necessarily expecting a handsome fee superior to the rich factory owner importing machines and employing ten thousand workers.

With obvious sarcasm, the pamphlet turns aside for a moment to consider the wealthy industrialist as ideal material for the comic dramatists of the future (Stendhal clearly took his own hint in the half-humorous portrayal of M. de Rênal in *Le Rouge et le Noir*) before appealing finally to a more balanced view of industry, not as the be-all-and-end-all of modern civilized existence, but as one of the enablers of social and political liberty. Yet even over this concept Stendhal hangs a significant question mark in the course of his masterly conclusion.

> In the life of a nation, each class becomes useful in turn. If Greece succeeds in freeing itself, thousands of merchants will settle there; they will bring icecream, mahogany furniture, prints, textiles etc. But as for the decent laws which allow trade to flourish, will it be these very same men who have the wisdom to make them? And the courage necessary for exterminating the Turks and putting such laws into practice, will that have been theirs as well?
>
> It is a mere six months since Santa Rosa* was killed at Navarino, and barely a year since Lord Byron died in trying to aid Greece. Where is the industrialist who has sacrificed his entire fortune in this noble cause?

* General Santorre di Santa Rosa was the leader of the abortive rebellion at Turin, whose wider repercussions drove Stendhal from Italy in 1821.

> The thinking class has this year inscribed Santa Rosa and Lord Byron on the tablet where the names of those destined to immortality are conserved. Here they are, a soldier and a nobleman: during this same period, what have the industrialists achieved?
>
> A worthy citizen has imported goats from Tibet.

The argument, we may say, has never stopped since. Stendhal, in his contribution to it, sounded, as always, an accent more twentieth than nineteenth-century. For 'the thinking class' the contemporary reader can substitute, by inversion and not without a shudder, that most vulgar and contemptible of contemporary catchphrases, 'the chattering classes', applied by right-wing populists to an articulate intelligentsia which dares to question, to criticize or to dissent. In our own time the same scorn for the 'uselessness' of art, learning and the impulses of the spirit has been loudly proclaimed by apostles of profit and financial acquisitiveness, and a comparable scepticism on the part of intellectuals has countered their larger claims to admiration. Stendhal, it seems (at least to the present biographer) remained firmly on the side of the angels.

It says something, both for the seriousness with which the subject was taken by the Parisian intelligentsia and for the growing importance of Stendhal's reputation that *D'un nouveau complot contre les industriels* was given significant coverage by reviewers both for and against. *La Pandore*, conceding his ability to handle the anti-industrial theme with verve and humour, censured the author for being 'preoccupied with the need to scatter his pleasantries everywhere'. Weightier and more severe in its disparagement, the mercantile *Journal du Commerce* took him to task for suggesting that the *industriels* were either uneducated workers or money-grubbing factory owners, rather than men whose imagination and spirit enabled them to reward merit when they saw it, a line similarly taken by the offended *Producteur* itself. Rather oddly for a newspaper fast turning towards Saint-Simonism, the *Globe* chose to issue what was effectively a new edition of the pamphlet, larded with comments, many of them favourable, by an anonymous reviewer who was probably known to

Stendhal.* Victor Jacquemont, much amused by the general brouhaha, asked his friend whether the now-established pen name had been altogether a wise choice. 'But what to do about it now? You have made it too famous to be given up. An altogether new effort is needed to regain some sort of reputation under another name. Yet *de Stendhal* is rather ridiculous. Frankly though, you quite like it, don't you?'

Between them, Jacquemont and Stendhal had other, more agreeable topics to discuss, political, literary and above all musical. In leaving Milan so precipitately in 1821, Henri had carried with him delightful recollections of his evenings at La Scala. He was fortunate enough, on settling in Paris, to find the capital's operatic life revitalized by a sequence of exceptionally brilliant seasons at the Théâtre Italien, bringing the latest lyric successes from across the Alps, interpreted by the foremost Italian and French singers of the day.

It was at the end of 1824 that Beyle himself became an opera critic, writing occasional reviews, over the next three years, for *Le Journal de Paris*, a moderate liberal paper much favoured by Destutt de Tracy and his satellites, with a large and loyal readership. The point has been well made that the Théâtre Italien itself concentrated elements of liberal opposition to the government, offering a hedonistic, sophisticated *bel canto* alternative to the officially sanctioned stuffiness of its established rival, the Opéra. Stendhal launched enthusiastically into his new role, furnishing a series of combative, acerbic pieces assessing not only the performance and the work itself, but the attitudes of the public besides, and bringing his own knowledge of Italy and Italian theatrical practice splendidly into play. Why does the Parisian audience applaud Rossini's *La Cenerentola* but not laugh at it? Because the French are more interested in preserving *le bon ton* than in showing real amusement. 'A young amateur from Berlin', Monsieur Meyerbeer, may undoubtedly display vigour, originality and a youthful grace of style in his *Il Crociato in Egitto*,

* In this connection, see his amusing letter to the editor of *Le Globe* (6 December 1825) on the introduction of the English word 'puff' – equivalent to our modern 'hype' – into French, signed 'Polybe Love-Puff'.

but 'the libretto on which he has expended such a wealth of harmony is of an absurdity uncommon even beyond the Alps'. As for poor Mozart, his operas are out of fashion because nobody can find anything truly smart to say about them any more.

Among the singers praised so judiciously by Stendhal the most exceptional by far was Giuditta Pasta, greatest of all dramatic sopranos in the age of *bel canto*, rivalled in the peculiar nature of her talents perhaps only by Maria Callas, with whom vocal enthusiasts have been tempted to draw interesting parallels, both as regards the two women's meteroic careers and in respect of their innate theatricality as performers. Having made her Parisian début in 1816 at the age of nineteen, in Ferdinando Paër's *Il principe di Taranto* at the Salle Favart, Pasta went on to alternate between regular engagements at the Théâtre Italien and at the opera in London, where she became a firm favourite. The timing and circumstances of her career offered her the advantage of triumphing first of all in the older repertoire of works by Mozart, Cimarosa and their contemporaries, and subsequently in the newer, more lightly textured romantic opera of the rising generation represented by Bellini and Donizetti. The former created his *Norma* expressly for her, the latter owed to Pasta's genius the success of *Anna Bolena*, the opera which confirmed his international reputation.

A highly intelligent, hard-headed Lombard, with strong patriotic instincts and a taste for living simply among congenial old friends, Pasta brought amazing intuitive skill to her various dramatic incarnations. There can be no doubt that her impact on the operatic stage revolutionized both the way in which other singers approached the whole business of histrionic performance and the approach to the lyric drama itself by audiences and composers alike. She was one of those remarkable figures who as it were find their just hour, and as such she was perfectly calculated to fascinate Henri Beyle.

His singular good fortune during 1822 and 1823 was to be the singer's neighbour and at length fellow lodger in Rue de Richelieu, where he moved in on the third floor of the Hôtel des Lillois, while she occupied rooms on the second and later the first floor. During his earliest miserable months of exile from Milan, it was

Pasta and her mother, Donna Rachele Negri, who had provided him with a lifeline to sanity by issuing an open invitation to their cosy Italian salon where, gambling heedlessly at the faro table and drinking in with delight the blessed sound of the Milanese dialect, the *lingua della minga*, till three in the morning, he could keep the blue devils away yet wallow to his heart's content in memories of Metilde.

In recompense, it was Stendhal who, together with Adolphe de Mareste, introduced Pasta to her admirer Alexandre Micheroux, a Neapolitan whose family hailed originally from Liège and who was now in exile after a sudden political fall from grace with King Francesco I of the Two Sicilies, in whose service he had formerly been posted as a diplomat. Attracted by Micheroux's good looks and polished manners, Henri was all the same struck by a singular coldness in his character which ironically made him the perfect partner for Pasta (who of course had a husband). The pair, he was convinced, spent their time talking about music rather than making love.

For though he declared her to be 'without vices, without faults, a simple character, full of integrity and spontaneity, and with the greatest tragic gifts I ever knew', Pasta was also, Stendhal perceived, 'too cold, too reasonable, not wild or affectionate enough'. Had he not, after all, made his customary play for her attentions and found himself indignantly rejected? The episode was swiftly forgotten and they became firm friends, if only because each was too intelligent and wordly to make a serious issue out of a mere embarrassment of this kind.

Stendhal was permanently smitten, besides, with a genuine admiration for the singer's artistry, rightly convinced that her talent was so original that the composers of operas in which she was currently starring could not possibly have foretold it. He had worshipped the tragic muse in the acting of Talma and Kean, but in a woman such genius touched deeper springs in him, and Pasta was in this respect 'pure, perfect, unadulterated'. He marvelled at her stillness, grandeur and technical control, as much as at the sudden accesses of pent-up emotion which drove her to tears after a performance.

Among other admirers of 'la gran donna' were several of his

best friends, Adolphe de Mareste, the exiled Neapolitan lawyer Domenico di Fiore and Victor Jacquemont, whose fluency in Italian made him welcome in Pasta's companionable salon and who was soon to fall seriously and unhappily in love with her young protégée and fellow star of the Théâtre Italien, Adelaïde Schiassetti. Jacquemont's particular musical passion was for the operas of Gioacchino Rossini, and this shared enthusiasm must surely have helped to inspire Stendhal in realizing his project for a full-scale biography of the composer, the *Vie de Rossini*, published in November 1823.

There is really no good excuse for writing the biography of a living person. The biographer, however much he or she may boast of having been given full access to personal papers, must always be hampered by that essential vanity on the part of the subject which has permitted this dubious exercise to go ahead in the first place. A balanced assessment of character and achievements is, under the circumstances, impossible, and the fear of lawsuits shadows every lightest assertion. Such an enterprise was in any case unlikely to appeal to Stendhal, the last writer one can possibly imagine trying to humour another man by slavishly tracing the high points of his career.

Had the two, in any case, actually met? Early in *Rome, Naples et Florence en 1817*, Stendhal describes a halt he made at Terracina, on his way south from Rome, where 'in the superb inn built by Pius VI' he falls into a musical conversation with a blond, balding man aged about thirty. He tells him that he hopes to hear Rossini's *Otello* at Naples and that he believes its composer to be the single great hope of Italian music. The man shows a certain embarrassment at this, and Stendhal realizes that he is indeed Rossini himself. They linger in talk till past midnight, and the writer parts from the musician with a certain melancholy, misquoting to himself Falstaff's words in Shakespeare's *Henry IV Part 1*: 'there live not three great men in England, and one of them is poor and grows old'.

Readers of this passage have tended to discount it for all sorts of reasons, starting with the simple fact, which could scarcely have escaped Stendhal, that Rossini was only twenty-five in 1817. The composer, what is more, firmly denied ever having met his biographer, and he has always been given the benefit of the doubt. Yet what of the evenings when the two of them dined with Monti in Milan, already referred to? The chronology in *Rome, Naples et Florence* may not be precise, but then, as we have seen, the whole book is a deliberate rearrangement of circumstances and events. With a somewhat foolish persistence, Rossini's later biographers have refused to take into account the possibility that, in a long life of much fame, travel and conviviality, he may easily have forgotten a few meals in the company of a Frenchman of (at that stage) no particular celebrity. What is more, they have treated the *Vie de Rossini* as though it were meant to be a straightforward narrative record of a life in music, grounded in a careful examination of actuality, as opposed to the unique Stendhalian mixture of journalism, polemic, memoir and criticism which lends the work its particular tone and outline.

Stendhal's greatness as a writer is based on his artistic lack of respect for facts as sacred in themselves. The notorious clarity of his literary style fashions another, often superior dimension of truth, even while it plausibly insists on an accepted authenticity. Once more, in the *Vie de Rossini*, we encounter a book which is not actually about the subject suggested by its title, and once more the clamour for release of Stendhalian ideas, on everything from national character to the inadvisability of piano lessons for young girls, dictates the project's engaging formlessness.

The starting point is once again Napoleon. Rossini becomes, in Stendhal's opening lines, the new Bonaparte, the youthful world conqueror. 'The glory of this man knows no bounds but those of civilization, and he is not yet thirty-two.' That much at any rate was true. Beginning with the double triumph of *Tancredi* and *L'Italiana in Algeri* in Venice in 1813, the young composer had contrived, during his Neapolitan years in association with the powerful-voiced soprano Isabella Colbran, whom he later married, to produce a sequence of masterpieces, *Otella*, *Mose in Egitto*, *Ermione* and *La Donna del Lago*, which created a foundation for serious opera on which both Verdi and Wagner were later to build. As for opera buffa, the worldwide triumph of *Il Barbiere di Siviglia*, after its initial fiasco in Rome in 1816, had established its creator as the past master of the genre.

In the *Vie de Rossini* Stendhal's acknowledged purpose was to investigate the causes of this meteoric success and to underline the paradox of a genius who, as framed by the book, emerges as an amiable, cynical, lazy *bon vivant* (which indeed he may have been). What he in fact produced was a marvellous series of little essays, in which Rossini's triumphs were set against Stendhal's own record of his personal response to the operas, within the context of a deep and immediate sympathy with the Italian social and cultural world surrounding them. Far from being a vulgar attempt to capitalize on the fame of a composer already widely celebrated by opera audiences in Paris and London, the book, whatever its faults, constituted a serious defence of the Italian musical spirit against those who wanted their ears tickled with evidence of more harmonic weight and learning. It was unquestionably the noblest tribute paid to Rossini during his lifetime.

As a contemporary witness to his music's impact on an informed, eloquent sensibility, the work is invaluable, and Stendhal's comments on individual numbers in the various operas have been endlessly quoted. What Henri Martineau calls its 'enchanting disorder' becomes one of its greatest assets. At moments such as Chapter XVII, where the author turns aside, between observations on *Il Barbiere di Siviglia* and *Otello*, to offer a sharp socio-political assessment of the relationship between art and popular taste in contemporary France, or the lovely opening to Chapter XXVI, with its evocation of a warm Neapolitan night under which a circle of elderly opera-lovers sits among the orange trees trying vainly to account for the blazing celebrity of this young man of the hour, we dawdle willingly in Stendhal's company because there is nobody else with whom we would rather spend the time. For lovers of the musician the *Vie de Rossini* may be less than perfect, for devotees of the writer, it will inevitably rank as a secondary work. Those who love both Rossini and Stendhal, on the other hand, will find themselves echoing a contemporary newspaper reviewer who described it as 'original, witty, amusing . . . a true dilettante cannot ignore this really fascinating book'.

CHAPTER 10

OUR ROMANTIC BARON

Certain writers take possession of the cities in which they live, staking them out like a personal territory. We can talk, for example, about Dickens's London or Joyce's Dublin, to the extent of being able to map out each town as a sequence of literary landmarks. Is there, however, such a place as Stendhal's Paris? He lived there during three crucial stages of his life, the last spanning almost a complete decade, and involved himself as intensely as he knew how in the capital's cultural life. Yet nothing he wrote has a distinctly Parisian flavour, in the same way as do the novels of his younger contemporary Honoré de Balzac, for whom the singular phenomenon of the city, captured by his unsparing gaze, provides a *raison d'être* for a vast array of characters and motives.

Even if Stendhal had no special love for Paris, we may nevertheless explore certain of its quarters and streets with that particular species of piety which delights to follow in the footsteps of this or that great artist. From the junction of Boulevard Montmartre with Boulevard des Italiens we can walk down Rue de Richelieu, where at various stages during the 1820s he lived at number 43 (*Souvenirs d'Egotisme* begins here), 61, (the former Hôtel des Lillois, no longer surviving in its original form, though a plaque tells the passer-by that this was where he wrote *Le Rouge et le Noir*), 69, 76 and 93. Round the corner are Delécluze's garret in Rue Chabanais (the house later became a brothel) and Place Boïeldieu, formerly Place des Italiens, where Stendhal stayed for a time at the Hôtel Favart, which still exists. Walking westwards down Boulevard des Capucines, we reach Rue Caumartin, and it was here, on the fourth floor of number 8, that *La Chartreuse de Parme* was begun and ended in a mere seven weeks of 1838.

It was to Italy indeed that the writer's thoughts turned in May 1825, when he was informed of the death in Milan of Metilde Viscontini Dembowski. When he heard the news, Stendhal wrote in English on a copy of *De l'Amour* the words 'Death of the author'. He did not of course die for another seventeen years, and the effect of this initially devastating loss seems not to have been as enduring as we might at first imagine. The fact is that his heart, for so long nursing the sentimental injuries it had received in Milan, was seriously engaged with a major love affair, one of the most arresting in his entire emotional history, if only for being one of the few in which his passion was, for some while at least, seriously returned.

Its object was a mature married woman of more or less his own age, with whose family he was already acquainted and who he had good reason to believe had loved him for almost two years before he had the courage to admit his own feelings for her. Clémentine-Marie-Amélie Curial was the daughter of Count Beugnot, a career bureaucrat under Napoleon whom Stendhal met in 1812 and always refers to in his personal papers as 'Doligny'. To her mother the Countess he had unsuccessfully paid court in 1814, in the light of an alternative to Alexandrine Daru as the mature woman with influence in high places who might help to advance his career. He gave Mme Beugnot the dedication of *Les vies de Haydn, de Mozart et de Métastase* and always claimed that after her lover, his friend Pépin de Bellisle, he was the person she was fondest of.

At the age of twenty, in 1808, Clémentine had married General Baron Philibert-Jean-Baptiste-Françoise-Joseph Curial, a Savoyard whose subsequent title of Count under the Empire was confirmed by Louis XVIII, whom he joined in 1814. Curial was one of the peers bold enough to vote against the execution of Marshal Ney during the following year, vain as such a gesture turned out to be. He appears to have retained the respect of the Bourbons, who rewarded him with various military posts before his death in 1829 as the delayed result of a carriage accident at Charles X's coronation.

The marriage was inevitably marked by General Curial's professional absences from home, periods when Henri Beyle could improve an acquaintance with the general's wife which had begun as long ago as 1814, when he had noted in his journal her 'eyes full of candour'. This impression had strengthened when, as her mother's guest at the Beugnots' country house at Bonneuil-sur-Marne, south of Paris, where he corrected the proofs of *De l'Amour*, he noted the steadiness of the gaze Clémentine fixed upon him. Mme Beugnot herself perceived this and somewhat obliquely told her daughter: 'Your glance rests on Beyle; if he was somewhat taller, it wouldn't be long before he was telling you that he loved you.'

'Menti' or 'Menta', as he refers to her in his notes, was arguably even more Stendhalian in all she was and represented than Metilde Dembowski had been. Hindsight of course makes it fatally easy for us to detect life imitating art, but in investigating this crucial episode in the writer's sentimental biography we can scarcely avoid feeling that Clémentine Curial was a woman who, like Napoleon, had found her hour, acting as a potent if unconscious influence on Stendhal's creative imagination.

Passionate, sensitive and highly intelligent, she was also strikingly beautiful. An anonymous *Biographie des dames de la cour* describes her as having 'a pretty face, fine black eyes, a handsome figure', and a terracotta portrait bust is characterized by an attractive hint of suppressed melancholy in the downward curve of the mouth and the sombre, visionary expression in those same admired eyes. The belief, long cherished among Stendhalians, that she had a big nose has been shown to derive from a fatal misreading of an original source, but the total effect of this unattributed sculpture amounts to something more powerful than mere drawing-room prettiness.

Clémentine sent Stendhal some 250 letters, of which only a tiny handful now survive. His well-meaning cousin and executor, Romain Colomb, took care to destroy whatever he could find of her share in the correspondence, leaving only tantalizing hints, in various notes made in reading, of the more colourful details. We know that Henri himself, inured through the bitterness of recent amorous experience, was more than usually diffident in declaring his passion, but by the middle of May 1824 the pair had obviously made their feelings known. A letter written on the evening of Thursday 18th shows him deploring the sad results of his excessive prudence, then rushing headlong to the vital question: 'How might I get to see you? When will it be suitable for me to appear at your house once more. I did not go there yesterday because, the day before, one of your servants heard me asking the porter whether you were there. Are you happy with my discretion? Was I appropriately indifferent? I'm angry with myself.' He asked for just one small sign, a shutter half closed, a blind half dropped, the merest signal from the boudoir window as he passed the house (memories here of Gina Pietragrua's Milanese signalling device of the towel and the shutters?) 'Must you really leave without me seeing you?'

Two days later Clémentine was asking him: 'How can we see each other before next Monday, if only for ten minutes? To leave for the country without having heard you say "I love you" seems to me a sacrifice well beyond my capabilities.' Maddeningly this is all Colomb chose to preserve from her presumably much longer letter, but a note by Stendhal makes it clear that the affair was finally consummated on Saturday 22 May, at the Curials' house in Rue du Faubourg Saint-Denis, an event which he believed had cured him of his melancholy over Metilde.

There was of course no question of Beyle's remaining in Paris while Clémentine stayed at her château of Monchy-Humières, near Compiègne. Her husband appears to have been obligingly absent for at least some of the time, and the lovers were soon reunited for a country holiday which hardly turned out to be a restful idyll. The long, tearful, not always coherent letter she sent him on 4 July, accusing him of trying to make her jealous, of sticking a dagger in her heart and of flirting with Mme Victor de Tracy, whom she detested, and (at any rate by implication) of being the father of the child with whom she believed herself to be pregnant, is smudged with her tears, and a comparably passionate sense of the dramatic surrounded Clémentine's introduction of Stendhal as a clandestine visitor into the château. According to Colomb's note, he was concealed for three days in the cellar, where she provided him with food and took it upon herself to empty his commode, climbing up and down a ladder she had to remove carefully on each occasion.

Far from being put off by such quixotic expedients, Stendhal fell ever more deeply in love with his 'Menti'. His friends knew all too well what was going on. 'Our romantic Baron de Stendhal,' wrote Jacquemont to Mme Victor de Tracy, 'is an inconceivable original . . . . in his Faubourg Saint-Denis he is currently far advanced in his crystallizations.' In the autumn a letter from Beyle to Adolphe de Mareste, staying with his wife's family in Normandy, begged for good advice, acknowledging 'I'm really in despair'. Whatever the tempestuous character of their liaison, it is clear that for both lovers, on the threshold of middle age, the continued possibility of deep emotional involvement was intensely exciting, underlining for them both the fundamental seriousness of their mutual engagement.

The pair were perhaps too similar ever to have been successfully compatible. Certainly the little surviving scraps of Clémentine's correspondence (she sent Beyle over 200 letters in two years) suggest that she understood better than most women his capacity for tenderness concealed beneath a mask of combative cynicism. By 1826, however, this affair was beginning to fray at the edges, and it was in the summer of that year that the lethal break-up took place.

Neither of them had really believed in each other's constancy, and though they spent Easter Sunday together in what one of Stendhal's earlier biographers calls 'a delirium of shared passion', by May he could no longer feel certain of Clémentine's devotion. Preparing to leave for a trip to England, Stendhal could scarcely have resisted the chance to call upon her at Saint-Omer in the Pas de Calais, where Count Curial was in charge of summer army manoeuvres. We know nothing of what happened there. All that exists is a few gloomy words from Beyle himself. 'The deepest misfortune *of his life*. Left Boulogne on 27th June 1826 at 2h. 40 minutes. Disembarked at Dover at 6h. 10 minutes, after a crossing of 3h. and a half. Storm at San Remo.' San Remo is of course Saint-Omer, but the storm may simply have been a real one. Whatever took place, the affair had begun its downward plunge, but the pair went on corresponding with one another, and met at least once more, ten years afterwards. By an ironic piece of good fortune, a single letter from Clémentine to Stendhal, dated 1834, by which time they had clearly settled into a loving friendship, survives as the result of interception by a suspicious censor in the Papal police, who made a copy of it, doubtless because she had included various observations on the current European political scene. We must make what we can of its envoi: 'Adieu, cher ami, tout à vous de coeur et pour toujours: vous le savez bien.'

Clémentine's later life was not especially happy. Her beloved daughter Bathilde, the bright little girl to whom Stendhal had once written a letter in praise of Cimarosa, succumbed to a mortal illness in 1827, aged only thirteen, and she worried over the amorous escapades of her neglectful son, Philibert. No wonder that when she herself died in 1840, her family were at pains to quash the rumour that she had committed suicide.

'Menti' would have been further saddened by the comments on her lover left by her second daughter, Marie-Clémentine, Marquise de Saint-Clou, in a manuscript memoir:

> Although he belonged to a set altogether opposed to ours, my mother now and then received a gentleman whom I could not stand. This was Monsieur Beyle, who later assumed the pseudonym of Baron de Stendhal in several more or less bad books he published. This personage, having lost a minor position held under the Empire, could never forgive the Bourbons for not having maintained him. My mother, who had first made his acquaintance . . . . at my grandmother's salons, continued to receive him, rarely indeed, but he was admitted to her house, which flattered him despite the egalitarian notions he flaunted. He was fat and common. People used to find him amusing, which I never understood. Talked little and threw out incoherent, sententious phrases in the way of conversation. One day, when we were discussing Charles X's recent concession of press freedom, he suddenly relinquished his calm manner and, rubbing his hands together, said rancorously: 'He won't get away, we've got him now.' 1830 arrived soon afterwards. For us all this was a bitter blow, and we saw it as an evil.

The fat and common 'Baron de Stendhal' made a far better impression in England, where his visit in 1826 distracted him, if only for a while, from mortifying reflection on the ravaged love affair. His companion on this occasion was Sutton Sharpe, a talented London barrister of radical sympathies whose acquaintance he had first made in Paris four years earlier. Enchanted with the gaiety and inexpensiveness of the French capital, Sharpe contrived to spend at least two months of every year there, and a natural charm, generosity and genius for friendship made him welcome in several of the salons frequented by Henri Beyle. He became a favourite companion of Mareste and Jacquemont, and dined regularly at La Rotonde in the Palais-Royal with a group that included, besides Mérimée and Stendhal, the painter Eugène Delacroix and the rising young poet Alfred de Musset.

Sharpe's contacts in artistic and literary circles on either side of the Channel were wide-ranging. As the nephew of the notoriously waspish banker-poet Samuel Rogers, he was acquainted with Shelley and Byron, made friends with the wildly eccentric but intellectually formidable Mrs Grote, wife of the classical historian, and enjoyed the company of General William Napier, brilliant chronicler of Wellington's Peninsular campaigns. Stendhal, flattered by Sharpe's enthusiastic reactions to *De l'Amour*, responded eagerly to his offers of help in forging links with English publishers, and the two remained in close touch for the rest of their lives.

One of our greatest regrets must always be that so few details survive of this English trip, since for the first time Stendhal was able to leave London and its environs for a really extensive tour of the kingdom. Essentially he appears to have accompanied Sutton Sharpe on his professional tour of duty as a barrister on the Northern Circuit, going first of all to Lancaster, where he witnessed the assize courts in session, thence to the lakes of Cumberland and Westmorland, over to York, and subsequently to Manchester and Birmingham. Here, in what Stendhal refers to in English as 'the plain of fire', they stayed with Sharpe's uncle, the ironmaster Daniel Rogers, at Cade Hill near Stourbridge, where he was much taken with 'the amiable Miss Rogers'.

The journey, much as he seems to have enjoyed it (references to York Minster and the moon on Lake Windermere turn up in his *Promenades dans Rome*) simply confirmed the dismal impression of England as a nation tyrannized by a relentless work ethic and fatally deluded by its myths of political freedom. While still in London Stendhal made a series of notes on the realities of British government and economy as he perceived them, which, in the light of all that has been said and written on these subjects since, make fascinating reading, more especially because of their understanding of that inexorable equation made by the English between property and civic status under the law.

His cynicism of five years earlier is now consolidated, more so indeed since the publication of *D'un nouveau complot contre les industriels*. Grotesque burdens of work laid both on artisan and employer have destroyed any chance England might have had for displaying *esprit* – that untranslatable French word meaning everything from liveliness and energy to a just enjoyment of life's pleasures. Heavy taxation increases the load of responsibility, exacerbated by the dismal climate and the institutionalized gloom of Protestantism, culminating in the hideous English Sunday, spent reading 'this collection of frequently disgraceful stories and sublime odes named the Bible'.

'Until American independence in 1773,' Stendhal concludes:

> England was the most emancipated country in the civilized world. Thanks to the freedom of the press and to the jury system, established in all its purity by Mr Peel, we may expect that freedom, by slow degrees, will crush aristocracy and superstition. Probably, for a century or two, except for some favourable accident, England will go on being cited as an example by all peoples marching towards liberty, but several of them, well before such a time, will have gained a far greater freedom.

This little essay, first published by Romain Colomb after the writer's death, deserves a modern readership, especially among those alarmed by the increasing erosions of liberty in the name of efficient government among the countries of the developed world.

Splenetic as he was on the miserable condition of England in one of its most inglorious and discreditable decades, Stendhal ought to have been pleased at the concession to him of one of London's choicest social privileges. Outlining his English journey, he mentions quite casually that he was introduced at Almack's, a detail which would have averted the attention of any sophisticated reader had he thought to publish *Souvenirs d'Egotisme* in his own lifetime. Almack's (inverting the surname of William Macall, the enterprising Scotchman who opened it in 1765) was a gorgeous entertainment complex in King Street, St James's, comprising a huge ballroom, concert hall, lecture theatre and smaller rooms for tea drinking and cards. The entrée to its Wednesday balls during the London season, notoriously difficult, lay under the scrutiny of a committee of aristocratic patronesses, who carefully reviewed each application before graciously issuing ticket vouchers. The end in view was a typically English combination of snobbery and meanness: as long as the air of rank and *bon ton* was rigorously preserved, economies could be made on the refreshments in the name of avoiding vulgar ostentation, and *habitués* learned to feast barmecidally off 'tepid lemonade, weak tea, tasteless orgeat, stale cakes and thin slices of bread and butter'. To have passed this major social hurdle, even as Sutton Sharpe's foreign guest, was thus something of a triumph for Stendhal.

More than a whiff or two of Almack's hung about the work on which he had been intermittently engaged since the start of 1826, and to which both the emotional upheavals in his liaison with Clémentine and his sampling of high life in the London of George IV contributed their due inspirations. At the end of January Stendhal had begun sketching out the first part of a fictional work to be set amid aristocratic Parisian salons of a kind he did not frequent, and written as his own contribution to a literary brouhaha which provided an absorbing topic for those he did.

Among the most successful of recent French novels were two by Claire Lechat de Kersaint, Duchesse de Duras, a leading hostess of the Restoration, noted for her interest in the social questions of the day. Both *Ourika* (1824) the story of a negress who marries a well-connected white man, and *Edouard* (1825), dramatizing a union which crosses the class barriers, were wildly popular – the former had drawn praise from Chateaubriand and given its name to fashionable bonnets and collars – and the Duchess was rumoured to have written a third book, dealing with the yet more controversial topic of sexual impotence.

This she had indeed done, but the tale, entitled *Olivier ou le Secret*, was kept in manuscript and read only to select gatherings of friends, the writer's own 'happy few'. At the end of 1825, another novel, also called *Olivier*, was published anonymously, purporting to be the very work on which the Duchess herself had been engaged. Its author was Hyacinthe Thabaud de la Touche, a minor literary figure best remembered as the reluctant addressee of poems by the lovelorn Marceline Desbordes-Valmore. Strenuously denying responsibility for the imposture as soon as it was suspected, La Touche was prepared to absolve the Duchess from authorship but claimed to know who had really written the novel as issued. The genuine *Olivier*, never published during the nineteenth century, turns out to be an epistolary romance involving a duel and a suicide among the French nobility of the period.

Stendhal, naturally absorbed by the scandal, with its gamey mixture of dupery, impropriety and gilt-edged gossip, hastened to turn it into hard copy for a magazine article. Readers of the *New Monthly Magazine* for 18 January 1826, found 'Grimm's Grandson' in fine flow, telling them – or rather, pointedly not telling them – about what the false *Olivier* (more popular among salon tattlers, apparently, than the death of Tsar Alexander or the rivalry between Pasta and Mme Mainvielle-Fodor) really dealt with. He seemed, what was more, to accept the Duchess's authorship, if only for the chance it offered of making captious remarks about her legitimist foibles and a smutty *jeu de mots* on the significance of her surname.

He would not leave it at that. The novel he began soon afterwards, his first completed work of fiction, which we now know as *Armance*, started as his own contribution to the *affaire*, but soon came to engross a great many other Stendhalian preoccupations, so that it appears much more than a mere literary *jeu d'esprit*, localized within a contemporary scandal. Among its author's least-known works, it has found comparatively few translators, and many readers who profess an admiration for *Le Rouge et le Noir* or *La Chartreuse de Parme* are seemingly unaware of its existence. Yet the case of *Armance*, what it achieves and what it fails to achieve, is an enthralling one, and among scholars and critics of Stendhal it continues to be hotly discussed.

The plot has certain coincidentally similar features to the two *Olivier* novels it was intended to emulate. Octave de Malivert, a gloomy young sprig of the nobility with an adoring mother, falls in love with a cousin, lovely, half-Russian Armance de Zohiloff. The pair of them spend much of the book (not especially long by 1820s standards, though the original appeared in the regulation three volumes) havering over the peculiar nature of their passion for one another, before Octave, failing to acknowledge the awful secret of his sexual incapacity, rushes off to take part in the Greek War of Independence and swallows a mixture of opium and digitalis as the ship nears the Morea. 'A smile was on his lips, and his rare beauty struck the very sailors entrusted with his burial. The nature of his death went unsuspected in France by all save Armance. A little while afterwards, the Marquis de Malivert having died, Armance and Mme de Malivert took the veil in the same convent.'

Thus abruptly the story ends, yet such curtness is typical of the book as a whole. Its flat, laconic style suggests that the author will only tell us as much about the characters as we absolutely need to know. Few of them, apart from Octave and Armance, are calculated to hold our interest in a fashion similar to the various figures in works such as *Lucien Leuwen* and *La Chartreuse de Parme* whom a few deft strokes so sharply define. A first reading of *Armance* is likely to leave many of us baffled, exasperated and all too ready to understand why it was almost completely ignored by contemporary French critics at its publication in 1827. As for reviewers *outre-Manche*, a scathing notice in the *Foreign Review and Continental Miscellany* reached similar conclusions of angry bamboozlement. Describing it as 'a piece of superfine sentimentality', the anonymous pen havocs the novel with merciless sarcasm.

> If anything like the 'goings-on' described in *Armance* be the common usages of Parisian company, they ought to cease to accuse us of amusing ourselves 'tristement', for anything more 'lugubre' than the doings of the salons of Madames de Malivert and Bonnivet cannot be conceived . . . . It is absolutely impossible to wade through the commonplace dullness of the second volume.

As for Octave's famous secret, 'this . . . he is proceeding to tell his mistress, when a cursed servant comes to announce that *le déjeuner va sonner*, and, wonderful to relate, the young lady prefers a *petit pâté* to a secret'. On the same topic, the review concludes witheringly: 'We are sorry that we cannot gratify [readers] by telling them poor Octave's secret, for we do not know it; and it must therefore remain with the authorship of Junius, the executioner of Charles I, and the Egyptian hieroglyphics, among the res incognitae of the world.'

That, alas, was the trouble. If Stendhal had not written to Mérimée on 23 December 1826, spelling out the nature of Octave's affliction (using the same word 'babilanisme' for impotence which applies in *Souvenirs d'Egotisme* to his own temporary misfortune) we should scarcely have been able to guess at it. As it is, whatever frankness he may have used in discussing the matter with his circle of worldly Parisian bachelors* vanished swiftly in the face of the challenge of having to canvas such a theme for the enlightenment of the novel-reading public.

How then should *Armance* be read? Some critics have been tempted to see its utterly deadpan style as fundamentally comic, shot through with concealed threads of pure Stendhalian irony. Others have taken Octave's impotence as an emblem of the sterility at the heart of Restoration society. Nearly everyone, coming face to face with a first novel by one of the most respected and influential practitioners in the entire history of the genre, has been disappointed by the sparse auguries of future greatness, by its ineptly handled plot and numerous technical weaknesses.

Considered as a synthesis, however, fusing several of Stendhal's personal preoccupations and mirroring others more general to his age, *Armance* holds its own fascination. On one level we can see it as his attempt at a novel in the English 'silver fork' style of Edward Bulwer Lytton, Catherine Gore and the young Benjamin

* 'In the year 1826, if civilization continues and I return to Rue Duphot [where Stendhal lived while writing *Armance*] I'll tell how Olivier bought a beautiful Portuguese dildo in elastic rubber, tied it to his belt, and with the said article, after giving complete ecstasy to his wife . . . . valiantly consummated his marriage.' Stendhal to Mérimée op. cit.

Disraeli, in which a dandyish hero and a soulful heroine play out their drama of amorous scruples against a background of smart drawing rooms and the sort of society one might expect to find there. Wildly popular in England, these gilded romances of fashionable life had an enthusiastic following in France, and we know that Stendhal himself had glanced at several of them, most notably Lord Normanby's *Matilda: a Tale of the Day* (1825), explicitly mentioned in the preface to *Armance*. The entrée to Almack's, so often used as a backdrop by the silver-fork novelists, must inevitably have lent some inspiration.

Another and far more significant thread in the book's texture is created by the style as a vehicle for the particular type of story the author sought to tell. Few readers can have escaped the impression that what they are actually experiencing is fiction of an age different altogether from the 1820s. A mere blink of the eye might serve to put Octave into a periwig, Armance and her friend Méry de Tersan into paniered skirts, and transpose the whole work into one of those *histoires galantes* from the reign of Louis XIV or his successor, the Regent Orléans, a period whose literary manner, whether in the form of the memoirs of the Duc de Saint-Simon or Saint-Réal's powerful fictionalizing of the tragic story of Don Carlos of Spain, so strongly influenced Stendhal.

In fact the obvious model, as he himself conceded, was Madame de La Fayette's *La Princesse de Clèves* (1678), a tragic love episode set in the sixteenth century, generally regarded as the first major French achievement in the field of serious fiction. More than is usually acknowledged, *Armance* self-consciously imitates La Fayette's manner, not just in such aspects as the baldness of the ending (both heroines seek solace in a convent) but in its deliberate avoidance of descriptive padding and theatrical confrontation, for the sake of thoughtfully analysed emotion and a sober insistence on statement as opposed to rhetoric.

Stendhal himself recognized the link. One of his most engaging habits as a literary artist was that of examining and commenting on his own works after they were published, with an unsparing lack of vanity in the contemplation of his own achievements. In the notes with which he interleaved a copy of *Armance*, he admits its resemblance to seventeenth-century novels, calls it 'délicat comme *La Princesse de Clèves*' and draws an interesting graph to show the progress of fiction upwards from Madame de La Fayette and downwards to his own time and the Duchesse de Duras' *Ourika*. As for the style, he was all too conscious here of his determined attempt to avoid 'modern banter' by cultivating a deliberate dryness of tone.

The most absorbing aspect of this puzzling fictional début is its ambiguous presentation of the hero. Octave de Malivert has many literary originals. The Byronic parallel is explicitly made through a reference to Thomas Phillips's painting of the poet in Albanian dress, there are evident traits drawn from German Romanticism as well as hints from the gloomy, hyper-refined lovers in the dramas and novels of the Grand Siècle, but the closest allusions are to figures peopling Stendhal's immediate world of 1820s Paris. It has been plausibly suggested that one of his living models was Astolphe, Marquis de Custine, the writer and traveller whom the Duchesse de Duras' daughter, Clara, had been on the point of marrying when rumours of his impotence began to circulate. In 1824 the bisexual Custine had been beaten up by a party of soldiers at Saint-Denis after having made overtures to an artilleryman, and Stendhal seems to make a covert reference to this episode in the novel's third chapter. Yet another sexually ambivalent avatar of Octave has been identified in the painter Anne-Louis Girodet de Trioson, part of Delécluze's circle, whose heroic canvases are charged with a not especially latent homoeroticism.

Octave is the earliest of those youthful and enchanting Stendhalian heroes whose glamour undoubtedly owes something to the wish-fulfilment of a fat, plain, balding man, and a good deal to their creator's own sexual complexity. The Romantic age is noted for the eloquence with which it expressed male homosexual sentiment and desire, whether in neoclassicism's emphasis on the appeal of athletic nudity in painting and sculpture, in the cultivation of friendships which sought deeper bonds than those of ordinary professional or social comradeship, in the self-conscious flaunting of masculinity in dress styles clearly intended to arrest male as much as female attention, or in the heavy publicity given to sexual unorthodoxy among several of the period's most distinguished figures.

Stendhal himself was hardly immune, if not to these specific preoccupations, then at any rate to feelings which only an absurdly protective biographer would shrink from identifying as homosexual. The subject in itself exercised a considerable fascination: he was convinced, it seems, that all great men were in some way visited by a penchant for their own sex, and was ready to produce an example in Napoleon himself. Scandals like that involving Custine, whose acquaintance he subsequently made, or the notorious case of Percy Jocelyn, Bishop of Clogher, who had fled to Paris after being caught *in flagrante delicto* with a guardsman in a London inn parlour, greatly interested him, and the figure of Lord Link in *Lucien Leuwen* suggests that he was well aware of Byron's eclectic tastes in this quarter.

His own sensitivity to male attractiveness was more than merely academic, compromised as it probably was by a consciousness of what he lacked in physical beauty. His writings are littered with references to the handsomeness and elegance of the men he met, observed or imagined, and as we have noted, the charm of a personality such as Victor Jacquemont, himself evidently one of the prototypes of Octave de Malivert, was palpably enhanced by youthful good looks.

At least one passage in the journals, notorious for the embarrassment it has caused certain writers on Stendhal, constitutes a frank acknowledgement of a homosexual impulse. On 26 May 1814, while in a state of complete uncertainty as to his future following the collapse of the imperial regime after the battle of Leipzig, Henri Beyle went to watch Mademoiselle Mars acting Rosine in Beaumarchais' *Le Barbier de Séville* at the Comédie-Française. Sitting beside him was a young Russian soldier, aide-de-camp to one of the generals commanding the force which had just taken control of Paris.

> This charming officer, if I had been his wife, would have inspired the most violent passion in me, a love like that of Hermione [the passionate heroine of Racine's *Andromaque*]. I felt the first stirrings of it, and at once grew timid. However much I desired him, I dared not look at him. If I was his wife, I'd have followed him to the end

> of the world. How different from a Frenchman my officer was! In the latter what naturalness, what tenderness!

Continuing to write admiringly of him as 'my officer', Stendhal goes on to declare that if a woman had made such an impression on him, he would have spent the whole night searching for her lodgings. Even Gina Pietragrua only sometimes had that effect, he admitted.

The customary question, 'Does this really matter?', generally designed to obviate discussion of a topic by which many otherwise enlightened readers are surprisingly embarrassed, answers itself. To the extent that Stendhal's personality interests us enough to want to achieve as complete a picture of it as possible, the issue has significance. Not predominantly homosexual, he was honest enough with himself to recognize the occasional charms of his own sex, and his superfine modern intelligence, transcending the banalities of religious and social taboo, coolly apprehended the reality of a homosexual impulse as a motivating force in certain of his contemporaries. His heroes, Fabrice, Lucien, Julien, are the more engaging for their ambivalent attractiveness, precisely because, it is implied, men as well as women respond to their allure.

Whatever the importance of Octave de Malivert considered as the first Stendhalian *jeune premier*, his impact on contemporary readers and reviewers in France was hardly spectacular. Regarding the former, Stendhal had rhetorically appealed to Mérimée, asking whether *Armance* had 'enough warmth to keep a pretty French marquise awake till two in the morning? *That is the question*. . . . If the novel isn't of a kind to spend the night over, what is the point of writing it?' The verdict of certain aristocrats was that he knew nothing of those salons his book purported to describe, according to the subtitle *Quelques scènes d'un salon de Paris en 1827* suggested by the publisher.

Even if he was genuinely treading on unfamiliar territory in trying to evoke the world of Restoration *haut ton*, Stendhal had widened still further his acquaintance with the drawing rooms of literary Paris, less socially exalted but far more interesting. At the lively Wednesday evening parties of the painter Baron Gérard, friend of everybody from Pasta and Balzac to Musset and Delacroix, he had made the acquaintance of Marguerite-Louise-Virginie Chardon, wife of the dramatist, poet and academicien Jacques Ancelot. Precociously talented during her convent schooldays, she had gone on to outstrip her husband in popularity as a writer for the stage, though the pair of them also collaborated on a successful series of comic vaudevilles.

Madame Ancelot's Tuesday salon in Rue Joubert off the Chaussée d'Antin was one of the most resilient on the capital's cultural map during the nineteenth century, a place at which almost everybody of note in 'la France artistique' was calculated to make an appearance, from the reign of Louis XVIII to the last years of the Second Empire. With entirely pardonable vanity, the hostess herself, exercising a modest talent for painting, occasionally took to portraying the various groups of august names she and her husband could summon together, such as Victor Hugo, Alfred de Vigny, the elderly Chateaubriand and Mme Récamier, the tragedienne Rachel and Eugène Delacroix. Though malicious tongues, including that of Mérimée, who declared her 'ugly as sin' and disliked her yapping, monotonous voice, hinted that she spent far too much time on intriguing to secure membership of the Academy for her protégés, the general impression, borne out by her letters and memoirs, is of a spirited, discriminating woman with an enviable gift for friendship. In Rue Joubert, as she told Stendhal's former fellow *auditeur* Amédée de Pastoret, 'you will find a little lodging, calm and retired, enjoying nothing of the splendour and bustle of the Chaussée d'Antin . . . . but a place where one can be happy, living among books and friends from every period of existence and every situation'.

Henri Beyle appears in her group portrait entitled *Salon of Louis-Philippe's reign: Rachel reciting verses in the role of Iphigénie*. It was some time before he had gained the entrée to Virginie Ancelot's drawing room. Though he suspected she was not inviting him because of his fling at the Academy in the expanded *Racine et Shakespeare*, she seems, in an amusingly coquettish fashion, to have been trying to make him want to gain admission while appearing to hold him at arm's length. When allowed finally to visit, he for his part insisted that the introduction should be made under whatever name happened to suit him that day. Since he had just sent her a copy of the *Vies de Haydn, de Mozart et de Métastase*, Stendhal was announced under the appropriate pseudonym of César Bombet.

Nothing, however, could have prepared the Ancelots for what ensued. The acting lessons with Dugazon were evidently not forgotten as their guest launched into a one-man show as Monsieur Bombet, supplier of cotton stockings and nightcaps to the army, extolling the glories of his commercial calling (was this a sardonic send-up of the mercantile pomposities attacked in the *Industriels* pamphlet?) and ardently discoursing on the vagaries of the nightcap trade. Mme Ancelot managed valiantly to retain her composure, but her poor husband retreated spluttering with laughter into the next room, while their guests listened mystified to the patter of the bogus manufacturer.

Stendhal soon became one of the chief conversational energizers of the Rue Joubert salon. One *habitué* who best appreciated his spirit without ever becoming a close friend, the critic Charles de Sainte-Beuve, wrote nostalgically of wonderful evenings when, at midnight, with most of the company already gone, Beyle could enchant the more intimate group who remained, making them either laugh or grow angry, according to his maxim that 'nothing is as nice as a few insults among friends'. Generously, Sainte-Beuve exclaims: 'How much this man, judged so unfavourably by those who hardly knew him, was loved by his friends: What fine characteristics, what an entirely liberal soul I knew him to possess: . . . At his best moment, from 1818 to 1830, what wit, what sagacity:'

From her surviving letters, we can see that Virginie Ancelot – Stendhal always called her 'Ancilla'* – was equally appreciative of this singular and unforgettable personality. The two nevertheless enjoyed a somewhat stormy relationship. None of his letters to her exists, but from the nine of hers which have been traced we can reconstruct a friendship in which frequent misunderstandings on either side could always somehow be smoothed over through

* Since the Latin word means 'maidservant', there may have been some reference here to her *bienséance* with the kind of literary establishment Stendhal disliked: his nickname for her husband was 'Ancillus'.

the agency of that articulate intelligence both so abundantly possessed. Looking back on her salon of the 1820s, Mme Ancelot showed little but indulgent admiration towards somebody she seems to have regarded as a brilliant middle-aged *enfant terrible*, worth enduring for the sheer pleasure of his company. 'Beyle was excited by everything and went through a thousand different sensations in a few minutes. Nothing escaped him, nothing left him cold, but his sadnesses were hidden under jesting and he never seemed as happy as when expressing the liveliest contradictions.'

Seasoned though they initially may have been with hopes of conquest, Stendhal's mature female friendships form one of the most appealing aspects of his life and at once set him apart from the large number of nineteenth-century French writers who mingled ferocious sexual pursuit with a barely suppressed misogyny. Several more of these intimacies sprang up during the late 1820s. Though Mary Clarke, for instance, may not have cared for him, it was on a visit to her that he was introduced to the daughters of a New York widow, Mrs Garnett, recently settled in Paris after her husband's death and well acquainted within literary circles. Harriet, second of the four Garnett girls, seems to have had a personal reason for disliking Stendhal – perhaps some unwelcome attention had been paid – but her younger sister, Julia, settled willingly enough into a bantering correspondence, and both he and Mérimée evidently fancied their chances of her hand in marriage. The latter, when he heard she was engaged to the King of Hanover's librarian, Georg-Heinrich Pertz, almost collapsed in a fit. Stendhal contented himself with remarking to Mareste: 'Well, there's Mlle Julia married. What a vexation to a sensitive soul!'

A more permanent link had survived, and was now renewed, from earlier Parisian days. The happiest memories of those boring evenings in 1810 at 'Shepherdrie house', the home of Mme Rougier de La Bergerie, were connected with her daughter Julie, since married to Louis Gaulthier, receiver-general for the department of Yonne. With 'Jules'* as he always called her, Stendhal

* Stendhalians always refer to her by this name, though she was christened Marie-Jeanne-Julie-Cécile.

embarked upon (or perhaps resumed) an affectionate exchange of letters, bearing witness to the growth of a singularly close relationship, not perhaps taken seriously enough by biographers more readily seduced by the marmoreal glamour of Metilde Dembowski or the raffish fascination of Gina Pietragrua. It may be sufficient, however, to cite the testimony of Romain Colomb, implying that she was the woman with whom, in the final analysis, Henri Beyle held the deepest spiritual ties. The last to sprinkle holy water on the coffin at her funeral at Montmartre in 1853, Colomb, entrusted with her Stendhal letters, described her effusively as 'so good, so lovable, of so fine an intelligence, of so charming and delightful a character'.

So indeed she was, a creature of exceptional sensitivity and alertness to her friend's gifts as a writer, and a correspondent honoured by him with an affectionate sincerity and freedom of address, his 'aimable et bonne Jules'. His letters to her during the late 1820s suggest that she had already become one of those intimate correspondents with whom he could enter on any subject and expect a rational response. From London in 1826, descanting on the hypocrisies of British justice and liberty, he wrote with horror of country houses where 'I've seen Englishwomen constantly treated as inferior beings. Their great virtue is devotion, the virtue of slaves.' Stendhal wanted nothing of this in his relationships with women, counting instead on the value of frankness and integrity in what became a sort of slow-burning *amitié amoureuse* between him and Julie Gaulthier. 'You'll allow me to be stupid, simple, natural: don't count on an entertainer, I haven't got that sort of talent, and even less so when I make an effort.' Elsewhere we find him humorously exclaiming: 'Women! women! you're always the same, but perhaps you would be less lovable if you were more reasonable', before he bids her: 'Be happy. If only I could contribute to your happiness!' and signs himself 'Le Léopard'.

The cultivated, self-assured Frenchwoman, armed with a sense of humour, a sophisticated awareness of her effect on sensible men of the world and an inexhaustible gift for lively conversation, represented one of the civilized marvels of the early nineteenth century, unparalleled elsewhere in Europe. We can only envy

Stendhal his extraordinary ability to create and sustain these strong female friendships, but we should recall at the same time the eminently favourable constellation of Parisian salons, with their prevailing air of ease and conviviality, in which such enduring alliances could readily be made.

Few among the she-*beylistes* presents a more immediately engaging personality than Sophie Duvaucel. Six years younger than Stendhal, she had hardly known her father, a *fermier-général* guillotined in 1794 alongside the great chemist Antoine Lavoisier, and grew up to become the secretary and amanuensis of her mother's second husband, Georges Cuvier, professor of comparative anatomy at the Jardin des Plantes. As well as achieving international eminence in his field, Cuvier was a trusted Bourbon functionary (Louis XVIII had made him Minister of the Interior, with an accompanying barony) and his suite of little rooms at the zoological institute and menagerie beside the Seine was thrown open every Saturday to a mixed crowd of distinguished foreigners, men of science and a great many of those who regularly dropped in on Delécluze, Baron Gérard, La Fayette and the De Tracys earlier in the week.

Though it may be that Cuvier himself never really saw the point of somebody like Stendhal, the writer was warmly received by the rest of the family, even the worn-looking, sombre Mme Cuvier, whose impassivity masked a kind heart. It was Sophie, however, who provided the real focus of attention, with her unfailing sociability allied to wit, perceptiveness and a beauty which had attracted the English portraitist Sir Thomas Lawrence to sketch her likeness to adorn an issue of the fashionable London annual *The Keepsake*. When her stepsister, Clémentine, died suddenly in 1827 on the eve of her marriage, Sophie rallied the shattered household and took over the running of her stepfather's daily affairs. The crisis, followed five years later by Cuvier's own death, prevented her from finally accepting an engagement to Sutton Sharpe which Stendhal and Mérimée had both tried to encourage.

Her relationship with Beyle was essentially that of an indulgent, practically minded sister to a disorganized but endlessly amusing elder brother. She found him a tailor to make his calico shirts, she sparred with him in conversation or through the post, she kept a solicitous eye on him via mutual acquaintances and understood the importance – and the difficulty – of keeping him entertained. During the summer of 1827, before Clémentine Cuvier fell ill, Sophie and Henri ate ices together and talked of Sharpe as 'the *only* likeable Englishman'. Later, with Mme Cuvier in tow, they went on one of the new Seine steamers upriver to Villeneuve-Saint-Georges to watch the landing of the giraffe which Mehemet Ali, the francophile Pasha of Egypt, had sent as a present to Charles X.

At the Jardin des Plantes Stendhal played his professional gadfly role for all it was worth. Adrien de Jussieu told the restless Jean-Jacques Ampère, currently in Germany, that the young man had a rival in his 'blague ironique'. 'Nothing can be funnier than listening to Beyle . . . . discussing with these girls the various merits of men and things, and especially of the *Globe*. Candour is hardly in his line, nor is anything in the way of admiration. But what would be shocking in a youthful enthusiast is pardonable in a stout Mephistopheles like him.'

Even Mephistopheles may now and then have needed a holiday, and it was Stendhal's object, during the 1820s, to ensure that he could eke out his earnings from journalism, added to his little income and army half-pay pension, sufficiently to be able to afford to return now and then to his dear Italy. In the autumn of 1823 he had contrived an extended journey across the Alps, via Geneva and carefully avoiding Austrian Lombardy (more particularly Milan) to Florence and Rome. In Switzerland he made contact with Metilde Dembowski's cousin, Bianca Mojon Milesi, who gave him most flattering letters of introduction (which he seems not to have used) to various Italian artists along his southward route. At Rome he met up with several friends, including Delécluze, enjoying an extended Italian tour, the journalist Prosper Duvergier de Hauranne, and Jean-Jacques Ampère, accompanying no less a figure than Julie Récamier, most illustrious salon-muse of the Empire, famous for her long-standing liaison with François-René de Chateaubriand and for her portrait by David, the archetypal image of imperial neoclassicism.

Now a ripe matron of forty-six, Récamier had succeeded in

capturing the heart of the twenty-three-year-old Ampère: Delécluze, meanwhile, aged forty-three, had fallen under the spell of her niece, Amélie Cyvoct, not yet twenty-one. Stendhal had, alas, nothing to say about these vernal-autumnal passions, but enjoyed himself with dining at the French embassy and going to the opera. He met the successful young composer Saverio Mercadante – 'he has his own style, that's something for a young man' – but could hardly understand why all Rome was singing airs from his *Elisa e Claudio*. Equally mystifying was the popularity of a certain Donizetti from Bergamo, 'a tall, handsome, cold young man without any sort of talent': the Romans had only applauded his *Zoraide di Granata*, thought Stendhal, because they wanted to spite the ambitious maestro Giovanni Pacini and his protectress Pauline Borghese, Napoleon's sister.

The fruit of this Italian journey, which lasted six months to March 1824, was a revised version of *Rome, Naples et Florence*, published three years later. As has already been pointed out, this is essentially a different work from its predecessor in shape and emphasis. The title is still misleading, since half the book focuses on Milan and Bologna and places in between, but there is a far greater sense of control, smoothness and serenity in the general organization, the considered labour of middle age as opposed to the frenetic scurrying of excited young-manhood.

Authenticity, nevertheless, remains low on the list of the writer's priorities. There is no serious attempt to correct the earlier text, simply a shift in balance from one place to another, and a far greater stress on the anecdotal quality of the various entries in this incomparable morsel of narrative fudging, a travel diary which is all the better for not being quite the thing it claims. Once again, and far more pertinently than in the case of *Armance*, we can ask: 'Does it really matter? Is the deliberate inaccuracy or outright lying less palatable to us than the reality it is intended to replace?' There is no need to excuse *Rome, Naples et Florence* (1827) as some editors have done, by claiming that its throng of *petites histoires* represents a kind of dry run for the imminent ventures into fiction. Since Goethe (who, incidentally, much admired this work) 'slipped out of Carlsbad at three in the morning' on the first leg of his momentous *Italienische Reise* in

1786, nothing had been written which more sharply and irresistibly conveyed the transfiguring experience of Italy. Stendhal's magnificent palimpsest has remained unsurpassed ever since in its vital apprehension of the place, in a physical, aesthetic or moral dimension, as a redemptive state of mind.

In the summer of 1827, soon after the new edition of *Rome, Naples et Florence* was published, he left once more on a long and this time still more varied Italian tour. A slipping-out à la Goethe was clearly in order, perhaps because he wanted to be at a safe enough distance when *Armance* emerged in August. At any rate nobody seemed to know where on earth he had got to, except for Sutton Sharpe, who was informed that he might be heading for Corfu or Palermo, but told not to say anything, even to Sophie Duvaucel. In the same letter Beyle suggested to his friend that he might care to join him, and solicited a few letters of recommendation to such useful contacts as Sharpe might possess in the British-governed Ionian Islands, with the idea of a journey to Athens.

As it turned out, Sharpe stayed at home and Stendhal got no farther than Naples. On the way he had lingered in the congenial company of the Marchese di Negro at Genoa, a generous host to foreign visitors whose receptions, Beyle told Mareste, were 'just like Delécluze's, only with ladies as well'. One stifling evening Di Negro had invited them all to dine in a grotto in his garden overlooking the sea, and on this or another occasion Stendhal had at last met Alessandro Manzoni, whose *I promessi sposi* (or *Gli sposi promessi*, as it was originally called) had earlier that year been sent by the novelist section by section to his friend Claude Fauriel in Paris, where Henri and Sophie were evidently agog to read it.

Taking a boat to Leghorn he went on to Naples, where he marvelled at the scenic effect of an eruption of Vesuvius forming the climax of Pacini's *Gli ultimi giorni di Pompeii* at the Teatro San Carlo, and afterwards spent ten days on Ischia, riding a donkey around the island and feeding the chickens belonging to the peasant owners of the cottage where he stayed. By the middle of October he was in Florence, a city he had increasingly started to feel at home in. Settling down for a stay of almost two months, he fell readily into the social rhythms of the Grandducal capital, with its agreeable round of 'delightful soirées, balls and dinners in abundance, with pretty Englishwomen, all stupid as clods. All the old fogeys of Europe ought to come here.' As usual in Italy, he was fascinated by the murders and executions (the boy at the Teatro Ognissanti who had knifed a comrade, the beheading of a man from Pistoia who had murdered his wife) but alert at the same time to the increasingly oppressive political climate in the surrounding states: 'Many arrests in Romagna: the times are severe.'

Tuscany under Grand Duke Ferdinand III was still comparatively liberal in permitting a modified freedom in the exchange of ideas among writers, intellectuals and technological experts. The place to which every traveller of any intelligence gravitated on arrival in Florence was the Gabinetto Vieusseux in Piazza Santa Trinità. Jean-Pierre Vieusseux, a Piedmontese descended from a French Huguenot family, had founded his scientific and literary library here in 1819, occupying three floors of the Palazzo Buondelmonti. From the printing house, which issued the liberal periodical *Antologia*, the visitor mounted to the first-floor reading room, above which was the study in which Vieusseux received his guests.

Stendhal had sent copies of the *Histoire de la Peinture*, the *Vies de Haydn, de Mozart et de Métastase* and *Racine et Shakespeare* to the enterprising publisher in 1823, with a polite request for the favour of a notice in *Antologia*, which had duly obliged by summarizing an article on the first of these from the *Edinburgh Review* and subsequently noticing *Racine et Shakespeare*. His own introduction to Vieusseux had arrived through the Belgian historian Louis de Potter, and he was now made welcome within a group of liberal Italian intellectuals, among them the Neapolitan poet Alessandro Poerio, Marchese Gino Capponi, co-founder of the magazine and later a key player in the Tuscan revolution of 1848, and Vincenzo Salvagnoli, the young Florentine lawyer who became one of Stendhal's closest friends during his last years in Italy. It was at the Gabinetto Vieusseux that he also met the poet Giacomo Leopardi: neither of them, alas, left any impression of the encounter.

A much more significant meeting during this stay in Florence took place between Stendhal and Alphonse de Lamartine. They had of course been earlier introduced by Victor Jacquemont, but the acquaintance had not so far been improved. Though Lamartine was by now legation secretary to the French minister to Tuscany, it was probably not simply the hope of gaining some profitable social introductions in the city which encouraged Stendhal to seek him out. They had more friends in common than Jacquemont alone, and this time it was a letter from Adolphe de Mareste which brought the two together.

For all Lamartine's initial misgivings regarding a man he believed was a godless cynic, he respected Stendhal at once for the absolute candour with which he stated the religious position to which the poet, with his ardent spirituality, always attached significance. It was true, Beyle admitted, that he held a reputation for atheism and mocking the name of God. He would neither acknowledge nor deny the Divine existence, simply that he knew nothing of it and that:

> waiting for God to reveal himself, I believe that his prime minister, chance, governs this sad world just as well . . . . I feel I am an honest man, and that it would be impossible to be otherwise, not for the sake of pleasing a Supreme Being who does not exist, but for my own sake, who need to live in peace with my habits and prejudices and to give purpose to my life and nourishment to my thoughts.

He confessed to envying Lamartine what he called his 'consoling illusions' and to basing his credo on literature and the fine arts. He ended with an irresistible 'Causons!', 'Let's talk!', and so of course they talked, as Lamartine says, 'without mystery and without anger'.

A mutual respect developed almost at once, and every evening before or after dinner Beyle would call at the poet's house in Via dei Boffi, near Porta Romana. 'We used to throw a branch of fragrant myrtle on the fire, and we talked with the intimacy which solitude and good faith inspire in men. I instilled in him certain doubts as to his unbelief, and he, as regards music, art and poetry, cast much light upon my ignorance.' Then Lamartine adds this extraordinary and penetrating tribute: 'It was then that I learned that he was a poet to his very fingertips.'

To one of Lamartine's more colourful expatriate friends, Hortense Allart, Stendhal offered his services as a literary agent. After a scandal involving an illegitimate child by her lover, a Portuguese count named Sampaio, she had thought it prudent to quit Paris for Italy where, perhaps predictably, she sat down to write a novel about her recent experiences, entitled *Gertrude*. Already published in Italy, it had, she assured Beyle, been a great success in Rome – 'I get letters 8 pages long' – and only awaited a French publisher. When Stendhal the next spring was as good as his word, she wrote from a friend's villa at Albano, exclaiming 'in my excitement I can tell you you're a *charming* man' and suggesting that he send her a few copies of *Armance* to distribute among her Roman acquaintances.

From Florence he moved on, via Bologna and Ferrara, to Venice, where, visiting the Accademia gallery, he admired Titian's great *Assumption of the Virgin* but pronounced Canova's monumental pyramid at the Frari to be 'the tomb of sculpture'. His natural eye for good art had meanwhile lighted enthusiastically on the work of the young Venetian painter Francesco Hayez, destined to become one of the most polished European portraitists of the nineteenth century and already famous for his historical scenes, which Stendhal had praised in *Rome, Naples et Florence*. Now the writer told his friend Alphonse Gonssolin that Hayez: 'seems to me to be nothing less than the greatest living painter. His colours gladden the sight like those of Bassano, and each of his figures shows some nuance of passion. . . . This painter teaches me something new about the passions he depicts.'

Hayez was then living and working in Milan, a place to which Stendhal dared at last to return. Quite what he expected in the way of a reception from the Austrian authorities, whose mounting suspicion had after all been one of the main causes of his hurried departure from the Lombard capital seven years earlier, is hard to say. As far as the Habsburg police were concerned, time had not softened his reputation as a dangerous subversive, and he was forthwith refused permission to remain in the city for longer than twelve hours.

The letter sent on this occasion from the police commissioner Baron Torresani-Lanzenfeld to Count Strassoldo, military governor of Milan, is eloquent, not only of the iron inflexibility with which Austria under Metternich viewed the least hint of liberalism, but also more sinisterly of its determined international surveillance of all potential critics or opponents of the regime. Noting the arrival of 'the celebrated Frenchman Enrico Bayle, 44 years of age, formerly auditor of the Council of State under Bonaparte', Torresani identifies him as:

> the author, I am assured by a reliable authority, of the notorious work entitled *Rome, Naples et Florence par M. de Standhal* [sic] 'in which, besides revealing the very worst political tendencies, he allows himself the most vehement and audacious sarcasms against the Austrian Government, neither does he shrink from heavily compromising a great many persons, both in our own province and in other Italian States, with the most blatant calumnies.

Stendhal had, it seems, presented himself at police headquarters, requesting a permit for fifteen days' stay, announcing that he was travelling for health and recreation. Ordered to leave as soon as possible, he was at least given what, under the circumstances, were perfectly valid reasons for the refusal. It was not, Torresani explained:

> his diatribes against the Austrian Government, which is too conscious of its strength and dignity to bother with such matters, but the temerity with which he dared to attack the honour and reputation of many subjects of this state, especially various respectable women, which determined the authorities to let him know, in this fashion, their contempt for his abuse of the hospitality shown him in Milan for so many years.

Evidently blustering at first, by disclaiming his authorship and declaring that, once back in Paris, he would seek redress and clear his name through the Imperial ambassador, Beyle acknowledged the amazingly naïve hope that he might be allowed to return to the city 'where he now thinks he might establish himself for good'. The unbending veto, however, allowed him merely to spend a night at the house of a friend, Luigi Buzzi, whom Torresani of course investigated and discovered to be the possessor of political opinions which 'tend to modern liberalism'. Interestingly, to his report on Buzzi for Strassoldo, he added some further notes on Beyle. From his first arrival in Milan in 1816 'he gained a reputation as an irreligious revolutionary, enemy of legitimism and all political order. He is also noted as the author of an infamous political work, printed in 1817 . . . . entitled *Histoire de la Peinture en Italie*.'*

Other friends of his offered to intervene on his behalf, but Stendhal preferred a prudent retreat to Lake Como, where he settled down for a quiet fortnight at an inn called Il Delfino on Isola Bella, to read the *Novelle* (among them the original story of Romeo and Juliet) by the Lombard Renaissance cleric Matteo Bandello. The clarity and liveliness of these tales enchanted him, but what he seems most to have admired was the fact that their author, as he believed, had invented nothing and that his stories were all founded on real events. The same principle was to govern Stendhal's own approach to fiction in works such as the so-called *Chroniques italiennes* and most notably *Le Rouge et le Noir*, where, as we shall see, a whole network of actualities underpinned the novel's imaginative structure.

At the end of January 1828 the traveller returned to Paris. However carefully he may have budgeted for his latest Italian tour (a meticulous itinerary drawn up for Romain Colomb's benefit suggests that Stendhal had been only too conscious of expense) he was now starting to feel once again the pinch of precarious finances. For some time his relations with Henry Colburn, London proprietor of the *New Monthly Magazine*, had been, to say the least, uncertain. Colburn himself was the archetype of that ageless figure, the enterprising and scrupulously dishonest publisher, praised for his vision and acumen by those who did well out of him, but viewed altogether more cynically by writers like

* As a footnote to this correspondence, it may be noted that *Rome, Naples et Florence* was placed on the Papal index in 1828. *Le Rouge et le Noir* 'and other works by the same author' joined it in 1864.

Stendhal whom he was increasingly reluctant to pay and quite prepared to swindle when it suited.

During the previous year Stendhal's English correspondence had been littered with complaints at Colburn's duplicity. The publisher soon became 'this animal', 'this demi-rascal' and the debts steadily mounted to well over a thousand francs. Bartholomew Stritch, his original intermediary and translator, was now arranging a new agreement for the author with *The Athenaeum* for a series of articles at the lump sum of £150 per annum, but this did nothing to assuage his rising fury at Colburn's dilatoriness – due, as it eventually turned out, to the commercial failure of the *New Monthly*, which soon ceased publication altogether.

To make matters worse, in June 1828 the Ministry of War suddenly stopped his regular military half pay and only began it again six months later, after Stendhal had been constrained to make out a detailed account of his entire army service, which, he maintained, had lasted exactly thirteen years, seven months and twenty-eight days. Clearly there had to be other, more reliable ways of making a living than periodical journalism, and Henri now asked Adolphe de Mareste's advice as to whether he should enquire about a 1700-franc post currently on offer at the Royal Archives, for which his name had been suggested. Even if this possibility was not pursued, friends and acquaintances were evidently on the lookout, though the unpaid post of 'Assistant Verifier of Armorial Bearings' conferred on him by Amédée de Pastoret, presumably as a well-intentioned first rung on the official ladder, would hardly remedy the pressing lack of what he referred to by the English word 'fish'.

His response to this material insecurity was characteristically robust and philosophical. One friend who marvelled at his irrepressible verve was Victor Jacquemont, newly returned from America in a state of extreme disgust at the place's sordid commerical vulgarity and delighted to be back, for the moment, in Europe. At Baron Gérard's Wednesday soirée, he told Sutton Sharpe: 'Beyle was on form and honestly deserved that we should each have given him ten francs for his effort, so amusing was he. Since I've been deprived for a month of any form of wit comparable to his, I probably found him funnier still.' Six weeks later Jacquemont had set off again, on the long and fateful Indian journey from which he was never to return.

Mérimée, among those bidding farewell to Jacquemont as he gaily boarded the Brest mail coach, also kept an eye on Stendhal. The pair had somewhat slackened in the assiduous but frankly cynical courtship they had so far kept up towards Mme Ancelot, and Mérimée was soon able to write to Sharpe with news of their friend's latest amorous interest:

> a lady beside whom Ancilla is nothing but a star of the third rank. B. is mad with love for her and spends all his evenings there. She is an extraordinary woman, very lively, pretty and quarrelling with her husband. She's only 24. What's more, she displays great frankness and discussed everything just like a man. An Englishwoman would be quite dumbfounded to hear her talk.

'Pretty' was scarcely the right word to describe the extraordinary woman in question, with her strong-boned face and thick braids of dark hair. Alberthe-Alexandrine de Rubempré, the wife of a financier whom she had married at the age of seventeen, had swiftly forsaken him to become the mistress of one artist, Tony Johannot, and later of another, her cousin Eugène Delacroix. It was with the latter that Stendhal was prepared at first to share her favours, entranced as he suddenly became with the siren he and his circle always referred to as 'Madame Azur' since she lived in Rue Bleue. The romance barely lasted the year: Alberthe was much too general with her favours to make him more than briefly happy, and a trip he took to Bordeaux, Toulouse and across the Pyrenees to Barcelona during the autumn, far from making her heart grow fonder, simply left the field free for others similarly struck by her wit, vivacity and intense beauty. When Stendhal returned at the end of November, he found Mareste firmly in possession of the field. Two months afterwards, writing in English to Sharpe, Mérimée gleefully outlined the state of play.

> I ought to leave you to your coalfire and give you no news, however as I am good I shall give you a brief bulletin of proper food for your wicked mind i.e. scandal. De Mareste is still in high favour with Mrs Azur. She is desperately in love with him. Mareste

is so proud of it that he becomes every day more unmerciful for Stendhal who is in love too and extremely jealous. Stendhal will not see her any more; he confirmed to me the story of the grand trio in which he played his part so well, and says he never knew before what pleasure was. Mareste will play only solos. . . .

Inseparable companions for eight years, Stendhal and Mareste now fell out, ostensibly over a political argument but more probably because of Alberthe, and as we might expect, the friendship was afterwards only superficially renewed. Stendhal sardonically reflected that 'the Baron' had at least managed by some miracle to keep Madame Azur faithful for two years, though he also believed that he himself had contrived to pass on his love for her not just to Mareste but to Mérimée as well.* 'I've an unhappy talent,' he wrote:

for communicating my tastes; often, in speaking of mistresses to my friends, I've made them amorous, or, which is worse, I've made my mistress amorous of the fiiend I really loved. This is what happened to me with Mme Azur and Mérimée. I was desperate for 4 days. When my despair subsided, I went to beg Mérimée to spare me pain for 15 days. He answered: 'For fifteen months I've had no interest in her, I saw her stockings wrinkled down her legs' – *en garaude*, like a slut, we'd say at Grenoble.

Even though, as a sort of revenge, Stendhal gave her name to a devout Marquise in *Le Rouge et le Noir*, he and Alberthe somehow remained close. He could forgive women more easily than he could pardon men.

His customary refuge from worries both emotional and material lay in concentrated literary work. In 1828, with encouragement and some assistance from Romain Colomb, he had begun a species of detailed vade-mecum, half guidebook, half traveller's companion, to that Eternal City with which he had dealt so cavalierly in the two versions of *Rome, Naples et Florence*.

* In *Souvenirs d'Egotisme* he says that he 'inoculated' Mareste with his passion for Alberthe. The verb is used in its old-fashioned sense, referring to the deliberate transference of infected tissue from smallpox victims to healthy bodies.

The frame surrounding his new book, to be entitled *Promenades dans Rome*, was created from the time-honoured device, first made famous in Boccaccio's *Decameron*, of presenting the material through the medium of a group of individuals, in this case four men and three women, French tourists in Italy accompanied by their servants. The female visitors are not particularized, but the men are clearly defined. There is Frédéric, who has 'much intelligence, kindness, indulgence and gentle gaiety' though 'in every day life we should term him a child', Paul, not yet thirty, 'a very handsome man, full of spirit, fond of the cut-and-thrust of conversation', and the more shadowy figure of Philippe, who occasionally lectures the company on historical themes.

In this amiable society, with Stendhal himself tagging pleasantly along, with no very deliberate attempt at topographical method, we wander through the city and its surrounding hill country, the whole tour spreading across two volumes and divided, like *Rome, Naples et Florence*, into a sequence of diary entries. The book is one of his longest, it relies heavily on material borrowed directly or at least suggested by the work of earlier authors, and it has evidently tried the patience of several writers on Stendhal. Yet since, as its most authoritative modern editor justly points out, *Promenades dans Rome* ranked among its author's best-regarded works in his own lifetime, it is worth examining some of the reasons for its continuing hold on the modern reader – who need not necessarily be either an ardent italophile or a dedicated *stendhalien*.

For one thing, we are not dealing here, any more than in the earlier Italian travelogues, with a guidebook in the traditional sense. There is, however subliminally, a constant insistence on continuity, on the present either replicating the past or else directly taking over from it, on the image of Rome not as a mere heap of colossal ruins and cavernous basilicas to which the names of dead emperors, consuls and popes are attached, but as a place vibrantly and intensely inhabited by real people, gossiping, loving, intriguing and now and then murdering, as such people tend to do. The truth of Stendhal's Rome is more than simply what the Italians call 'urbanistic', a matter of brick, stone and archaeology: when the seven travellers arrive in the city, one of the subjects about which they eagerly enquire is its political condition, and, as the author correctly implies, it would be wholly unconvincing were they not to do so. 'I talk about politics with regret,' he claims, 'but as soon as there's the slightest chance of an intimate conversation, nobody in Italy talks about anything else.' More clearly than many other contemporary writers, Stendhal saw the dangerous paradox in the existence of the restored Papal theocracy side by side with the gathering pace of nineteenth-century reform, and could at least hint at coming storm clouds even if he shrank from too much open canvassing of political themes throughout the book.

Another animating force in the *Promenades dans Rome* is of course the presence of the author himself. There is something addictive about Stendhalian digressions, and again and again this most opinionated of ciceroni ravishes us with sheer mental vigour. At Castel Gandolfo, for example, rather than having to bother with describing the place's charms, he entertains us with a disquisition on his favourite theme of Italian sexual spontaneity, as opposed to the monotonous proprieties of the northern nations. A mention of brigands sets him wondering whether Italy would not be a more boring place without them. He moves airily from the ignorance and incompetence of Roman cardinals to discussing the best route from Paris through Switzerland, predicting great things for the young composer Vincenzo Bellini, and reproducing, for our appalled delectation, the grim text of the Duke of Modena's recent law introducing censorship to guard against 'the moral contagion of books imported from other nations'. When Stendhal, telling us to look in other guidebooks if we want an exact account of all the artistic curiosities exhibited in Rome, says that their authors were 'frightened of offending', we know that the reason we enjoy reading his loose, baggy Roman charivari so much is because he has no such fear.

On the same September day in 1829 that the publication of *Promenades dans Rome* was announced in the *Journal de la Librairie*, Stendhal's cousin and lifelong benefactor Pierre Daru died at his country house at Bècheville, north of Paris. Daru, having lost none of his credit and eminence at the fall of Bonaparte, settled down after 1815 to write a long, fanciful history of the recently extinguished Venetian Republic, a work whose eleven volumes gave currency to several hardily perennial legends as to the Draconian government of a state which Napoleon and the Habsburgs had so ruthlessly dismantled.

Daru's incredulity, referred to earlier, in the face of Stendhal's newly displayed literary talent was matched by the younger man's disdain for him as a boring old academic pen-pusher. Henri was at his usual café, the Rouen, which had recently moved its premises to Rue du Rempart, facing the Théâtre-Français, when he opened the paper to discover the announcement of Daru's death. Initially thunderstruck, he soon jumped into a cab, his eyes filling with tears, and hurried to the family house in Rue de Grenelle. His general feeling was one of entirely comprehensible shame at the way in which he had consistently avoided his cousins, and when he reached his destination and was met by a weeping footman, he himself started to cry. Yet such was the effect on him of the house in mourning that, with what later seemed the rankest ingratitude, he put forward his departure for Bordeaux so as to avoid having to 'die with sorrow'.

Pierre Daru's last kindness on Stendhal's behalf had been to use his influence with Joseph Dacier, administrator of the Royal Library, to gain the job of assistant conservator in the department of manuscripts. The death, on 5 May 1829, of Dominique-Martin Méon, a noted medievalist and first modern editor of *Le Roman de la Rose*, left a place vacant which, in the usual course of events, would have been filled in an entirely orthodox sequence of upward movements by existing library staff. Encouraged, however, by support from influential figures such as Pastoret and Cuvier (Edouard Mounier having churlishly declined assistance), Stendhal proceeded to apply, sending Dacier copies of his works and carefully pointed out that 'time, *edax rerum*, has much modified my political opinions, and even in my youth, employed in fairly serious business, I became acquainted with all necessary discretion'. He need not really have bothered, either with this *douceur* or with the exemplary letter of application to the Interior Ministry which followed. Méon's post had already been given to a colleague, Paulin Paris, and the auxiliary job from which the latter transferred was quickly filled by a resident underling.

Nine years after Stendhal's death the library offered a belated amends for this recourse to the immemorial practice of making in-house appointments while seeming to court the interest of external candidates, when it purchased the manuscripts of the *Chroniques italiennes*. The title is one of convenience, applied by Roman Colomb in 1855 to a disparate group of translations, little histories, short stories and novellas gathered together by Stendhal over a decade from 1829 onwards. Their Italian setting is not the only unifying factor. Taken together, they express various facets of the writer's consistent vision of Italy as a place animated and empowered by violent physical response, expressed through sex or murder, a land which after three centuries continued to rehearse the cloak-and-dagger melodrama of the Renaissance as a kind of vitalizing rhetoric.

The first of these pieces, the story *Vanina Vanini*, completed in December 1829, admirably illustrates both this concept of an Italy governed by laws of desire, and Stendhal's unique, sometimes frankly exasperating methods as a storyteller. The tale purports to be set in modern times: Vanina, beautiful daughter of the Roman aristocracy, seeks in vain for glamour and energy among the young men of her class and tells her admirer Prince Savelli that rather than marry any of them she would prefer the handsome *carbonaro* Missirilli who has just escaped from prison. She later finds him hiding in her father's attic, the pair fall in love under the somewhat bizarre conditions ordained by the proud Vanina, and the tale subsequently incorporates a scheming cardinal, sexual bribery and Missirilli's patriotic martyrdom.

Reading *Vanina Vanini*, it is hard not to feel that, as with *Armance*, Stendhal's imagination is really appealing to an older world than that of the 1820s, costuming the characters, so to speak, in the ruffs, doublets and farthingales of the sixteenth century, as opposed to the waistcoats, bonnets and 'inexpressibles' of the nineteenth. There are daggers, there is blood and talk of poison, and the game of sexual ambiguity is played between Missirilli, who first appears disguised as a woman, and Vanina, who dresses up as a page to seduce the cardinal in order to rescue her lover. Yet the crisp tone of the story is ruthlessly contemporary, showing no patience with the kind of romantic convention which seeks to adorn style as well as characters. When Stendhal cannot be bothered with having to tell us what Vanina's father says to her at the ball, or to hint in more than the sketchiest detail at the reasons why the wounded, dragged-up Missirilli should have found his way to the palace attic in the first place, he simply passes on to a more significant phase in the narrative. The last sentence, baldly announcing that after Missirilli's death, Vanina married Prince Savelli, is either masterly in its ironic concision or else simply maddening in its cavalier refusal to explain or elaborate usefully. You either relish Stendhal or you do not, but as a test case *Vanina Vanini* offers the perfect model.

The creative impulse which set off the composition of this story, perhaps during the author's autumn journey through southern France and into Spain, inspired another short work, more complex and at the same time more obviously flawed, which Stendhal completed, then set aside altogether, in the early months of 1830. *Mina de Vanghel* exploits a contrast dear to its creator, between the sentimental, emotionally responsive soul of the Teutonic heroine and the formal, precise coldness of modern French society, with its view of marriage based on money and position as opposed to affairs of the heart.

The succession of women with whom Henri Beyle became romantically involved were nearly all destined to appear, at some stage or other, in his imaginative works. A contractual engagement, as it were, made them Stendhalian heroines before they actually became such, and it was a mere matter of time before this inexhaustible human resource could be drawn upon to provide some of the most powerfully depicted female figures in nineteenth-century fiction. For his eponymous Mina, Stendhal turned to a girl he had known and loved over twenty years previously, the adored Wilhelmine von Griesheim of his Brunswick days, from whom (together with touches drawn from certain of her friends) he had formed his impression of the German soul, so innocent, so constant, so direct.

'Mina de Vanghel was born in the country of philosophy and imagination.' The story's opening words throw down a challenge, and the heroine, like many other Stendhalian protagonist, is all set to take on the world. An idealistic adventuress, she journeys to France in search of the kind of ennobling love which will fulfil her highest expectations. 'For all the polished savagery of its inhabitants, Paris delighted Mina', yet the French, however amusing, fail to stir her soul. Where, she enquires, is true feeling, unalloyed by self-consciousness? Falling heavily for Alfred de Larçay, rich, dull and married, she pursues him to Aix-les-Bains, gets herself hired, in disguise, as his wife's maid, bamboozles another admirer into compromising the entirely virtuous Madame de Larçay and flees to Italy with Alfred. It becomes obvious that she has made a bad choice: Alfred, slave to convention, utterly fails to understand the massive sensual imperative which has governed the heroine's actions. Discovering that his wife has been made the innocent victim of a grotesque deception, he leaves Mina. 'This is what great souls are exposed to,' she concludes, watching him go, 'but they have their resources.' She goes into his room and shoots herself through the heart. 'Was her life a false calculation? Her happiness had lasted eight months. Hers was too ardent a soul to content itself with the reality of life.'

The failure of *Mina de Vanghel* is almost entirely structural. Whereas *Vanina Vanini*, a story written along similar lines, works precisely because Stendhal strips the plot to its essentials, its successor staggers under an overloading of dramatic vicissitude. There is enough material here to make a full-length novel, as he later perceived when dusting it down to form the basis of the long narrative fragment *Le Rose et le Vert*. What draws us to both works is the overwhelming force with which the writer makes the case for women as the active, dominant agents in fiction, driving the story forward in their capacity as amorous outlaws and buccaneers, bold, imaginative and magnificently scornful of stereotype or cliché. Except in one or two isolated cases, he had no models for this kind of heroine, and the central tradition of the nineteenth-century novel in France, Russia and England was to reject this aspect of his creativity completely (in comparison with their Stendhalian counterparts, even Anna Karenina and Dorothea Brooke are essentially passive). Figures like Mina and Vanina and their later avatars Mathilde de la Mole and Lamiel are vindications, if any were needed, of the lonely singularity in Stendhal's peculiar claim to genius.

One way out of his current financial difficulties – and one which, ironically his Amazonian heroines would have disdained – was to contract marriage with a comfortably established partner. A marginal jotting in a copy of the *Histoire de la Peinture*, made on 10 January 1830, shows that he had discussed the possibility with friends, who had helped him to produce a budget – 1800 francs for the 'toilette de Madame', 3000 for 'imprévus et maladies', 1000 for hire of furniture et cetera – making a total of 12,000 francs. It was more than mere mercenary calculation nevertheless which brought him together again with Giulia Rinieri de' Rocchi, a young Italian woman from Siena whose acquaintance he had first made three years before.

Giulia was the ward of Daniello Berlinghieri, the elderly Tuscan Minister to France, whose distinguished career had included service with the Knights of Malta against the Barbary corsairs and the rectorship of Siena University. A platonic attachment to Giulia's mother resulted in the girl being consigned to his guardianship, presumably with the idea that she would eventually marry him. Given the disparity in their ages – Berlinghieri was nearing seventy while his ward was in her twenties – the adoption needed to be made official, and under this dispensation he could bring her to Paris and instal her as a species of diplomatic hostess and housekeeper. Though he apparently refused to meet his neighbour La Fayette (perhaps less for political reasons than because of the grizzled hero's reputation as a ladykiller among impressionable young girls), Berlinghieri became a friend of Baron Gérard and the Cuvier circle at the Jardin des Plantes. From a letter written to him by Stendhal in Italian in 1827, we can surmise that he also came on the steamer ship with Sophie Duvaucel to greet Mehemet Ali's giraffe, though Giulia herself stayed at home.

No less sensitive and accomplished than Sophie or any of Beyle's other female friends, Giulia Rinieri de' Rocchi appears to have grown genuinely interested in him, and the attachment, in one form or another, was lasting between them both. Surprisingly, in view of some of his earlier baffled assaults on women's susceptible hearts, it seems to have been her initiative which, during the early months of 1830, lifted their friendship onto an altogether more serious footing. Stendhal was frankly astonished by her reception of him on 21 January, and two days later, on his birthday, wrote: 'How to explain this goodness? It is at forty-seven that Dominique perceives the brilliance he possesses. He never suspected it at 28. *Il tempo e galantuomo* (time is a gentleman) and will tell me why Dominique receives such a welcome.' On the 27th he exclaims: 'What! *four days after 47 a young girl* says: I love you.' The archaeology of his marginal jottings leads us yet further, to the moment at which, on 3 February, she stood before him holding his head in her hands and saying, 'I know, I've known for a long time, that you are ugly and old', then bending to kiss him. On the 22 March his cryptic note in English '*a time, first time*' implies that the pair had become lovers in earnest.

While this crucial liaison was gathering strength, Stendhal, his confidence undeniably boosted by Giulia's regard, luxuriated in the life of the literary boulevardier which, even with so little money, he could now count on enjoying. One major Parisian artistic figure with whom his acquaintance was ripening into a friendship based on sound mutual respect was Eugène Delacroix. Their connection extended a good deal further than a share in the love of Alberthe de Rubempré. They had first met in 1824 at Baron Gérard's, though at that stage Delacroix was disinclined to admire the *Vie de Rossini* and Stendhal, in his review of that year's Salon, was unenthusiastic about *Le massacre de Scio*, the evocation of an episode on the island of Chios during the Greek independence struggle which ranks among the painter's most compelling early achievements. 'I cannot admire M. Delacroix and his *Massacre de Scio*. This work always seems to me to be a painting originally intended to portray a plague which the artist, in response to news in the papers, has turned into a Massacre on Chios.' A noble soul, incapable of meanness, Delacroix was entirely ready to forgive Stendhal's severity, especially since the latter had gone on to praise his feeling for colour and movement, which he said reminded him of Tintoretto.

Both men were present at the Théâtre-Français on 25 February 1830, at the event which sealed the belated triumph of French Romanticism, the first performance of Victor Hugo's *Hernani*. The notorious fracas which had broken out in the auditorium between the conservatives, shocked by the author's assault on the precious classical *règle* which hitherto ordained the outline and structure of French serious drama, and the young Romantics, thrilled by the play's iconoclastic energy, had undoubted political undertones which merely served to enhance the air of *succès de scandale* instantly surrounding the piece. Stendhal, who had reservations about the play, left no impression, alas, of the famous 'Bataille d'*Hernani*', at which almost everybody who mattered on the contemporary Parisian literary scene, from Alexandre Dumas to Théophile Gautier, distinguished by his scarlet waistcoat, seems to have been present. Doubtless Beyle was pleased to see the heroine Dona Sol being played so dashingly by his much-admired Mademoiselle Mars, now a mature tragedy queen of fifty.

Stendhal had been introduced to Victor Hugo by Sainte-Beuve, who soon realised that the meeting was one between entrenched differences rather than like minds. Drinking tea at Mérimée's apartment, the pair, according to Sainte-Beuve, had skirmished like 'two wild cats facing each other from opposing gutters, on the defensive, hackles raised, and not sheathing their claws without infinite precautions beforehand'. Hugo's later verdict on Stendhal that he was 'an intelligent man who was also an idiot' gained reinforcement from his impression of *Le Rouge et le Noir* as a formless creation, written in bad French. 'Every time I try to make out a single phrase of your favourite work,' he told a friend, 'it feels as though one of my teeth were being pulled out . . . Stendhal never suspected for an instant what writing really involved.'

If Hugo absolutely failed to see the point of Stendhal as a man, it was unlikely that he would be able to grasp the essence of his greatest work, in the process of completion, ironically, around the time of their encounter *chez* Mérimée. It was at Marseilles, on the night of 25 October 1829, that the idea had first begun to develop for a novel provisionally entitled *Julien*, centred around the figure of an ambitious young man whose career across the horizons of love, politics and religion would end in the attempted murder of his mistress and his own execution. When at length it was published just over a year later, this working title had been altered to *Le Rouge et le Noir*, under which enigmatic label the world has since acknowledged one of those rare works whose resolute singularity of tone and viewpoint teaches novelists a lesson in the mysteries of their art.

Writer after writer on Stendhal has sought to crack the riddle of his two colours – assuming, indeed, that it is there to be solved. The most popular interpretation relates red to a military uniform and black to the priestly soutane donned at one stage by Julien Sorel, though the French army, under Napoleon or the Bourbons, never actually wore red tunics. Equally plausible is the idea of black as a colour of gloomy political reaction and legitimist formality, as opposed to the vivid scarlet symbolizing liberal opposition. Others have seized on the gambling game rouge-et-noir, suggesting that Julien's career is meant to be seen as a matter of chance and luck, while one highly convincing hypothesis is based on the hoisting of a red-and-black flag by the insurgents of the July Revolution. Yet even this last theory does not fully explain the intention behind the title, and the best we can say is that its apparently deliberate vagueness is entirely appropriate to a novel whose author does not always find it necessary to answer all the questions which he raises.

The germ of *Le Rouge et le Noir*'s plot lay in two murder cases which had caught Stendhal's attention in the *Gazette des Tribunaux*, a daily report of proceedings in the nation's law courts. Writing in the *New Monthly Magazine* in 1826, he had indicated this as prescribed study for an English visitor to France at all curious as to the make-up and manners of modern society, emphasizing its value as a mine of detail and a thoroughly good read in its own right, with absorbing narrative, precision and immediacy guaranteed throughout.

The earlier of the two *affaires* which provided Julien Sorel with real-life prototypes was that of Antoine Berthet, a young man of the 'pale but interesting' type, the son of a blacksmith, who had trained as a priest in a Grenoble seminary before entering the household of the prosperous bourgeois Michoud family as a tutor. Dismissed for obscure reasons, he applied to another seminary, from which he was soon expelled. Angry and desperate, he sent Madame Michoud a blackmailing letter, implying that she was the mistress of his successor in the tutorial post. When Monsieur Michoud found Berthet a job teaching the children of the Cordon family, his wife took care to denounce the young man to his new employers, who were in any case suspicious of his growing interest in their daughter.

Once again dismissed, Berthet now threatened to murder Madame Michoud, and on a Sunday morning in July 1827, he entered the church where she was at mass and succeeded in severely wounding her. Turning his double-shotted pistol on himself, he only managed to break his jaw. The courtroom at his trial was thronged with smartly dressed *grenobloises*, attracted by the murderer's delicate youthfulness. Any hopes they might have established of judicial leniency were dashed by the death sentence for premeditated homicide, and Berthet was executed, despite several attempts at obtaining a royal pardon, on 28 February 1828.

Adrien Lafargue, protagonist in the second case, had already figured, however incongruously, in the *Promenades dans Rome*, where Stendhal, making no serious apology for obtruding some dozen pages of résumé from the *Gazette des Tribunaux*, reported the details of the affair as a means of padding out his second volume. A handsome young cabinet-maker working at the spa town of Bagnères-de-Bigorre in the Pyrenees, Lafargue, having found his mistress in bed with one of her former lovers, shot at her twice, then cut her throat. Found guilty, he was given a comparatively brief prison sentence, a fact which seems to have impressed Stendhal less than the sheer zeal and fearlessness with which Lafargue carried out his murderous revenge. It was this, he noted, which contrasted the lower-middle-class Lafargue with the altogether passionless aristocracy of modern France. Poor and without social advantages the cabinet-maker may have been, but at least he was energetic, imaginative and well educated. 'Probably all great men from now on will arise from the class to which M. Lafargue belongs. Napoleon, in the past, blended similar conditions: a good education, an ardent imagination and extreme poverty.'

This sense of Lafargue as essentially an historical figure, heightened by the allusion to Napoleon, is something Stendhal readily transferred, not just to Julien himself, but to the overall character of *Le Rouge et le Noir* as a work of fiction, insistently grounded in actuality. Whatever his contempt for Sir Walter Scott's Tory politics and his impatience with the novelist's apparent lack of spontaneity when it came to engaging with ordinary human emotions, he had justly admired books such as *Old Mortality* and *The Bride of Lammermoor*, and whether consciously or otherwise, reflected this admiration in his own novels. For just as Scott had underlined the dimension of historical truth as a determinant factor in his characters' lives, creating imperatives and defining motives – his most signal achievement indeed as a novelist – so Stendhal is concerned to locate the dramatis personae of *Le Rouge et le Noir* firmly within the recognizable context of a contemporary France, whose prevailing atmosphere governs their passions, ambitions and prejudices.

Not for nothing is the novel subtitled *Chronique du XIXe siècle* on its title page and *Chronique de 1830* at the head of its opening section. The objection that Stendhal did not include the July Revolution of that year as an integral component of the book is malapropos. Much of *Le Rouge et le Noir* was already written by the arrival of summer, and the '1830' element has broader implications than those tied with any sort of Hegelian inevitability to the advent of political upheaval. Verrières, the town in the Franche-Comté of which M.de Rênal is mayor, thought to have been modelled on Dôle, a small city in the same region, is both modern and timeless in its provincialism. Here, the author declares, 'the tyranny of public opinion (and what an opinion!) is as stupid in the small towns of France as in the United States of America'. Its very plane trees, trimmed and lopped, symbolize a prosaic repressiveness; the Mayor, in any case, considers trees useless unless they 'yield a return', a phrase on which Stendhal seizes as the embodiment of that mercantile evangelizing, the enemy of pure beauty, which he had earlier pilloried in *D'un nouveau complot contre les industriels*.

Paris, Julien discovers, is no better. The Hôtel de la Mole, where he makes his début in smart company, is a mausoleum of spiritless elegance, in which the merest glimmer of original intelligence becomes instantly suspect, and where 'the young men who came to offer their respects, nervous of referring to anything which might lead to their being suspected of thinking, frightened of betraying some prohibited reading or other, fell silent after a few fine words on Rossini and the weather'. Riddled with legitimist snobbery and scorn, the world of the Restoration aristocracy horrifies Julien with its deadly self-regard. Nobody could now accuse Stendhal, as in the case of *Armance*, of not knowing his Parisian salons. Whatever his precision of detail in creating a *mise-en-scène* for his hero's bizarre social triumph as a suitor for Mathilde de la Mole, he consistently emphasizes the young man's willingness to compromise with an established value system for the sake of an intoxicating ambition, stifling all notion of Julien as the sort of engaging chancer whose career we might be tempted to applaud on the assumption that each audacious leap will always find a safe landing.

The most astonishing achievement of *Le Rouge et le Noir* is not necessarily in the sturdy historicity of its re-enactment of scenes and confrontations among the nobility and bourgeoisie of Charles X's disastrous reign. Neither does its peculiar hold on us as a work of art rely exclusively on its author's resolute grasp of motivation, determined as he is to make us know why his characters speak and act in the way they do. The book's command of its readers' respect, the constant impression of uniqueness it conveys, for all its diversity of source material, as a work which dictates its own critical terms, goes much deeper than these issues of authenticity and technical competence.

What Stendhal contrives, partly through paring away the traditional layers of narrative and description from the body of the novel, is to create a constant awareness of a work of art in the making rather than something finished and by the same token inviolate. The story's insistent immediacy, the sense that we are there as it unfolds, the importance of our not knowing, or even being able to guess, as we might in the work of other novelists, what is going to happen to Julien or Mathilde or Madame de Rênal, are all features of a personal idiom, essentially that of a relation offered to us as the facts stand, and one in which 'author' need not necessarily imply 'authority' clad in the full omniscient confidence of a Balzac or a George Eliot.

The style itself mirrors the hero's impatience, that peremptoriness peculiar to an existence which, for all the grandiose glimpses into a successful future, seems consciously or otherwise to foresee its abrupt and early end. So curt are the chapter openings – 'The children adored him, he cared nothing for them', 'As they left the drawing room around midnight . . .', 'He hurried to brush his coat . . .', 'Julien read over his letters . . .' – that it almost feels as though young Sorel himself were guiding the pen.

Yet Stendhal's point is of course that this is not the all-conquering *jeune premier*, that this pushy, cynical, contemptuous youth, whose attitudes we find ourselves sharing only because the opinions and responses of those around him are so venal and commonplace in comparison, is another kind of hero altogether, whose death consecrates the eternal impossibility of reconciling the tyrannical imperatives of all-creating fancy with the achievement of a reasonable happiness. Thus there is a ghastly comedy in the book's sublime coda, not so much in the apparitions of Mathilde carrying Julien's head on her knees as in the fact that this vessel of the intelligence which has driven the book now becomes a theatrical prop in the young woman's historical tableau, as if she were absurdly determined, at the last moment, to try to convert a modern novel into a Romantic costume drama. We are left applauding Madame de Rênal for the flawlessly Stendhalian plainness, or as he might have called it 'dryness', with which she terminates the narrative flow with her death. 'She did not try in any way to take her own life; but died three days after Julien, while embracing her children.'

Stendhal himself was not Julien, any more than Verrières was Grenoble, yet as various studies have shown, *Le Rouge* was toughened by its construction on an armature of reference to the people, events, places and feelings which held an idiosyncratic personal meaning for him. The path of worldly advancement followed by his hero was one which, for various reasons, he had not taken, and there can be no doubt that his peculiar manner of offering the young man for our approval while simultaneously withdrawing him from it owes something to the special nature of that backward glance he cast over his own life in comparison to those of boyhood friends such as Mounier, Faure and Crozet, all of them with established professional careers.

The fact was, nevertheless, that after fifteen years during which he had been able to establish a literary reputation and to live without positively starving on a mixture of earned and unearned income, Stendhal still coveted some sort of official post which would pay him a fixed salary, ensure a degree of social respectability and enable him perhaps to marry. Even though the librarianship had eluded him, some other combination of cachet and emolument must surely lie within his grasp, if only an influential friend were to come up with a suitable offer.

In the end it was history rather than string-pulling which produced the desired result. No great gift of prophecy had been required to foretell a short and catastrophic reign for Charles X, the very incarnation, some might have said, of the famous verdict on the restored Bourbons that they 'learned nothing and forgot nothing' from their years in exile. Though not in himself a vicious or cruel man, he was fatally lacking in the kind of realistic awareness of his subjects' political volatility which might have helped him to achieve the necessary compromises between hard-nosed pragmatism and a readiness to humour the more extreme right-wing elements among the governing élite.

The royal nomination, in August 1829, of three highly unpopular ministers, among them the arrogant and morbidly Catholic Prince Jules de Polignac, to head a new government, laid the foundations of the monarchy's collapse. Charles's ill-advised attempt to undermine the principles of the Charter which had set his late brother on the throne of France was challenged by a vote in the Chamber of Deputies, followed in turn by the King's equally foolish decision to dismiss parliament and stage an election. The foregone outcome of an increased opposition was met by a suicidal show of strength on the part of monarch and ministers. On 26 July 1830 a set of emergency ordinances was passed, abrogating press freedom, dissolving the newly elected Chamber, drastically reducing the number of deputies and restricting still further the already too limited franchise. By the next day the first barricades were going up, Marshal Marmont, Paris's military governor, had called out his troops, the poorest citizens were looting rifles from gunsmiths to arm themselves, and the aged La Fayette was once more being talked of as a champion of liberty. Charles X's ultimate unwisdom was first of all to believe that none of this really mattered, then to agree too late to a change of ministry, then to retreat from his palace at Saint-Cloud to Rambouillet, still putting his trust in Polignac's crazy assurance that the Blessed Virgin would somehow see them through. On the 29th, Marmont's regiments, having met with fierce resistance, went over to the rebels, and the following day the young *marseillais* politician and historian Adolphe Thiers, who was to enjoy a career of quite remarkable buoyancy for nearly half a century more, declared Louis-Philippe, Duc d'Orléans, scion of the cadet branch of the Bourbons, 'a citizen king'. Charles promptly abdicated in favour of his grandson, the Duc de Bordeaux, and left hurriedly for a gloomy exile in Edinburgh.

This so-called 'July Revolution' confirmed the ascendancy of Romanticism. Many of the fighters on the barricades had come from that rudderless younger generation described at the beginning of Alfred de Musset's novel of the period, *La Confession d'un enfant du siècle* (1836) as having, in a sense, arrived too late for Napoleon, youth whose blood was now stirred by the chance of a fight to the death with the forces of reaction. The most memorable works to emerge from the conflict were the noble *Symphonie funèbre et triomphale* composed by the young Hector Berlioz for the state funeral of the revolutionary martyrs, and Eugène Delacroix's *Liberty leading the people*, the classic painterly image of this and all other popular uprisings, exhibited at the Salon of 1831.

Delacroix had in fact been a somewhat timid spectator of the July days, and so indeed had Stendhal. Even if he could write exultantly to Sutton Sharpe a fortnight later, extolling the boundless courage of the young Parisians, he had nevertheless remained in his apartment at 71, Rue de Richelieu, during the worst of the fighting, reading Las Cases' *Mémorial de Sainte-Hélène*, that most popular of all essays in nostalgic Bonapartism. At each new round of shots, he scribbled a comment in the margin, on page 147 'fusillade from firing parties while I read this page 1.15 p.m. 28th July 1830', on page 171 'complete coolness under fire on the part of the people', on page 195 'beginning of rifle shots which I can hear while reading this page. It is the Jesuits who make them shoot', and so on.

With what now seems astonishing rapidity, Stendhal's fortunes altered abruptly as a direct result of the creation of the July Monarchy. Though an audience with the new Interior Minister, François Guizot, on 3 August failed to secure him the comfortable prefecture he craved, a more promising answer came on 7 September from the Foreign Minister, Louis-Mathieu de Molé, who assured Beyle that a request for a consular post at Naples, Genoa or Leghorn would be properly considered. Loyal friends had used what influence they could, especially Mme Victor de Tracy, who knew Molé's mistress, Comtesse de Castellane, and the Neapolitan exile Domenico di Fiore. The former urged him not to waste time and to be specific, since appointments were being begged by 'victims, martyrs, God knows who'. With the sagacity Stendhal always admired in her, the Englishwoman forced him to make up his mind once and for all as to whether he really wanted the Italian posting for which she had been so solicitous with Molé on his behalf. The appointment came through in the nick of time, by royal ordinance, on 25 September, when he was chronically short of funds. Henri Beyle was named His Most Christian Majesty's consul-general at the Austrian Imperial port of Trieste, with a salary of 15,000 francs per annum. A week after he left Paris, the *Journal de la Librairie* announced the publication of *Le Rouge et le Noir*.

CHAPTER 11

TOO MUCH SUNLIGHT

In the bustle surrounding his departure for Trieste, Stendhal had not forgotten Giulia Rinieri de' Rocchi. The relationship between the pair seems to have grown still warmer during the late summer of 1830: a note in an autobiographical sketch made three years afterwards tells us that on 29 July he spent a protective evening with her as the noise of revolution swept through the streets around them. On 6 November, the same day that he left Paris for Trieste, he felt sufficiently emboldened to write a letter to her guardian, Daniello Berlinghieri, asking for her hand in marriage.

'It is perhaps a great temerity in me, poor and old as I am, to confess to you that I should consider my life's happiness assured were I to obtain the hand of Mademoiselle your niece.' Daring indeed it was, but Stendhal's proposal, in its candour and warmth, undoubtedly merited respect. When he wrote of himself, 'I view it as a miracle that I should be loved at forty-seven', nobody but the most hardened cynic could have seen such a declaration as merely an attempt to gain respectability through the sort of cosmetic wedlock with which certain bachelors, for whatever reason, seek to enhance their career prospects. Henri loved and admired Giulia for what she was, and the affection, as we have seen, was returned. There was no reason to despair, given his willingness to allow her, once married, to spend six months of every year with Berlinghieri, and an equal readiness to sign, without reading it beforehand, whatever contract was presented to him.

The Tuscan diplomat was either far too possessive of his ward or perhaps too much a calculating man of the world to countenance a middle-aged French consular functionary, with little more than his official salary to fall back on, as a prospective husband for a nubile daughter of the Sienese aristocracy. The letter Stendhal received in reply has survived, a model of courtly politeness, in which the inevitable refusal is wrapped up in a sequence of exquisite tributes to his noble soul, honourable character, qualities of spirit and heart et cetera et cetera, and the issue is made entirely to depend on Giulia's own response to the offer. The wily 'uncle' does not exactly say no, but a reference to the instability of the current French political situation suggests that he was by no means convinced that Stendhal's new-found position was in any way secure. Giulia evidently took her guardian's advice and rejected the proposal, but this did nothing to lessen the intimacy, and when she returned to Italy Beyle was a guest at her family's villa of Vignano, in the Chianti east of Siena.

The journey to Trieste took more than a fortnight, involving a two-day wait at Lyons after the Rhône steamboat crashed into a bridge, a brief stop at Nice, where Stendhal felt a '*vif sentiment de* happiness' in the company of the likeable consul Aimé-Thérèse-Joseph Masclet in his flourishing rose garden, a journey by sea to the Piedmontese port of Oneglia and thence, as he hoped, a quick posting to Lodi and Brescia. As it turned out, an interfering Austrian police official at Pavia, noticing that his passport lacked the necessary visa, made him wait for clearance from Milan, where he retrieved his papers only after the French consular representative, Baron Denois, had put pressure on the authorities. Following a night in Verona, he hastened north to Udine, arriving at Trieste on 25 November.

A light *bora* was blowing as he came into the city, that cruel wind whose gusts have always been invoked as a pretext for the bleaker moods of the Triestines. If Stendhal knew anything about this free port of the Habsburg Empire, it was surely that the place had provided the backdrop for the murder, in 1768, of Johann Winckelmann, whose ideas he had challenged in the *Histoire de la Peinture*. He was likely also to have associated it with the Bonaparte family: Napoleon's brother Jérôme, King of Westphalia, and his sister Elisa Baciocchi, Princess of Tuscany, had lived here at various times, and a less fortunate sister, Caroline, widow of Joachim Murat, King of Naples, was still in residence. Otherwise the city, sober and severe under its citadel and cathedral of San Giusto, offered little in the way of cultural or social inducements, and 'the Hamburg of the Adriatic' as certain visitors chose to call it, held few potential charms for the newly arrived consul.

He had come furnished with letters of introduction from influential acquaintances. The composer Giacomo Meyerbeer, whose father owned a sugar refinery at nearby Gorizia, recommended him to Princess Porcia, wife of the Austrian governor, and Bianca Mojon Milesi arranged that he should meet her relative by marriage Costanza Reyer, who kept a liberal salon and maintained links with Viennese intellectual circles surrounding Schubert and Grillparzer. Stendhal described her admiringly to Mareste as a woman of thirty-six:

> who has plenty of ideas . . . . and a large drawing room painted in fresco where, at ten o'clock, twenty glasses of Cyprus wine and thirty of lemonade are brought in, accompanied by excellent slices of *gateau de Savoie*. I visit this salon four times a week and shall end up going six times. It is not, and never will be, a matter of love: but in the whole of Paris I can't find a house like this one!

Otherwise he could solace himself with his membership of the Triestine Club, the Casino Vecchio, and patronize the opera at the Teatro Grande. Among that season's offerings, which included Rossini's *L'inganno felice* and the often-performed *Romeo e Giulietta* by Niccolo Vaccai (Stendhal, hearing it in Paris as a vehicle for Pasta, had judged its earlier sections tolerable for the sake of its beautiful third act) was *La straniera*, the second really successful opera by the young Vincenzo Bellini, somewhat harshly written off in the *Promenades dans Rome* two years earlier. That verdict, far from being revised by hearing the piece again in Trieste, was reinforced in a letter to Mareste which interestingly dismissed the composer, whom many regard as the very incarnation of Italian *bel canto*, in terms of a second Gluck, incapable of melody or arresting orchestration and writing merely in prolonged recitative. Stendhal's comments emphasize the limitations of his aesthetic when confronting this new, more nakedly dramatic style which, though he must have known the extraordinary skill and orginality with which Rossini had handled it in his later Neapolitan operas, seemed garish and coarse in comparison with Cimarosa and the masters of an earlier generation.

If he saw *La straniera* and Bellini's popularity in general as simply another example of the Italian obsession with novelty, and disliked the work more because it was taken from Vicomte D'Arlincourt's ludicrous novel *L'Etrangère* which he had pilloried in a *London Magazine* article, he was interested nevertheless in the diva interpreting the title role, the remarkably versatile artist Caroline Ungher. At the age of twenty-one, Ungher had been chosen by Beethoven to sing the soprano part in the first performance of his Ninth Symphony, and it was she who induced the deaf master to acknowledge the applause he could not hear. Rossini described her as having 'the ardour of the south, the energy of the north, a voice of silver and a talent of gold', attributes genuinely appreciated in the Italian opera houses where she pursued a triumphant career. Though Stendhal found her lacking in vocal sweetness or smoothness of tone, he was responsive to her personal charm, but apparently failed in his attempts at securing a reciprocal fascination. 'She is admirably pretty, she has ideas, is twenty-three or twenty-four years old; she has known all the diplomats, but she's too strong in mathematics. I tried to persuade her that 48=25, which wasn't in the least admissible.' Ungher later became involved with the poet Nicholas Lenau, who committed suicide for her sake, and then married a French painter sixteen years her junior who, as an elderly widower, insisted on having the bed in which she had died (in 1877) brought all the way from Florence to France so that he himself could spend his last moments in it.

Bored as Consul Beyle was with Trieste and depressed by its hostile winter climate which brought on his rheumatism, he was good at his job, and under other circumstances might have settled comfortably enough into a professional routine. His earlier training as an imperial bureaucrat stood him in good stead, and he kept the French Foreign Minister, Comte Sebastiani, well informed on everything from the price and availability of wheat in the Croatian Banat, the English purchase of Apulian olive oil and the exact number of hectolitres of corn bought by the Austrians for provisioning the fortress of Mantua to the arrival of foreign ships in the port and the passage towards Gorizia of twenty-five carts loaded with Congreve rockets. His vigilance and attention to duty were surely enhanced by the volatile political situation elsewhere in Italy, which soon afterwards spilled over into scattered outbreaks of revolution (most notably in the Duchy of Modena, providing valuable hints for *La Chartreuse de Parme*) and by the spread of the great cholera epidemic which was to haunt European cities throughout the succeeding decade.

There was no chance, however, that he would be allowed simply to get on with the tasks assigned to him. Even if, as he assured Sebastiani, the government here was 'not at all troublesome', the police were 'wise and intelligent' and the disturbances of neighbouring states merely an object of curiosity, his own position, or the lack of it which soon became apparent, was evidence of a growing nervousness on the part of the Austrians regarding anyone with the remotest hint of liberal sympathies or opinions. The absurd fact emerges that almost as soon as he arrived in Trieste Stendhal was labelled *persona non grata* by the authorities, and that his tactful, persistent and painstaking discharge of official business was carried out under a gathering cloud of disapproval.

All diplomatic representatives in the Austro-Hungarian empire, as in other states, required an *exequatur*, a permit from the government implying that they were cleared from any taint of political subversion and could thus carry out their duties without interference as expatriate residents. Given what the authorities already knew of Stendhal, and his reputation as an author of 'dangerous' books, there was no question of this facility being granted him, something made clear as early as 21 November 1830, four days before the consul reached Trieste, when Prince Metternich wrote to the Austrian ambassador Count Apponyi:

> However disposed the Court of Vienna may be to gratify the French government, it is in the common interests of both recipro-

> cally to refrain from consigning the management of public affairs in their respective states to persons whose principles and antecedents are calculated to excite a justified suspicion. Such is nevertheless the case as regards M. Beyle. Your Excellency will not be ignorant of all he has published under the name of Stendhal against the Austrian government in Italy.

Further evidence that Habsburg officialdom was fully alerted to the potential danger comes from Josef Amberg, director of the Venetian police force, who wrote to Prince Porcia, governor of Trieste, to tell him that during a December fortnight Beyle had spent in Venice, he had been placed under the most vigilant surveillance.

Amberg was fully aware of the warning issued two years earlier by his Lombard counterpart Torresani-Lanzenfeld when Stendhal had attempted to revisit Milan. It was evidently this, more than anything else, which hardened the government's resolve not to allow such a dangerous creature as 'il noto francese Enrico Bayle' to stay any longer than was absolutely necessary in the imperial domains, and it was this indeed to which Count Sedlnitzky, the Viennese chief of police, referred when writing to Metternich on 30 November 1830, refusing the *exequatur*. Five days later, in the *Journal des Débats*, an announcement confirmed the refusal 'to M. de Bayle de Stendhal', though Mérimée told Mareste that he thought this was merely a malicious invention 'by the great man's enemies'.

Stendhal was left in the bizarre position of occupying a post in which he was officially unacceptable until the French Foreign Ministry should stir itself to find him a job elsewhere. His letters to friends in Paris became shot through with gloomy cynicism. One written to Sophie Duvaucel, in which he laughed at the *Débats*'s linking of Beyle to Stendhal, ended with a gruesome tale of a local girl who had been buried alive. Another, to Virginie Ancelot, began, 'Alas, I'm dying of boredom and cold'. He told Domenico Fiore that as he grew older he felt in need of a warm place in which to be consul, Palermo perhaps, Naples or Cadiz, and complained to Mareste that never so much as now had he realized what it was to be without money because of his father's financial incompetence. 'To be obliged to tremble with apprehension over keeping a position in which one is perishing with boredom!' He was too poor to employ a cook: at the hotel where he stayed, L'Aquila Nera, now Hotel Milano*, he was expected to dine alone, to support his consular dignity, and the food was vile. An enormous capon was followed by half-cooked sole, a woodcock killed yesterday and rice boiled up with garlic sausages. 'My entire life at present is represented by my dinner.'

The notion of the wretched consul solitarily munching his way through an enormous, largely inedible meal, while the ridiculous paranoia of an authoritarian regime condemns him to official nullity, is obviously not lacking in pathos, but Stendhal had other matters to distract him. *Le Rouge et le Noir* was now out, and finding – or not finding – the readership its author had hoped for. The interest and admiration of his friends was tempered, as always when somebody writes a novel, by rather too much readiness to see the author as his own hero and thus to take issue with him as if he shared Julien Sorel's character and attitudes to the smallest degree. Mérimée indeed took it upon himself to point out that the sheer truth to life of Julien's calculating ruthlessness would prove repugnant to most readers. It was not the business of art, he claimed, to demonstrate this aspect of human nature.

When the reviews appeared, these reflected a similar mixed reaction. *La Gazette littéraire* commended the book's distinctiveness, while remarking on its decidedly uneven narrative style. Like several of Stendhal's friends the critic of *L'Artiste* advised his readers against the second of the two volumes, noting prophetically however that 'this is a book which will one day be successful'. The more conservative *Gazette de France* baldly remarked, 'M. de Stendhal is not stupid, though he may write stupid books', but the more liberal *Revue encyclopédique* was scarcely more enthusiastic, observing dismissively that since the story was set within the context of a political dispensation which

* The story told by Stendhal's first English biographer, Sir Archibald Paton, in 1874, that the hotel manager accused him of stuffing his dirty linen down the water closet, is probably not true.

had now been swept away, its historical aspect must make it seem rather out of date.

Two of the most appreciative notices were published in the *Journal des Débats* and *Le Temps*. The former was by the influential young critic Jules Janin, whom Stendhal admired and had met on various occasions in Paris, as well as enjoying his burlesque thriller *L'âne mort*, one of the literary successes of 1829. His spirited résumé of the early chapters shows a keen grasp of the author's intentions, but what comes across most powerfully from Janin's essay is a sense of the work's dramatic novelty, of its impact on contemporary readers as something unique in the annals of French fiction, an attempt at testing their reactions to certain social realities by offering these to them as a sequence of deeply incised sketches and semi-satirical portraits. *Le Rouge et le Noir* may well be vastly exaggerated in its merciless depiction of provincial life, not to speak of its Parisian scenes, Janin implies, but its power compels us to believe in it. As an example of its fearful credibility he singles out the episode at the Besançon seminary, proclaiming: 'It is impossible to conceive of so hideous a picture, one which struck me as forcibly as the earliest ghost story told me by my nurse.' The review's magisterial concluding paragraphs shrewdly and passionately accuse Stendhal of being a brilliant despoiler, someone happy to believe in nothing so long as this enables him to respect nothing, a writer whose malign potency is like that of some genie in an Oriental tale irresistibly dragging you towards destruction while showing you enchanting visions on the way.

> Add to this invincible need to represent everything as ugly and to raise his voice so as to appear more fearful the fact that M. de Stendhal is a maker of paradoxes. At the truest point of his fiction, at the very instant he sees us to be attached and interested he suspends his narrative, breaks the flow, stops short and coolly drops you into an unexpected paradox.

Some may feel that Janin has perfectly summed up here one of the writer's most important characteristics, but many later readers might number this among Stendhal's strengths rather than categorize as a weakness so original a manipulation of fictional method.

If Alfred de Musset really did write the review in *Le Temps*, which some doubt, he was equally enthralled by the novel's singular storytelling style. The author 'is scathing without being bitter, and says things with the most dispassionate air which make your blood boil: he is the devil of a man, who makes monstrosities appear in his magic lantern, all this in a simple, sometimes naive fashion'. The critic was as enchanted as the rest of us by Mathilde de la Mole, seeming to understand the way in which she consistently tries to design her existence as the centrepiece of the kind of thrilling, violent fiction from which the narrative constantly pulls away. He ended, however, by pointing out that the genuine red and black lay in the style itself, a matter of blood and mourning which seemed also to affect the characters. 'M. de Stendhal is a disenchanter par excellence; he loves to desolate his world: he delights in the unforeseen. . . . This is an admirable *tour de force*.'

The question of where Beyle would go next if he was not to remain as consul in Trieste was decided in early February 1831. Discussing possibilities in a recent letter to Mareste, he had dismissed the port of Civitavecchia in the Papal States as 'an abominable hole' and ventured, while writing to Sophie Duvaucel, the idea of either Rome, Naples or Florence as serious propositions. On 11 February his assignment to Civitavecchia was confirmed in an official document signed by King Louis-Philippe, making special mention of his 'intelligence, probity, zeal and fidelity in our service', but it was a month before he was officially told by Sebastiani that he might leave Trieste and that an *exequatur* had been requested from the Pontifical government. The salary, to his dismay, was set at 10,000 francs, one third less than what he currently received, though as it turned out, he was able to live comfortably on the combination of a monthly wage with his small income.

On the day the appointment was approved by Louis-Philippe, Stendhal was enjoying a stay in Venice, frequenting the salon of the elderly Countess Isabella Teotochi Albrizzi, a Corfiote Greek married to a Venetian patrician, who in earlier years had numbered Byron, Alfieri and Foscolo among her friends. It was to

Venice that he returned on 31 March, beginning the earliest part of his two-week journey to Civitavecchia, but on this occasion he was not allowed to stay more than a night in the city before moving on towards Padua, Rovigo and Ferrara. The whole question of what route he should adopt was fraught with difficulty, owing to the series of revolutionary upheavals which had broken out during the winter across the Papal States, the Duchies of Modena and Parma and parts of the Kingdom of the Two Sicilies. Zigzagging southwards, the keen-eyed consul compiled a dossier for Sebastiani on the nervous political mood of the various scarcely pacified towns through which he passed, Padua seething with anti-Austrian hatred, Ferrara cowed and awaiting retribution from the Government, Bologna where an angry crowd killed a wretched porter for cheering the Imperial troops and Florence where the prudent citizens hedged their bets as to the likely success of a rebellion against the popular Habsburg Grand Duke Leopold. On 17 April Stendhal came at last to Civitavecchia.

The town where he was to spend much of the eleven years remaining to him could never, by any stretch of the imagination, have been called attractive or exciting. If Civitavecchia was not quite the abominable hole Beyle required his friends to imagine, it was without either the graces of an Italian art city or the lively, cosmopolitan society which animated seaports like Leghorn, Ancona and Genoa, in any of which he might have been a good deal more at his ease. He made few friends here, developed no sentimental attachments of any note among the inhabitants, and registered no special feelings of devotion to the place itself.

Yet the port had its distinctions. Founded, or at least built up by the Roman emperor Trajan as Centumcellae, it had been given renewed importance by the Renaissance popes, consolidating the Church's temporal power with the creation of a fortress, originally planned by Bramante in 1508 for Julius II and completed in 1557 by Michelangelo as one of his last works. A girdle of ramparts was raised by Antonio da Sangallo, and in the early seventeenth century the harbour had been graced with a new lighthouse and a tower built at the behest of Urban VIII, whose Barberini coat of arms featuring bees in flight inspired Stendhal to refer to the town in his letters as 'Abeille'.

Raised to the status of an episcopal see in 1825, Civitavecchia gained more material advantage as a port of call for steam packets on the western Mediterranean routes. Murray's *Handbook for Travellers in Central Italy*, issued in 1843, a year after Stendhal died, notes that 'a large proportion, if not the majority, of travellers land here on their first entrance into Southern Italy' and calculates the arrival of thirty steamers a month, distributed among five different lines from Marseilles, going on to Naples, Malta and the Levant. 'The brightness of the ramparts and the lazzaretto, and the massive architecture of the buildings around the basin, give it a striking appearance as we approach it by sea, but the anticipations to which they give rise are not realized by the town itself.' Passengers landing for the journey to Rome on either of the two diligences (an eight-hour trip) were subjected to the rigmarole, then customary throughout Italy, of having to pay a series of small fees to police and customs officials, as well as a charge for a consular passport visa. 'It will hardly, therefore, be a matter of surprise that in many instances the recollections of Civita Vecchia are not of the most agreeable kind.'

Society and amusements among a population of some six thousand inhabitants seem to have been limited. Murray observes that the town possesses the largest prison in the Papal States and that visitors are admitted to a sight of the brigand Gasparone, who has been rounded up and put behind bars together with his twenty followers. Necessary permission may be obtained through the consul, and the bandit 'is visible between the hours of ten and twelve'. Stendhal cynically told Domenico Fiore that out of every hundred foreigners passing through, 'fifty want to see the celebrated brigand Gasparone and four or five to see M. de Stendhal'. There was a theatre, the Teatro Minozzi, named after the architect who built it in 1786, an ugly, uncomfortable affair, whose orchestra, the Accademia Filarmonica, was made up of amateur players, controlled by the same strict government regulations which threatened unruly members of the audience with six months' imprisonment. Otherwise strangers to the town were struck by its general air of seediness and poverty. During the watermelon season ragged urchins gnawed at the pieces of green rind they picked up off the street, and in the same torrid summer months while Stendhal's consular office hopped with fleas, the poorer inhabitants had to be allowed a special licence to eat snails when every other foodstuff failed. 'The fever-stricken people, with their tattered clothes, positively sweating with wretchedness, made me miserable,' wrote a French tourist in 1841, but Stendhal would have to learn to live with them and make the best of it.

His predecessor, Baron Charles de Vaux, was not the kind of bureaucrat who would move quietly and efficiently aside to make room for his replacement, as Beyle himself had dutifully done for M. Levasseur, named to succeed him at Trieste. A loyal supporter of the Bourbons*, on whom the Papal government had looked benignly for his *bien-pensant* views, the Baron hung on with reproachful patience until the *exequatur*, somewhat unwillingly granted in the light of the new consul's known liberalism and the abhorrent tendency of his various publications, was confirmed on 25 April. Retreating to Rome, De Vaux sent Stendhal a letter, scarcely a model of repressed emotions, splitting hairs over the exact date when his official period of service might be deemed to have ended, hoping that his consular uniform would be of use to his successor as a model (please accept the buttons as a gift) and describing himself as 'having been too attached to my duties'.

In his capacity as a consul Stendhal has more often than not been represented as insufficiently attached to his duties. His lengthy absences, not merely from Civitavecchia but from the Papal States and Italy as well, have been calculated as amounting to four and a half years out of the eleven during which he occupied the post. What need to be considered in making any sort of judgement on his professional dedication are, first of all, the nineteenth-century view of consuls and their functions; secondly, the relative efficiency with which Henri Beyle, when actually at his desk, carried out his appointed task; and finally the mitigating circumstances of Civitavecchia's unquestionable dullness, surely sufficient to provoke even the most dedicated second-rank diplo-

* Stendhal told Sophie Duvaucel that De Vaux, on hearing of Charles X's fatal ordinances of 25 July while in Civitavecchia's only café, had actually started dancing with joy.

mat into climbing aboard the Rome diligence whenever the opportunity allowed.

If a consular post in Italy was not a sinecure, it was seen by many as affording the chance to live in relative comfort, supported by rank and social position, amid a congenial, pleasure-loving society enlivened by the presence of a continually changing throng of foreign visitors. The strain of official business, even in a busy port like Civitavecchia, was never immense, and some of Stendhal's work involved that less easily qualifiable but always necessary consular duty of gathering local news and gossip in order to keep the home government alert to the prevailing socio-political mood, in the Papal States and elsewhere across Italy. If his dispatches were not especially *bien vus* at first by the Foreign Minister, this was because he found it difficult to detach himself from the cynical, journalistic tone he tended to adopt in letters to friends. An analysis of the attitudes among the various classes of Roman society which states baldly that 'European civilization stops dead at the Tuscan frontier' or the authoritative breakdown of Papal government finance which suggests that a more sophisticated banking system is unlikely to work because of the Holy Father's unworldliness, are indicators that Stendhal was having difficulty in finding an appropriate tone for such communications and may explain why historians of Risorgimento Italy have been reluctant to draw on his official correspondence as a reliable source.

His day-to-day responsibilities as a consul were normally connected with such matters as the issuing of passport visas and various sorts of marine certificate, such as quarantine clearance declarations, as well as recording the arrival and departure of ships in the port. Only very occasionally was he required to exercise his authority in a less humdrum context. One opportunity for this occurred in November 1834, when a certain Bernard Alphonse, a French subject arrested at Rome for political activities and removed to the prison at Civitavecchia, wrote asking whether Beyle might intervene on his behalf to procure him the right to take open-air exercise. Writing to the Apostolic Delegate, Monsignor Peraldi (a frequent recipient of the consul's courteous request for permits and validations), he asked that Alphonse be transferred to the citadel, adding 'such a kindness, depending on your humanity, would diminish this man's present misery. You will see, from his attached letter, Monsignore, that he seems to have acquired some education, and I do not believe him to be seriously at fault'. Peraldi agreed to Stendhal's suggestion: some time later Alphonse was returned to France, but appears to have jumped ship *en route*.

Stendhal's sphere of influence spread much wider than the consular district of Civitavecchia. French agents everywhere in the Papal States, from Rimini and Ravenna in the north to Anzio and Terracina in the south, let alone Sinigaglia, Loreto and Ancona on the eastern seaboard, were expected to report to him, and once he had settled into a working routine he sent them all a circular reminding them of their duties.

> Never put off till tomorrow whatever information you may be able to submit on any given day . . . . a delay of 24 hours could cause another of a week in the sending of a despatch to Paris . . . Never be afraid to write at length. Plenty of detail is appropriate. A detail which may often seem insignificant to the writer will assume importance when joined with others received by a higher authority.

The tone is that of the model bureaucrat, learned in part from the late Pierre Daru, but the last remark suggests the novelist rather than the civil servant.

He was always conscious of being underpaid for his work, a feeling exacerbated by having to contribute to a government pension fund and to pay the wages of an assistant. Much has been written about the secretary of the French consulate at Civitavecchia during the 1830s, most of it not very charitable and some of it downright unjust. When Stendhal arrived, Baron de Vaux had recently dismissed from the post of *chancelier* (secretarial assistant) a young man named Lysimaque Mercure Caftangioglou*-Tavernier, the son of a French mother and a Greek father who had fled a Turkish massacre at Salonika with the surviving members of his family and sought refuge at Marseilles. Lysimaque

* This Turkish surname means either 'son of a caftan-wearer' or 'son of a caftan-maker'.

had rendered himself obnoxious to De Vaux for several reasons, one being his adherence to the Greek Orthodox faith, unacceptable to the Papal government, another being a reputation acquired by his mother, Fanny Tavernier, for dishonest commercial dealings with local merchants, besides which he was known to favour liberal political opinions. The last point may have swayed Stendhal in a decision to reinstate him, which induced De Vaux to issue a warning of possible future difficulties between them, implied in the opening remarks of his letter quoted earlier: 'I have done my duty, you have been informed and will be incapable of assigning any blame to me should you one day have cause to regret your choice.'

The recent publication of Lysimaque's surviving letters to Stendhal during the latter's various absences has revealed an undeniably conscientious, alert and intelligent secretary and consular substitute, quick to inform his superior of everything which mattered in local affairs via clear, readable dispatches, even though his written French was occasionally faulty and his spelling decidedly erratic. Regrettably, however, his assiduity was not confined to a satisfactory fulfilment of his allotted tasks. Tavernier was a mean-spirited, sly intriguer, quick to capitalize on Stendhal's neglect of his duties in order to advance his own career (which, by a satisfying irony, he failed to do), mixing fawning, insolence and greed in his approaches towards his chief and generally showing himself to be unworthy of the confidence initially placed in him. As will be seen, the relationship between the two, beginning in an atmosphere of formal politeness, degenerated to an absolute mistrust and disharmony some three years later.

There were few in Civitavecchia whom Stendhal was likely to find friendly, sympathetic or remotely *beyliste* in outlook and attitudes, though at least two newly formed local acquaintances more than proved their worth in terms of loyalty both before and after the writer's death. One was the *cavaliere* Pietro Manzi, a man of considerable wealth and standing, whose travels abroad had included a period spent as the slave of Tunisian pirates and whose skill in languages and general air of the cosmopolite made him an interesting contrast with most provincial Italian aristocrats of his epoch. Two years younger than Stendhal, he also had been a career civil servant under the Empire, and his experience later rendered him useful to Baron de Vaux, who had recommended him for the post of honorary vice-consul.

Stendhal, obviously esteeming him highly, left Manzi a bequest of volumes from his library. Those the *cavaliere* might have chosen would perhaps be connected with archaeology, his particular passion and one which, as we shall see, his friend Beyle took up with lively enthusiasm. On the opposite side of Piazza San Francesco, Civitavecchia's main square, onto which the French consulate faced, was the shop belonging to Donato Bucci, a local antiquarian, the collector and vendor of artefacts turned up by excavators of the countless Etruscan tombs scattered across the surrounding Latian countryside. Bucci's original visit to Stendhal had been in a professional capacity. 'Knowing the newly arrived consul by his literary repute, I went to pay him a call and offer him my services. He received me especially well . . . . and from this moment onwards we contracted a friendship for one another which lasted until his death.' Bucci, still fairly young, soundly liberal in his political outlook, well read and in touch with current developments in France, was noteworthy also for his consistent devotion to Stendhal's interests, becoming a faithful correspondent when his friend was away in France and displaying a singular respect in supervising the disposition of his manuscripts, books and possessions after the writer's death in 1842.

The friend who turned out to have recommended Bucci to Stendhal was the Swiss painter Abraham Constantin, described in the *Promenades dans Rome* as 'the man of our day who has best understood Raphael and best copied him'. A specialist in painting on porcelain and enamel, Constantin had worked at the Sèvres factory for over a decade before obtaining, via Baron Gérard, a prestigious commission from Charles X to create a series of Raphael copies at a salary of 40,000 francs a year. It was at Gérard's studio in Rue Bonaparte that he and Stendhal probably met each other, and their friendship now resumed in Italy on a more regular footing. In the company of this honest, patient, perceptive soul, Beyle began to explore anew the Roman scene which he had depicted with such verve in the *Promenades* and which now lay so tantalizingly close, a few hours' journey by diligence.

Rome became Stendhal's town, the place where, even if the Romans themselves hardly came up to the mark set by his particular requirements of sophistication and good company, he could depend on the presence of an international society formed of artists, writers, aristocrats and professional travellers from the rest of Europe, giving the city a tone, an elegance which it never wholy recaptured after its metamorphosis in 1870 into the sprawling metropolis of the Kingdom of Italy. Those who knew it then, but who had first made its acquaintance when it was still the Papal capital, indulged an unashamed nostalgia for the compact huddle of ruins, palaces, fountains and gardens nestling within ancient walls, a Rome where, as it seemed, everyone who was not a prince or a priest was a beggar, and everybody else was an artist or a tourist.

This old Rome at first seemed the ideal refuge from Civitavecchia's workaday dreariness. Plunging avidly into smart society, Stendhal inevitably found himself able to shock its more sober representatives with his outrageously voiced opinions. The painter Horace Vernet, director of the French Academy at Villa Medici, told Mareste that 'le grand homme', easily bored, wanted to talk as frankly as in any Paris salon.

> He discusses, he dissects, he discourses according to his fashion. The poor Romans, terrified of compromising themselves with their amiable government, block their ears and flee. Their interlocutor, left alone, doesn't know what to do. You know how necessary an audience is to him. He tells me that he's ill, very ill, that he has rheumatism, fears cholera etc. etc. etc. which all means: I'm eaten up with boredom. Lately he has sent me a fat notebook containing some quite amusing details about these pimps of Cardinals and Monsignori. Clearly if this is the sort of consular diplomacy he's engaged in, he is likely to find few friends here.

Mareste may well have been right in supposing that Stendhal's various illnesses were less actual than psychosomatic, though he does seem to have been increasingly prone, in this last decade of his life, to nagging minor ailments which constituted further variations on the enduring venereal theme. The notorious malaria, to which all but the hardiest residents in the region succumbed, must surely have played its part (he seems to have had one attack annually) but whatever its menaces to health, his repeated visits to Rome imply a genuine affection for a city about which he had already written with such abundant warmth and a feeling that, however treacherous the climate, the place itself did him good.

He kept some sort of Roman lodging throughout the entire period of his consulate, either renting rooms, or else living in an hotel. For a time he shared lodgings with Abraham Constantin near the Caetani palace in Via delle Botteghe Oscure, then lived in Palazzo Cavalieri in what is now Largo Arenula. After 1835 he favoured Palazzo Conti, the present-day Albergo Minerva, close to the ancient church of Santa Maria sopra Minerva beside the Pantheon, but four years later settled himself in the second-floor apartment of a print-seller's house in Via Condotti.

His early visits to Rome included, as a matter of course, occasional attendance on the French ambassador, Louis-Clair de Beaupoil, Comte de Sainte-Aulaire, who had taken up his post only a few days before Stendhal's arrival in Civitavecchia. Sainte-Aulaire, born in 1778 and already a noted public servant and politician, stayed only two years at the Rome embassy before moving on to Vienna, where he wrote some incisive memoirs of his dealings with Metternich and the Imperial government. Stendhal was delighted to find in his chief, whom he had already met briefly as the guest of Ludovico Di Breme in Milan fifteen years earlier, a man of broad sympathies, considerable cultivation and the kind of intelligence likely to be well disposed towards a consul so emphatically unlike others of his diplomatic breed.

With the Comtesse de Sainte-Aulaire there was a stronger connection altogether, for had not her grandmother, Mme de Brizon, the wife of an army officer stationed at Grenoble, retained Dr Gagnon as her personal physician? The ambassador's second wife (his first, ugly, bad-tempered and rich, had died when still in her teens), she was a blonde beauty, still extremely attractive in middle age, whom Mary Clarke, Stendhal's inveterate enemy, called 'very passionate and very graceful'. From the beginning she treated Consul Beyle with great kindness, making him a frequent guest at her dinners and salons and acting as one of those mother-sisters, like Alexandrine Daru and Comtesse Beugnot, with whom he enjoyed a quasi-amorous relationship. In a sketch for a novel, *Une position sociale*, begun in 1832 and heavily based on his Roman embassy world, Stendhal presents Mme de Sainte-Aulaire as the Duchesse de Vaussay, who was:

> carried by her fiery temperament towards a ferocious abandonment to every sort of pleasure, but always held the highest notion of duty, a notion rather superstitious than reasonable, a notion whose basis had never been properly examined and one which had seized hold of her capacity to be emotionally stirred.

The portrait of the 'Duchesse' as a woman who did not choose to have love affairs but was easily manipulated into them may simply be wishful thinking on Stendhal's part, but his ambassador's wife fascinated him sufficiently to furnish suggestions for another fictional character, the Byronic siren Mme Grandet in *Lucien Leuwen*. Here not every detail coheres with reality (the author was besides, in the portion of the novel which never got written, prepared to turn her into a spiteful, vindictive *intrigante*) but we can surely find enough of the Comtesse de Sainte-Aulaire in 'the slender blonde beauty, like Paolo Veronese's young Venetians' to whom falling in love was a bore, who looked incomparable at nine in the morning when she had just got out of bed after dancing the night away at a ball and for whom opera buffa was a serious pleasure.

For most of the last six months of 1831 Stendhal was wandering to and fro across Italy, with comparatively short stays at Civitavecchia in between. The tenderness towards Giulia Rinieri de' Rocchi had not lessened as a result of her guardian's tactful put-off regarding a marriage proposal, and now that she herself had returned to her native Siena, her admirer saw no reason not to pursue his advantage as best he could. During the next two years he would make several excursions into Tuscany – watched and noted as always by the local police – staying from time to time at Berlinghieri's villa of Vignano in the *contado senese*, and twice attending the Palio, the nail-bitingly exciting horse race around the inward sloping rim of the city's central Campo which forms the highpoint of the Sienese year. Such was the nature of Stendhal's continuing links with Giulia and her family that Mérimée was soon able to tell Sophie Duvaucel 'they say everywhere that M. Beyle is married ! ! ! . . . to an Italian lady, very rich and very charming'.

Sophie, given her understanding of this same M. Beyle, might perhaps have been more sceptical of this news, in any case untrue. The closeness and sincerity of their friendship, even at such a distance, can be gauged from two letters, one of which he wrote on 28 April 1831 in response to a criticism from her, now unfortunately lost, on *Le Rouge et le Noir*, the other Sophie's ardent, angry denunciation of the new political order in France, frankly revealing of her conservatism in a way which seems to assume that Stendhal will at least respect her point of view even if he cannot share it. 'Your letter' he tells her:

> is infinitely more sincere than anything else you have written to me. You don't sufficiently criticize the novel in question. You have sugared the pill. You should have written as soon as you read it. At Venice there was once a man who, so as to love his wife, got her to box his ears. I am that man. Nothing bores me more than a compliment. If I had ten thousand such, I fancy they'd have made me a baron or an academician. But what use are one or two bundles of sticks? They're not enough to light a stove. Therefore I beg you, Mademoiselle, be sincere with me.

And indeed, after a fashion, she was. In a letter whose rhetorical sweep across a single massive paragraph is set in motion by what sounds like an alexandrine verse line:

'Du tout, du tout notre homme, tenez-vous bien pour dit', Sophie pitched ferociously into the hypocrisy and destructiveness, as she saw them, of the latest liberal ideas. 'You dare speak to me of the sovereignty of the people! A fine sovereign forsooth! I'd prefer grand dukes, I'd even prefer the grand Lama of Tibet! But for your smock-frocked riff-raff I've nothing but disgust.' She assured him of her complete sincerity in condemning his Julien Sorel, adding: 'The day when you can be honestly natural and true, then maybe we shall understand each other.' In a postscript she urged him, in his own interest, to be more discreet when writing to her and not to involve himself in anything except whatever directly concerned him, ending in English: 'This is a real piece of friendship which you must receive as kindly as it is given.'

Her anxiety was scarcely misplaced. The situation in Italy was still unstable after the failed revolutionary upsurge of 1831, whose brutal repression in the Duchy of Modena would contribute significant hints towards the background of *La Chartreuse de Parme*. In the Papal States, where Austrian troops had been swiftly dispatched into Romagna, the European powers, most notably Britain and France, had tried to apply pressure to the pontifical regime to improve its standards of justice and efficiency, currently abused to a point at which Metternich, nothing if not realistic at this point in his career, could detect a fundamental menace to the whole of Italy. A further problem was now created by the arrival on 23 February 1832 of a French fleet in the port of Ancona, which, after landing 1500 troops, seized the city without firing a shot, an action calculated to warn Austria against treating the Papal States as an imperial fiefdom and to send a message to the Pope to change his mode of government or else face practical opposition from a monarchy which now assumed the role, less convincingly adopted by Great Britain, of freedom's champion.

This sudden bullying gesture towards a peaceful sovereign state was by no means well received elsewhere in Europe, and international opinion almost immediately demanded a climb-down by the French. The Comte de Sainte-Aulaire thoroughly disapproved of the expedition on entirely practical diplomatic grounds, and his burden was made no easier by the need to deal directly with the expedition's expenses. The commanding officers having used up the funds available to the vice-consul in Ancona, Frédéric Quilliet, a request for more money was passed on to his immediate superior Henri Beyle of the Civitavecchia consulate (the relevant loan being arranged ironically with the Papal banking house of Torlonia). After a week or so, matters had grown so pressing that Stendhal himself received orders from Sainte-Aulaire to leave at once for Ancona and take charge of the whole payment operation.

Arriving on 8 March, he stayed the rest of the month in the

splendidly situated Papal city, with its cathedral of Saint Cyriac topping the headland, the harbour dominated by a Roman triumphal arch and the great lazzaretto designed by Gasparo Vanvitelli, and churches rich with the works of Titian, Lotto and the Bolognese school. Stendhal was scarcely in a position to enjoy any of this: he wrote peevishly to Sainte-Aulaire, claiming that he was being treated with insufficient respect and demanding to be returned to his post. Meanwhile he bombarded vice-consul Quilliet with notes emphasizing the importance of prompt payment in sustaining the national honour of France. No wonder that when at last he was able to get back to Civitavecchia on 31 March, Sainte-Aulaire lauded him to Count Sebastiani in Paris. 'His zeal,' he wrote, 'inspired him to undertake this disagreeable and difficult commission, which he carried out with much skill and intelligence.'

The considerable volume of official correspondence surrounding this Ancona episode, and his letters to Quilliet in general, show Stendhal in an interesting though not especially endearing light. The cynical, free-ranging commentator on Italian affairs who so irked his Foreign Ministry chiefs at home disappears, to be replaced by a frosty diplomatic martinet, curt and magisterial in his requests for greater stylistic clarity and in his constant injunctions to employ 'soin' and 'zèle' (this to a septuagenarian consular official whose already phenomenal assiduity resulted in the sending of 625 letters in a single year). Glacially unsympathetic as to Quilliet's money worries, Consul Beyle could be devastatingly attentive, on the other hand, to his epistolary shortcomings. Pulling apart a message from Ancona on the subject of a cholera scare, he peppers his reply with the sort of impatient criticisms a schoolmaster might scribble on an essay: 'Lack of clarity!', 'What magistrate? Pontifical or Venetian?' 'at a moment when the government is receiving so much false or at least exaggerated news, I urgently request that letters directed to me should possess the merit of being exact, precise and clear. . . . Write to me on small sheets and with an Italian address'. The whole tone of this correspondence, only made public in 1955, appears almost repulsively formal and inhuman in its rigidity, conveying the impression that Stendhal either could not be bothered with

Quilliet as a mere underling or – which is possible – that he actually enjoyed adopting this posture of the nitpicking, bureaucratic bully, nagging his junior over faults in accounting and pulling him up short on lapses in his official prose.

In the face of European feeling on the issue, France eventually backed off from its show of force, and none other than Clémentine Curial's father, Count Beugnot, was sent to supervise the withdrawal of the occupying force, making Quilliet the scapegoat for various problems connected with the enterprise. Stendhal meanwhile, even though acknowledging to Mareste that his Anconetan mission had not lacked interest, needed something more substantial with which to anaesthetize the stultifying boredom of Civitavecchia, and found it now, as he would find it increasingly during these last Italian years, in the exercise of his pen.

It was doubtless inevitable that in a society so hopelessly limited he should try to recapture and anatomize the essence of his Parisian life, begun under the shadow of a retrospective misery but soon vitalized by his triumphs as an author and literary personality, culminating in the publication of a work which he knew to be a masterpiece. Accordingly, on 20 June 1832, while staying in Rome, he sat down to write a memoir of this crucial time, in order to confront himself both as he seemed then and as he was now, the precious fragment which we know as *Souvenirs d'Egotisme*.

He needed, as he confessed, to undertake this kind of project because 'without work, the ship of human life has no sort of ballast', but also because he genuinely felt that he was addressing a particular species of reader, the responsive *beyliste* yet unborn or else still a child, the sort of mind he compared to his idol, the great memorialist and victim of the French Revolution, Madame Roland, or to his adored mathematics teacher in Grenoble, Gabriel Gros. Unlike many another autobiographer Stendhal was frank enough to acknowledge from the outset that he would never have begun had it not been for this distinctive sense of an audience.

The *Souvenirs* are, by their nature, only a superficially organized arrangement of events and characters from his metropolitan life during the early 1820s. It is just possible that had he completed the book, instead of abandoning it at a point somewhere around 1824 during an account of Delécluze and his salon, he might have pulled his materials more tightly into line, but that would in its turn have spoiled much of our pleasure in reading what, under its present guise, sounds like Stendhal thinking aloud, a spontaneous meandering from one association to the next without too much of that overrefining impression of order and control which so often makes us question the truth of autobiography. Stendhal may be inexact – when precisely did he meet Claude Fauriel and when was the rift with Mary Clarke? – and he may become hopelessly entrapped by his own irrepressible readiness to say something about everything (see, for example, his long digression on the actor Talma in Chapter VII) but we never have any reason to feel, in the *Souvenirs d'Egotisme*, that he is telling a lie.

As episodes and Stendhalian dramatis personae pass before us, the visit to the Lambeth brothel, the evenings *chez* Pasta, correcting the proofs of *De l'Amour*, descriptions of Mareste, of Mérimée, of Delécluze, all done with delicious gusto, we may wonder what the object of a work in which so little appears to be recollected with pleasure of satisfaction honestly was. The clue to its true nature as a species of self-explicator comes at the end of Chapter XI, after Stendhal has been riding the crest of an extended recollection of his uncle, Romain Gagnon. If only he had taken the advice about women given him by the elegant ladykiller as he prepared to board the Lyons mail all those years ago, to begin his first trip to Paris! But then perhaps, as he says, he might have grown dry and cynical towards the sex as a result. 'Instead, as regards everything concerning women, I am lucky enough to be made a dupe just as I was when aged 25. This is why I shall never destroy myself out of boredom or disgust. In my literary career I have still a host of things to achieve, work sufficient to fill ten lives.'

He left off the *Souvenirs* on 4 July, his brain dulled by the intense heat of a Roman summer enlivened only by the presence in the city of the diva Maria Malibran, whose sensational career, ending with a tragic death in Manchester in 1836, when she was twenty-eight, as the delayed result of a riding accident, seemed to epitomize all the frenzied brilliance of a romantic life in art.

Stendhal may have met her in Paris as one of the Marquis de La Fayette's youthful protégées, and doubtless knew that Ludovic Vitet, the *globiste* who had criticized *Armance* so sternly, had like so many others fallen madly in love with her. His own admiration of her gifts had been expressed in a letter to Sutton Sharpe in 1828. 'Mme Malibrand [sic]-Garcia, whom you know, will be the greatest singer in the world if she does not abuse her higher register. Her strength is in the lower notes.' Now she was in Rome with her husband, the Belgian violinist Charles de Beriot, and as well as seeing her perform at the Teatro Valle (in one of her best-known roles, Desdemona in Rossini's *Otello*) Stendhal may have met her at the Sainte-Aulaires' or at the Villa Medici, where Horace Vernet painted her portrait.

Much of that summer and autumn were spent, as during the previous year, in Italian jaunts, to Albano, a favourite spot for Roman *villeggiatura*, to the Abruzzi, and yet again into Tuscany. At Florence once more he met Leopardi, who told his sister, Paoline, of having 'seen again your Stendhal, who, as you know, is the French consul at Civitavecchia', and improved his friendship with the lawyer and contributor to Vieusseux's *Antologia*, Vincenzo Salvagnoli. In October he told him that he was getting up an article on *Le Rouge et le Noir*, with the idea that Salvagnoli should translate it for the magazine, partly as a reaction to the French reviews of the book, which he felt had misunderstood its true character, especially the notice by Jules Janin in the *Journal des Débats*. *Antologia* had already done Stendhal a favour by publishing, in its issue of September 1830, a long and enthusiastic review of the *Promenades dans Rome* by the leading Italian critic of the day, Giuseppe Montani, who had earlier written a similarly detailed notice of *Armance*. In printing Salvagnoli's version of the author's own critique of his latest work – and it is actually more an extensive plot résumé preceded by some tart observations on modern French novel-reading habits – Vieusseux and his editors may or may not have spotted the numerous scarcely ironic coincidences between Stendhal and the Janin review, which he had simply adapted whenever it suited him. In an Italian postscript he told Salvagnoli: 'it is up to your gracious eloquence to harangue the readers of *Antologia* and persuade them that this work is the finest in the world, worthy of taking its place in the libraries beside the immortal *Tom Jones.*'

Fielding had always been among Stendhal's particular passions and touches of him colour the novels both in terms of the way scenes and confrontations are imagined and in the detached ironic tone struck by the writer. Amid his consular duties there was plenty of time for reading, and as always he scratched comments and autobiographical notes in the books currently engaging him. Selective and highly critical in his attitude to modern authors, he turned with pleasure to the literature of the past. Jacques Amyot's translation of Plutarch (on which Lord North's English version, famously quarried by Shakespeare, is based), Pierre de Bourdeille de Brantôme's *Vies des grandes capitaines* and Montaigne's *Essais* were in his library, as were his beloved *Princesse de Clèves* and the always admired Corneille. As for Pascal, he used him as a sovran antidote to the stylistic vulgarity of the newspapers through which he had to wade each day, or to the affectation of Chateaubriand, for whose writing and personality Stendhal had always nourished a resolute dislike.

Besides books there was always the occasional distraction of a visitor to Rome for whom Beyle, with his intimate knowledge of the city, could act as a cicerone. In 1831 he had welcomed his Paris salon acquaintances Jean-Jacques Ampère and Adrien de Jussieu, taking the former to excavate Etruscan tombs near Corneto (modern Tarquinia) and the latter on a journey to Naples, where they climbed Vesuvius and Stendhal purchased what he believed to be a marble bust of Tiberius. Now, in the last weeks of 1832, he played Roman host to a distinguished Russian traveller, Count Alexander Turgenev*, met originally among the network of Paris salons including those of Baron Gérard, Mme Ancelot and the Jardin des Plantes, where he was presented to Cuvier by the explorer Humboldt and made a firm friend of Sophie Duvaucel. After an imperial decree forbidding Russians to reside in France for fear of contamination by the principles of the new regime under Louis-Philippe, he visited England and Italy,

* He was apparently not related, except perhaps very distantly, to his more famous namesake the novelist Ivan Turgenev.

where he arrived in Rome on 5 December. With Beyle as his guide he explored everything from churches like San Pietro in Montorio to the grand antique sites of Tivoli and the Villa d'Este. Stendhal was evidently an ideal tour-leader, full of information whether on matters historical, local politics or the relations between saintly, naïve, reactionary Pope Gregory XVI and his cardinals, as well as offering Turgenev useful advice on possible naturalization as a French citizen. To his friend Prince Wiazemski the count wrote exclaiming: 'Impossible to find a better companion. . . . He is not liked here because of the truth he utters and the *bons mots* with which he seasons it, but in my humble opinion it is his judgment which in the end is the correct one.' Wiazemski, who had met Beyle at Comte Molé's house in Paris, enthusiastically agreed.

> Not for nothing has your fate brought you close to Stendhal . . . . you resemble each other greatly, but you haven't the stature for writing *Le Rouge et le Noir*, one of the finest novels and most remarkable images of our age. Have you read it at last? I have loved Stendhal since his *Vie de Rossini*, so full of fire and with as much ardour as his hero's music.

Such Russian *beylisme*, had he known of it, might have revived in Henri his old scheme from 1814 of seeking a job at St Petersburg, where indeed the poet Alexander Pushkin had spent May and June of 1831 reading *Le Rouge* and swiftly enlisting among the happy few.

While the friendship grew between Stendhal and Turgenev, the former temporarily slipped out of Rome in February 1833 for another visit to Tuscany. 'All these jaunts to Florence and Siena were due to thoughts of Giulia,' he noted, but she herself remained tantalizingly silent following his return southwards, until 1 April, when an archly oblique letter beginning 'Mio caro amico' awaited him on his arrival at Civitavecchia. The purport was to let him know that, as she put it, her heart was in danger, from which he could scarcely be expected to divine that she was indeed preparing to become engaged, and to a man she had met only a week earlier, her guardian's legation secretary, Giulio

Martini. From the remarkably fervid epistles she began sending Martini almost immediately, the image emerges of Giulia as a romantic manipulator, capable of playing the passionate lover with gusto but distinctly calculating in all her moves.

Though Stendhal referred to this in English as 'the fatal letter of Pietrasanta', the town in northern Tuscany where Giulia was staying with a married sister, he was determined to wear a brave face and delayed answering for ten days, after which he sent her a cheerful, gossipy note. A brief sentence – 'Well then, we shall just be good friends' – shows that he had got the bearings of the situation. The letter was written on 20 April and on the 26th news arrived that the marriage was off, after which it was quickly *sur le tapis* again when in May her engagement to Martini was announced. Such technicalities seem not to have mattered greatly to Giulia: even if she was not the mysterious 'Rietti' who, on the 13th of the month, sent him a 'demand' which he 'refused' two days later with great relief, she continued to maintain a relationship with Stendhal whose undertones suggested that their former intimacy was by no means at an end. Yet another Tuscan trip in late May and early June was evidently made in hopes of seeing her once more: presumably the letter he read behind the cypress trees outside an inn at Antella, near Bagno a Ripoli, was a put-off from Giulia, who married her personable young diplomat on 24 June.

As the summer drew to a close, Beyle prepared to take a three-month leave granted to him the previous year by the new Foreign Minister, his old colleague in Napoleon's Council of State, Charles-Achille-Victor-Léonce, Duc de Broglie, who had succeeded Sebastiani in 1832. The duchess, a daughter of Mme de Staël, had once summed up *Armance* as 'the work of a man of low social tone', but her husband and Stendhal understood each other well enough on Italian political questions, and the latter was able to write with a good deal less restraint in making his reports to Paris.

It was indeed to France that he planned to return. 'I'm off to Lutetia [the ancient Roman name for Paris] to look at the streets, the *bouquinistes*' stalls and the theatres running new plays and new actors, after thirty months,' he told Domenico Fiore. The object of the exercise was plainly to recharge that intelligence and alertness which he sensed were growing dull in the sultry little parishes of Civitavecchia and Rome. His friends meanwhile got ready to welcome him, but it was not until 11 September that he arrived once more in Rue de Richelieu, and Mérimée, who told Sophie Duvaucel that 'the baron' looked 'a bit thin, but otherwise flourishing', invited Stendhal to his thirtieth birthday dinner in the company of some 'very charming ladies from the Opéra and other such excellent schools of good behaviour'.

Among those with whom he renewed contact after nearly three years' absence from Paris was Clémentine Curial, who asked him to stay at her château of Monchy where she had once concealed him in the cellar as her lover. A frequent guest at the Wednesday dinners she gave at her town house, he was observed by Comtesse Dash, whose memories paint a spirited picture of fashionable life under the July Monarchy. Clémentine, she was amused to see, delighted to pit Stendhal against the so-called Marquis de Courchamps, an impostor who, from a position as majordomo in a Breton nobleman's family, had successfully wormed his way into smart society, eventually securing a dubious fame as author of the fraudulent memoirs of an eighteenth-century marquise. The genuine literary article, mocking, atheistical and thoroughly modern, provided a perfect foil for the bogus item, a religiously inclined monarchist, and their hostess lost no opportunity in egging them on to vigorous argument. Noting wryly that when Stendhal laughed 'it was hardly in the manner of an eighteenth-century dowager', Comtesse Dash, evidently quite taken with his physical appearance, regretted later that she had not made more of this meeting with 'one of the era's most distinguished figures'. Clémentine, on the other hand, enjoyed her friend's visit to the full, and on the evening of 1 December 1833, a note in English, 'a delicious conversation with Menti from half past ten until midnight', followed by the words '2 at my lodgings', implies that some spark of life endured in a relationship officially ended seven years earlier.

Stendhal's homeward journey took him to Lyons, thence to Geneva, where he consulted Abraham Constantin's friend, the leading Swiss physician Jean-Louis Prévost. Of all the doctors whose advice he had sought on his various minor ailments and bouts of illness (many of them related to his continuing syphilis), Prévost, trained in Paris, Edinburgh and Dublin, and famous for his work on rheumatic diseases, was the expert Henri Beyle came most to respect, and his good advice, especially on the simple question of diet, surely helped to prolong the writer's existence in the context of an unfriendly climate and a not always regular way of life.

Returning to Lyons to take the steamer down the Rhône to Avignon, Stendhal happened upon two of his more distinguished fellow authors, preparing, like him, to set off on an Italian journey. For some months literary Paris had been agog with details of a developing liaison between the novelist George Sand (Aurore Dupin) and the poet Alfred de Musset, whose mother had been persuaded to let him leave for Florence and Venice in the company of a woman whose prodigious creative energy was probably less celebrated at that stage of her career than her fondness for tobacco and her artful adaptations of male attire. The affair with Musset, besides evoking several of his finest poems and, indirectly, her enchanting travel sketches *Notes d'un voyageur*, became one of the most notorious incidents in Sand's career as the result of the amorous triangle involving a handsome young Italian doctor she summoned to the poet's bedside when he fell ill at their Venetian hotel.

Like so many others who met Henri Beyle, Sand was put off by his habitual cynicism and his need to establish himself as, in some sense, superior to those with whom he talked by attempting to unmask their supposed pretensions. He instantly began mocking her expectations of Italy, telling her she would soon grow tired of it and warning that she was unlikely to discover any sort of intellectual stimulus in the form of interesting books, newspapers or conversation. Listening to him, she observed compassionately: 'I could well understand what was missing for an intelligence like this one, so charming, so original, such a performer, far from the kind of companions who could appreciate and provoke him . . . . I don't think he was bad at heart: he made too much of an effort to seem so.' When they reached Avignon he took the two travellers to look at a painted wooden Christ in the cathedral, exclaiming violently against 'these repulsive images whose barbarous ugliness and cynical nudity the Southerners cherish' and saying he wanted to attack it with his bare fists. In a village inn where Stendhal got 'equitably drunk' and cut a grotesque figure as he danced round the table in his fur-lined boots, Musset drew a brilliant little sketch of the capering consul, one of the most memorable images of him we possess.

The lovers took their leave at Marseilles, not especially saddened to see him board the diligence for Genoa, where they preferred the boat, owing to his fear of sea voyages. So tired indeed was Sand of his penchant for obscenity that if he had suddenly decided to take to the water, she felt she would probably have travelled by land. 'He was otherwise an outstanding figure, of a sagacity more clever than just in its assessments, with a true and original talent, a bad writer, but one who said things in such a way as genuinely to impress and interest his readers.'

The year stretching before Stendhal, a year of humdrum consular business alternating with prolonged periods of truancy in Rome, was substantially enlivened by a return to novel-writing, though in a form he could scarcely have foreseen when he quit Paris. He brought back to Italy with him a manuscript work of fiction submitted to him for criticism by his friend Julie Gaulthier, entitled *Le Lieutenant*. The original has never been traced, and we know nothing of the story beyond what is suggested by a frankly critical letter Beyle sent his 'chère et aimable amie' from Civitavecchia on 4 May 1834, telling her to revise it in its entirety as if she were translating a book into German. He slated the dull ending, the preponderance of aristocratic surnames, the overuse of superlatives, urging her always to think of something real whenever she engaged in descriptions, and to recount her narrative as if she were writing a letter to him.

Le Lieutenant, whatever his view of its merits, had given him an idea. Three days before writing to Julie Gaulthier, he had decided to begin his own novel, using the surname Leuwen she had adopted for her hero, and on 8 May, as he sat awake at midnight, the resolution was confirmed. For the next eighteen months he worked steadily to produce his longest fictional work, and what, had it been completed, would have been one of the most imposing achievements of its period in the field of the serious novel.

What we now know as *Lucien Leuwen* enjoyed a whole sequence of working titles, beginning with *Les Bois de Prémol*, which then became *Le Télégraphe*, *Le Chasseur Vert* (both later used as titles for the two volumes Stendhal managed to finish of the projected three), *Le Rouge et le Blanc*, *Le Bleu et le Blanc* and *L'Amarante et le Noir*. Not content with these, the novelist told Sainte-Beuve that he had written a work called *L'Orange de Malte*, a name employed in the eighteenth century as a euphemism for money. Under these various labels, the book's creation went forward to the accompaniment of continued marginal comment from the writer himself, standing back to judge his own achievement with that severity of self-analysis which ensures one of his strongest claims to greatness as a man. While he wrote, what was more, Stendhal sought ceaselessly to authenticate the characters and incidents he devised, and the resulting apparatus which adumbrates most of the better published editions of the work* represents a unique glimpse of a literary artist in the process of fashioning his own experience and observation into a viable imaginative construct.

The design of *Lucien Leuwen* was intended to accord neatly with the standard three-volume form popular with French and English readers of the period. Lucien, the son of a banker, expelled from the Ecole Polytechnique for taking part in an inopportune republican demonstration by certain of his fellow students, is enabled to join the army. When his regiment is posted to Nancy, he literally falls in love with the superb, Metildean widow Mme de Chasteller by tumbling off his horse in front of her window, but sees no significant action beyond confronting a surly band of discontented workers in an outlying village. Returning to Paris, he becomes the principal private secretary of a cabinet minister and is sent to Normandy to manipulate a local election so as to ensure that a generally admirable opposition deputy will not be returned and thus embarrass the government. Though Mme de Chasteller is not forgotten, Lucien conducts a politic – one might

* An attempt at a complete publication first appeared in 1894 but the full text was not established until 1926.

almost say prophylactic – affair with Mme Grandet, the beautiful wife of an industrial plutocrat. Her meddlesome importunity and his consequent boredom drive him to seek a diplomatic post as far from Paris as possible; the novel's third, unwritten volume would have taken the young man to a thinly disguised Rome, where the ambassador's wife would eventually engineer his downfall, with the book ending in his redemptive marriage to Mme de Chasteller.

There are plenty of reasons for considering this the finest of all unfinished novels, and for placing it, purely in terms of a fiction constructed out of the richest and most complex fabric of contemporary realities, among the central achievements of Stendhal's career. The fact that this already immense work, distinguished by its extraordinary density and seriousness of intention, was never released for publication during his lifetime (though initially he does seem to have toyed with the idea of issuing the novel as it stood) is one of the more remarkable aspects of his last mature phase as a novelist. Over few other books did he labour with so much meticulous attention to detail: every character and incident is carefully located and grounded, with an acuteness which must surely have owed something to the author's advantage of distance, at any rate in geographical terms, from the world he laid bare. There are strong echoes, for example, of the increasing industrial tension under the July Monarchy which had led to a direct confrontation, during the autumn of 1831, between the weavers of Lyons and troops acting in the name of the government and the manufacturers, alarmed by the workers' determination to organize and threaten strikes. The cynical 'enrichissez-vous' atmosphere of mercantile capitalism and the new bourgeoisie under Louis-Philippe is invoked as a backdrop to a cast of performers almost every one of whom, Stendhal's notes make clear, was based on somebody he had met or observed at close quarters.

The Marquise de Puylaurens, 'a tall woman of thirty-four or thirty-five, perhaps more, with superb eyes, a magnificent skin, and an air, what was more, of laughing heartily at all the theories in the world' is a portrait of Clémentine Curial, while the sprightly 'natural' Mme de Hocquincourt, whose brilliant salon

Lucien seeks out as a sop to his vanity when humbled by Mme de Chasteller, finds her origin in Stendhal's Milanese friend Nina Viganò, whose efforts at flirting with him he always pretended not to understand. The merest observation by a secondary character will as often as not reproduce what the writer himself overheard: when Mme Grandet, in Chapter 64, dismisses the hero's social charm by acidly remarking, 'It isn't difficult to become popular when you allow yourself to say anything whatever', these are in fact the words of Baron Cuvier on Stendhal himself, who happened to be listening at the time.

Yet for all this authenticity, or perhaps because of it, *Lucien Leuwen* never quite becomes the sum of its parts, however many of those may be unsurpassed individually in the entire range of Stendhal's writing. Banally summarized, it is a tremendous romance of love and politics, an obsessively detailed diorama of modern France in the manner of an historical novel, a book in which the hiss and clank and whirr made by the intricate machinery of its creator's formidable, not to say overweening intelligence can be heard frantically at work. Yet there is also a strong suggestion of him trying, as it were, to atone too heavily for the apparent formal solecism of *Le Rouge et le Noir* by constructing a traditional novel in the manner of Fielding, whom he so adored, and of Scott, with whom his relationship was more ambiguous and possibly more profound. We feel here, as we never feel in the earlier book, a sense of constraint, of looking over the shoulder, which is not induced simply by hindsight and the advantage of the writer's own working notes as a constant subtext.

Why in the end did Stendhal abandon this, the most ambitious project he ever undertook (unless we except the *Histoire de la Peinture en Italie*)? Though, after a year's painstaking attention to it, he made up his mind early in 1835 to suppress Volume III, for which a few sketches had already been drawn, because, as he said, 'it's only in the first flush of youth and love that anyone could swallow an exposition and fresh characters', and though he was clearly intending publication of the existing volumes when he returned to Paris in 1836, the novel suddenly seems to have lost relevance for him and nothing more is heard of it after that year.

It has been suggested that the work's very topicality in some sense overtook it, but it seems more likely that the novelist simply perceived that it was not his line of business to write a disciplined modern drama of socio-political forces and expect a character as charming and fundamentally harmless as Lucien to function adequately as its hero. In the eighteenth century, manipulating this amiable, intelligent, inoffensively vain young man as an innocent entering upon 'the world' like Joseph Andrews or Wilhelm Meister, Stendhal might have managed to convince himself. But this was 1834, and the rising star of Honoré de Balzac was about to give French readers Eugène Rastignac and Lucien de Rubempré, both of whom, in their entirely different guises, issued a more effective challenge, as men of their hour, to their meticulously defined social universe than the subaltern of the 27th Lancers, riding to his destiny at Nancy, could possibly contrive.

During his long Roman sojourns of 1834 and 1835 Stendhal consolidated still further the advantages held out to him by the capital's cosmopolitan society. He willingly accepted dinner invitations at the palace of the banker Alessandro Torlonia, whose Auvergnat family origins made him well disposed towards the French, and negligently informed Julie Gaulthier, in the same letter criticizing her *Le Lieutenant*, that he was spending his evenings with a nineteen-year-old marchesa, whom he dismissed as 'very comfortable, like a nice sofa'. Doubtless this was the same 'prettiest, youngest, richest and, towards me, best-disposed young woman in Rome' with whom, in a note on the *Leuwen* manuscript a year later he says he was bored to death, and left her lying in her bed at one o'clock the previous night. She has alas never been identified.

With two Roman noble families his relationship was a good deal more lively. The Caetani, Dukes of Sermoneta, one of the oldest princely clans in the city and boasting Dante's *bête noire* Pope Boniface VIII on a branch of their genealogical tree, had always cherished artistic interests. Don Enrico, the present duke, and his duchess Donna Teresa Gherardo de' Rossi, had been friends of Paul-Louis Courier, whose political integrity Stendhal so much admired, and four of their five children (three sons and two daughters) became friendly with Beyle. His closest links were with the second of the young princes, Filippo, to whom, in one of his various wills, he left all the books he kept at his Roman lodgings and who, by a singular irony, was destined to die (in 1864) at Civitavecchia.

Filippo's lively, ardent nature had drawn him into an affair wth Hortense Allart, for whom Stendhal had acted as an agent with French publishers in 1828 after meeting her in Florence. Worldly, pleasure-loving and bright, he made an ideal companion for the errant consul, and the pair, together with the eldest Caetani brother, Michele, jaunted agreeably up and down the city to dinners, dances and theatres, the charm of the association undeniably seasoned by Beyle's delight in rubbing shoulders with the Roman aristocracy, freely admitted in letters to friends, and by the clubbable, unsnobbish disposition of the Caetani themselves, apparently not above cooking meals and making coffee for their friends.

It was through this lucky association that Stendhal grew more closely acquainted with a young couple whom he may already have met at the French Embassy, Count Filippo Cini and his wife, Giulia, the daughter of a Roman house which could trace its ancestry to the medieval tribune Cola di Rienzi and which later in the nineteenth century counted Pope Leo XIII among its members. The countess, vivacious, sociable and very attractive, soon became a decided favourite with Stendhal, who referred to her as 'la contessa Sandre', playing on the similarity of her surname to the Latin word *cinis* – ash – French *cendre* – 'Sandre'. Though the two were never actually lovers, he was seriously captivated by her from the summer of 1835 onwards, until on 17 February 1836 he resigned himself to the fact that she was not reciprocating and that Filippo Caetani, with whom he had briefly quarrelled after a ball and then made up, had a more serious share in her favours. As we shall see, however, Stendhal's passion for Giulia Cini was not dead but sleeping.

The prince's mother, the Duchess of Sermoneta, was a noted amateur archaeologist, and Stendhal would no doubt have discussed with her his own ventures in the field, in the company of Donato Bucci and Pietro Manzi. Visits to the Etruscan sites around Civitavecchia provided one of the few diversions from the prevailing dullness of 'Abeille', which was becoming almost nightmarish to him. A growing interest in the ancient civilization of classical Rome's chief enemies in its earliest years as a city state was beginning to draw scholars, historians or merely the curious traveller to the Papal States to investigate the tombs and settlement sites which inquisitive but not always very scrupulous diggers were now turning over. Among them was Bucci, whose honesty as a dealer in archaeological relics is commended in the pioneering classic of Etruscology, George Dennis's *Cities and Cemeteries of Etruria*, published in 1848.

Dennis writes scathingly of Civitavecchia:

> What more wearisome than the dull, dirty town . . . . and what traveller does not pray for a speedy deliverance from this den of thieves, of whom Gasperoni [sic] though most renowned, is not the most accomplished? Civita is like 'love, war and hunting' according to the proverb – it is more easy to find the way in than the way out.

He is equally hard on the highway to Rome, which Stendhal traversed so many times, declaring 'as far as intrinsic beauty is concerned, it would be difficult to find in Italy a road more unattractive, more bleak, dreary and desolate; and to one just making acquaintance with that land of famed fertility and beauty, as so many do at Civita Vecchia, nothing can be more disappointing'.

Anyone landing at Civitavecchia, says the opinionated and super-informative English cicerone, should not fail to visit the Etruscan necropolis of Corneto a mere thirteen miles off, across 'a desert of undulating heath, overrun with lentiscus, myrtle and dwarf cork trees, the haunt of the wild boar and the roebuck'. Stendhal himself, making the journey in the autumn of 1834, sent a detailed account, with little drawings, to Sophie Duvaucel. 'This is . . . . the Père La Chaise of the Tarquinii, from whom derived that Tarquin whose son is so celebrated in the history of female virtue.' He and his companions poked about among the tomb chambers, crawling in on all fours, across the ashes of cremated

Etruscans, to find that in most cases the graves had already been pillaged, though he did promise to send Sophie some pottery fragments, and described a recently discovered effigy, in the characteristic reclining position, which he praised for its naturalness in comparison with the rigidity of Greek sculpture, adding a little dig at 'this orator without ideas, but not altogether cold, named Winckelmann, the first Baron de Steindhal'.

The consul's periodic returns to his office at Civitavecchia during 1834–5 were followed invariably by sharp spurts of bureaucratic assiduity, in which he could demonstrate his gift for assuming any one of a wide range of official disguises. In November 1834, for example, a long dispatch to Admiral de Rigny, the former Navy minister who had succeeded the Duc de Broglie at the Foreign Office that spring, described in the most vivid detail the effects of yet another famine in the Papal States, including a riotous mob surrounding the Pope's carriage, shouting 'Olio! olio!' and immense untended flocks of sheep which had wandered down from the hills to the shoreline around Civitavecchia in search of something to eat. In April 1835, with the recrudescence of cholera warnings, which had taken on a seasonal regularity in Mediterranean ports during this period, Stendhal was required to deal sternly with the local health inspector, Romanelli, who had carried out, to the letter and beyond, a government directive imposing eleven days' quarantine on all ships hailing from France. 'I am not aware of what M. Romanelli's conduct may be towards the shipping of other nations, but it should be pointed out that this functionary has taken upon himself the task of making absurd difficulties over French vessels.'

So absurd indeed that the brig *Malouine* was held up for an hour and a half on its entry into Civitavecchia harbour, 'which is contrary to the dignity of the French flag', and the captain was ordered to unload his supply of coal before the passengers' passports were even looked at. 'The *Malouine* was obliged to heave-to outside the port for more than an hour, this beneath the gaze of an inquisitive populace gathered all around . . .' What was more, as Beyle, good religious sceptic though he was, had no scruples in pointing out, the ship's officers, devout Catholics to a man, were thus seriously incommoded from going to Rome to witness that year's Easter celebrations.

Shipping naturally occupied much of the consul's attention. On 12 December 1834, the *Henri IV*, one of the regular steamers from Leghorn and Marseilles, struck a reef off the peninsula of Monte Argentario on the Tuscan coast. The cargo had been rescued and the ship, though seriously holed, might perhaps be refloated, but the crew and passengers, clambering to safety, had been forced to spend thirty-six hours on the rocks, owing to the deliberate inaction of the Grandducal quarantine officer, fearing lest it should be a Neapolitan vessel carrying cholera. Stendhal, who only got the news three days later, was wonderfully prompt in response, mobilizing local workmen in Civitavecchia to fashion seventy pumps, sending three ships and sixty men to the rescue, and dashing off letters to all the relevant authorities. His action was perhaps the swifter for knowing that his friend Jean-Jacques Ampère was on board, to whose father, the illustrious physicist, he sent a reassurance that no lives had been lost. To Sophie Duvaucel, who had recently married the elderly Admiral Ducrest de Villeneuve, he sent a sardonic summary of the episode, describing 'our poor friend Ampère who has just taken part in a shipwreck and spent 36 hours on a rock, in a freezing wind, kept there by the charming quarantine laws', while to Sainte-Beuve he dispatched a more graphic account, complete with details of the captain's Gascon boastfulness and the likely difficulties of convincing the Marseilles insurance office of the seriousness of the loss. The whole correspondence surrounding the loss of the *Henri IV* deserves to be read in detail as a superb demonstration of Stendhal's inimitable letter-writer's gift of adapting his style to the recipient – when he chose.

Alas, for all his resourcefulness and persistence as a consul doing his duty, there were moments when his diplomatic and ministerial superiors seemed less than helpful or benign, and when, as he saw it, those beneath him were all too ready to betray his trust. Chief among these was his secretarial assistant Lysimaque Caftangioglou-Tavernier, whom he re-employed after Baron de Vaux, for the most dubious of reasons, had dispensed with his services. In the summer of 1834 there took place between the consul and his *chancelier* a quarrel in which many Stendhalians have pinned the blame squarely on the latter, but which the evidence, viewed dispassionately, suggests was as much Beyle's fault as Tavernier's.

The cause of the dispute was a review of the consular accounts, sent on 19 May by Admiral de Rigny, questioning the inclusion among claims for expenses of such items as the payment of the office cleaning woman, the cost of firewood and the transporting of ambassadorial dispatches. Beyle, rounding on his wretched understrapper, accused him of mismanagement and blamed him directly for the ministerial reprimand. Tavernier, suitably nettled, pointed out that the accounts had been approved by his superior and ended a letter of mounting indignation by handing in his notice, 'deeply wounded by your ingratitude and the injustice of your proceedings'.

Stendhal scornfully accepted Tavernier's resignation and sent notes to Rigny and to Auguste de Tallenay, chargé d'affaires at Rome in the ambassador's absence. 'Le Grec' meanwhile hastened to write his own letter to the Foreign Minister, taking the precaution of sending copies of Beyle's original angry remonstrance and his own reply. After Tallenay sent a polite but firm reminder that notice should not have been served without first consulting the embassy, Tavernier directed a further obsequious vindication to Rigny, emphasizing the 'honour . . . duty . . . . respect for His Majesty's ordinances and the orders of Your Excellency' which had induced him to take such a course.

The previous year a new ambassador had succeeded the Comte de Sainte-Aulaire, posted to Vienna. Stendhal's relations with Justin-Pons-Florimond de Fay, Marquis de La Tour-Maubourg, were on an entirely different footing from those maintained with his friendly former chief and the dashing, sociable Mme de Sainte-Aulaire. Whatever their formal distance, La Tour-Maubourg was an able diplomat and diplomacy was as crucial in settling a tiff between two consular functionaries as it was in smoothing the path of Franco-Papal relations. Together the ambassador and Tallenay (who wisely reminded Tavernier of the old story of the pot calling the kettle black) now sought to conciliate both parties, but the damage was more or less permanently done. Even if the irritated secretary and the embarrassed consul were at length persuaded to make up, it was hardly with a kiss, and the mutual rancour expressed itself in, among other things, the icy formality of Tavernier's official bulletins sent to Beyle during the latter's long absences from duty.

Among the less attractive sides to Stendhal's character was an implacable hostility towards those who, for whatever reason, had given him offence. He was not magnanimous, was as capable as anyone else of bearing grudges and, as we might expect in somebody whose most loyal friends could, when he felt in the mood, be damned with faint praise or derided for their inability to meet the exorbitant demands of *beylisme*, he seldom forgave an injury. Lysimaque Caftangioglou-Tavernier was thrown accordingly into the outer darkness of the unredeemed, to be referred to indignantly as 'Sinon le Grec', an allusion to the notorious betrayer of Troy in Homer's *Iliad* and condemned with that deadliest of Stendhalian epithets, *fat*, meaning conceited or foppish. Stewing with rage, a note in a copy of Shakespeare the writer happened to be reading in November 1834 exclaims: 'Once a *man* has the misfortune to pass for a person of intelligence, all his professional superiors who lack this defect try to avenge it by making him angry.' The disgrace implicit in the whole affair, by which he felt diminished and less secure, is reflected in the succeeding remark: 'This mistake is one of those which can never be washed away.'

In the sense that Stendhal felt that it had been made to seem that he was disobeying that unwritten but universally acknowledged eleventh commandment, 'Thou shalt not be found out', Tavernier was undoubtedly to blame. Had he acted with greater prudence, posterity might have been less harsh with him. As it was, the younger man took his revenge, during his employer's* remaining years at Civitavecchia, by constantly sneaking on him to the officials at various French embassies and consulates in the Mediterranean, making it appear, however obliquely, that Beyle was simply frittering away his time in flagrant dereliction of duty

* Stendhal paid Tavernier's salary from his own pocket, something De Vaux had never done.

and seeking to represent himself as the faithful guardian of a neglected command-post. Stendhal's vengeance was more subtle, that eternal doom which makes the enmity of a competent writer perhaps the most fatal of all to those foolish enough to incur it, for was not Tavernier one of the various contributors to the creation of that most repellent of characters in *La Chartreuse de Parme*, the Fiscal Rassi?

A footnote to the whole affair of 'le Grec' and his disloyalty is provided by a letter to Romain Colomb written sixteen years after Stendhal's death by Donato Bucci (to whom he had indeed offered Tavernier's job on receiving his resignation). Bucci initially praises the secretary for his efficient office management in the consul's absence, but discloses that as soon as La Tour-Maubourg arrived *en poste*, passing through Civitavecchia to Rome, Tavernier fawned on the ambassador to the point of seeming 'un véritable domestique de place' in hopes of improving his prospects. Worse still, he not only told tales on Stendhal to the French government but denounced him to the Papal authorities as 'an atheist in religion and a revolutionary in politics', asserting that Bucci's own shop was a hotbed of conspiracy to foment rebellion in the States of the Church. It was scarcely any wonder that 'M. B.', as the letter refers to Beyle, once exasperatedly declared: 'I'd rather you had given me fifty strokes of the road than have made me take this infamous rogue Lysimaque for my secretary.' After Stendhal's death – and we have no good reason to doubt his friend's word – Tavernier, having prevailed on Bucci to lend him the keys to the consul's apartment, stole bank drafts from a desk and took possession of a bundle of letters from Victor Jacquemont which he subsequently had the gall to read and show to others in Bucci's presence. When the inventory of the dead man's effects was being taken and the secretary let fall some remark derogatory to his memory, the loyal Donato could restrain himself no longer. Quoting, with a heavy irony, Stendhal's own words, he burst out:

> 'only an infamous rogue like you could speak ill of so worthy a man, to whom you owe all you possess from your shoes to your hat!' I was so angry I'd have caught him a blow across the face if he

> hadn't got quickly away. . . . Yet, would you believe it, vile, grovelling and sly as a true Greek of the later Empire, some hours after this incident he dared to return to my house as though nothing had happened, begging me to continue helping him with the inventory.

The quarrel with Tavernier soured still further a period of Stendhal's existence when the dreariness of his days in Civitavecchia, the realization of advancing age and the harshness of southern summers with their fleas and glare and sleep-disturbing nocturnal heat were all starting to weigh upon him. 'I have seen so much sunlight!' he exclaimed. Obesity was also proving a problem, and he already possessed a special armchair, ordered from the Parisian furniture-maker Derville, custom-made for his large bottom. His scribbled notes on the pages of *Lucien Leuwen* or in the books he read, Saint-Simon, Fielding, Scott or Mrs Trollope, are almost like constant reminders to himself that he is still actually alive and not entirely numbed to surrounding varieties of experience. Fish dinners, gout attacks, the *tramontana* blowing, the smell given off by a young monk, a new kind of ink, dalliance with an actress, white trousers, a requiem mass for the recently dead Vincenzo Bellini, the first cup of coffee after nineteen months' abstinence, a delicious stroll on the Pincio, where 'dark clouds hide the sun and the sky shows clear above the dome of Saint Peter's, picked out in velvety darkness against the weak blue heaven, an admirable thing worthy of Claude', dinner with Alexandre Dumas and a resultant hangover from too much champagne, the Tiber in flood, a mysterious 'Tékla. Guernesey' and not relishing the 'maudite élégance académique' of Gibbon's *Decline and Fall of The Roman Empire*'.

Perhaps it was also, at least in part, for evidence of himself as a living person that he sat for his portrait to the young Italian painter Silvestro Valeri, a work which passed first of all to Mérimée, thence to the Empress Eugénie and is now in the Musée Stendhal at Grenoble. The consul is shown in his braided official uniform, wearing the ribbon and cross of the Légion d'honneur, conferred on him by royal decree on 15 January that year in his capacity as a man of letters. Curiously, in view of the strenuous efforts he had made in the past via Mérimée and others to obtain the medal, he seems to have been disappointed in this citation, seeing it as a reward more appropriately given for his consular service, something the Foreign Ministry, at any rate under Rigny's ascendancy, would surely not have considered.

Valeri's portrait, which Stendhal said made him look like 'an old hardboiled general', brings out the combative strength of character in that ugly face, with its narrow mouth, pug nose and the mongoloid eyes, the 'quelque peu de Kalmouck' referred to by one of his friends, which had caused Gina Pietragrua to nickname him 'the Chinaman'. By those who knew him the likeness was considered less faithful than that effected in 1841 by the Swedish army colonel Olof Johan Södermark, judged a masterpiece by the sitter and presented after his death to Romain Colomb by Donato Bucci, though many latter-day *beylistes* enjoy the intimacy of Henri Lehmann's pencil sketch made in the same year at Civitavecchia, even if the arms appear ludicrously out of proportion to the rest of the body. To these, for a consensus on what he actually looked like, we can add Jean-Louis Ducis' somewhat coarser representation, showing Stendhal as the smart *habitué* of Roman palaces in 1835, sporting a black cravat borrowed from Count Cini and a silver-topped cane, the characterful medallion made in Paris in 1829 by his friend the sculptor David d'Angers and the buoyantly youthful 'physionotrace' profile of 1807.

Not every painter in Rome, a city where during the early nineteenth century most of the large expatriate population was engaged with easel and sketchbook, cared for Stendhal's company. Jean-Dominique Ingres, who succeeded Horace Vernet as director of the French Academy at Villa Medici, had the novelist shown the door after he imprudently remarked that there was no such thing as a tune in Beethoven, and told his servants not to readmit him in future. Beethoven's greatest French admirer, the composer Hector Berlioz, had been similarly disenchanted. Watching the carnival crowd in Piazza Navona, he asked:

> And who is this rotund little man with the malicious smile, who wants to appear serious? It's a man of spirit who writes on the

imaginative arts, it's the consul of Civitavecchia who thinks himself obliged by *fashion* to leave his post beside the Mediterranean to come and swing in a carriage around the sewer of Piazza Navona; he's thinking up some new chapter for his novel *Le Rouge et le Noir.*

A sour footnote clarifies the reference to 'M Beyle, who wrote a life of Rossini under the pseudonym of Stendhal, together with some of the most irritating stupidities as to music, for which he fancies himself to have a taste'.

Whether it was merely as a result of the cumulative effect of his current existence in Rome and Civitavecchia or else the result of his growing frustrations with *Lucien Leuwen* we cannot know for certain, but on 23 November 1835, laying the novel aside, he started to work on a detailed record of his life, the autobiography which he entitled *Vie de Henry Brulard.* The pseudonym, uniting a family surname with an occasional variant of his forename, was partly intended as another of his onomastic efforts at bamboozling the police: on various pages of the manuscript, now in the Bibliothèque de Grenoble, we find a series of bogus title page inscriptions, '*Vie de Henry Brulard écrite par lui-même. Roman imité du Vicaire de Wakefield*', with a message to 'M.M. de la Police' telling them that the hero's wife was 'la célèbre Charlotte Corday', assuring them that the work contains no politics and that Brulard himself eventually becomes a priest. A subsequent series of conditions attached to the book's release into the public domain decrees that it is not to be published until after his death, that the names of all female figures are to be changed so as to avoid scandal, but that all male names must remain as written.

Stendhal's own version of how *Vie de Henry Brulard* came to be started is, as we might expect, somewhat factually distorted. He deliberately pushes back the date three years to 1832, and sets the scene with meticulous precision in the manner of one of the period's own novelists. Outside the church of San Pietro in Montorio, on the Janiculum, under a sky across which a light sirocco blows a few little white clouds, he looks across to Frascati and Castel Gandolfo, down towards the orange groves of the Capuchin convent and the Tiber, to the tomb of Cecilia Metella and the pyramid of Cestius. The splendid view comprises the whole historical experience of Rome as capital of an ancient empire and city of the Popes, and this sense of a chronological map unrolling before him inevitably brings Stendhal to confront the reality of his own middle age. In three months he will be fifty years old, and what has he done with his life? 'It is about time I got to know myself. What have I been? What am I? Truly I should be embarrassed to speak of it.' He turns to the contemplation of his various sentimental relationships, as if these alone validated his existence, and the grandeur of Rome, antique and modern, becomes a correlative landscape of past experience. 'Was I intelligent? Was I good at anything in particular?' Under a light evening mist, Stendhal goes home to his lodgings at Palazzo Conti: he is wearing a pair of white trousers made of English cloth, and on the inside waistband he has inscribed the cryptic legend 'J. vaisa voirla5[e]', that is to say 'Je vais avoir la cinquantaine'*

Yet how to begin? He wants to avoid too much 'I' and 'Me', so as not to become like Chateaubriand, 'ce roi des égotistes', to make sure that his book does not go the way of Byron's memoirs, ending up on the fire after having been entrusted to 'that milksop Thomas Moore', to obviate the time-honoured autobiographer's habit of lying (he disarminlgy owns up to having lied at least once already with his claim to have been present at the battle of Wagram) and to write 'without deceiving myself, and with pleasure, as if writing a letter to a friend'.

Because Stendhal, as far as we can tell, stuck firmly to these latter principles, *Vie de Henry Brulard* became one of the sharpest of all self-delineations, the better surely for its imperfect state, a working mansuscript which gives us the first seventeen years of the author's life unpurged of digressions, seeming irrelevancies, sudden sideswipes at the immediate present and occasionally confusing chronological leaps. Much of its central corpus of detail has been utilized profitably by successive biographers, but it is the work's remarkable opening and closing sections, with their air of musical improvisation on the Stendhalian theme – we recall his

* Cf. his inscription on his braces of the date and time of his conquest of Angela Pietragrua in 1813, and the English words 'Iam Gre.at' ('I am great') scribbled on a notebook for the *Histoire de la Peinture en Italie*.

ravishing image of the soul as a violin – which both underpin and exalt the factual substance of a remembered boyhood. After the Roman prelude of Chapter 1 there follows an astonishing excursion across the entire human muddle of Stendhal's existence – falling with Napoleon, love for Metilde, the July Revolution, the consulate, Brunswick and Moscow, his father's death – reduced at last to the names of the women he loved, their initials traced in the sand of the lake shore at Albano, those of Virginie Kubly, Mélanie Guilbert, Mina von Griesheim, Metilde, Menti, Giulia, with others less signficant like Adèle Rebuffel and Angéline Bereyter.

The signs thus scratched resemble the magic letters in a fairy tale, whose decipherment conduces to some spectacular illumination or advantage for the hero. We feel Stendhal in the actual process of beginning to understad the peculiar cast and complexion of his existence, using the very exercise of writing as a window of perception in the same way that he had sought to comprehend his experience of love through the composition of *De l'Amour* or to encapsulate his unique vision of Italy via the seemingly aleatoric structure of *Rome, Naples et Florence*. The free-flowing, unsystematized self-assessment forming Chapter 2 – Stendhal as 'unhappy lover, fond of music and painting', as *homme d'esprit*, 'that fine quality which has made me so many enemies', his constant lack of money balanced against a comparative paucity of debts, his profound contempt for the bourgeoise – is an attempt after all to arrive at the particular distillation of the truth he needs to set him going on the actual business of narrative. Even if it does not take him quite as long as Tristram Shandy to get himself into the world, he sounds an ironic echo of Sterne's hero by announcing, in the chapter's final sentence 'after so many general considerations I am about to be born'.

Stendhal did not finish *Henry Brulard* in the orthodox sense which might have entailed at least two further volumes to bring his life record up to date. What we witness taking place in the final chapter (46) is an almost literal dissolution of the narrative beneath the radiance of an achieved happiness, 'un intervalle de bonheur fou et complet'. He has left Grenoble and within a short space he is over the Alps and strutting proudly and contentedly by Martial Daru's side along the streets of Milan. A process of redemption has in some sense been achieved, because it is here that he is able to find himself at last, and in his ecstasy he allows the chronometer to start wobbling dizzily out of control. The name of Angela Pietragrua, who really belongs to a decade later, is sounded and the paragraphs break up into a series of disconnected sentences, all bearing witness to the writer's sudden feeling that he can no longer express the essence of what really happened to him in the great emotional crucible of Milan. At one point he implies that he has had to get up from his desk and walk to and fro for a quarter of an hour before sitting down to write again. He makes frantic appeals to the reader for pardon and sympathy, claiming to compose 'as Rossini composes his music . . . writing each morning whatever I find before me in the libretto'. Some half a dozen lines later the book, so to speak, fades from view.

There was another, more immediately practical reason why *Henry Brulard*, so merciless, so tender, so brutally precise in its registers of hatred, contempt or the sense of injustice, yet often so ardent and lyrical in the expression of a fleeting joy, its episodes mapped out for us in the accompanying series of little lettered diagrams, had to come to an end. On 26 March 1836 Stendhal was told that the leave he had long since asked for had finally been granted, and wrote in a footnote to the last manuscript page: 'The imagination flies elsewhere; this work is thus interrupted. Boredom numbs the spirit, too worn down during the years 1832 to 1836 at Rome. This enterprise, endlessly interrupted by professional tasks, surely demonstrates the effects of such a numbness.' In May he was off at last to Paris.

CHAPTER 12

THE LAST OF HIS LIFE

The order of release, issued by the new Foreign Minister, Adolphe Thiers, officially on health grounds, was not likely to pass without comment among Stendhal's diplomatic colleagues. The previous year Admiral de Rigny, in writing to him on the subject of his worsening relations with Lysimaque Tavernier, had issued a stern reprimand on the subject of his frequent absences from Civitavecchia: 'I do not intend to shut my eyes to so obvious and prolonged a violation of orders except in the hope that it will not be repeated.' Such derelictions of duty, perhaps thanks to Tavernier himself, corresponding with other consular officials behind his superior's back, were noted elsewhere in the Mediterranean. In July 1836 Stendhal's old army colleague Joseph Canclaux, consul at Nice (then part of the Kingdom of Sardinia), sent a letter to his opposite number at Genoa, Tellier de Blanriez, pointing out to him a revised version, in a Toulon newspaper, of an article originally published in *Le Constitutionnel* on the subject of the unfortunate tendency of French consuls in Italy to absent themselves from their posts. The writer was commander of the corvette *Diligente* who had picked up the relevant gossip on a recent cruise (though without calling at Civitavecchia). While not naming names, he plainly glanced at Beyle in mentioning a certain secretary who had regularly to be managing the office 'in the absence of the consul who resides continually at Rome. Lately, this consul having obtained leave to come to France, the secretary has witnessed the arrival of an apprentice consul to take over the direction of the consulate.'

So far was Stendhal from bothering with such criticisms that he did not return to Italy for another three years, an extended leave owing much to Comte Molé's return to the Foreign Ministry in September 1836. Ageing and infirm though he might be, he was setting off to Paris as an acknowledged literary celebrity who could afford to be selective over whom he saw and where he went. A detailed plan was drawn up for the trip – 'buy 6 handkerchiefs at Leghorn and 20 pairs of yellow gloves from Cagiati at Rome', 'maybe go to England, at least to Brussels, possibly to Edinburgh', with expressed intentions of going on a diet and lodging in Rue Taitbout, worth the extra 200 francs' expense. He would call on Balzac, on the critic Philarète Chasles and on Alphonse Levavasseur, publisher of *Le Rouge et le Noir*, as well as touring his constellation of female intimates, Julie Gaulthier, Clémentine Curial, Virginie Ancelot and, most exciting of all to him, Giulia Rinieri de' Rocchi, now residing in Paris with her complaisant husband, Giulio Martini, who always maintained cordial relations with his wife's lover.

Arriving in Paris at the end of May, he seems to have tried at once to pick up again the thread of his relationship with Clémentine Curial. The pair, as has been noted, never abandoned each other following the break-up of their affair in 1826, that mysterious 'storm' at Saint-Omer (Stendhal's 'San Remo') which was clearly a red-letter disaster in his amorous calendar. She was not encouraging, however: he noted her 'profound coldness' when they met on 9 July, and by the end of September he was telling himself that 'this little recrudescence of love is altogether cured, but to find myself close to Menti without touching her pretty hands would put me under a disagreeable constraint'. Once again we owe to Romain Colomb's tiresome delicacy the fact that her letter telling Beyle that a fire could be rekindled from the ashes, that the feeling of 1826 was dead and buried and that he should content himself with friendship, exists merely as a two-line summary of a vanished original.

That October Stendhal made another of his various attempts at securing a wife. The object this time was the widowed Eulalie-Françoise Réal, Baronne Lacuée de Saint-Just, a friend of Mérimée's mother, a woman of more or less the same age as her would-be husband and therefore likely to appreciate the decidedly philosophical tone in which he sought to engage her heart. Telling her not to be afraid of that 'reputation for singularity falsely attributed to me', he continued somewhat archly: 'It seems to me that we both have a road to follow. This road leads more or less in the same direction . . . Would you accept a travelling companion, a sort of majordomo, charged with ordering the post-horses and, if necessary, of riding them.' The baroness was, it seems, resistant to these and subsequent coy nudges in the same vein, choosing soon afterwards to marry Mérimée's cousin, the engineer Léonor Fresnel.

Beyle had not much more success in his pursuit of Julie Gaulthier, with whom his intimacy had understandably fostered hopes of a warmer relationship. A glance at some words she sent him in October 1836 suggests that she was not above flavouring her messages with a zest or two of coquetry, if only because this was the style in which a Frenchwoman of the period ordinarily enjoyed rallying her male acquaintance, and because Stendhal was plainly accustomed to it. Yet phrases like 'I believe in you, my dear Henri, haven't I proof of your devotion?' or 'real heroes, true friends, don't talk, they act' must have set him thinking more seriously. We do not know exactly what happened between them at her house at Saint-Denis on Christmas Day, but the tone of the letter which followed is carefully conciliatory, conscious of a need to tread softly after the rebuff she had evidently administered, assuring him of her continuing friendship and ending with a moving protestation of faith in his sterling excellence. 'Beyle, call me a complete idiot,' she writes:

> a cold female, silly, frightened, stupid, everything you want, insults like these won't ever efface the happiness of our divine conversation . . . . believe me, you're a hundred thousand times better than people suppose, than you yourself suppose, than I supposed two hours ago!

Otherwise, apart from his continued attentions to Giulia, who, between journeys to Italy with her husband, was always obliging, there seems to have been no fresh pursuit. A cryptic allusion, in writing to his Roman friend Count Cini, to 'a mistress who very much resembles mme Martini . . . and costs me 120 fr. a month' may simply refer to this ongoing affair rather than to some unidentified Parisian 'lorette'. Elsewhere he settled back with the greatest of ease into the gratifying rhythms of his old metropolitan life, dining at the Café Anglais with Sutton Sharpe, Mareste and Adrien de Jussieu, often in the company of Delacroix and the German doctor David-Ferdinand Koreff, a ubiquitous figure in the Paris of the Romantics, and joining the club founded by Mérimée, the Cercle des Arts in Rue Choiseul, which, as well as his friends Etienne Delécluze and Baron Gérard, included among its members such choice spirits as Balzac, Meyerbeer and Nodier. He went to the Louvre to sample the 'austere truth' of the Murillo and Velázquez canvases which Baron Taylor had smuggled out of Spain in bales of wool, heard *I puritani* and *Anna Bolena* on successive nights at the Théâtre-Italien, and picked up the latest morsel of scandal about a certain countess being surprised in a fiacre outside the Invalides at one in the morning to pass on to friends in Rome.

His old enthusiasm for the theatre was now suddenly rekindled by the appearance on the Parisian stage of a remarkable young actress, born Elisabeth Félix but known 'in art' as Rachel, who, from the humblest of beginnings as a poor Jewish girl, awed and enthralled mid-nineteenth-century audiences during a cruelly brief career by her performance of the great Racinian tragic roles. Describing her to Cini as 'a poor little beggar of 18, very thin', Stendhal claimed that she played tragedy as if inventing whatever she said, and that the box-office takings at the Théâtre-Français had shot up since she joined the company. Her triumph was in the part of Hermione in *Andromaque*.

> She expresses irony in a sublime manner. While she's in fashion, a dinner guest may well say 'I can't come tonight, I've a ticket for Mlle Rachel'. . . . Her genius confounds me with amazement each time I see her act; it is two hundred years since such a miracle was seen in France.

One of Mme Ancelot's group paintings, designed to celebrate her successful hunting of cultural lions and lionesses, shows

Rachel, sombre-eyed and dressed in black, reciting lines from the same play to an illustrious audience, a drawing room gathering that includes Chateaubriand, Mme Récamier, Tocqueville and, in the right-hand corner unmistakably, Beyle himself, eyes bright with absorption.

It was Mérimée, another of the salon's *habitués*, who introduced Stendhal to what proved one of his most rewarding later friendships. From Aix-la-Chapelle, whence he was about to set off on a summer jaunt into the Rhineland, 'Clara' undertook to present 'le Baron' to a Spanish lady (with whom he was at pains to point out that there had been no question of sex), 'a most finished and beautiful example of an Andalusian woman'. Doña Maria Mañuela de Guzmán Palafox y Portocarrero, Condesa de Montijo, was the wife of a Spanish nobleman who had been imprisoned for his liberal sympathies by King Ferdinand VII and then released when it became opportune for that less than admirable sovereign to curry favour with the progressive element throughout Spain. She had come to Paris with her two daughters in 1835, ostensibly to provide them with a decent education, but also for the sake of a little tranquillity, at a safe distance from a country racked by civil war and the visitations of cholera. Ironically she seems to have been less enchanted with French liberalism than her husband, though it was he who returned to Spain almost immediately, leaving the girls to enjoy a variety of schools, including a fashionable convent in Rue de Varenne, the wildly progressive Gymnase Normale, Civile et Orthosomatique, and, briefly and disastrously, an English boarding institution in Bristol.

The elder of the children, Maria Francisca, known as Paca, later became the Duchess of Alba, wife of one of the premier grandees of Spain. The younger, Maria Eugenia, 'Eouki', the child whose red hair earned her the nickname 'Carrots' from her cruel English schoolmates, married the man who in 1852 assumed the title of Napoleon III, Emperor of the French, and in doing so found her place in European history as Empress Eugénie. Whatever the failings underlined by historians, she was a woman of strong character, animated by intense loyalty and gifted with a long memory for favours done and insights received from those whose company she enjoyed.

One of these, an enduring influence on her till his death in 1870 during the last days of Napoleon's reign, was Mérimée. Having originally befriended the Montijo family while in Granada, he became their valued mentor and confidant when they moved to Paris, and his notion of cementing a friendship between Beyle and the two precocious little Spanish girls (Paca was eleven and Eugénie ten) proved exactly the right one. Stendhal's life may not have brought him much into contact with children, but an earlier tenderness and charm shown towards Clémentine Curial's daughter, poor sickly Bathilde, indicate that he was not the traditional crabby old bachelor frowning on the young in unacknowledged envy of the attention given them.

For the Montijo sisters he became instead an adoptive uncle, sensibly refusing to talk down to them and treating each almost as though she were another Sophie Duvaucel or Julie Gaulthier. His love for Paca and Eouki was the stronger because he clearly valued their innocence, a relief, no doubt, to somebody made colossally cynical by so much sardonic scrutiny of adult prevarication, manoeuvring and hypocrisy. 'I love you,' he told them, 'because you're children. When you're grown women you'll be false like all women and I shan't love you any more.' The girls adored him in return, delighting in his visits for the stories he told them of Napoleon. Writing to her father in Spain, Paca announced: 'We've made the acquaintance of a gentleman called M. Beyle, who is charming and very nice to us. In Napoleon's time he was employed at court and did all the Emperor's business for him, so that he tells us all sorts of things that happened during the Empire.' These Thursday evenings he spent with them made a profound impression on Eugénie, whose marriage to Bonaparte's nephew ten years after Stendhal's death was such an oddly coincidental fulfilment of the enthusiasm with which, as she later acknowledged, the writer had intoxicated her during childhood.

It is always said of the Empress that she never read a line of Stendhal's works, and the story of her visit to the museum at Grenoble is often quoted, in which, on being shown what was described as 'a portrait of Stendhal' she exclaimed: 'No, no, that's M. Beyle, I knew him well.' This was in 1860, but she was destined to live on, the doyenne of ex-sovereigns and survivors from a vanished political order, until after the First World War. By the beginning of the twentieth century she had evidently done her old friend the justice of reading and enjoying his work, and politely reproved a young French diplomat in 1910 for not following her example. 'With him,' she said:

> you're at a good school; he is my favourite author. Do you know that it was he who gave me a taste for literature at an age when I was more disposed to think about dancing and travel? I'm grateful to him for having taken the trouble to show me (I was a very young girl then) the consolation reading can bring on those evenings when one witnesses the collapse of one's highest hopes.

To her husband's relative Count Primoli, Eugénie, yet warmer in her praise, exclaimed 'Do I remember M. Beyle! He was the first man who made my heart beat, and how violently!' She remembered the excitement of being allowed to stay up an hour longer on Thursday nights, the sound of the door bell and the two girls grasping the writer's hand and leading him to the drawing room where, installed in a fireside armchair, he took them on his knees and continued the thrilling imperial saga left off the previous week. 'We wept, we laughed, we trembled, we went crazy. . . .' When their mother, trying to calm them, laughingly told Stendhal it was his fault for letting two children tyrannize him, he replied, 'It doesn't matter', and gave them both a kiss. 'Nobody understands great matters better than little girls; their approval consoles me for the criticisms made by fools and bourgeois.'

It was this Napoleonic enthusiasm which revived Stendhal's own interest, never exactly dormant, in the heroic career of his former master, and he was indeed to dedicate the magnificent Waterloo episode of *La Chartreuse de Parme* to Paca and Eouki. A more immediate outcome of his Thursdays with the Montijos was a second attempt on the project first undertaken nearly twenty years earlier of an extended study of the Emperor and those closest to him. Beginning in November 1836, he carried on these *Memoires sur Napoléon* until the June of the following year when, though he had made an initial agreement with the publisher

François Buloz, editor-in-chief of the *Revue des Deux Mondes*, a sense of the task's sheer magnitude may have started to impinge, let alone a wish to be realizing other literary plans entirely. The extent of the new source material, inevitably mushrooming since he last tried his hand at a book on Napoleon, was immense: Las Cases' famous *Mémorial de Sainte-Hélène* alone ran to eight volumes, and it seemed as if almost everyone connected with the Corsican hero from his secretary Bourrienne to each lesser-ranking army officer, had hurried into print, not to speak of the historians both in France and England.

Experience and self-knowledge should have taught Stendhal that he was not cut out for this sort of work. It was one thing to engage critically with the memorialists, as he had done in a brilliant *London Magazine* review in 1825 of the Comte de Ségur's *Histoire de Napoléon et de la Grande Armée en 1812*, invoking the authority of his own personal witness as a participant in the Russian campaign. It was another entirely to try tacking together his various sources in a long historical essay while at the same time seasoning the text with a typically Stendhalian scatter of pertinent – or impertinent – observations and excursions. When he showed the book's preface to Mérimée in February 1837, the latter was appropriately scathing as to its rampant inconsistency in layout and substance.

Yet, as with everything he ever wrote, certain portions of the *Mémoires sur Napoléon* redeem the enterprise, however doomed from the outset, by their clarity and originality of insight, not to speak of the ways in which they so nakedly reflect their author's personal engagement with his theme. For instance, whatever his continued private expressions of scorn for what he deemed the pedantry and pomposity of his cousin Pierre Daru, he echoes here an admiring reference made in the Ségur review to the minister's personal integrity, and while pointing out his political cautiousness, commends him as 'a prodigy of orderliness and hard work', the only man who dared to speak up to Napoleon's all-powerful field marshals. Stendhal was able, what is more, to work into his seventh chapter an exuberant evocation of Milanese life and atmosphere at the time of the French invasion in May 1796 which fascinatingly prefigures the joyous opening to *La Chartreuse de Parme*.

The project supervening in the preparation of the Napoleon book was altogether more successful, if only because it sprang so directly from inherent restlessness. Soon after Beyle's arrival in Paris the previous year, Mérimée had described him to Sutton Sharpe as being 'powerfully tormented by the need for locomotion' and Donato Bucci, in the letter to Romain Colomb quoted earlier, speaks of 'the locomotive habits of M.B., who used to fall a prey to spleen if he had to remain long in the same place'. The chance to indulge this lifelong passion which, assisted either by necessity or choice, had carried him from the Yorkshire Dales to Posillipo and from Barcelona to Smolensk, arose once more when during the summer of 1837 he embarked on a series of journeys through provincial France which were to culminate in one of his most expansive texts, the *Mémoires d'un touriste*, finally published at the beginning of July 1838.

As with *Rome, Naples et Florence*, the appeal of the book was to a distinctive market for travel literature, which had continued to grow since 1815 and whose best examples were works such as Lady Morgan's *France in 1829 and 1830* or her earlier glance at Italy which tended to adopt a detached and markedly critical stance towards the landscapes, towns and societies through which the traveller moved, rather than simply expatiating on their beauties or historical associations. The singularity of *Mémoires d'un touriste*, despite the blandness of its title, owes much to Stendhal's deliberate avoidance of a unified viewpoint, of having perpetually, as it were, to face the camera directly as opposed to adopting more oblique angles and approaches. For his own purposes he pretends to be somebody else, a member of that very class whose pretentions he had questioned in *D'un nouveau complot contre les industriels*, a certain Monsieur L. . . ., 'commercial traveller in iron' who, according to the author posing as editor, 'has the defect of calling things somewhat too readily by their own names'. Both this device and the journal format developed from his earlier travel books enable the writer to speak plainly and to avoid having to mention those features which, for various reasons, happen not to interest him. Another more significant reason for adopting this ploy, this ink-and-paper version of the joke he had once played in Mme Ancelot's salon by dressing up as the cotton-nightcap-merchant Bombet was that it enabled him to look more coolly at the provincial world of Louis-Philippe's France, after seven years of a constitutional monarchy with its system of checks and balances in the English manner, an increasingly powerful bourgeoisie and a growing industrial working class which had already established itself as a force to be reckoned with in the disturbances at Lyons and Grenoble touched on in *Lucien Leuwen*.

The delightfully loose structure of *Mémoires d'un touriste*, which makes it the most grateful to the casual browser of Stendhal's books, allows him to insinuate a whole range of social and political observations, running the gamut from open criticism and detailed analysis of systems and opinions to the merest incidental detail whose implicit irony almost, but not quite, escapes notice. Having told us how miserable the sight of unemployed silk workers in the streets of Lyons has made him, 'the tourist' carefully sidesteps the responsibility of speaking out in reference to the riots of 1831 and 1834, with the result, of course, that we read volumes into his ostentatious silence, as indeed we do into his remark several pages later, while on a Rhône steamer: 'I do not know where to find suitable terms in which to depict the growing prosperity that France enjoys under the rule of Louis-Philippe. I am afraid I shall appear a pensioned hack.'

For the whole of May and June 1837 Stendhal explored central France, Brittany and Normandy, visiting Bourges and Tours, sailing up the Loire to Nantes, and returning to Paris by way of Le Havre, Coutances and Rouen. The early part of the trip was made in the company of Mérimée, who had been appointed to the prestigious post of Inspector of Ancient Monuments, a job for which his wide-ranging cultural curiosity admirably suited him and one in which he was able to exercise a profound influence over the conservation and restoration of much that might otherwise have fallen victim to official philistinism or general neglect. Mérimée had contributed besides to the wealth of expert information on which Beyle was able to draw for adumbrative detail in the new book. A whole series of notes and sketches was prepared by the younger man as a kind of crash course in Gothic art, though his friend's ultimate response to the beauty and majesty of medieval church architecture, if the ambiguous observations on the cathedral at Valence are anything to go by, seems to have been less than wholehearted. Elsewhere Stendhal applied to his friend Dr William Edwards for details of French prehistory and ethnography, to Louis Crozet and Adolphe de Mareste for *faits divers*, anecdotes and Napoleonic material, to the Marquis de Custine for a story told by his uncle about a monkey, a cat and a cheese, and to his Parisian dinner companion, the polymathic Adrien de Jussieu, for notes on volcanoes.

The reviews of *Mémoires d'un touriste* were not surprisingly mixed, given the book's various slants, political, social and religious. *Le Commerce* compared him (and it was not the first to do so) with Diderot, but no doubt justly pointed out that the loose structure of his work and the constant sense of the author trying to engage the reader with the sharpness of his wit and intelligence militated against it being taken seriously. *La Presse*, however charmed by Stendhal's style, of which its critic Francis Wey offered a singularly minute analysis, was mystified by an antithesis between implicit humour and ceaseless triviality, as well as by the curiously old-fashioned tone of anticlericalism. In *La Revue de Paris* Arnould Frémy praised that 'instinct towards the beautiful, the fanaticism for all which is truly noble and exalted among arts and letters' which 'breathes throughout the book', while in the provinces Amédée de Roussillac, critic of *La Revue du Lyonnais*, held up the Tourist's observations on Lyons to the ridicule and disgust of his readers, concluding 'It seems useful to us to indicate the *Mémoires d'un touriste* as a work of ignorance and bad taste, not to speak of bad faith'.

A futher volume, covering the deep south of France, may indeed have been planned, but it seems likely that Stendhal's object, in the journey undertaken during the spring and summer of 1838, was to produce an altogether different, more cohesive and personal work than the *Mémoires*, with their heavy reliance on borrowed material. Not published until 1927, the *Voyage dans le Midi de la France* has all the intimacy and detail we value in the writer at his most relaxed, that quality later praised by Henry James (an admirer of the *Mémoires*) when speaking of 'this absorbing passion for example, anecdote and illustration that constituted Beyle's distinctive genius'. Yet it is a different Beyle as diarist from the young assistant commissary on his way to Vienna, or even from the sophisticated *italianizzato* of *Rome, Naples et Florence*, who speaks from these pages. His concerns are those of an elderly man fretting somewhat over the quality of his dinner and put out by the impoliteness or even by the coarse good manners of the Provençals. At Montpellier the butter looks like pomade, at a dismal concert at Toulouse, where the women are all unaccountably ugly, he stares gloomily at the audience through his opera-glasses, at Grasse the streets are filthy and his boredom at the inn is full of the smell of boiled resin from the scent factories. Touches like these enhance the value of *Voyage dans le Midi* as an indicator of Stendhal's sensibilities in late middle age. The journal alas ends abruptly at Valence, and there are none but the sketchiest hints as to the rest of the tour, carrying him at last into Switzerland and far up the Rhine.

Even while deeply imbrued in compiling his travel book, Stendhal had turned his thoughts once more towards fiction, more specifically to the rich resource uncovered during his idle hours among the libraries, archives and bookstalls of Rome. In a letter of March 1835 addressed to Romain Colomb, who was asked to hand it on to Domenico Fiore, he had expatiated at some length on the pleasures of browsing through old manuscript accounts of the scandals, murders and criminal exploits of the great Italian families in the sixteenth and seventeenth centuries, the sort of material which formerly excited the English dramatists of Shakespeare's age. The layers of dust on these volumes, he told his friends, were solid, the text made his eyes swim and 'every time my shirt turned dark grey'. Sometimes he had to read them on the spot, locked into the library by the archivist, but on other occasions he was actually able to purchase the manuscript, as in the case of a book of confessions written by a young *abbate* named Don Ruggiero, bastard son of a noble house, around the time of Queen Christina of Sweden's arrival in Rome in 1655.

By 1836 and his departure for Paris he had gathered together enough of these *historiettes*, anecdotes and memoirs of a late-Renaissance Italy of ruffs and farthingales, dagger-brandishing bravoes, blighted loves and midnight assignations to begin plundering them in earnest for contributions to French magazines, eager by now for the sort of costume-drama novellas and short stories which on the other side of the Channel had become staple fare for those watered-silk-bound annuals, 'The Keepsake', 'the Book of Beauty' or 'the Amulet', dominating fashionable literature in 1830s London. In March 1837 the *Revue des Deux Mondes* published *Vittoria Accoramboni*, Stendhal's translation of an outline narrative of the life of the famous courtesan around whom John Webster's tragedy *The White Devil* is woven, and in July of that year the same periodical offered its readers his version of the hideous brew of incest and murder making up the tale of Beatrice Cenci, out of which Percy Bysshe Shelley some twenty years earlier had tried not altogether successfully to fashion a verse drama. Further tales were either completed or partially sketched during the next two years, *La Duchesse de Palliano*, *L'Abbesse de Castro*, *Suora Scolastica* and *Trop de faveur tué*, all of them nowadays included among the *Chroniques italiennes*, the blanket heading devised by Romain Colomb when he issued them, together with *Vanina Vanini* and the sinister *San Francesco a Ripa*, completed in 1831, after Stendhal's death.

The temptation is obviously to dismiss these short fictions as mere morsels of sophisticated hackwork designed to keep their creator's hand in, until such time as he chose to turn towards more substantial inventions. In the case of *L'Abbesse de Castro* and *Suora Scolastica* this was patently not the case, and each can be seen as an attempt at deepening his experience of that novella or 'long story' medium which other contemporary writers, Mérimée, Balzac or Nodier in their widely differing modes, were able to master and stamp with significant individuality. Even *Les Cenci* and *Vittoria Accoramboni*, ostensibly direct renderings into French from Italian originals, convey a sense of Stendhal peering fascinated into the glass of bygone barbarities, torture, treachery, spiritual blackmail and the hierarchical pomps and vanities of a world far removed from the prosaic realities of steam navigation, the electric telegraph, elastic loops on trouser-bottoms, franchise reform, bicameral government and C-spring carriages, surrounding Henri Beyle in the late 1830s.

It may also be that, once more in the swim of his old Parisian life, he experienced again the inevitable concomitant of such an existence for him, an imaginative yearning for the ageless allure of Italy, however eagerly he might have hastened to France to scrape off the corrosion of Italian squalor, parochialism and political backwardness. Something of the old ferocity, violence and passion was still aflame among ordinary Italians, as he well knew. A year or so earlier in Rome, on a Sunday in April, he had been sitting in his lodgings neare the Corso reading a book by the archaeologist Jean-Antoine Letronne on the cosmology of the early Church Fathers, when he was told that a young girl had just been murdered in the doorway of a nearby trattoria. Hurrying to the scene he found her:

> still lying in the middle of the street; at the base of her head there was a pool of blood about a foot in diameter, foaming at its centre. The trickle of blood began from beside a cart guarded by a gendarme. . . . If the Pope and his ministers earned a scudo from every murder committed, I could understand their lack of concern. Three days ago a man was killed at the Trevi fountain for the sake of a single dried fig.

The implication of episodes such as these had its destined influence on Stendhal as a novelist. His last major attempt at fiction, *Le Rose et le Vert*, begun and abandoned in 1837, had been a leisurely reprise of the *Mina de Vanghel* story worked out in smaller compass some years before. This time the heroine was called Mina Wanghen, the daughter of a banker, who spreads a rumour after his death that her family has lost all its money, so as to deter the young men anxious to secure her fortune, and persuades her mother to take her to Paris. After the introduction of various key characters, a scheming abbé, a young duke, both essentially clichés of Stendhalian invention, and the development of Mina into a woman as red-blooded and combatively independent as her former avatar in the 1830 version, he relaxed his grip, leaving tantalizing evidence in a series of plans as to how the work was to have been carried on.

What obviously mastered him far more strongly at present was the image of Italian intrigue, passion and murder distilled through his magazine stories, fuelled as these were by the reading of manuscript chronicles, the very stuff, it must seem, of romance, yet all based on historical fact. During August 1838, the month in which the *Revue des Deux Mondes* published *La Duchesse de Palliano*, he had been looking over a seventeenth-century account of the meteoric rise of the Farnese family from almost complete obscurity to the enjoyment of immense power and wealth as sovereign dukes, cardinals and consorts of European royalty. On a page of the text he jotted the English words, highly significant as these turned out to be, 'to make of this sketch a romanzetto'.

The material in its crude form as *Origine delle grandezze della famiglia Farnese* lay magnificently to hand. The sensational story of the beautiful Vandozza, mistress of Rodrigo Borgia, later Pope Alexander VI, and her nephew Alessandro, who carried off a beautiful young girl after killing one of her attendants, was imprisoned in Castel Sant'Angelo, had a brief liaison with a woman named Clelia and ended as Pope Paul III, seemed to offer all Stendhal needed for the fashioning of a full-blooded historical romance. His imagination had dwelt on this, what is more, for several years, and we must make what we can of his subsequent assertion that the work which eventually emerged was really begun in 1830.

August passed into September, he renewed his agreeable visits to Giulia, called on Astolphe de Custine, living with his English lover Edward Saint-Barbe (whose handshake Stendhal found unsettling) in 'the perfection of the countryside only an hour and three quarters from the Opéra' and passed a critical eye over Alfred de Vigny's novel *Cinq-Mars*, an episode from the reign of Louis XIII. Such tales were now in high vogue, and it was only a year or so before Alexandre Dumas would consecrate the genre in France with his marvellous sequence of romances from the same period of history, beginning with *Les Trois Mousquetaires*.

Yet however Beyle might have embarked on turning the story of young Alessandro Farnese and his sexually freebooting aunt into an acceptable fiction, the emergent novel, rather like *Vanina Vanini*, managed to fuse the elements of sixteenth-century palace intrigue with a *mise-en-scène* firmly orientated in his own age, vibrant with echoes of his own experience, a drama whose political power drew its vitality from the reader's awareness – surely also the writer's own – that certain aspects of Italian life and feeling remain unchanged from one age to the next. What easier transformation therefore than to turn Vandozza Farnese into Gina Sanseverina, that archetype of the Stendhalian feminine dynamic, and her nephew into Fabrice del Dongo, the best-loved of his heroes, though probably for the wrong reasons? What more piquant beginning, among a bundle of dusty folios, for the work Stendhal eventually called, with a relevance justified only by its appearance in the book's final pages, *La Chartreuse de Parme*?

The circumstances of the novel's composition are among the most famous in the annals of modern literature. Every writer must wish for some infusion of the amazing creative oestrus which seized hold of Stendhal between 4 November 1838, when, shutting himself away in his rooms at Rue Caumartin, he began work on *La Chartreuse*, and 26 December, when he sent the '6 énormes cahiers' containing the completed book to Colomb, commissioned with finding him a publisher. In these fifty-two days, shutting out visitors and only allowing himself the occasional distraction of an evening at the opera and the Théâtre des Funambules or a call on the Montijos for a party and some Spanish songs, he followed the method employed with most of his other books, writing a rough draft of each section, then dictating a finished version to a copyist. On 24 January 1839 he signed a contract with Ambroise Dupont with an advance of 2500 francs in return for a cession of rights for five years, and the work was advertised two months later for sale at fifteen francs a copy as 'by the author of Le Rouge et le Noir'.

Skilful publicist though Dupont may have been (*Le Constitutionnel* of 17 March featured a 'taster' in the shape of the Waterloo episode), he was also, as noted in the case of the *Mémoires*, a merciless pennypincher when it came to the printed text. In order to reduce *La Chartreuse* to a manageable two volumes, Stendhal was compelled to cut the work either through paring down the already extant manuscript or else by suppressing various features he might have felt inclined to add at the last moment. The result was a final chapter of singular abruptness, in which the easy progression of the narrative is suddenly reduced to a headlong sequence of events whose seriousness, in the context of what has happened earlier between Fabrice and Clelia, is betrayed by the all-too evident need to wrap up the narrative within the confines of a second volume. In the space of a single page the young lovers' little son, Sandrino, dies, followed eight lines later by his mother. Fabrice, disposing of his property, retreats to the eponymous Charterhouse. Gina, retiring to a Lombard villa (significantly named Vignano, in allusion to Giulia Martini's country seat) where she 'united all the apparatus of happiness'*, dies soon after her nephew, who, we are told, only spent a year in his Charterhouse. Parma's prisons are empty, Count Mosca is immensely rich, and the new Duke Ernest V adored by his subjects. With a commendation 'to the happy few' the work ends.

Among those engaging instantly with *La Chartreuse de Parme* even in what Stendhal called its 'strangled' form, as a major achievement in the fiction of the age, was Honoré de Balzac, by now the lion among French novelists and someone whose critical opinions the author was bound to value. On 11 April 1839, a sunny spring day with an east wind blowing, according to Stendhal's note, they had met each other in the street and Balzac, complimenting him on the book and suggesting that he suppress the identity of 'Parma', told him there had been nothing like it for forty years. Such praise merely echoed two letters he had already written him, extolling *La Chartreuse* as 'a great and beautiful book', acknowledging its opening longueurs but asking Stendhal, in the event of a second edition, to take the opportunity to develop the hugger-mugger finale. If Machiavelli was writing a modern novel, he declared, it would be *La Chartreuse*. As for the difference between them as novelists, 'I make a fresco and you make statues', Balzac shrewdly opined.

These ideas and others on the book were expanded by the younger writer in a sixty-two-page critical account of the work published in the *Revue Parisienne* of 25 September 1840. Dividing

* The coincidence between Stendhal's 'tontes les apparences de bonheur' and Jane Austen's 'all the apparatus of happiness' used to describe Mrs Elton in *Emma* is striking, especially since he apparently never read her. Who was their common source?

contemporary literature into three classes, those of images, ideas and eclecticism, he placed Stendhal in the second class, alongside Mérimée, Béranger, Musset and Nodier, writers working in a manner defined by Balzac as inherently eighteenth-century, distinguished by concision, abundance of facts and sobriety of images. *La Chartreuse* was the masterpiece of the literature of ideas and its author was indeed the modern Machiavelli. Here was a work which could only have been conceived and executed by a man of fifty 'in the full potency of middle age and the maturity of all his talents'. We might add here that only a writer as prodigiously versatile as Balzac could have written this review, perhaps the profoundest tribute ever laid at Stendhal's feet. Translation does no sort of justice to paragraphs such as the one beginning: 'Entrons dans le terrible drame italien qui s'est lentement et logiquement préparé d'une façon charmante' – the whole experience of the novel, in its counterpoise of the terrible and the enchanting, captured in a single sentence. The novelist-turned-critic grasped quite uncannily the essential inspirations bringing the characters to life, the literary ancestry of the doctor Ferrante Palla, a *risorgimentale* liberal modelled partly on Stendhal's Milanese friend Rasori, in the high-stomached Balfour of Burley from Scott's *Old Mortality*, or the fact that Gina Sanseverina owed her vibrant authenticity to a real woman – or rather, as students of Stendhal's life may guess, to a whole gallery of them. 'It is time to do justice to M. Beyle. Our epoch owes him a great deal. . . .'

When Stendhal received the *Revue Parisienne* article off the steamer at Civitavecchia, he went into ecstasy combining delight at the genuine fervour of Balzac's admiration with a certain measure of embarrassment at having to explain his working techniques and imaginative flashpoints to someone whose enthusiasm had been offset by several serious reservations as to the narrative style of *La Chartreuse*. All three drafts exist of the letter he eventually nerved himself to write in reply, and these form not merely a vindication of certain debatable aspects of the book's structure and tone, but an invaluable guide to Stendhal's literary aesthetic, defined by a perspective stretching back unmistakably to his earliest childhood years under the tutelage of his enlightened grandfather, Dr Gagnon, his great-aunt Elisabeth with her lofty *espagnolisme* and the elegant libertinage of his uncle Romain.

It is obvious, from reading these letters to Balzac and from a glance at the host of corrections and addenda with which he annotated the copy later belonging to Victor Jacquemont's friend Achille Chaper, that Stendhal was not happy with *La Chartreuse de Parme* as it stood and felt that even without his fellow novelist's strictures on its formal shortcomings, the book needed greater consistency and polish. Yet what, in the end, should we have gained, or graver still, what might have been sacrificed from this, the best-loved of all the author's works, so well known indeed among a certain kind of reader that mere mention of a place name such as Sacca or Grianta will instantly conjure up the precise Stendhalian association? If Balzac's advice had been followed, we should probably have lost that superb opening, a lyrical overture of *bonheur à la Beyle*, a joyous Napoleonic orgasm, flinging us irresistibly, with the young Henri himself, into the midst of the sensuous Italian vortex. Fabrice, everybody's favourite cute young cub, might by the same token have accumulated heavier touches of chiaroscuro around his character especially towards the close, but such a technical adjustment would certainly have been at the cost of that naturalness and spontaneity in the growth of so unpredictable a hero which serve to enhance the work's momentum.

We would rather *La Chartreuse de Parme* triumphant over its notional imperfections than scrubbed into a decorous artistic urbanity. The rugged grandeur of its design and performance recalls the distinction once made between Corneille and Racine, the former portrayed as a grizzled veteran glorious amid his wounds, the latter as an elegant smooth-tongued ambassador: appropriately for a writer whose preference was for the warrior of *Le Cid* rather than the courtier of *Iphigénie*, the novel's spirit seems emphatically Cornelian rather than Racinian. A vast Stendhalian palimpsest scribbled over with countless strands of memory and association, it enfolds everything from the inspiration of his love for such widely diverse muses as Angela Pietragrua, Metilde Dembowski and Giulia Rinieri de' Rocchi to the harshest of political realities (instantly spotted by Balzac) embodied in the obvious parallels between Ranuce Ernest and the iniquitous Francesco IV, Duke of Modena, whose regime was a byword for repressive obscurantism in Stendhal's Italy. Yet this same Italy, as envisaged by the author, transcends the inventive multitudinousness with which he intially engages our admiration. If Stendhal chose to discard Balzac's suggestion that he suppress the specific identity of the Parmesan setting, it was not simply because he had certain precise spots in mind, but because much of what happens in the book and many of its characters, among them the morally tortuous Count Mosca and of course Gina herself, appear inconceivable without the dimension of Italy in those crucial early years after Napoleon's fall, historical only in the sense that they were not immediately contemporary with the writing of the book. Benedetto Croce's objection that Stendhal was giving us 'the Italy of his dreams' rather than the real thing is unjustified when we see how faithfully, both in its largeness of gesture and in the indulgence of its comic irony, *La Chartreuse* replicates the spirit of that Milanese romantic world, the world of Ludovico di Breme, Silvio Pellico and others, in which he had most authentically known who he was. We do not require much hindsight to feel that with the advance of age and the encroachments of mortality he wanted to remember what it had all been like.

At least one early reader of *La Chartreuse de Parme* was moved to record a poignant reaction to the work – in a purely biographical light indeed, the most poignant of all – only a month before the *Revue Parisienne* article appeared. During the August of 1840, Félix Faure had gone to the spa of Uriage-les-Bains, some ten miles from Grenoble, to take the waters, noted for their efficacy in the treatment of rheumatism and skin diseases. It was almost certainly more than a decade since 'Happy' had seen his old schoolfellow Henri Beyle. He was now a peer of the realm, president of the Royal Court of Justice at Grenoble, and the owner of a country estate at Saint-Ismier inherited from his father.

Though he had brought the best of his legal skill to the tangled business of trying to recover something from Chérubin Beyle's estate which should console Henri for the 'Jesuit's deceptions, the unfavourable outcome had strained an already weakening friendship. When in 1834 Faure had become centrally involved, in his capacity as a newly-created peer, in the business of passing sentence on those most implicated in the recent industrial unrest at Lyons and Grenoble, Stendhal's confused resentments found an outlet in the series of high-minded denunciations of his friend as a government lackey which litter *Vie de Henry Brulard*.

At Uriage, seating in the shade of a popular avenue, Faure started to read *La Chartreuse de Parme.* Given the naked immediacy of Stendhal's personal engagement with his readers, the experience was bound to prove traumatic. Félix can scarcely have avoided feeling a certain bitterness when their friendship lessened, and it must have induced something of a shiver to hear, in such articulate clarity of enunciation, this voice once dear to him, now lost. Perhaps this was why he felt moved to record at some length his reaction, not so much to the book as to its author.

Judging Stendhal to be striving too hard after effect, he discerned links between such laboured artificiality and the author's failure to make a public career for himself after the fall of Napoleon. The resulting rancour, he believed, was what now induced Beyle to denigrate the upper classes and vilify the present social order. 'I recognize here, not the original Beyle, so loyal, so good, so frankly generous, created by nature and by his respected grandfather Dr Gagnon, but a Beyle angry, embittered disillusioned through being deceived'. The villains, Faure maintained, were the lying, Jesuitical Chérubin and the libertine Martial Daru, early role model for Henri in his amorous adventures, and to them might be added the philosopher Helvétius, whose theories of self-interest in hum an motivation formed the basis of the youthful Beyle's 'system'. As for the style, it was that of the writer's own conversation, recognized at once in phrases such as 'fou de bonheur', '*fou de joie*', and in its overall quality of free-flowing carelessness. In the margin of his critique Faure wrote: 'Say no more of Beyle as he is now, but speak instead of the early Beyle I knew. As for his present condition, I do not know what has become of him.'

In the late June of 1839 Stendhal's long Paris *congé* came to an end. By way of Switzerland, Turin and Genoa he descended into Italy, resuming his consular duties at Civitavecchia in mid-August. He had been kept up to date with office business and local affairs by letters from Tavernier, whose tone was always respectful, but he can have been under no illusions as to the possibility of further trouble between them. Donato Bucci had already taken the trouble to tell him that on the day after his departure for France in 1836, 'le Grec' had picked the lock of his study, but on being confronted with this in the presence of Stendhal's servants Toto and Susanna, had imperturbably denied it, even though Bucci had found several books scattered on the floor and nibbled by rats. Susanna's information that Tavernier had stolen several of the consul's shirts was soon afterwards confirmed by a further note from the ever-loyal Bucci.

Further proof of Tavernier's dishonesty was furnished by an episode which took place just before Stendhal's return. In advance he had sent off from France, by the steamer *Sully*, several boxes of books and personal papers, news of which reached the ear of one of the cardinals, Lambruschini, who gave orders to the Apostolic Delegate at Civitavecchia, Monsignor Grech Delicata, to open the packing cases and send an inventory. Delicata, of whom Beyle seems generally to have thought well, replied that the books had been deposited with the police by Tavernier – surely not activated by any motives other than compromising his already politically suspect employer – and that the secretary, doubtless so as to give himself a character for absolute integrity, declined to assist at the opening of the boxes. When the Cardinal repeated his order, Delicata, failing to get Bucci to witness the exmination, carried it out in the presence of two police officers.

What they found constitutes the most valuable testimony we possess to the full scope of Stendhal's reading. As well as dictionaries, guidebooks, maps and almanacs, there are his favourite authors, Shakespeare, Montesquieu, Pascal, Napoleonic memoirs, English novels (including Dickens's recently published *Pickwick Papers*, all three lines of its serpentine full title faithfully copied out) works by the writer's acquaintances such as Duvergier de Hauranne, Astolphe de Custine and the leading critic Arnould Frémy, odd volumes of Muratori's *Annali d'Italia*, Cervantes and Chateaubriand, a miniature library of French and English classics in seventy-eight parts, a whole scatter of ancient authors, Horace, Virgil, Livy and Dionysius of Halicarnassus, the complete works of Xavier de Maistre, a satire written in Toulousain dialect, the letters of Mme du Deffand and William Robertson's *History of Scotland*.

Among these, promiscuously bundled up and now unceremoniously rummaged through so that a list could be made of works deemed subversive or at least worthy of the censor's scrutiny (the final roster of such items runs to eight pages) were the manuscripts of several unfinished Stendhalian projects, including *Le Rose et le Vert*, *Suora Scolastica* and *Le Chevalier de Saint-Ismier*, a historical tale set in the Richelieu period so profitably mined by Dumas, and adapted from a story by the Spanish playwright Tirso de Molina. What was not listed was an altogether more serious and groundbreaking attempt at a new novel, in the wake of *La Chartreuse*, which the writer had started a month or so before leaving Paris.

The incomplete torso which has come down to us as *Lamiel* took its earliest inspiration from a prostitute whom Stendhal identifies as 'Amiel', spotted in the Rue Saint-Denis near the Bastille, but its roots are far more deeply planted in recollections of his early love Mélanie Guilbert and certain details of her life and character. The story reflects the impact, both of the kind of picaresque Spanish romances on which *Le Chevalier de Saint-Ismier* had been based and of Balzac's novel *Le Père Goriot*, published in 1834. Lamiel, a Norman village girl of dubious parentage, is taken on as a companion by the recently widowed Duchesse de Miossens. Eloping to Paris with the Duchess's son, Fédor, she falls seriously in love with the notorious criminal Valbayre. After being tried and sent to the galleys, he orders her, via an accomplice, to rob the young Duke Fédor, whom she is eventually compelled to marry through the agency of the grotesque hunchbacked Dr Sansfin, a character apparently based as much on Stendhal's notions of himself as on hints from elsewhere. Valbayre, having regained his freedom, returns to Paris, is sentenced to death for murder and commits suicide. To avenge his death Lamiel burns down the Palais de Justice and her charred corpse is discovered in the ruins.

Only the first sixteen chapters of this sensational outline were ever completed, though a recent Gallimard edition of *Lamiel* (1983) contains a detailed reconstruction by Anne-Marie Meininger of its fragmented process of composition, which continued almost to the day Stendhal died. The materials are far too complex to include here, but Meininger's implication that through his imaginative recovery of the lost image of Mélanie via Lamiel he was led at last to abandon the novel seems not altogether plausible. The heroine herself was far too interesting a figure for Stendhal to let go: a lineal descendant of Mathilde de la Mole, Mina de Vanghel and Vanina Vanini, she is an astonishing mixture of venturesome innocence, casual brutality and emotional coldness, in which she is partly tutored by the satanic Sansfin. 'The book's real interest,' Stendhal wrote at the beginning of one of his various plans, 'will arrive when there is genuine love.' In fact the heroine, identified elsewhere in his notes by her 'dégoût profond pour la pusillanimité' and her 'hardiesse dans l'orgie', represents one of the most distinctive and potentially forceful realizations of the female by a male writer in the entire tradition of the nineteenth-century novel. Regarding the tone, if, as the author told Balzac, he had deliberately cultivated his stylistic plainness in *La Chartreuse* by regularly reading the official parliamentary bulletins while composing it, in *Lamiel* he adopted an even harder-edged manner, à la Sansfin, as we might say, exemplified in that celebrated scene in Chapter XI where, mystified by the whole phenomenon of love and sex, she nonchalantly forfeits her virginity.

The whole episode is richly comic, but the humour is bitter, *grinçant*, almost an essay in Beylian self-mockery. Having heard the peasant girls talk about 'going for a walk in the woods' Lamiel arranges an assignation with a strapping blond yokel whose Norman money-grubbing soul cannot resist her ten-franc bribe. They meet as agreed, he kisses her and she tells him: 'I want to be your mistress.' 'Ah, that's different,' said Jean with a businesslike air, and so without excitement or love the young Norman made Lamiel his mistress. 'Is that all?' said Lamiel. 'That's all,' answered Jean. 'Have you had lots of mistresses?' 'I've had three.' 'And there's nothing else?' 'Not as far as I know.' He leaves after being given a further five francs. 'Lamiel sat down and watched him go. (She wiped away the blood and hardly noticed the pain.) Then she burst out laughing as she repeated to herself, "So that's all this famous love amounts to!"' At which point, with brilliant dramatic timing, young Fédor de Miossens makes an appearance.

No sooner had Stendhal resumed work on *Lamiel* in October 1839 than Prosper Mérimée arrived to pay a visit. Close as their association was, no friend of Henri's had ever been safe from his private litany of complaint at the shortcomings of those he supposedly held dear, and Mérimée was now destined, like others before him, to be found wanting in that barely definable quality which redeemed choice spirits from the commonplace. The nickname 'Clara' had been replaced by 'Academus' – one supposes Stendhal was jealous of his fellow writer's successful absorption into the French cultural establishment – and on a trip to Naples the older man fretted at the younger's appalling vanity. The jaunt was not a success: Beyle had always been ambiguous in his feelings towards the Neapolitans and now he found the autumn sun too strong, the Teatro San Carlo 'destestable from every aspect' and the women positively hideous, incapable of passion or emotion.

This was all included in a private letter. His consular dispatches, addressed to Marshal Soult, Duke of Dalmatia, that indefatigable survivor from the days of Napoleonic *gloire* who was now briefly Foreign Minister and had represented France at Queen Victoria's coronation, took on an altogether greater sobriety and detachment than those tattling man-of-the-world gazettes he had dashed off in the past to Mole and Broglie. When François Guizot took over at the end of 1840 a rather more skittish tone came discreetly into play. Guizot plainly expected a more intensive flow of political and commercial information from his consul, which the latter was at pains to supply, yet even here a sly aside could enliven the dreariest bulletin. Did a smile cross the features of 'Monsieur le Ministre' when he read the report, for example, of Civitavecchia's relatively pacific condition in the context of Italian political edginess and caught Stendhal ironically observing that its inhabitants 'are interested merely in earning money and getting double or triple the price for articles sold to travellers arriving off the steamers'?

The journeys to Rome had resumed almost as soon as Beyle returned *en poste*, and it was in December 1839 while working on

Lamiel at his lodgings in Via Condotti that Stendhal fell seriously in love for the last time. On this occasion it was a graver matter than something which might have been scribbled in the margin of a book or on the leaf of his manuscript (though we can indeed glean the usual harvest of relevant notes from both these sources). Now he actually set out a logbook of the affair, which as he said 'reminded me of the situation of 1819 and 1820, *in the time of* Metilde', yet the result is more surrealistically cryptic than any of his other private memorials, and certain aspects of it, despite the considerable detective work carried out by François Michel in 1953 on the notebook and its accompanying marginalia remains baffling to Stendhal scholars.

With prophetic decisiveness the cahier is headed in English 'The Last Romance' and the object of the writer's passion is identified here and elsewhere solely by the name 'Earline', which caused Romain Colomb, reading through it some years afterwards, to think that the woman in question was English. One such candidate has been suggested in the form of a Mrs Hugh Caldwell, wife of an Indian Army colonel resident in Rome, whose maiden name was Mary Anne Earle, but no real evidence exists to support this, and in any case a far likelier figure seems to fit almost perfectly into the frame. This was a woman already well known to Stendhal, an authentic Italian society beauty, flirtatious, enchanting, fond of parties and dancing, no less than his 'Contessa Sandre', Giulia Cini.

To her husband he had written a number of friendly letters from Paris, perhaps partly with the idea of ingratiating himself so as more easily to pursue the Countess when he got back to Rome. His relations with them both, already close, grew still warmer during the 1840 carnival season of February and March, when he visited the family nearly every day, met them regularly at social gatherings, made toy soldiers for their children and was even able to touch his 'Earline' on the knee while fingering the material of her dress. The fly in the ointment, however, remained Don Filippo Caetani, still in amorous attendance on the Countess and now referred to in the cahier as 'Valri' – *rival*, by that system of inversion beloved by Stendhal whereby for example Rome becomes 'Mero' or 'Omar' and the Papal Secretary of State Cardinal Bernetti is turned into 'Nettiber'.

Not for nothing had he entitled his 'Earline' notebook 'The Last Romance'. The ambiguity here is significant, for it is both the record of a late-flowering passion, a stirring of that irrepressible Stendhalian spark of love which validated his existence, and also a final attempt at a novel, notes towards the story of an elderly man, a young woman in the prime of her beauty, and a youthful *cavaliere servente*, with a husband most inconveniently neither odious nor foolish, and a meddling mother-in-law who, one comment implies, may have helped to poison whatever chances the writer fancied himself to possess.

In their inchoate scrambling of emotion, introspection and memory, and in the sense so potently conveyed of the act of writing either as a means of capturing an impression before it escapes or as a species of ritual calculated to exorcise the dangerous intensity of sensation, the 'Earline' manuscripts are a poignant illustration, if any were needed, that Stendhal's heart was the same tenderest of organisms it had been since those terrible earliest moments of joy and anger during his Grenoble childhood. There is something intolerably moving, for anyone who loves this man and his books, in his constant reference here to earlier ideas and experiences of passion. The old magic of 'crystallization' from *De l'Amour* is invoked more than once, and there are cryptic references to Alexandrine Daru, to Metilde Dembowski and to 'la saison des évènements de Saint-Remo par Menti'. Perhaps the most heart-wrenchingly honest note of all, scribbled on the 16 June 1840, reads: 'Character of Dominique, his habitual indulgence in the art of seeking *the happiness*. He dreams incessantly, and his greatest sorrow comes from detaching himself from such dreaming.'

Under the spell of Giulia Cini, Stendhal set out, on 10 April, that extraordinary list of twenty-three articles headed *Les Privilèges* which amounts essentially to a self-portrait of someone whose main problem had always been that he was far too intelligent to suffer fools gladly. God, he thought, might give him the privileges of never having to suffer serious illness, only three days' indisposition a year and death in bed while asleep. His penis would be allowed to grow erect at will, be two inches longer and give him pleasure twice a week. A magic ring would enable him to make any woman fall in love, he would have fine hair, excellent teeth, good skin, play whist, billiards and chess to perfection, sit a horse well and be a skilful fencer. He could change into any animal he chose, become invulnerable and run five leagues in an hour. Every day there would be a gold napoleon in his pocket, he would no longer be plagued by fleas, scorpions, mosquitoes and mice, and he would have the power to change a dog into a woman with the wit of Virginie Ancelot and the heart of Mélanie Guilbert. Two hundred times a year he would have a lynx's eyes and the physical agility of the *funambule* Deburau.

The reality, alas, was that he was learning instead to compromise with life as it was. He no longer hoped for a change of consular posting, honestly admitting to himself that he preferred staying in Civitavecchia and Rome to moving anywhere else. A little lark-shooting in the company of the dogs he now kept for the sake of having something to love – the one a black, melancholy English spaniel, the other, called Lupetto, coffee-coloured and playful – a spot of archaeology (he wrote excitedly to Soult about a group of huge marble statues discovered at Cerveteri and described his collection of antique bronze medals to Eugénie de Montijo) work on touching up *La Chartreuse* and rereading favourite authors such as Saint-Simon and Buffon, provided Beyle's *menus plaisirs*, as well as, of course, the consolation of good singing at the opera. At Civitavecchia's theatre the sensation of 1841, in Donizetti's *L'esule di Roma*, was the contralto Luisa Mollica, whom he could hear practising 'one square and two streets away'. All the local girls hated her because she was so gay and talkative and charming, but the consul was enchanted, the more so because his servant Toto had fallen in love with her. Toto, it should be added, was something of a liability: he had stabbed his former mistress, and Stendhal had saved him from a severe sentence by contriving to get rid of the dagger.

Meanwhile, whatever the ongoing Roman drama of his feelings for Countess Cini, it was the continuing lure of the other Giulia, formerly Rinieri de' Rocchi, now Signora Martini, which drew him once again to Florence. If he needed a pretext for a further Tuscan trip during the summer of 1840, it was offered by a joint project with Abraham Constantin for turning the latter's notes on Renaissance painters into a readable text, to be published by Gian Pietro Vieusseux as *Idées italiennes sur quelques tableaux célèbres*, though Stendhal was not exactly optimistic about the chances of such a book selling in Italy. It was in his Florentine lodging in Borgo San Lorenzo that he could meet once more with Giulia, and the pair were reunited a month later after his brief homeward dash to Civitavecchia, when he noted in his copy of *La Chartreuse*: '4th Sept. *she a time* 6th Sept *I a time*, Sunday, rain. I insist on her staying a while, *the husband* present, otherwise I'd have gone.' Giulia's constant devotion to Henri was indeed impressive: the following year, at almost the same time, after hearing a performance of Bellini's *Beatrice di Tenda*, the pair slept together at the Albergo Porta Rossa (still happily in existence as a hotel) where he recorded ominously that the occasion was 'perhaps the last of his life' as in fact it turned out to be.

His eye could still be caught by a handsome woman, and in July 1841 he was delighted to hail the arrival in Civitavecchia of Mme Bouchot, daughter of the famous operatic bass Luigi Lablache, to whom Stendhal pays tribute in *Le Rouge et le Noir* and married to a French painter. Her forename was Cecchina (recalling that of the maidservant in *La Chartreuse de Parme* which the author inexplicably insists on phoneticizing to the un-Italian-looking 'Chékina') and he was soon referring to her as 'Miss Bouche' or 'mme Os', from the Latin *os, oris*, a mouth. By 5 August she had become 'an oasis in the desert of life at Civitavecchia' and the consul had enjoyed her favours. Soon afterwards her lover, the French-naturalized German artist Henri Lehmann arrived on a sketching trip and drew a rather awkwardly proportioned but highly characterful head-and-shoulders of Stendhal, the last likeness ever taken of him. It was Lehmann who became the object of what may have been a slightly spiteful joke on Beyle's part. One evening, when Mme Bouchot had been complaining to a gathering of her compatriots about a thieving chambermaid, Stendhal with mock pomposity declared:

> Yes, Madame, in my capacity as consul I must confirm your suspicions. The information at my disposal allows me to declare

> that your days are in danger, and by virtue of the powers invested in me by my function, I order my compatriot M. Lehmann, here present, to lend you his assistance in case of need at the critical moment: this very night, and henceforth until the departure of the next boat to Naples, he is to sleep in your bedroom.

A closer inspection of Lehmann's sketch, beneath which Stendhal's remark about the oasis is inscribed, reveals something wrong with the right side of the face, a slight upward twisting of the features as if part of a general facial rictus, evidence that the sitter had indeed suffered from a recent stroke. During work on *Lamiel* the previous year he fainted and fell into the fire, later telling Fiore that he was taking belladonna for a series of migraines and had bought himself a gun. 'In short, is it worth the bother of living?' Consulting various doctors, he began a homoeopathic regime, with a course of arnica, nux vomica and bryony, cold baths and mustard plasters, but in March 1841 he had his first 'brush with nothingness' in the shape of a serious stroke. Writing to Fiore, now his chief confidant in such matters (Mareste, once such a cherished alter ego, disappears altogether from the existing correspondence after 1836) he observed, with a fine flourish of his old Moscow courage: 'It's only the immediate sensation which is disagreeable, and this horror arises from all the stupid nonsense put into our heads when we're three years old.' He had had four memory lapses in a year, little intervals of six to eight minutes when 'the mind works well enough, but without words'. While dining at a restaurant with Constantin he had to make incredible efforts to recall the word for a glass. 'During the last attack but one, at dawn, I continued getting dressed to go shooting. As well to be knocked out there as anywhere else.'

Now he started to feel faint at least four or five times a day: every night he lay down to sleep he wondered whether he might not wake up again. 'I haven't asked the doctor the name of this illness, so as not to have to think about it.' By 19 April 1841 the letters to Fiore had assumed a distinctly valedictory turn. The Pope's personal physician, Dr Clemens Alertz of Aix-la Chapelle, came to see him, and the kind and ever-attentive Constantin called each day. 'He gilds the pill for me, which isn't too bitter; I hope to recover. But in case this letter turns out to be *L'ultima*, I want to make my farewells to you. I really love you, and you're not exactly one of a crowd. Adieu, make the best of whatever happens.'

As things befell, this was not quite the end, but Stendhal wanted now to consult the one doctor he really trusted, Jean-Louis Prévost of Geneva, whose intervention, he believed, had rescued him from serious decline years previously. Writing to Guizot on 9 August, he begged for leave as soon as Tavernier should return from a journey to Constantinople, and a week later this was granted. Leaving Civitavecchia for ever on 22 October, with all his papers in order, he arrived two days afterwards at Marseilles, where a rendezvous had been arranged with his old Florentine friend Vincenzo Salvagnoli, who was instantly struck by the consul's air of fretfulness and exhaustion. At Geneva Stendhal seemed so ill that Salvagnoli had to give up the idea of a walk along the lake shore, and when they at length reached Paris early in the morning of 8 November, Romain Colomb, meeting his cousin after two years, was horrified to see how old and sick he looked. The single ironic compensation was that the old Beylian asperity seemed somewhat softened under the pressure of physical suffering. 'He understood better those little duties which sustain social relationships and carried them out more punctiliously; everything about him appeared more communicative and affectionate. In short, the changes in him worked to the advantage of his sociability.'

Others too, though forcibly struck by the alteration, agreed with Colomb. Virginie Ancelot's sixteen-year-old daughter, Louise, towards whom Stendhal played the role of a bantering uncle, observed: 'If his spirit has diminished, his heart seems to have gained.' Mme Ancelot herself, an inveterate string-puller in the Parisian literary world, had the idea of putting him up as a candidate for the French Academy, an honour as unlikely as it was richly deserved, but though he obviously took the suggestion seriously, he confided to his interleaved copy of *La Chartreuse*: 'I haven't any reputation at all in 1842. . . . Literary life such as it is in the 1840s is a wretched business. It reveals the most contemptible instincts of our nature and those most productive of minor unhappiness.' Nevertheless he continued to work the novel over and to complete his Italian tale *Suora Scolastica* for a collected edition of his shorter fiction, as well as writing a new preface for *De l'Amour*.

If this was holding back the inevitable, so too were his trips to the theatre or to hear the first performance in Paris of Rossini's *Stabat Mater*, in January 1842 in front of a rapt audience with a line-up of star soloists including Giulia Grisi and her lover Mario di Candia, the aristocratic tenor so adored by the young Queen Victoria. In former years Stendhal, great Rossinian as he was, might have penned an appreciative magazine article, like his friend Delécluze, who reviewed the piece for the *Journal des Débats*, or at least entered his opinions in a journal or a letter – the work was, after all, a rare late blossoming from a talent which its owner had otherwise suppressed after his 'retirement' with *Guillaume Tell* in 1829. As it was, Beyle merely scribbled the words 'Stabat Grisi le 19 Janvier 42'.

Rossini would live on, a cheerful if always enigmatic bon vivant, for another quarter of a century: Stendhal's life had almost run its course. On 22 March 1842, having dictated some more pages of *Suora Scolastica* to the copyist earlier in the day, he went out to dine with Guizot at the Foreign Ministry. Dinner then was not the late occasion it has become in these final years of our own century, and he left the Ministry, the Hôtel Bertin in Rue Neuve-des-Capucines, around seven in the evening. Outside the building he was suddenly overtaken by a severe apoplexy and collapsed on the pavement. Carried into a shop across the road, he was first attended by a German doctor named Weiland, hastily summoned from round the corner in Rue Caumartin. About twenty minutes later, either by an extraordinary coincidence or because someone there knew of his connection with Beyle, Romain Colomb arrived and had his already unconscious cousin carried to his lodgings at the Hôtel de Nantes in Rue Neuve-des Petits Champs, an elegant eighteenth-century house which still survives. There, at two o'clock in the morning of 23 March, Stendhal died at the age of fifty-nine. 'I find that there's nothing ridiculous,' he had told Fiore in a letter written soon after his first stroke, 'about dropping dead in the streets, as long as one doesn't do it deliberately.'

In the nineteenth of his twenty-one wills, Stendhal had expressed a wish to be hurried straight to the grave without unnecessary expense. Colomb quite correctly ignored this, and the funeral service took place in the church of L'Assomption in what is now Place Maurice-Barrès, joining Rue Saint-Honoré and Rue Duphot. The invitation to the ceremony was issued on behalf of the writer's sisters Pauline Périer-Lagrange and Zénaïde Mallein. The former inherited, under the terms of the twenty-first will, three-quarters of whatever might result from the sale of Stendhal's property entrusted to Donato Bucci. Presumably she attended the funeral, but it is hard to accept Mérimée's statement that only three people (the other two being himself and Colomb) followed the coffin to its rest.

This in any case was only temporary. Stendhal had wanted to be buried either at Andilly, outside the city, or else at the cemetery of Montmartre, in those days a peaceful, half-rustic graveyard among inns and windmills, and Colomb, faithful to the memory of a cousin who had always rather patronized him, was determined to arrange things properly, though without undue expense. The body was finally interred in the cemetery's lower and cheaper section, with a marble plaque replaced somewhat more grandly on the fiftieth anniversary of Stendhal's death by a monument incorporating the sculptured medallion portrait by David d'Angers, topped by the urn from the original tomb bearing the initials 'H.B.'. By the 1920s the Cimetière de Montmartre itself had long been absorbed into the Parisian urban sprawl, and the general air of grimy neglect overhanging Stendhal's corner of the graveyard caused concern to his admirers, but a scheme to replace the monument with something grander fell victim to a spiteful intervention by no less a *stendhalien* than Henri Martineau. Only in 1962 was the grave opened, the surviving remains reinterred in a small coffin and the tomb re-erected.

Three of the wills had been quite specific on the subject of an epitaph, and the inscription has achieved its own celebrity in French literary annals. In 1822, while profoundly nostalgic for Milan and Metilde in the course of reading Ermes Visconti's *Dialogo sulle unità dramatiche di tempo e di luogo*, which he adapted for the first version of *Racine et Shakespeare*, Stendhal had sought to encapsulate his own understanding of who he really was and what honestly mattered to him by making up a mock memorial inscription. This appears again at the end of an autobiographical sketch written in Paris during his long *congé* and in the wills of 1836, 1837 and 1840. The outline of its opening words is basically the same in each case – 'Arrigo Beyle, Milanese, visse, scrisse, amo' – though in the 1822 version the name is rendered in its more common Italian form as 'Enrico'. The epitaph's general significance hardly needs underlining. Its three verbs, 'lived', 'wrote' 'loved', in that order, emphasize mounting degrees of importance, while the use of Italian and the localizing adjective *Milanese* show Stendhal's deepest emotional loyalty to have remained unchanged with the passing of years.

In *Souvenirs d'Egotisme*, telling us that he had originally dreamed up the inscription in Milan in 1820, he adds to the original words a sentence in Italian meaning 'This soul adored Cimarosa, Mozart and Shakespeare'. The officious Colomb was certainly having none of this: though he allowed the *Milanese* to pass (in spite of declaring later, as a result of a calumny made up by Tavernier, that Stendhal had chosen the adoptive citizenship as a protest against France's humiliation over the Eastern Question in 1840) the verbs were reshuffled, with writing first, followed by love, and life taking the lowest place.

Whatever Henri Beyle's dim view of his contemporary fame, he would have been wryly amused by the widespread reporting of his death in the French newspapers. Most of them agreed that he was 'un homme de talent' who had published several novels under the pseudonym of 'Frédéric Stendhal', though one referred to 'Baron de Stendhal' and warned its readers against confusing him with a certain 'Frédéric Styndall', hero of a novel by a M. de Kératry – which was precisely what the shorter obituaries had done. Far worthier and more extensive tributes were published in the *Revue des Deux Mondes* by Auguste Bussière and in *Le Courrier Français* by Paul Merruau, who ended his noble lament by saying: 'If he sought for happiness, which we all pursue, principally in the pleasure of the mind; if he brought together every kind of emotion in his somewhat materialist philosophy, yet he never neglected those impressions which address themselves to the nobler instincts of the soul.' The journalist and critic Paul-Emile Forgues, writing in *Le National* under the alias 'Old Nick', in the past a judicious reviewer of Stendhal's works, was similarly admiring, the tone of his article shadowed by indignation at those editors who could not even be bothered to get the dead man's name right, the name of:

> a studious observer of human passions . . . the only man to whom Diderot, were he alive today, would stretch out his hand . . . the ingenious analyst to whom we owe the truest definition ever given of love . . . . author of two novels which connoisseurs have already singled out from all the rubbish produced in the genre by our dismal age of magazine serials.

Colomb, who was to produce his own Stendhal memoir in due course, was more immediately concerned with disposing of the writer's meagre estate and arranging with the admirably scrupulous Bucci as to the sale of effects left behind at Civitavecchia, in rooms the egregious Tavernier had sealed with an officiousness that in his case seemed decidedly suspect. The main object of both executors was evidently to provide, as far as the will allowed and sometimes beyond that, for Stendhal's sister Pauline, his principal legatee. The 'cara sorella' was now an elderly, almost blind and semi-invalid widow, living in the most straitened circumstances at Enghien-les-Bains outside Paris, where she worked as an attendant at the spa baths. Doubtless she was happy to receive the extra money offered by Bucci from his own share in the legacy derived from selling the consul's books, as well as to be given the proceeds of Colomb's sale of Stendhal's clothes, one overcoat, a pair of braces, four pairs of stockings, sixteen shirts, four waistcoats and a few other items, making a mere 130 francs. In the end, after Mareste, Alberthe de Rubempré and others had clubbed together to provide her with an annual pension of 100 francs, Pauline returned to that very Grenoble from which she, like Henri, had been so eager to escape, and died in 1857, aged seventy-one, in the care of Zénaïde, the *rapporteuse*, the other sister, conspicuously unloved but possibly more content with life than either of her two more colourful siblings.

The fate of Stendhal's surviving friends and relatives was to recall, with increasing indulgence and regret, mingled with rueful amusement, their eccentric, opinionated and – with all his faults – adored *grand homme*, and in such recollection to sense an irreparable loss. Against the captious remarks of the few who stubbornly refused to recognize his stature, such as the *littérateur* J. P. Viennet, whose contemporary memoirs damn Stendhal to perdition with such comments as 'he made up stories for his dinner' or 'an attack of apoplexy delivered us from him on the 24 March' (all because Stendhal had accused him of not understanding Romanticism) could be set a whole array of moving testimonies to his effect on hearts and minds.

If Mérimée, who chose to publish his spirited memoir *H. B.* anonymously in a twenty-five-copy edition in 1850, took a dim view of the likelihood that later generations would appreciate Stendhal, and thus laid himself open to the charge that he had never really understood the man himself, a less guarded view was taken by Bucci, growing old in his little shop at Civitavecchia among his Etruscan vases and dusty inscriptions. Visited one boiling August afternoon in 1861 by the Russian diplomat Felix Meyendorff on his way to Rome, who described him as 'a doctrinaire liberal who has outlasted his epoch . . . the only really interesting article in his shop', he yielded to a flood of affectionate reminiscence. Meyendorff, with a truly Russian feeling for Stendhal, deduced that the writer had suffered from some unidentified hurt which forced him to take refuge in Civitavecchia like a storm-tossed ship. 'There is a chord vibrating mournfully throughout his works. . . . Endowed with a heart which stayed young despite his years, he underwent the sadness of a deep deception. It was too late for him to learn resignation. The knife seems to have stayed in the wound it made, which never closed up.' Bucci, giving Meyendorff a volume from Stendhal's edition of Lanzi's history of painting, the origin of the *Histoire de la Peinture en Italie*, told him that Stendhal's death had left an irreparable sense of emptiness.

For certain *beylistes* the loss was more ambiguous. Louis Crozet, telling Colomb, a few months after Beyle died, that he was the one who really understood the man and his ideas and tempting fate with the remark that 'I am perhaps the sole individual with whom our friend never played the fool', came into possession of a trunkful of several autograph manuscripts. Among them was *Vie de Henry Brulard*, which he forthwith sat up the entire night to read with mounting horror, riven by the utter mercilessness with which Stendhal dealt with Grenoble and the *grenoblois*, and warning Colomb afterwards not to show the work to anybody. Everyone, said Crozet, apart from the pair of them and their friend Louis de Barral, had been sacrificed without pity.

With Julie Gaulthier, 'L'aimable Jules', the act of memory was touched only by the purest love and understanding. Writing to Colomb, who was trying, in his splendidly conscientious fashion, to gather together a collection of Stendhal's correspondence, she recalled: 'He had such a deliciously relaxed manner in intimate conversation and was never so agreeable as when you forced him to get to the bottom of an idea. Add to this his horror of fools, his dislike of interrogations which obliged him to explain what he had thrown to the winds without premeditation.' Praising those flashes of genius endlessly lighting up his conversation, she exclaimed: 'Poor Henri; poor Beyle! he was destined to every sort of robbery, and people have stolen from all his works . . .' At her funeral in 1853 – she too was buried in Montmartre – Colomb, overcome with grief at hearing the handfuls of earth cast on the coffin by the mourners, turned away to weep for 'this woman, so good, so lovable, of so fine an intelligence, of a character so entrancing and so dear'.

Others among Stendhal's most intimate women friends lived on, silent for the most part amid their memories. Alberthe de Rubempré lamented him in the company of Delacroix – 'Où est le pauvre Beyle?' – Sarah Newton de Tracy bitterly regretted burning the letters she received from him. Sophie Duvaucel, having continuously cuckolded Admiral Ducrest de Villeneuve, died in 1867 a rich old widow, as indeed was Giulia Martini, whose husband had achieved a certain mournful distinction as an unflinchingly loyal supporter of the deposed Grand Duke Leopold of Tuscany whom Stendhal commended for building such good roads across his duchy. As for Eugénie de Montijo, hers was a grander, more sombre fate as Empress of the French, vilified for her supposed part in fomenting the war with Prussia which brought about Napoleon III's downfall. Widowed and living in English exile, she survived, an enthralled witness of whirlwind changes on the political stage of the world, until 1920, dying in her ninety-fourth year, the last surviving *beyliste*. It may be that at the time of writing there are still one or two very old people alive who recall having seen or even met her, a woman remarkable, among other things, for having sat on Stendhal's knee.

The advice she gave to the young diplomat in 1910 to read and learn from Stendhal was already well taken in France, and his reputation, both in his own country and elsewhere, is secure against serious assault on his position as one of the most consummately original figures in the entire literature of the world. His novels have been filmed and turned into television serials, Henri Sauguet made *La Chartreuse de Parme* into an opera in 1926 and Jacques Laurent forty years later attempted to finish off *Lamiel*. Gina Sanseverina's name found its way onto the labels of a line of female beauty products and an Italian psychiatrist devised the 'Stendhal syndrome' to refer to the state of emotional collapse, analogous to the writer's own, experienced by certain tourists in Florence visually overdosed on the city's aesthetic delights. Stendhal became, for better or worse, the author of a thousand epigrams and *bons mots* he had never made, and his writings provided the playground for lucubrations as diverse as that of Jean Sarocchi of Toulouse University, whose '*L'énergie syllabique ou l'ARA énergumène*' (1986) speculates most entertainingly on the prevalence of the letters a-r-a in the varous book titles, or of Jacques-Louis Douchin, investigating the significance of the numbers 7 (=Beyle) 3 (=his mother) 4 (= Chérubin and bad luck) in his *Esquisse de numérologie stendhalienne* (1984).

Perhaps all this reflects the spirit of what Stendhal once told Delacroix: 'Don't neglect anything which might make you great.' Yet there are times when, in our desire to invoke him as a protomodernist transcending those two worlds of Enlightenment and Romanticism in which he swayed uneasily from one foot to the other throughout his life, we forget the man himself in probing the mesmeric singularity of his textual inventions. While the object of this biography has been to place those same texts in their temporal framework and relate them here and there to particular inspirations, human, historical or topographical, and while I have tried to suggest to the reader that there may indeed be Stendhalian life, vast, gorgeous tracts of it, beyond the twin pillars of the inevitable *Rouge* and *Chartreuse*, my aim has also been to correct, however slightly, the view of him which he himself now and then tended to encourage, as simply a kind of literary anatomist, desiccated, cynical, eternally preoccupied with calculating his effects. I have tried instead to underline the ultimate integrity, the ardour of engagement with sensation, the massively humane curiosity which, even at his worst, stiff-necked with pride or festering in contempt, he never strove to stifle. His greatness, at the last, lay in having successfully found himself out. In his journal of 1805, he had summoned up the image of the ideal friend, with whom the initial excitement of shared enthusiasms was never dampened by propriety and convention. For many of us this perfect companion will be found in Henri Beyle, the hunter after happiness whose head was a magic lantern.

NOTES

Chapter 1

p. 1 I have written: *Oeuvres intimes* II, Bibliothèque de la Pléïade, Paris, Gallimard, 1982, *La Vie de Henry Brulard*, p.970.

p. 2 Dauphinois character: *Brulard* op. cit. p. 562; also *Voyages en France*, Bibliothèque de la Pléïade, Paris, Gallimard, 1992, *Mémoires d'un touriste* p. 388.

p. 3 Beyle family: Paul Arbelet: *La jeunesse de Stendhal*, Paris, Champion, 1919 vol. I pp. 12–14; see also Baron Borel du Bez, *Les armoiries et la particule de Stendhal*, in *Journées Stendhaliennes internationales de Grenoble* 1955, Paris, Le Divan, 1956 pp. 83–93.

p. 4 Grenoble: Félix Jourdan-Clet: *La Ville de Stendhal, Grenoble à la fin du XVIII siècle*. Le Divan no. 242. April-June 1942 pp. 191–5.

p. 5 Mme Pison du Galland: *Brulard* op. cit. pp. 550–1.
'Why couldn't the doctors': Ibid. p. 563.

p. 6 Chérubin Beyle: Ibid. pp. 595–7.
Deformed his character: Arbelet *Jeunesse* op. cit. I. p. 97.

p. 10 Death of Séraphie: *Brulard* pp. 735–6.

p. 11 Zénaïde tell-tale: Ibid. pp. 642–3.

p. 21 Death of Lambert: Ibid. pp. 674–9.
'A city of Provence': Ibid. p. 603.

p. 13 Gagnon family: Arbelet *Jeunesse* I pp. 40–5. H. Chobaut & L. Royer:
La famille maternelle de Stendhal, les Gagnon. Grenoble, Arthaud, 1938.
Dr Gagnon: Marie-Henriette Foix: *Vie grenobloise du grand-père de Stendhal, Henri Gagnon*, Stendhal Club number 55, April 1972 pp. 257–72, Victor del Litto: *Les études médicales du docteur Henri Gagnon*. SC 2, January 1959, pp. 118–22.

p. 16 'Voltaire, extremely': *Oeuvres intimes* II op. cit. pp. 53–4.
Elisabeth Gagnon: *Brulard* p. 600.

p.18 'Young, brilliant': Ibid. p.571.
Félicia: Ibid. p.699.
p.19 'It was for me': Ibid. p.658.
Stay at Echelles: Ibid. Ch. XIII.
p.21 Abbé Raillane: *Brulard* pp.604–11, Gilbert Dalet: *Donnons la parole à l'abblé Raillane*, SC 98, January 1983 pp.165–80, Yves Armand: *L'abbé Raillane maître de pension*, SC 123, April 1989 pp.229–32.
p.24 Execution of Louis XVI: *Brulard* pp.632–4.
p.25 Execution of Ravenas & Guillabert: Ibid. pp.691–2.
p.26 Amar & Merlino: Vital Chomel: *En marge du chapitre XI de la 'Vie de Henry Brulard*, SC 126, January 1990.
Chérubin Beyle's imprisonment: see note by V. del Litto in SC 108 pp.315–6.
'Amar put you down': *Brulard* p.639.
p.27 Ecole Centrale de Grenoble: Arbelet *Jeunesse* I pp.241–53.
p.28 Dubois-Fontanelle: Ibid. pp.256–72.
p.29 Gattel: Ibid. pp.279–85.
Mathematics: Brulard p.596. François Michel: *Stendhal mathématicien*, in *Etudes stendhaliennes, deuxième édition augmentée*, Paris, Mercure de France, 1972, pp.386–403. Gilbert Dalet: *Deux sans-culottes grenoblois, Falcon et Gros*, SC 125, October 1989, pp.32–8.
p.30 Gros as Gauthier: *Lucien Leuwen* Ch. 7.
Falcon: Dalet, *Deux sans-culottes* op. cit.
p.32 Duel with Odru: *Brulard* pp.824–8.
p.33 Attack on Fraternity Tree: ibid. pp.844–50.
p.34 Virginie Kubly: Arbelet *Jeunesse* I pp.355–66, *Brulard* pp.760–70. Stendhal places this before the Fraternity Tree episode, though it evidently took place afterwards.
p.35 'Twelve years ago': *Oeuvres intimes* I p.791.
p.36 S. & the Bigillions: *Brulard* pp.781–4.
p.37 'In those days': Ibid. pp.841–2.
p.38 S.'s maths exam: Ibid. pp.865–6.
p.39 'At this moment': *Souvenirs d'Egotisme* in *Oeuvres intimes* op. cit. II pp.578–9.
'The sole impression': *Brulard* p.869.

Chapter 2

p.40 'My idea was': *Brulard* p.869.
p.41 'I never met': Ibid. p.872.

p.42 Pierre Daru: Bernard Bergerot: *Qui était Pierre Daru?* SC 88, July 1980, pp.242–50; see also Bergerot's full-scale biography, *Daru, intendant général de la Grande Armée*, Paris, Tallandier, 1991.
Selmours: For surviving fragments of this play, a comedy *à l'anglaise*, see Stendhal: *Théâtre I*, in *Oeuvres complètes, Nouvelle édition*, Geneva, Cercle du Bibliophile, 1971.
p.43 First impressions of Paris: *Brulard* pp.873–4.
p.44 Racine vs. Shakespeare: Ibid. pp.911, 914.
Ministry of War: Ibid. pp.916–7.
p.45 Lime trees: Ibid. p.910. For S.'s attachment to trees, see Robert Chessex:
Un touriste qui aime les arbres, SC 65, October 1974, pp. 17–36.
p.46 Journey to Milan: *Brulard* pp.394–47.
p.48 Opera at Novara: *Brulard* pp.951–2; see also Ottavio Matteini: *Stendhal e la musica*, Italy (no place of publication indicated), Edizioni Eda, 1981, pp.33–49.
p.49 'Do I enjoy': *Brulard* p.890.
p.50 'Vibrating on my soul': *Oeuvres intimes* I p.454.
p.51 'I don't know how many': *Brulard* p.763. For S.'s devotion to Cimarosa, see Matteini op. cit. pp.45–7, Luigi Magnani: *Le teorie estetiche di Stendhal*, in *Omaggio a Stendhal, Atti del VI congresso internazionale stendhaliano, Parma 22–24 maggio 1967, Aurea Parma* fasc. 2, May–December 1967, p.197, and Francis Claudon: *Stendhal e Cimarosa*, in *Stendhal e Milano*, Florence, Olschki, pp.563–91.
p.52 'There is no place': John Moore: *A View Of Society and Manners in Italy*, in *The Works of John Moore MD*, Edinburgh, Stirling & Slade, 1820, Vol. 2, pp. 420–1.
S. on Milan: *Mémoires sur Napoléon*, ed. Louis Royer, Paris, Champion, 1929, vol II pp.143–71.
p.53 'I was spellbound': *Brulard* p.54.
p.54 S.'s recollections of youth in Milan: *Oeuvres intimes* I pp.735–9.
p.55 'You can scarcely': *Correspondance* ed. Henri Martineau & Victor del Litto, Bibliothéque de la Pléïade, Paris, Gallimard, 1962, ol. I p.16.
p.56 S. on Gafforini: *Vies de Haydn, Mozart et Métastase, Oeuvres complètes* op. cit. Vol 41, p.386.
p.57 Daru to Oudinot: V. del Litto: *Une lettre de Pierre Daru*, SC 21, October 1963, pp.3–5.
p.58 Michaud's renewal of S.'s commission: Arbelet *Jeunesse* II, pp.145–50.

p.59 S.'s Goldoni translation: Manlio D. Busnelli: *Stendhal traducteur de Goldoni*, Editions du Stendhal Club 18, 1926.
p.60 'Let us enjoy': *Oeuvres intimes* I pp.17–18.
p.61 'While she is lying': Ibid p.20.
p.62 Depetazzi: Albert Maquet: *M. Depetas, l' 'excellent médecin; de la ville de Saluces*, SC 45, October 1969, pp.69–72.

Chapter 3

p.63 Victorine Mounier: Paul Arbelet: *Les amours romantiques de Stendhal et de Victorine*, Paris, Emile-Paul, 1924.
'I believed': Letter to Edouard Mounier, Corr. I p.79.
p.65 'I am 18¾': Ibid. pp.1085–6.
p.66 'Je fous Mme R.': *Oeuvres intimes* I p.39.
Delphine: Corr. I p.64.
Timoleone: Ibid. pp.72–3.
p.67 De-Gagnonize: *Oeuvres intimes* I p.152.
Helvétius: Victor del Litto: *La Vie intellectuelle de Stendhal*, Paris, Presses universitaires de la France, 1959, Jules Alciatore: *Stendhal et Helvétius, les sources de la philosophie de Stendhal*, Geneva, Droz-Giard, 1952. Also Corr. I pp.84–5.
p.69 Geoffroy on Duchesnois: Arbelet: *Premier voyage de Stendhal au pays des comédiennes*, Paris, Cahiers de la quinzaine 16, Series 18, L'Artisan du Livre. Expanded version of this published in 1934 as *Stendhal au pays des comédiennes*, Grenoble, Arthaud.
'Matters came to a head': Arbelet, *Stendhal au pays des comédiennes* op. cit. pp.32–41.
p.70 S. to Mounier: Corr. I pp.59–60.
p.71 S.'s meeting with Duchesnois: *Oeuvres intimes* I pp.67–8.
p.73 List of plays: *Journal littéraire* I, *Oeuvres complètes* op. cit. 33, pp.341–2.
p.74 'Le Faux Métromane': Corr. I, pp.97–100.
Letellier: For the various drafts and related material, see *Théâtre II, Oeuvres complètes* 43, pp.29–200.
p.76 'And you have': Ibid. p.131.
p.77 S.'s expenses: *Oeuvres intimes* I, pp.127–36.
'My father's unfeeling': Ibid. p.134.
Napoleon's coronation: Ibid. pp.156–7.
p.78 Little rhetorical flourish: Ibid. p.157.
S. & Victorine: *Oeuvres intimes* I, pp.157–9.
p.79 Dugazon: Arbelet: *Stendal au pays des comédiennes* op. cit.

pp.99–127
Pursuit of Victorine: *Oeuvres intimes* I, pp.176–80.
p.81 'If I have not': Ibid. p.198.
p.82 Mélanie Guilbert: André Doyon & Yves du Parc: *De Mélanie à Lamiel*, Aran, Switzerland, Editions du Grand Chêne, 1972.
p.84 On 9 February: *Oeuvres intimes* I, pp.204–6.
p.85 'She was divine': Ibid. p.225.
Fortuné Mante: V. del Litto: *Pourquoi Stendhal n'a pas été épicier à Marseille*, SC 28, July 1965, pp.257–76. Also Corr. I, pp.1097–1100.
p.87 S.'s journey to Marseilles: *Oeuvres intimes* I, pp.336–40.
'How can these people': letter from Mme Mante to Charles Meunier, quoted in Del Litto article op. cit. p.265.
p.88 A faithful account: Mante to S., Corr. I, pp.1103–5.
'Does the profound': Ibid. pp.1105.
'What goodness!': Ibid. p.1107.
p.89 Letter to Pauline: Ibid. pp.216–21.
Picnic with Mélanie: Ibid. 221–3, *Brulard* p. 689.
p.90 Mme Cossonnier: Yves du Parc: *Madame Cossonnier ou les prestiges de la diplomatie*, SC 83, April 1979, pp.213–27.
p.91 'I base my tranquillity': Corr.I, p.127.
'We looked at the bats': *Oeuvres intimes* I, pp.457–8.
p.92 Mélanie's later career: Doyon & Du Parc op. cit. pp.120–99.
'If I wish my tomb': Full text of Mélanie's will in ibid. pp.184–9.

Chapter 4

p.93 'Fell with Napoleon': *Brulard* p.540.
p.94 Gagnon to S.: Corr. I, pp.1163–5.
'Commerces humiliantes': Ibid. p.325.
p.96 S. at Montmorency: *Oeuvres intimes* I, pp. 459–60.
p.97 'Imagine a great': Ibid. p. 1030 (*Voyage à Brunswick* pp.1030–48).
p.98 S. at Brunswick: André-François Poncet: *Stendhal en Allemagne*, Paris, Hachette, Les Soirées du Luxembourg, 1967.
p.100 'Never was life': Charles Simon: *Les souvenirs du Baron de Strombeck et Louis Spach sur Stendhal*, Paris, Editions du Stendhal Club 9, 1925.
'He has the air': *Oeuvres intimes* I, p.488.
p.102 Journey to Wolffenbüttel: Ibid. pp.480–3.
p.103 'A delightful café: *Lucien Leuwen* Ch. 23.
p.104 'Never had so much': *Mina de Vanghel*, in *Le Rose et le Vert* etc. Paris, Gallimard, 1982, p.118.

p. 105 'I have no more': Corr. I. p. 347.
Official correspondence:Ibid. pp. 377–512.
p. 106 'Their principal defect': *Oeuvres intimes* I p. 506.
'Four years ago': Corr. I p. 482.
'Born for his art': Ibid. p. 366.
p. 107 'I have much loved': Ibid. p. 517.
p. 108 'After the storm': *Oeuvres intimes* I p. 518.
'He'll never like': Ibid. p. 526.
p. 109 'As we started': Ibid. p. 534.
'A very handsome': Ibid. p. 535.
p. 110 'Still not a moment': Corr. I p. 532.
p. 111 'But I haven't': Ibid. p. 535.
p. 112 S. at Haydn's memorial service: ibid. p. 536.
S. and Viennese music: see Richard N. Coe: *Lisbeth folle par amour*, SC 39, April 1968, pp. 249–64, 40, July 1968, pp. 315–30.
S. & Babet: Coe op. cit.; also Corr. I p. 539.

Chapter 5

p. 114 Alexandrine Daru: Henri Martineau: *Petit dictionnaire stendhalien*, Paris, Le Divan, 1948, pp. 161–2.
'Cette fraîche cousine': Martineau op. cit. p. 161.
p. 116 Journal du Kahlenberg: *Oeuvres intimes* I p. 540.
'In the next': Ibid. pp. 541–2.
Climbing the Kahlenberg: Ibid. pp. 542–4.
p. 118 Letters to Pauline: Corr. I, pp. 556–7, 563–4.
'I've just seen': *Oeuvres intimes* I p. 551.
Rougier de la Bergerie: André Doyon & Yves du Parc: *Amitiés Parisiennes de Stendhal*, Collection Stendhalienne II, Lausanne, Editions du Grand Chêne, 1969, Ch. I.
p. 119 'Not the least idea': *Oeuvres intimes* I p. 554.
p. 120 Stendhal chez David: Ibid. p. 552.
'The chambers of the Palace': Ibid. p. 608.
p. 121 A likely budget: Ibid. p. 605.
Auditorship: René Dollot: *Autour de Stendhal*, Milan, Istituto Editoriale Italiano, 1948, pp. 243–73. Also Corr. I pp. 582–3, *Oeuvres intimes* p. 612.
Daru to Duc de Bassano: Ibid. pp. 613–4.
p. 122 S. at Plancy: Ibid. pp. 625–9.
S. to Faure: *Oeuvres intimes* I pp. 628–9.
p. 123 'My tower': Ibid. pp. 629–30.

Inspector of Crown Furniture: Elaine Williamson: *Stendhal inspecteur du mobilier de la couronne*, SC 128, July 1990, pp.337–64.
p.124 'At the name': Corr. I p.598.
p.125 For Pauline's benefit: Ibid. pp.600–2.
p.126 'This capital': *Oeuvres intimes* I, pp.669–70.
p.127 Trip to Normandy: Crozet & Faure journals are in *Oeuvres intimes* I pp. 1080–92.
'We travelled': Ibid. p.675.
Bècheville: Elaine Williamson: *De Bècheville à Saint-Cloud, Stendhal secrétaire de la Comtesse Daru*, SC 114, January 1987, pp.140–55.
p.128 'History of the battle': *Oeuvres intimes* I pp.678–89.
p.129 Histoire d'une partie de ma vie: Ibid. pp.1058–79.
p.130 'All men are cold': Corr. I pp.609–10.
Pauline's lesbianism: André Doyon: *Henri et Pauline Beyle, histoire de la 'cara sorella'*, SC 93, 94, 95, October 1981, January, April 1982, pp.41–65, 181–99, 239–57.
p.131 'I felt the ferocity': *Oeuvres intimes* I p.724.
'Until now I rejoiced': Ibid. p.728.
p.132 'Should I say': Ibid. p.736.
p.135 S. at Bologna: Ibid. pp.771–6.
p.136 'There is doubtless': *Rome, Naples et Florence en 1817* in *Voyages en Italie* op. cit. pp.94–5.
S. in Florence: *Oeuvres intimes* I pp.779–93.
p.140 Gina at Varese: Ibid. pp.802–8.
'Just a line': Ibid. p.811.

Chapter 6

p.142 'He spoke to me': André Doyon: *Stendhal dans la correspondance intime du Comte Pierre Daru*, SC 48, July 1970, pp.289–95.
'I thought': Doyon article op. cit.
p.143 Musée Napoléon: Thérèse Imbert: *Henri Beyle et l'inventaire du Musée Napoléon*, SC 105, October 1984, pp.9–20.
Memorandum to Duc de Cadore: pp.628–31.
p.144 'Ah! my dear': Corr. I p.621.
A long rambling sequence: *Oeuvres intimes* I pp.821–3.
Chérubin's house: André Doyon: *La maison de Chérubin Beyle*, SC 98, January 1983, pp.151–64.
p.147 'In this ocean of barbarity': Corr. I pp.656–7.
S. in Russia: Prosper Mérimée: *H.B.* in Charles Bellanger, *Notes*

stendhaliennes suivies de 'H.B.' de Mérimée, Paris, Editions du Myrte, 1948.

p. 148 'We left the city': *Oeuvres intimes* I pp. 832–3.
Letter to Faure: Corr. I, pp. 658–60.
Uexküll's diary: *Arms And The Woman: The intimate journal of an amorous Baltic nobleman in the Napoleonic Wars* by Boris Uxkull, trans. Joel Carmichael, London, Secker & Warburg, 1966.

p. 149 Reading Livy: Note made on 23 July 1832, quoted in Ferdinand Boyer: *Les Lectures de Stendhal*, Editions du Stendhal Club 14, 1925.
'The more I advance': Corr. I p. 672.
'You wouldn't recognize us': Corr. I p. 675.

p. 150 Piece of suet: Mérimée, *H.B.* op. cit.

p. 151 Crossing of the Beresina: The incident noted here is reported in detail in Mérimée *H.B.* op. cit. Though many Stendhal biographers have tended to place it further ahead, during his service in Saxony in 1813, I see no reason to doubt Mérimée. The question of the number and date of meetings with Napoleon remains unresolved.

p. 152 'I'm very well': Corr. I p. 688.
Cold passionlessness: *Oeuvres intimes* I p. 835.

p. 153 Hamlet: Ibid. pp. 848–9.
'Chagrin d'ambition': Ibid. p. 851.

p. 154 Battle of Bautzen: Ibid. pp. 867–71.
Görlitz: Ibid. pp. 1093–4.

p. 155 S. at Sagan: Ibid. pp. 873–80. Leszek Slugocki: *Les problèmes du séjour de Stendhal à Sagan* in *Communications présentées au Congrès Stendhalien de Civitavecchia (III Journée du Stendhal Club)* Sansoni, Florence, Didier, Paris, 1966, and (by the same author) *Stendhal à Sagan, une lettre inédite*, SC 24, July 1964, pp. 248–54, *Une fille naturelle de Stendhal à Sagan*, SC 70, January 1976, pp. 177–8.

p. 156 'Only in this': *Oeuvres intimes* I p. 885.

p. 157 'Is it your business': Ibid. p. 88.

p. 158 'From the moment': *Le Rouge et le Noir*, Classiques Garnier edn. ed. Pierre-Georges Castex, Paris, Bordas 1989, pp. 48–9.

p. 159 S. to Duc de Cadore: Corr. I p. 714.
'in order that': Ibid. p. 761.

p. 160 S. & Vivant Denon: Crozet's journal extract is in *Oeuvres intimes* I pp. 1095–7.

p. 161 S.'s adherence to the acts: Henri Martineau: *Le Calendrier de Stendhal*, Paris, Le Divan, 1950, p. 145.
Letters to Blacas: Corr. I pp. 771–2, 777–8.
'I asked for nothing': *Souvenirs d'Egotisme*, op. cit. p. 431.

p. 162 'A stout lad': see François Michel: *Le policier qui espionna Monsier de Beyle?*, in Etudes stendhaliennes op. cit. pp.218–22.
p. 163 Haydn, Mozart & Metastasio: No adequate modern edn. outside the well-annotated *Oeuvres complètes* vol. op. cit.
p. 164 Carpani & plagiarisms: The Carpani-Bombet controversy is fully covered in ibid. pp.451–508.
p. 165 Quérard: J. M. Quérard: *Les supercheries littéraires dévoilées*, Paris, Paul Daffis, 1869, vol I p. 547.
p. 167 'I fully perceive': *Oeuvres intimes* I p.906.

Chapter 7

p. 168 S. at Turin: Corr. I pp.780–1.
Fabio Pallavicini: Petre Ciureanu: *Stendhal et Fabio Pallavicini*, SC 37, October 1967, pp.23–43.
p. 169 Marchesa Pallavicini: Giuseppe Marcenaro: *Genova con gli occhi di Stendhal*, Cassa di Risparmio di Genova e Imperia, 1984, pp.89–90.
'Madame P.': Corr. I pp.785–6.
Rivages de la mer: L'italie en 1818 in *Voyages en Italie* op. cit. pp.275–8.
p. 171 Peach trees: Corr. I p.787.
Letter to Comtesse Beugnot: Ibid. p.784.
p. 172 Meeting with Gina: *Oeuvres intimes* I pp.915–6.
L'esprit des lois: Ibid. p.923.
'Ah! my dearest': Corr. I pp.800–1.
p. 173 Daru to Stendhal: Ibid. pp.1239–40.
'The avarice of the tender father': Corr. I p.805.
p. 174 S. at Padua: *Rome, Naples et Florence en 1817* op. cit. pp.112–3.
Pacchierotti: Angus Heriot: *The Castrati in Opera*, London, Calder, 1960 pp.163–71 – no source given for Mount Edgcumbe.
p. 175 S. on Venice: *RNF 1817*, pp.119–31.
p. 176 News of Waterloo: *Oeuvres intimes* I pp.936, 941–2.
Break-up with Angela Pietragrua: Mérimée's version in *H.B.* op. cit.
p. 177 A. P.'s letters to S.: Corr. I p.1241.
'Her loss is immense': *Oeuvres intimes* I p.961.
p. 178 Letter to Crozet: Corr. I pp.814–6.
'Having finished': *Oeuvres intimes* I p.958.
p. 179 S. & Richerand: André Denier: *Richerand médecin consultant de Stendhal*, SC 2, January 1959, pp.101–8.

p. 182 Di Breme: Ludovico di Breme: *Lettere*, ed. Piero Camporesi, Turin, Einaudi, 1966.

p. 184 Sismondi: Obituary notice in *Revue Encyclopédique*, quoted in Di Breme, *Lettere* op. cit. p. vii.
Italian Romantics: *Manifesti Romantici e altri scritti dell polemica classico-romantica*, ed. Carlo Calcaterra, 1950, augmented edn. by Mario Scotti, 1979, Turin, Utet.
Letter to Crozet: Corr. I pp. 818–24.

p. 185 Sismondi: Victor de Litto: *La Vie intellectuelle de Stendhal*, Paris, Presses universitaires de la France, 1959, p. 509 n. ref. to his *Epistolario* II pp. 336–7.
Pellico: Ibid. p. 508 n. ref. to L. Rinieri: *Della vita e delle opere di Silvio Pellico* vol. I p. 244.
S. & *Edinburgh Review*: Del Litto: *Vie intellectuelle* op. cit. Part III, ch. 2.
'Eat one meal less': Corr. I p. 831.

p. 186 'I have dined': Ibid. p. 832.
Byron in Milan: Leslie A. Marchand: *Byron, A Portrait*, London, John Murray, 1971, pp. 255–8. See also Marchand's edn. of Byron's *Letters & Journals* Vol. 5, London, Murray, 1976.
'All society in Milan': Byron *Letters* op. cit. Vol. 5, p. 123.

p. 187 'A young man about thirty': John Cam Hobhouse, Lord Broughton: *Recollections of a Long Life*, ed. Lady Dorchester, London, Murray, 1909, Vol 2, p. 41.
'Gloriosissimo successore': Di Breme: *Lettere* op. cit. p. 376.
Di Breme's dinner: Hobhouse: *Recollections* op. cit. pp. 47–9, Stendhal: *Lord Byron en Italie*, Revue de Paris, March 1830. Text is in *Oeuvres complètes* 46, pp. 239–54.
S.'s Russian anecdotes: Hobhouse: *Recollections* 2, pp. 52–7. Extracts censored by Lady Dorchester are in George M. Rosa: *Stendhal Raconteur*, Studi Francesi Vol XXII 65–6, May–December 1978, pp. 358–64.

p. 189 Polidori episode: Byron: *Letters* Vol. 5 op. cit. pp. 121, 124. *The Diary Of Dr John William Polidori*, 1876, ed. William Michael Rossetti, London, Elkin Matthews, 1911, pp. 173–7. S.'s account in *Lord Byron en Italie* op. cit.
Meeting with Byron: *RNF 1817* op. cit. pp. 124–5.

p. 190 S.'s 1824 Byron memoir: *Souvenirs sur Lord Byron* in *Oeuvres complètes* 35, pp. 167–73. For Hobhouse's assault on S. and a thorough though extremely partisan examination of S.'s Byroniana, see Doris Langley Moore: *The Late Lord Byron*, London, John Murray, 1961, Ch. XI, pp. 372–96.

p.194 Di Breme to Pellico: *Lettere* op. cit. p.633.
'The abbé de Breme': Corr. I p.1036.
Di Breme–Hobhouse–Foscolo: De Breme: *Lettere* op. cit. pp.653–73. Also Erald Reginald Vincent: *Byron, Hobhouse and Foscolo*, Cambridge, University Press, 1949.

Chapter 8

p.195 George Alexander Otis: *Oeuvres intimes* I p.970.
'A hundred strokes': *RNF 1817* p.22.
p.196 Cardinal Consalvi: Ibid. pp.28, 60–1.
'You wander through': Ibid. p.46.
'Despite its three hundred': Ibid. p.58.
p.197 Death of Périer-Lagrange: André Doyon: *Henri et Pauline Beyle* article op. cit. p.240.
In a single letter: Corr. I pp.814–16.
p.198 'Your lively remarks': Ibid. pp.1242–3.
p.199 'The thing which makes': Ibid. p.853.
Letter to Crozet: Ibid. pp.818–23.
'The happy few': Paul Hazard: *Mélanges offerts à E. Huguet*, 1940, pp.394–6.
p.200 *Histoire de la Peinture en Italie*: No recent publication. 2-vol. edn. by Henri Martineau, Paris, Le Divan, 1929
p.203 Sistine ceiling: Op. cit. Vol. 2, pp.276–81.
p.204 Reviews of *Histoire de la Peinture*: Dealt with in great detail by Paul Arbelet in *L'Histoire de la peinture en Italie et les Plagiats de Stendhal*, Paris, Calmann-Lévy, 1914, Chapter 1.
See also C. W. Thompson: *Note sur la diffusion de l'Histoire de la Peinture jusqu'en 1833*, SC 51, April 1971, pp.207–17.
p.205 Alexandre Lenoir: V. del Litto: *Un exemplaire de l'Histoire de la Peinture en Italie interfolié et commenté par Alexandre Lenoir* SC 52–9.
p.206 Schmidt's journal: *Oeuvres intimes* I pp.1098–1108.
p.208 'Is it possible': *Souvenirs d'Egotisme* op. cit. p.494.
p.209 Egron to S.: Corr. I p.1248.
Paul Léautaud's pseudonym list: in *Stendhal, les plus belles pages*, Paris, Mercure de France, 1908.
p.212 'L'italie morale': This is the running title given in the Pléïade edn. pp.137–45.
p.213 Countesss of Albany: Carlo Pellegrini: *Stendhal e la Contessa d'Albany*, Aurea Parma op. cit. pp.62–9.
'The author will find': Corr. I pp.1250–1.

p.214 'It is the spirit': *RNF 1817* p.161.
p.215 S. on Mareste: *Souvenirs* op. cit. pp.435–8.
p.216 Open letter: *Journal littéraire Vol. 3*, op. cit. pp.53–5.
p.217 'Do you read': Corr. I pp.951–3.
S. & Italian Romanticism: *Del Romanticismo nelle Arti* ed. Pierre Martino, Editions du Stendhal Club 1922, I.
p.218 Des périls de la langue italienne: *Journal littéraire 3*, op. cit. pp.55–102.
p.219 'Qu'est-ce que le romanticisme?' dit M. Londonio: Ibid. pp.106–30.
p.221 S. & Mme de Staël: Jacques Félix-Faure: *Stendhal lecteur de Mme de Staël*, Collection Stendhalienne 16, Editions du Grand Chêne, Aran, Switzerland, 1974.
p.222 'This poor woman': Corr. I p.844.
Rasori: Ibid. p.908. Also Bruno Pincherle: *Lo stendhalesco dottor Rasori*, in *In Compagnia di Stendhal*, Milano, All'Insegna del pesce d'Oro, 1969, pp.79–171; also Francesca Kaucisvili Melzi d'Eril: *Una conoscenza milanese di Stendhal: G. Rasori*, in *Stendhal e Milano* op. cit. I pp.454–64.
p.223 Vie de Napoléon: Borsieri's critique in *Stendhal e Milano* op. cit. I pp.170–2.
L'Italie en 1818: Full surviving text in *Voyages en Italie* op. cit.
p.225 'The great evil': Ibid. p.238.
p.226 Elena Viganò: Corr. I p.897.
p.227 Metilde Dembowski: Annie Colet: *Stendhal et Milan*, Paris, Corti, 1986, Vol. I and the same author's *Metilde Viscontini; du mariage à la séparation*, SC 99, April 1983, pp.345–50. Also George Jessula: *Metilde Dembowski avant Stendhal*, SC 115, April 1987, pp.265–70, and Michel Crouzet: *Metilde, muse stendhalienne*, in *Stendhal e Milano* op. cit. I pp.49–76.
p.230 'One really striking part': Corr. I p.940.
'I have a charming': Ibid. p.943.
p.231 'For I can count': Ibid. pp.947–8.
p.232 S. at Volterra: Ibid. pp.969–73.
p.234 'Everything which the deepest': Ibid. pp.985–8.
p.235 'I'm spending my evenings': Ibid. p.1000.
Graph: Reproduced in *Oeuvres intimes* II p.9.
p.236 Casin di San Paolo: René Dollot: *Autour de Stendhal* op. cit. pp.158–63.
'An unequalled freshness': *RNF 1826* in *Voyages en Italie* p.311.
p.238 'Milanese good humour': Corr. I pp.1030–1.
p.239 S. on Scott: Ibid. pp.1053–4, 1056. See also K. G. McWatters &

C. W. Thompson: *Stendhal et l'Angleterre*, Liverpool, University Press, pp.159–75.

p.240 St Gotthard Pass: *Souvenirs* op. cit. p.433.

Crozet to Mareste: V. del Litto: *Textes et documents inédits 3: La 'calomnie'*, SC 130, January 1991 pp.165–8.

p.241 Confalonieri's evidence: Partially reproduced in Pincherle, *In Compagnia di Stendhal* op. cit. *Metilde nel Processo dei Carbonari*, pp.145–207.

p.242 Metilde's last days: Pincherle op. cit., Colet: *Stendhal et Milan* op. cit. pp.96–111.

De l'Amour: Fully annotated edn. by Henri Martineau, Classiques Garnier, Paris, 1959. The Gallimard Folio series edn., 1980, has excellent intro. and notes by V. del Litto.

p.245 S. & Hazlitt: Robert Vigneron: *Stendhal et Hazlitt*, Modern Philology vol. 4, May 1938, pp.375–414.

Chapter 9

p.248 Assassinating the king: *Souvenirs* op. cit. p.434.

p.249 My good sense: Ibid. p.438.

Visit to the brothel: Ibid. pp.444–6.

p.250 Babilan: see note in ibid. pp.1252–3.

Lolot: Ibid. p.446.

'I needed to put a hill': Ibid. p.474.

p.251 Lucy Hutchinson: Richard Bolster: *Stendhal et les Mémoires de Lucy Hutchinson*, in *Stendhal et l'Angleterre* op. cit. pp.149–57.

p.252 Westminster Bridge Road: *Souvenirs*. pp.483–9.

Philippe Berthier: *Stendhal et les demoiselles de Westminster Road*, in *Stendhal et l'Angleterre* op. cit. pp.295–304.

p.254 English magazines: For general intro. to this phase of S.'s career, see K. G. McWatters & René Denier: *Stendhal, Chroniques pour l'Angleterre, Contributions à la presse britannique*, Vol I, pp.5–28, Grenoble, Publications de l'université des langues et lettres de Grenoble, 1980.

p.257 D'Arlincourt: *London Magazine*, March 1825, in McWatters & Denier op. cit.

Mister Translator: Corr. II pp.66–9.

p.258 Stritch: *Souvenirs* pp.510–11.

François Michel: *Stendhal chroniqueur clandestin au 'New Monthly Magazine', lettres inédites*, in Nouvelles Soirées du Stendhal Club, Paris, Mercure de France, 1950, pp.218–62.

p.260 Paris salons: André Jardin & André-Jean Tudesq: *Restoration and*

Reaction 1815–1848, Cambridge, University Press, 1983, pp.70–3 (originally issued as *La France des Notables*, Editions du Seuil, Paris, 1973).

p.261 'It was at this inconvenient': *Souvenirs* pp.520–1 S. on Delécluze: Ibid. p.521.

p.262 Delécluze on S.: *Journal on Delécluze* 1824–1828 ed. Robert Baschet, Paris, Grasset, 1948 pp.421–5. D.'s portrait of S. is in *Carnet de route d'Italie (1823–1824): Impressions romaines*, ed. Baschet, Paris, Boivin, 1942, pp.102–6.

p.266 'His wife has taken': *Souvenirs* p.468.
S. & Mérimée: Thierry Ozwald: *Le Beyle de Mérimée*, SC 129, October 1990, pp.14–34.
Victor Jacquemont: An excellent biography is by Pierre Maes: *Un ami de Stendhal, Victor Jacquemont*, Paris, Desclée de Brouwer, 1935.
S. on Jacquemont: *Souvenirs* pp.459.

p.268 De Tracy salon: Ibid. pp.452–6.

p.271 Mary Clarke: Margaret Lesser: *Clarkey, A Portrait in Letters of Mary Clarke Mohl*, Oxford, University Press, 1984.
S. on Mary Clarke: *Souvenirs* p.467.

p.272 'I'm horrified': Lesser: *Clarkey*, op. cit. p.42.
'When you have': *Brulard*. op. cit. p.625.

p.273 'A servile disciple': Charles de Rémusat: *Mémoires de ma vie*, Paris, 1959, Vol 2, pp.141–2.
S. & *Le Globe*: Jean-Jacques Goblot: *Paul-François Dubois, Stendhal et 'le Globe'*, SC 54, January 1972, pp.121–43. See also S.'s *Grimm's Grandson* essay, *London Magazine*, 18 December 1824.
Dubois on S.: Goblot article op. cit.

p.274 English troupe: For an account of this episode in its socio-artistic context, see F. W. J. Hemmings: *Culture and Society in France 1789–1848*, Leicester, University Press, 1987, pp.160–3.

p.276 Racine et Shakespeare: *Oeuvres complètes* op. cit. vol. 37, p.1–51.
Lamartine to Mareste: Ibid. pp.291–5.

p.278 Racine et Shakespeare II: Ibid. pp.51–159.
Delécluze on R & S II: E. J. Delécluze: *Souvenirs de soixante années*, Paris, Michel Lévy, 1862, pp.156–8, 231–6, 258–62.

p.280 '*D'un nouveau complot*': The full text of this pamphlet is in Fernand Rude: *Stendhal et la pensée sociale de son temps*, Paris, Gérard Montfort, 1983, which also contains a thorough account of the surrounding controversy. See also articles by Robert Diver, in SC 75, Kichiro Kajino in SC 74, Alain Chantreau in SC 31 and V. del Litto in SC 20.

p.283 'In the life of a nation': Rude op. cit. p.342.

p.285 S.'s opera reviews: *Notes d'un dilettante* has been issued separately in a recent edition by Jacques Bonnaire as '*L'Opéra Italien*', Paris, Editions Michel de Maule, 1988.

p.286 Giuditta Pasta: Best short account of her career is in *Enciclopedia dello Spettacolo VII*, Rome, Casa Editrice Le Maschere, 1960, pp.1758–9.
S. on Pasta: *Souvenirs* op. cit. Ch. 7 passim.

p.288 *Vie de Rossini*: A modern edn. by Pierre Brunel, Paris, Parution, 1987. Meeting with Rossini: *RNF 1817*. op. cit. p.28.

Chapter 10

p.291 S.'s Paris: Henri Martineau, *Calendrier de Stendhal* op. cit. contains detailed year-by-year information as to Stendhal's various residences, together with street plans. For a Stendhalian tour of Paris, see Nicolas Tredell: *Remembering Harry Beyle*, PN Review Vol 18, No. 6, July/August 1992 pp.6–7.

p.292 Clémentine Curial: Martineau, *Petit Dictionnaire*, op. cit. pp.149–55. See also Marie-Jeanne Durry: *Une passion de Stendhal, Clémentine*, Editions du Stendhal Club 22, 1927.

p.293 'A pretty face': Jean Théodorides: *Lectures estivales* SC 37, October 1967 p.71.

p.294 'How might I': Corr. II pp.30–1.
'How can we': Ibid. p.783.
Long tearful letter: Ibid. pp.790–2.
Colomb's note: Ibid. p.792.

p.295 'Our romantic Baron': quoted in Henri Martineau: *Le coeur de Stendhal*, Paris, Albin Michel, 1953, Vol 2, p.80.
'I'm really in despair': Corr. II p.52.

p.296 'Adieu, cher ami': Ibid. pp.921–3.
'Although he belonged': Victor del Litto: *Un témoignage inédit sur Stendhal*, SC 102, January 1984, pp.193–4.

p.297 Sutton Sharpe: Doris Gunnell: *Sutton Sharpe et ses amis français*. Paris, Librairie Ancienne Honoré Champion, 1925.
'Plain of fire', 'amiable Miss Rogers': Corr. II p.123.

p.298 S.'s notes on England: *Oeuvres complètes* op. cit. Vol. 45. pp.295–300.

p.299 Almack's: Alison Adburgham: *Silver Fork Society*, London, Constable 1983, pp.102–7.
'Tepid lemonade': Lord William Pitt Lennox quoted in ibid. p.104.

p.300 *Olivier*: Text and full apparatus published by Denise Virieux in *Madame de Duras: Olivier ou le secret*, Paris, Corti, 1971.

p.301 *Armance*: Standard text is in Classiques Garnier edn., Paris, 1950, ed. Henri Martineau.
'A smile was on': Op. cit. p.245.
'If anything like': K. G. McWatters: *Armance en Angleterre en 1828* SC 20, July 1963 pp.309–15.

p.302 Letter to Mérimée: Corr. II pp.96–9.

p.303 *Armance & La princesse de Clèves*: V. del Litto: *Stendhal lecteur d'Armance*, SC 71, 72, April, July 1976.

p.304 Astolphe de Custine: C. W. Thompson: *Les clefs d'Armance et l'ambivalence du génie romantique du Nord*, SC 100, July 1983, pp.522–47.
S. & homosexuality: C. W. Thompson: *Stendhal connaisseur de l'"improper'*, SC 114, January 1987, pp.113–39. Also Philippe Berthier: *Stendhal et la Sainte Famille*, Geneva, Droz, 1983, pp.209–19.
'This charming officer: *Oeuvres intimes* I p.904.

p.307 Virginie Ancelot: *Les Salons de Paris, Foyers éteints*, Paris, Tardieu 1858. Also Henri Martineau: *Stendhal et le salon de Mme Ancelot*, Paris, Le Divan, 1932.
You will find': Martineau: *Ancelot* op. cit. p.77.

p.308 S. as Bombet: Ancelot: *Les salons de Paris* op. cit. pp.64–5.
Sainte-Beuve on S.: Sainte-Beuve: *Correspondance*, Paris, Calmann-Lévy, 1878, Vol 2, pp.378–80.

p.309 'Beyle was excited': Ancelot op. cit. p.62.
S. & the Garnetts: James Fred Marshall: *Les dames Garnett amies de Stendhal*, Le Divan 272, pp.172–87, and his Du nouveau sur les dames Garnett, SC 78, January 1978, pp.120–30.
Julie Gaulthier: Doyon & Du Parc: *Amitiés parisiennes de Stendhal* op. cit. Ch. I.

p.310 'You'll allow me': Corr. I p.89.

p.311 Sophie Duvaucel: Martineau, *Petit dictionnaire* op. cit. pp.206–8.
See also Louis Royer: *Stendhal au Jardin du Roi*, Grenoble, Arthaud, 1930.

p.312 'Nothing can be funnier': Jean Théodorides: *Stendhal observé par Adrien de Jussieu*. SC 25, October 1964 pp. 43–4.

p.313 S. on Mercadante & Donizetti: Corr. II. p.24.
RNF 1826: Modern, fully annotated edn. in Pléïade *Voyages en italie* op. cit.

p.314 S. at Genoa: Giuseppe Marcenaro: *Geneva con gli occhi di Stendhal* op. cit.

S. on Ischia: Jacques Boulenger: *Du Stendhal inédit*. Candidature du Stendhal Club. Paris, Le Divan, 1926, pp.103–4.

p.315 Vieusseux: Pierre Jourda: *Vieusseux et ses correspondants français*, Editions du Stendhal Club 16, 1926.

S. & Lamartine: Lamartine: *Cours familier de littérature* XVII, Paris, 1864, Entretien CII pp.419–25.

p.317 Hortense Allart: Corr. II pp.832–3, 834–5.

S. on Hayez: Ibid. p.133.

p.318 Attempted visit to Milan: Charles Simon: *Stendhal et la police autrichienne*. Editions du Stendhal Club 2, 1928.

Colburn: François Michel: *Stendhal chroniqueur* op. cit.

p.320 'Beyle was on form': Pierre Maes: *Lettres de Victor Jacquemont à Stendhal*, Paris, Poursin, 1933, p.74.

p.321 'A lady beside whom': Mérimée: *Correspondance Générale*. ed. Maurice Parturier, Paris, Le Divan, 1941, Vol I pp. 43–4.

Alberthe de Rubempré: Mathieu Méras: *Autour d'Alberthe de Rubempré et d'Adolphe de Mareste*. SC 98, January 1983 pp.187–204.

'I ought to leave': Letter published in full by A. W. Raitt, *Prosper Mérimée*, Eyre & Spottiswoode, 1970, pp.367–8. This remains the best biography of Mérimée.

p.322 'I've an unhappy talent': *Souvenirs* op. cit. p.482.

p.323 *Promenades dans Rome*: Modern, fully annotated edn. in Pléïade *Voyages en Italie* op. cit.

p.324 Death of Pierre Daru: *Souvenirs* op. cit. p.442.

p.325 'Time, edax rerum': Corr. II p.166. Louis Royer: *Stendhal candidat à la Bibliothèque Royale*, Editions du Stendhal Club 32, 1931.

p.327 Mina de Vanghel: Text in *Le Rose et le Vert, Mina de Vanghel et autres nouvelles* op. cit. pp.115–57.

p.329 Giulia Rinieri de' Rocchi: Luigi-Foscolo Benedetto: *Indiscretions sur Giulia*, Paris, Le Divan, 1934.

Marginal jottings: *Oeuvres intimes* II, pp.121–6.

S. & Hugo: H. Rochefort: *Les aventures de ma vie*, Paris, Vol 11, p. 54.

p.331 *Le Rouge et le Noir*: Best modern edn. is by Pierre Castex in the Classiques Garnier series already referred to.

p.332 Sources of *Le Rouge et le Noir*: An extensive range of these will be found investigated throughout SC numbers. To them may be added René Fonvieille: *Le véritable Julien Sorel*, Arthaud, Grenoble, 1971, and Claude Liprandi: *L'affaire Lafargue et Le Rouge et le Noir*, Lausanne, Editions du Grand Chêne, 1961.

p.337 July Revolution: Good account in M. D. R. Leys: *Between Two Empires*, London, Longmans, 1955.
p.338 'Fusillade from firing parties': Ferdinand Boyer: *Stendhal et les historiens de Napoléon.* Editions du Stendhal Club 17, 1926.

Chapter 11

p.340 'It is perhaps': Corr II. pp.193–4.
Berlinghieri's answer: ibid. p.857.
p.341 Stendhal at Trieste: René Dollot: *Stendhal Consul de France à Trieste.* Editions du Stendhal Club 23, 1928. Nora Poliaghi: *Stendhal e Trieste.* Florence, Olschki, 1984.
p.342 Constanza Reyer: Corr. II p.198.
S. on Bellini: Ibid. pp.234–5.
p.343 Caroline Ungher: Pierre Sabatier: *A propos d'une rencontre à Trieste, Stendhal et Caroline Ungher.* SC 23, April 1964, pp.216–220.
'she is admirably': Corr. II p.259.
p.344 'However disposed': Metternich to Apponyi translated in Dollot (*Stendhal Consul* op. cit.) from Anton Bettelheim: *Biographewege, Reden und Aufsätze*, Berlin, 1913, pp.198–214.
p.346 'My entire life': Corr. II p.215.
Reviews of *Le Rouge*: These are in Garnier edn. op. cit. pp.688–708.
p.349 Civitavecchia: Ferdinando Barbaranelli: *La Civitavecchia di Stendhal*, in *Communications* op. cit. pp.17–39.
Also V. del Litto: *Stendhal consul de France à Civitavecchia* in ibid. pp.7–17, and *The Handbook for Travellers in Central Italy*, London, John Murray, 1843, pp.165–6.
p.350 Teatro Minozzi: Ferdinando Barbaranelli: *Le théâtre de Civitavecchia au temps de Stendhal*, SC April 1965, pp.201–7.
p.351 De Vaux to S.: Corr. II p.871.
p.352 S.'s consular letters: Georges Dethan: *De la valeur pour l'historien de la correspondance consulaire de Stendhal. Communications* op. cit. pp.53–65.
Bernard Alphonse: Annie Colet: *Une lettre inédite de Henri Beyle consul de France*, SC 103, April 1984 pp.217–20.
p.353 Lysimaque Tavernier: Yves du Parc: *Il Signor Lisimaco, Chancelier de Stendhal*, in *Dans le sillage de Stendhal*, Lyons I.A.C. 1955, pp.71–142. Also *Lysimaque Tavernier, Lettere a Stendhal* ed. Rosa Ghigo Bezzola, Schena/Nizet, Fasano/Paris, 1991.
p.354 Manzi & Bucci: Ferdinand Boyer: *Les amis de Stendhal à*

Civitavecchia, Nouvelles soirées du Stendhal Club op. cit. pp.105–17.

p.356 'He discusses, he dissects': Mareste quoting Vernet: in Gunnell: *Sutton Sharpe et ses amis français* op. cit. p.213.

p.357 Sainte-Aulaire: Roger Boppe: *Stendhal à Rome, les débuts d'un consul*, Paris, Les Editions de France, 1944.

p.358 'Une position sociale': in *Le Rose et le Vert etc.* op. cit. pp.185–229.

p.359 Two letters: Corr. II pp.280–3, 872–4.

p.360 S. at Ancona: George Dethan: *Un consul et un vice-consul, Stendhal et son agent à Ancone, Frédéric Quilliet.* Revue d'histoire diplomatique 69, October-December 1955, pp.292–312.

p.362 *Souvenirs d'Egotisme*: Fully annotated modern edn. in *Oeuvres intimes* Vol 11 op. cit. See also Pierre Martino's most useful edn. of 1954, Paris, Imprimerie Nationale.

p.363 S. on Malibran: Corr. II p.139.

p.364 Leopardi to Paolina: *Epistolario di G. Leopardi*, Firenze, Lemonnier, 1934–41, VI p.209.
S. to Salvagnoli: Corr. II pp.482-n4, 484–5.
Giuseppe Montani: Review of *Promenades dans Rome* is in Giuseppe Montani, *Scritti letterari*, Turin, Einaudi, 1980 pp.217–39.

p.365 Alexander Turgenev: Martineau: *Le coeur de Stendhal* op. cit. II, pp.241–3, Tatiana Müller-Kotchetkova: *Stendhal et Alexandre Tourgueniev*, SC 62, January 1974, pp.113–26.

p.366 'the fatal letter': Corr. II pp.907–8.

p.367 'I'm off to Lutetia': Ibid. p.515.

p.368 'A delicious conversation': *Oeuvres intimes* II p.185.

p.369 'I could well understand': George Sand: *Histoire de ma vie, V, partie III*, in *Oeuvres autobiographiques II* pp.204–5, Paris, Bibliothèque de la Pléïade, Gallimard.

p.370 S. on *Le Lieutenant*: Corr. II pp.643–4.

p.371 *Lucien Leuwen*: Good modern edns. by Henri Martineau in Les Classiques du Monde, Paris, Hazan, 1950, and by Henri Debray & Michel Crouzet in the Flammarion GF series, Paris 1982.

p.374 S.'s Roman friends: Pietro Paolo Trompeo: *Nell'Italia Romantica sulle orme di Stendhal.* Rome, Casa Editrice Leonardo da Vinci 1924 pp.215–331.

p.376 S. to Sophie Duvaucel: Corr. II pp.711–4.

p.377 Romanelli affair: Corr. III pp.68–76.

p.378 Wreck of Henri IV: Corr. II pp.752–68.

p.379 Rigny to S.: Ibid. pp.913–4.
'deeply wounded': Ibid. p.916.

p.380 'Once a man': *Oeuvres intimes* II p.209.

p.381 Bucci to Colomb: Letter included in Casimir Stryienski: *Soirées du Stendhal Club*, Paris, Société du Mercure de France, 1904, Vol I. pp.235–51.

p.384 *Vie de Henry Brulard*: Fully annotated edn. in Pléïade *Oeuvres intimes* II op. cit. See also useful edn. by Beatrice Didier in Gallimard Folio series, Paris, 1973.

Chapter 12

p.388 Canclaux to Tellier: Francis L. Mars: *Les rencontres niçoises de Stendhal*, SC 6, January 1960, pp.277–80.

p.389 'This little recrudescence': *Oeuvres intimes* II p.282.

p.390 'It seems to me': Corr. III p.221.
Julie Gaulthier to S.: Corr. III, pp.535–6, 536–7.

p.391 S. on Rachel: Ibid. pp.271–3.

p.392 Eugénie de Montijo: Harold Kurtz: *The Empress Eugénie*, London, Hamish Hamilton, 1964. Also Comte (Joseph) Primoli: *L'enfance d'une souveraine*, Revue des Deux Mondes, 15 October 1923, pp.770–1.

p.394 'With him you're at': V. del Litto: *L'Impératrice Eugénie, Stendhal et Mérimée*, SC 36, July 1967, pp.350.

p.395 *Mémoires sur Napoléon*: Champion edn. by Louis Royer is sole modern publication of text.

p.396 *Mémoires d'un touriste*: Modern edn. is in *Voyages en France*, ed. Victor del Litto, Bibliothèque de la Pléïade, Paris, Gallimard, 1992.

p.399 Letter to Colomb & Fiore: Corr: III pp.18–21.
Chroniques italiennes: Best modern edn. is by Beatrice Didier in Garnier Flammarion GF series, Paris 1977.

p.401 Roman murder: *Oeuvres intimes* II pp.191–2.
Le Rose et le Vert: Modern edn. in *Le Rose et le Vert etc.* op. cit. with annotations and apparatus.

p.402 *Origine delle grandezze*: Text supplied in Luigi-Foscolo Benedetto: *La Parma di Stendhal*, Florence, Sansoni, 1950, which contains the major Italian source materials for *La Chartreuse*.
La Chartreuse de Parme: Standard modern edn. is by Henri Martineau, Classiques Garnier, Paris, 1961.

p.404 Balzac to S.: Corr. III pp.555–6, 557–8.
Revue Parisienne article: reprinted in Honoré de Balzac: *Etudes sur La Chartreuse de Parme de Monsieur Beyle*, Castelnau-le-Lez,

Editions Climats, 1989.
S. to Balzac: Corr. III, pp.393–405.

p.407 Félix Faure on *La Chartreuse*: Jacques Félix-Faure: *Un compagnon de Stendhal*, Aran, Switzerland, Editions du Grand Chêne, 1978, pp.161–9.

p.409 Bucci to S: Corr. III pp.267–8.
Tavernier's dishonesty: V. del Litto: *Un épisode inconnu de la vie de Stendhal*, SC 34, January 1967, pp.119–30.

p.410 *Lamiel*: Excellent modern edn. with full apparatus by Anne-Marie Meininger in Gallimard Folio series, Paris, 1983. This is based on the fundamental text and related materials established by V. del Litto in his edn. of 1971.

p.413 *Earline*: Full text given in François Michel: *Etudes stendhaliennes* op. cit. pp.278–307. See also Michel's introductory article in ibid. pp.251–78.

p.414 *Les Privilèges*: *Oeuvres intimes* II pp.982–9.

p.416 Mme Bouchot: Martineau: *Coeur* op. cit. II pp.389–91.

p.417 'It's only the immediate': Corr. III p.434–5.
'He gilds the pill': Ibid p.438.

p.418 'he understood better': Roman Colomb: *Notice sur la vie et les ouvrages de H. Beyle*, quoted in Pierre Jourda: *Stendhal raconté par ceux qui l'ont vu* op. cit. pp.175–9.
'I haven't any reputation': *Oeuvres intimes* II p.423.
Stendhal's death: André Doyon: *Le dossier de la mort de Stendhal* SC 36, July 1967 pp.317–21.

p.420 S.'s wills: Texts given in *Oeuvres intimes* II pp.989–1008.
Epitaph: V. del Litto: *Enrico Beyle milanese*, SC 87, March 1980, pp.197–207.

p.424 'I am perhaps': Jacques Félix-Faure: *Stendhal, Félix Faure et Louis Crozet, ou les tribulations d'Alceste*, SC 29, October 1965, pp.44–61.
'he had such': Doyon & Du Parc: *Amitiés Parisiennes* op. cit. pp.56–74.

p.425 Stendhal syndrome: This interesting phenomenon is fully discussed in Graziella Magherini: *La sindrome di Stendhal*, Florence, GEF, 1989.

INDEX